Essential Biological Psyc

Also in the *Essential Psychology Series:*

Essential Health Psychology
Mark Forshaw

Essential Behaviour Analysis
Julian C. Leslie

Essential Personality
Donald Pennington

Essential Biological Psychology

G. Neil Martin MA PhD FRSA

Principal Lecturer in Psychology, Middlesex University

First published in Great Britain in 2003 by
Arnold, a member of the Hodder Headline Group
338 Euston Road, London NW1 3BH

http://www.arnoldpublishers.com

Co-published in the United States of America by
Oxford University Press Inc.,
198 Madison Avenue, New York, NY 10016

British Library Cataloguing in Publication Data
A catalogue record for this book is available from the British Library

Library of Congress Cataloging-in-Publication Data
A catalog record for this book is available from the Library of Congress

ISBN 0 340 808977

1 2 3 4 5 6 7 8 9 10

2007 2006 2005 2004 2003

Typeset in 10 on 12 Sabon by Dorchester Typesetting, Dorchester, Dorset
Printed and bound in Malta.

What do you think about this book? Or any other Arnold title?
Please send your comments to feedback.arnold@hodder.co.uk

For Angela and Gilbert and, in memoriam, Eirian and Gwilym

Acknowledgements

The author and publishers would like to thank the following for permission to reproduce the material in this book: Talairach for Figure 2.1 and Dr Nicola Brunswick, Middlesex University for Figure 2.3. Every effort has been made to trace and acknowledge ownership of copyright. The publishers will be glad to make suitable arrangements with any copyright holders who it has not been possible to contact.

Contents

Preface

If you ask any student of psychology to describe what biological psychology means to them, they might tell you that it was a hard-nosed, science-based branch of the prolific, fructiferous arboretum that is psychology. Although this view seems intuitively appealing, it is not entirely correct. First of all, psychology itself is the scientific study of behaviour, and most of its great discoveries have been based on adopting the scientific approach to study behaviour. Biological psychology, the study of the role of physiological processes in behaviour and vice versa, seems more scientific than social or developmental psychology, say, because it seems to deal with physical matter: the brain, the cardiovascular system, the immune system, skin conductance, and so on. Perhaps because the subject matter of biological psychology is more observeable or measurable, it may be perceived to occupy a higher scientific plain than other branches of the discipline. Don't be fooled.

The findings of studies in biological psychology usually provoke more questions than they answer (as any good progressive scientific study does). If we knew all the answers, we could lock up the labs, pack up our papers and go home. But, because of the richness and complexity of the subjects studied in biological psychology, their study generates question after question. Does the brain have different regions for perceiving different types of object? Where are memories stored? Can memories be stored? How does ageing affect our intellect, and how is this related to physiology? How does injury to the brain and spinal cord affect our behaviour? Is there a sensitive period for developing language? Does biochemistry or neuroanatomy determine our sexual orientation? Does excessive amounts of the hormone testosterone make us aggressive? What is consciousness? Does faulty biochemistry cause depression, anxiety and schizophrenia?

This book hopes to provide you with some possible answers to all of these questions and much more. The book is called Essential Biological Psychology because its aim is to provide you with essential information about, and analysis of, topics in biological psychology. It is packed to the gills with up-to-date and fresh research, which is always needed in order to gain an understanding of this branch of psychology. Each chapter has key features to help you study. For example, the 'What you will find in this chapter' and 'What you should be able to do after reading the chapter' sections at the beginning of each chapter give you an outline of the topics covered in each chapter, and the level of understanding and knowledge you should be able to show after reading it. In each chapter, there are two features designed to give you a flavour of recent research findings in a specific area or to provide you with in-depth analysis of a key topic; these are the 'Research update' and 'Focus on …' features, and you will find at least one of each in each chapter (apart from Chapter 1, which introduces you to the subject and the subsequent chapters).

This book was written in the summer of 2002 and, as I write, the British government is proposing the establishment of banks of stem cells for use in research, which could lead to the elimination of degenerative illness such as Alzheimer's disease or Parkinson's disease. While the world of book publishing moves slowly, the rest of the world moves on rapidly. Do let me know what you think of the book; you can contact me by writing to me c/o Psychology Academic Group, School of Health and Social Science, Middlesex University, Enfield, London EN3 4SA, England, UK, or email me at n.martin@mdx.ac.uk.

Finally, as is customary in all prefaces, the thanks. Immeasurable thanks go to Christina Wipf-Perry and Emma Woolf at Hodder Arnold, exemplary editors who know how to use and appreciate a sense of humour. For comments on the first draft, grateful thanks to Dr Nicky Brunswick, Dr Nick Le Boutillier and Prof. Nigel Foreman. For distraction when it was needed, I thank Gleneagles and Rhod Sharp (who was a good-humoured lucubratory companion, even though he did not know it at the time). And last, but by no means least, I would like to thank Paula, who provided the cushion for number two and, now, for number three.

G. Neil Martin
September 2002

What is Biological Psychology?

WHAT YOU WILL FIND IN THIS CHAPTER
- a definition of biological psychology and related disciplines
- a brief description of the milestones in the history of biological psychology and neuroscience
- a description of the scientific method and how this approach is adopted in biological psychology

WHAT YOU SHOULD BE ABLE TO DO AFTER READING THE CHAPTER
- define biological psychology and describe what biological psychologists do
- describe the scientific method and explain why it is the favoured method of study in biological psychology
- be aware of the major discoveries and milestones in the history of neuroscience and biological psychology

1.1 ESSENTIAL BIOLOGICAL PSYCHOLOGY

When you think of the term biological psychology, you probably have in mind a number of words and phrases: the body, the mind, the brain, thinking, understanding others, the title of this book. The phrase suggests a marrying of two scientific disciplines – biology and psychology – and, in a sense, this is correct.

Biological psychology is the branch of psychology that investigates the biological bases of behaviour. From measuring heart rate in response to an emotional stimulus, to recording the activity of the brain during thinking or the activity of the hormones in the body in response to stress, to specifying the types of brain cell (or neuron) found in a region of the brain that is responsible for visual perception, the range of behaviours studied by biological psychologists is wide. For this reason, many of them specialise in a specific sub-area of biological psychology. For example, they may study the effects of the brain's chemicals on behaviour, the cell structure and organisation of the brain, the body's hormonal system, the blood flow or electrical activity of the brain during various tasks such as seeing, thinking, feeling, hearing, touching, and so on. Table 1.1 gives you a very brief idea of the types of behaviour that biological psychologists study.

Table 1.1 Some of the subjects studied by biological psychologists

- Vision
- Audition (sense of hearing)
- Gustation (sense of taste)
- Olfaction (sense of smell)
- Somatosensation (sense of touch)
- Structure and activity of neurons (brain cells)
- Communication between neurons
- Dysfunctions of the nervous system (such as Alzheimer's disease and Parkinson's disease)
- Stress
- Mental illness (such as depression, anxiety, schizophrenia, personality disorder, etc.)
- Neural transplanation
- Recovery of cognitive function following brain damage
- Decision-making
- Planning
- Reasoning
- Creativity
- Object perception
- Face perception
- Perception of space, form and motion
- Disorders of perception
- Obesity and eating disorders
- Memory acquisition, recall, recognition and retrieval
- Learning
- Ingestion and ingestive processes
- Sexual behaviour and orientation
- Emotional expression and recognition
- Reward and punishment
- Neurosurgery
- Production and comprehension of language
- Developmental and acquired language disorders
- Immune system functioning
- Neural correlates of consciousness
- Movement and movement disorders
- Genetic basis of behaviour and behavioural disorders
- Sleep
- Hypnosis
- Attention
- Aggression
- Social interaction and cognition
- Personality

1.2 THE BRANCHES OF BIOLOGICAL PSYCHOLOGY

As the variety of topics in Table 1.1 suggests, biological psychologists specialise in the topics that are of interest to them. There are some terms used to describe specific types of biological psychology (and, therefore, biological psychologist) and there are other terms that are synonymous with it. Some of the terms that are interchangeable with biological psychology include psychobiology and physiological psychology – to all intents and purposes, all of these terms refer to the same discipline. Other terms that refer to specific areas of biological psychology include neuroscience, neuropsychology, histology and psychoneuroimmunology.

Neuroscience

Neuroscience is an area of study where psychology, physics, chemistry and biology converge. It refers to the study of the neural basis of behaviour, and much of the work in the area is cellular in nature. Neuroscientists are interested in how specific brain cells, types of brain cell or groups of brain cells contribute to brain function and to behaviour. For example, neuroscientists may be interested in discovering whether specific types of cell are involved in specific behaviours (such as object or face recognition); they might be interested in discovering which chemical systems in the brain become active or inactive during certain psychological states such as sleep, mental impairment, depression, schizophrenia, and so on. It is sometimes prefaced by 'cognitive' to indicate that the study involves the neural basis of aspects of cognition such as using language, recognising objects, places and faces, recognising and experiencing emotion, performing mental arithmetic tasks, engaging in visual imagery, and so on (Posner and DiGirolamo, 2000).

Some psychologists combine what seem on the surface to be entirely different branches of the discipline, such as neuroscience and social psychology. Social cognitive neuroscience, for example, involves the study of the social processes that influence behaviour, the information processing that gives rise to social behaviour and the neural basis of the cognitive behaviour that involves information processing (Ochsner and Lieberman, 2001). Some of the topics that interest social cognitive psychologists include the role of specific brain regions in socio-emotional behaviour, and the role of neural mechanisms in regulating aggression, dominance and bonding.

Neuropsychology

Neuropsychology is the study of the relationship between the brain's structure and activity, and its function (Martin, 1998a). Many studies in neuropsychology are based on the consequences of human brain injury or on studies of healthy participants who are observed behaving while specialised equipment, such as brain or neuroimaging scanners, measure brain activation. The meat and drink of neuropsychology, however, is the single-case study. A psychologist will observe an impairment of function (which could be cognitive, emotional, perceptual or motoric) in a person with brain injury, and create a hypothesis about the association between the damaged brain region and the function disrupted. He or she will then administer or create another series of tests to test this hypothesis, and draw a conclusion about the significance of the underlying brain region to the disrupted function.

Other methodological approaches

Psychophysiology refers to the study of the body's physiological processes and their relation to behaviour. Usually, psychophysiologists use specialised equipment (such as electrodes connected to an ECG monitor or an EEG amplifier) that records changes in the electrical activity of the body as it responds to a stimulus. Histology is the study of brain cells and their structure and activity. You will learn more about the study of cells later on in Chapter 2 and in the chapters on neuroanatomy and neurotransmission. Finally, psychoneuroimmunology refers to the study of the body's immune system processes and the ways in which they react to psychological variables. Psychoneuroimmunologists may, for example, look at the effect of stress on wound healing, the development of an illness or on the maintenance of good health; they may study variables that mediate these effects, such as sex, age, personality, ability to cope, and so on. All of these sub-areas – in themselves, large areas of study – come under the umbrella of biological psychology.

1.3 BIOLOGICAL PSYCHOLOGY'S APPROACH TO BEHAVIOUR

Like all sciences, biology, psychology and biological psychology have their roots in the philosophy of the Ancient Greeks and were fashioned by the various philosophical schools of thought that developed from this. At the heart – and, indeed, the brain – of biological psychology is a phenomenon called reductionism (or biological reductionism).

1.4 REDUCTIONISM

Reductionism refers to the idea that the subject matter of science can best be understood by reducing it to its smallest parts. Biological reductionism argues that we can only understand biological processes by looking at the physical components and mechanisms that give rise to these. Applying this approach to biological psychology, the prevailing view is that an organism's behaviour can best be understood – some biological psychologists argue, can *only* be understood – by studying the biological basis of behaviour. In effect, you are reducing the study of behaviour to its most basic building blocks: the cells, organs, systems and brain regions that give rise to behaviour. Aristotle, for example, believed that behaviour was governed by the heart and heart only (an approach called cardiocentric or heart-centred), a view that was superseded by the ideas of the Ancient Greek physicians, Galen and Hippocrates, who argued that the brain was responsible for behaviour (this view was called the cephalocentric view).

Reductionism is closely related to another philosophical concept called materialism – the idea that reality can only be understood through an understanding of the physical world. This phenomenon was prevalent in the mid-nineteenth century and came to a head in the thinking of the Scottish philosopher James Mill, who argued that there was little difference between animals and humans, both being composed of substance and, therefore, subject to the physical laws of the universe.

1.5 THE MIND–BODY PROBLEM AND THE 'GHOST IN THE MACHINE'

This thinking had developed some way since the French mathematician and philosopher, René Descartes published a thesis arguing that 'mind' and 'matter' were two different, separable entities. This view of the mind and the body is known as dualism or Cartesian dualism (after Descartes) and is the philosophy most widely associated with the mind–body problem. Descartes was a rationalist – that is, he believed that the best way of accruing and understanding knowledge was not through the senses (which could be deceptive) but through logical argument, deduction and reasoning. The mind–body problem, simply put, concerns whether the mind and the body are the same as each other, are different but interact, or are different but do not interact. According to Descartes, although mind and body were two different entities, they did interact (a phenomenon called interactionism). He called physical bodies 'extended things' and minds 'thinking things'. The interaction between the two occurred in a small structure in the brain called the pineal gland. Other philosophers, such as Spinoza, held a different view (believing that the mind and body were one and the same thing). Which, if any, view is correct?

Like many problems in psychology and other sciences, answers to difficult questions such as the mind–body problem depend on the terms you use and how you use them. A popular idea in biological psychology (actually, it's a philosophical idea) is 'identity theory'. Identity theory argues that behaviour X is like having cells Y and Z acting in ways A, B and C. Essentially, it is an extension of reductionism and argues that there is no distinction between so-called mind and so-called body – they are one and the same thing. This argument was at the centre of Gilbert Ryle's famous book, *The Ghost in the Machine*: the ghost was the mind and the machine was the brain; the implication was obvious (Ryle, 1949). Identity theory is a persuasive argument because it suggests that terms such as mind, emotion, perception, and so on, are more usefully seen as metaphors for what the brain does rather than entities in and of themselves. These are terms we use for the behaviour the brain produces when its cells and chemicals interact in specific ways. This is an ambitious hypothesis and it will take scientists more than decades to accrue evidence to support it fully and to develop sophisticated techniques to test it, but it is an eminently testable hypothesis and the evidence to date supports it.

Much of the work undertaken by neuro-scientists in the nineteenth century to the mid-twentieth century was geared towards studying the behaviour of brain cells – describing them and their types, and finding ways of highlighting parts of them. Later, techniques were developed that allowed scientists to discover new things about cells, the brain and the body, such as how brain cells (neurons) communicate (electrically) and how they send messages to each other (via chemicals called neurotransmitters). In the 1800s, an Italian physician, Camillo Golgi, and a Spanish histologist (a scientist who studies cells), Santiago Ramon y Cajal, described in detail the structure of the brain's nerve cells. Golgi, using a method of identifying cells called staining (described in more detail later), revealed the structure of brain cells under a microscope, showing how the cell comprised different elements (described in Chapter 2). Ramon y Cajal used Golgi's staining technique to show that brain cells were connected and proposed the influential 'neuron doctrine': the notion that neurons are the basic communication elements of the nervous system.

In the late eighteenth century, the Italian physicist and physician, Luigi Galvani, made another important discovery: he found that cells in muscles and nerve cells could produce electricity, a finding that was further developed by Johannes Muller and Hermann von Helmholz who found that cells communicated with each other via electrical signals. All of these exciting discoveries in the nineteenth century created an impressive picture of how the cells in the brain were constructed and operated.

At around the same time, neurologists and physicians were reporting case studies of individuals with brain injury who presented unique (and interesting) symptoms. Franz Joseph Gall and Caspar Spurzheim, authors of the doctrine that was phrenology, proposed that specific regions of the brain were responsible for specific functions. The essence of phrenology (or anatomical personology as they called it) was that specific brain regions became overactive if a person was adept at a specific function. If a person was a gifted mathematician, for example, the brain area responsible for mathematical reasoning would be overactive and create an indentation or bump in the part of the skull above. A person's mathematical ability, therefore, could be measured by palpating the skull. At the specific level, as we now know, the proposition is ridiculous (active brain areas do not cause bumps in the skull). However, Gall and Spurzheim's contribution to neuroscience was important for a more general reason. Behind phrenology was the idea that functions could be localised in the brain, a tenet that is considered an inviolable truth in the twenty-first century. (Gall also made other valuable discoveries but he will perhaps be best known for phrenology.)

Gall's proposition is called localisation of function; but his notion did not go unchallenged. Pierre Flourens reported that the removal of any part of the brain could cause a disruption in function and that all regions of the brain participated in mental functioning (an idea called equipotentiality – each brain area has the equal potential to undertake specific functions). This view is not entirely supported by studies from modern neuroscience but it became a dominant view for a while in the nineteenth century and the beginning of the twentieth, when scientists such as Karl Lashley and Henry Head reported experiments purporting to show that no single region of the brain undertook the task of learning or processing language.

In the early to mid-nineteenth century, a series of studies was published that seemed to provide support for Gall's view of localisation. The British neurophysiologist John Hughlings-Jackson reported that different motor and sensory processes were localised in specific and different parts of the brain. Pierre Paul Broca and Marc Dax reported patients who were able to understand speech but not produce it. Broca's study is probably the more famous because it illustrates one of the most well-known examples of localisation of function in neuropsychology: that the ability to produce speech is localised on the left side of the brain. In 1861 and 1864, Broca published studies of a patient called 'Tan' (his real name was Leborgne), so called because after being admitted to hospital, this word was almost all he would utter. He was unable to produce fluent speech. When Leborgne died, an autopsy found a lesion – an injury – to the left side of the brain near the front. This region is now known as Broca's area, and is found near the brain's motor area. A little later that century Carl Wernicke reported patients with the seemingly opposite problem: they could produce speech but could not comprehend it. These patients were also found to have damage to the left side of the brain but a little further back from Broca's area. We now know that this region – called Wernicke's area – is crucial for our processing of the sound of words. Wernicke suggested that simple, perceptual and motor activities were localised in specific parts of the brain but more complex behaviours were more distributed, involving interconnections between brain regions. Both of these examples illustrate another concept in biological psychology: lateralisation of function. This refers to the notion that a function 'resides' in one side of the brain.

In fact, Wernicke proposed that Broca's and Wernicke's areas were linked (by connective tissue called the arcuate fasciculus). Wernicke hypothesised that the auditory and visuospatial aspects of language (how it sounds and how it looks) were formed in different parts of the brain. Neural representations of these aspects are sent to an area of the brain specialised for visual and auditory information processing. Spoken and written words are converted here into a common neural representation. This information is then sent to Wernicke's area where it is recognised as language and its meaning understood. From here, information is relayed to Broca's area where the sensory information is converted into motor information, which leads to speech production. Wernicke hypothesised that if the connections between Broca's area and Wernicke's area were severed or disrupted, the brain-injured individual would show lapses in the use of language (paraphasias). He or she would be able to comprehend properly and would be able to speak but not speak correctly – he or she might omit parts of words or substitute incorrect sounds and be aware of doing this but not be able to do anything about it. This is called conduction aphasia and Wernicke's hypothesis is supported by evidence from patients: severing the connection does indeed cause these language disruptions. Chapter 9 looks at language difficulties such as these in more detail.

These case studies formed the basis of modern neuropsychology. Now, they complement fairly sophisticated brain imaging techniques such as Positron Emission Tomography (PET) and functional Magnetic Resonance Imaging (fMRI). Studies using PET and fMRI have allowed us to observe the activity of a living, healthy (and unhealthy) human brain as it processes sounds, sights, smells, words, music, feelings, movement, decision-making, memory retrieval, and a constellation of other simple and complex behaviours. The next chapter describes some of these techniques and methods, with examples of how they have helped our understanding of the biological basis of behaviour.

Before you go on to the next section in this chapter, take a look at Table 1.2. This gives you a brief outline of the major discoveries and ideas in biological psychology and neuroscience from 3000 BC onwards and reviews some of the milestones described in this chapter.

Table 1.2 A brief history of neuroscience and biological psychology

3000–2500 BC	Estimated age of manuscript (the Edwin Smith Surgical Papyrus) describing 48 observations of brain injury and its treatment; contains the first description of various parts of the brain and is the first scientific document to feature the word 'brain'.
430–350 BC	Hippocrates proposes that the brain is responsible for behaviour and, in *The Sacred Disease*, states that 'the brain is the most powerful organ of the human body'.
384–322 BC	Aristotle argues that the heart is the organ responsible for behaviour, having connections to all sense organs; the brain is bloodless, without sensation, not connected to sense organs and regarded as not essential for life.
AD 200	Galen proposes that mind is divided into faculties called sensation, reasoning and memory; the mind is located in the brain, not the cavities within it.
1500s	Andreas Vesalius publishes drawings of brain (and other neuroanatomical) dissections; these reveal the cavities of the brain.
1600s	René Descartes proposes that a small brain structure, the pineal gland, is where sensory information converges before going on to the 'soul'.
1791	Luigi Galvani discovers that living or excitable nerve tissue and muscle produce electricity.
1800s	Camillo Golgi uses a staining method (now named after him) to identify parts of the nerve cell; Santiago Ramon y Cajal uses the same technique to demonstrate that nerve cells are connected.
1808	Franz Joseph Gall proposes that functions reside in specific brain areas. With Caspar Spurzheim, Gall suggests that highly active brain areas produce indentations on the skull; by measuring these bumps, the strength of the underlying

function could be determined. This was called anatomical personology – or phrenology; 37 separate functions were identified.

1828	Pierre Flourens proposes aggregate field view of the brain – all brain regions participate in mental life and no site is exclusively responsible for specific functions.
1848	John Harlow describes the case of Phineas Gage who sustained damage to the prefrontal cortex and consequently showed impaired social behaviour.
1852	Emil du Bois-Reymond and Hermann von Helmholz discover that nerve cells communicate via electrical signals.
1861	Pierre Paul Broca reports a case of a patient with left frontal hemisphere lesions who was unable to produce speech.
1870	Gustav Theodore Fritsch and Eduard Hitzig become the first scientists to report that the neocortex can be selectively excited by electrical stimulation.
1875	Richard Caton records electrical potentials from the scalp of living monkeys, cats and rabbits.
1876	Karl Wernicke reports that damage to the left hemisphere near the top of the temporal lobe results in impaired ability to comprehend language. He suggests that this area and Broca's area are neurally connected.
1879	The first laboratory in experimental psychology is set up by Wilhelm Wundt in Leipzig, Germany.
1888	John Hughlings-Jackson discovers that motor and sensory processes are localised in different parts of the brain; he proposes that the brain is hierarchically organised with the cortex having responsibility for higher-order behaviour and simple brain structures assuming responsibility for lower-level behaviour.
1891	The word neuron is introduced.
1892	Dejerine reports the first case of a split-brain patient.
1906	Santiago Ramon y Cajal proposes the neurone doctrine – the idea that the nervous system comprises interconnected nerve cells.

Alois Alzheimer reports a case study of a woman who suffers from degenerative brain disease and shows evidence of severe cognitive impairment.

1909   Karbinian Brodmann publishes a cytoarchitectonic map of the brain; this divides the brain into 52 regions based on cell type and cell organisation.

1929   Karl Lashley fails to localise maze learning in rats, which leads to the theory of mass action – brain mass is important for function, not individual brain regions.

1928   First study of increased blood flow to regions of the brain during cognition.

1929   Hans Berger is the first person to record electrical activity from the human brain.

1930s   Edgar Adrian records electrical activity from single sensory and motor neurons.
Otto Loewi, Henry Dale and Wilhelm Feldberg discover that chemicals called neurotransmitters are released by presynaptic neurons.

1937   Alan Hodgkin discovers that the action potential leads to depolarisation.
Santiago Ramon y Cajal discovers that neurons communicate with each other via synapses, the spaces between them.
Wilder Penfield shows that electrical stimulation of the cortex can produce behaviour, such as the recollection of memories, in humans.

1949   Donald Hebb proposes that learning occurs through the strengthening of synapses.

1955–60 Vernon Mountcastle, David Hubel and Torsten Wiesel record activity from single neurons in the sensory cortex of cats and monkeys; Hubel and Wiesel discover that depriving the eye of stimulation leads to reorganisation of the visual system.

1957   Brenda Milner reports the case of HM, a patient who had part of the temporal lobe removed and showed a failure to learn new information after the surgery.

1958   Avid Carlsson discovers the neurotransmitter, dopamine.

1960s   Joseph Bogen carries out first split-brain operations on humans to alleviate epilepsy. The resulting behaviour is studied by

Roger Sperry and Michael Gazzaniga who discover that the two cerebral hemispheres appear to operate independently.

1960	John Wada and Theodore Rasmussen develop the Wada test in which the carotid artery is injected with anaesthetic that anaesthetises the same side of the brain.
1963–73	Allan McCormack (1963) and Godfrey Hounsfield (1973) independently develop the technique of x-ray computerised tomography.
1965	Stephen Sutton and colleagues report a brain potential called the P300, which is elicited by decision-making.
1970s	Study of *Aplysia* (the sea slug) shows the importance of synapses in learning and memory.
1980s	Positron Emission Tomography (PET), a technique for studying neural activity via the measurement of blood flow, developed.
1982	Linda Ungerleider and Mortimer Mishkin propose that two different routes in the visual system undertake the perception of an object's qualities and its location, respectively.
1988	S.E. Petersen and colleagues publish the first neuroimaging study of single-word processing.
1990s	Segi Ogawa and others develop functional Magnetic Resonance Imaging (fMRI), a technique that measures neural activity by recording the oxygenation of blood arriving at active neurons.
1993	The gene for Huntington's Chorea is identified.

Sources: Martin (1998a), Kandel and Squire (2000)

1.6 THE SCIENTIFIC METHOD

Central to any science is experimentation. That is, scientists try to find things out by performing experiments. An experiment is a way of providing objective measurement but is not the only method of measurement a scientist can employ. He or she may – like Charles Darwin – make naturalistic observations of organisms, and form hypotheses and theories based on such observations. This approach involves no direct intervention from the scientist. Correlational observation is a form of measurement that involves drawing a statistical conclusion about the relationship between two variables. For example, a balanced diet may be correlated with good health and intelligence. Correlation, however, does not mean the same as causation – if you find a correlation between diet and health and intelligence, you cannot conclude that diet causes health and intelligence (the causal relationship may go the other way!). To draw a more certain conclusion about diet and health, you would need to ensure that you had a group that you fed healthy food, another that ate 'unhealthy' food and a group that ate what it liked. After taking baseline measures of intelligence and health – to make sure everyone was starting at the same level – and having taken a history of individuals' eating habits and preferences, and their educational level, age, sex and socio-economic status, you would then observe the effect of manipulating diet on various measures of health and intelligence over a period of months and (ideally) years. In other words, you would perform an experiment, the only effective way of identifying cause and effect relationships.

In the experiment just described, the group of individuals allowed to eat what they wanted would constitute a control group – there is no direct intervention from the experimenter; the other two groups are experimental groups because the scientist is deliberately manipulating the variable he or she is interested in (in this example, diet). Having a proper control group is crucial in experiments. Say, for example, that a scientist hypothesises that aerobic exercise is just as effective as listening to exciting music in improving creativity and increasing heart rate. She designs an experiment in which two groups complete creativity tests and have their heart rate monitored. One group performs aerobic exercise, the other listens to music. The results from both conditions are compared and the scientist discovers what she expects. From what you know of the scientific method, what is slightly wrong with this experiment? Before you go on to the next paragraph (which has the answer), take a moment to think about this.

(The experiment lacks a control group that did not listen to music or exercise; the scientist might have taken creativity and heart rate measures before and after the interventions – music and exercise – and in this way the participants act as their own control group. However, ideally, a control group whose creativity and heart rate is recorded before and after a period of 'doing nothing' would be included so that the experimenter can be certain that the effect was due to the intervention and not due to chance.)

In an experiment, a scientist does not merely observe, he or she intervenes in some way to make something happen. The scientist does this because he or she wishes to test a hypothesis. A hypothesis is a statement or argument made on the basis of a theory that is based on evidence. For example, one current theory in the literature on the neuropsychology of emotion proposes that emotions aroused by seeing pleasant or unpleasant images generate activation in different parts of the brain, and that these brain changes reflect general responses to stimuli that are pleasant or unpleasant. If this is true, we can hypothesise that any stimuli that elicit these emotions (such as music) should produce similar differences in brain activity (in fact, this study was recently reported by Schmidt and Trainor (2001) and we will come back to it in Chapter 8 when we look at the biological basis of emotion).

Experimentation is an essential part of the process of discovery in any science, whether it is chemistry, biology or psychology. You will see how biological psychologists conduct experiments in their own field throughout this book. In the next chapter, you will see how some of the methods and techniques are used by biological psychologists to test hypotheses and help them try and understand the biological bases of behaviour.

SOME USEFUL FURTHER READING

Carter, R. (1998) *Mapping the Mind*. London: Weidenfeld and Nicholson.

Cowey, A. (2001) From ancient to modern. *The Psychologist* 14(5), 250–4.

Della Sala, S. (1999) *Mind Myths*. Chichester: John Wiley.

Kandel, E.R. and Squire, L.R. (2000) Neuroscience: breaking down scientific barriers to the study of brain and mind. *Science* 290, 1113–20.

Kinsbourne, M. (1998) Unity and diversity in the human brain: evidence from injury. *Daedalus* 127(2), 233–56.

Kosslyn, S.M., Cacioppo, J.T., Davidson, R.J., Hugdahl, K., Lovallo, W.R., Spiegel, D. and Rose, R. (2002) Bridging psychology and biology. *American Psychologist* 57(5), 341–51.

Martin, G.N. (1998) *Human Neuropsychology*. Hemel Hempstead: Prentice Hall Europe.

Ochsner, K.N. and Lieberman, M.D. (2001) The emergence of social cognitive neuroscience. *American Psychologist* 56(9), 717–34.

Solso, R.L. (1999) *Mind and Brain Sciences in the 21st Century*. Cambridge, MA: MIT Press.

SOME USEFUL JOURNALS TO BROWSE

Brain
Cognitive Neuropsychology
Journal of Cognitive Neuroscience
Journal of the History of Neuroscience
Nature Neuroscience
Neuroimage
Neuropsychologia
Neuroreport
Psychological Science
Psychoneuroimmunology
Psychophysiology
Science
Trends in Cognitive Science
Trends in Neuroscience

2 Approaches to Studying Biological Psychology

WHAT YOU WILL FIND IN THIS CHAPTER
- a description of the major techniques and approaches in biological psychology, including neuroimaging techniques, psychophysiological techniques, lesioning and histology
- illustrations of the usefulness of these techniques to our understanding of the biological basis of behaviour

WHAT YOU SHOULD BE ABLE TO DO AFTER READING THE CHAPTER
- describe each of the main techniques and methods in biological psychology
- be aware of how each technique helps us to understand different aspects of the biological basis of behaviour, and be aware of the advantages and limitations of each

2.1 THE TOOLS OF BIOLOGICAL PSYCHOLOGY

One of the greatest advances in neuroscience and biological psychology in the past 20 years has been the development of neuroimaging: an umbrella name that describes fairly expensive and sophisticated equipment that allows scientists to view the activity and structure of living tissue. It may seem surprising to learn that the first brain imaging study was only published in 1988 (Petersen *et al.*, 1988).

What was novel at the tail end of the 1980s is now relatively widely used in hospitals and research centres. There are even journals (such as *Neuroimage*) dedicated to publishing research using these techniques exclusively and variants of these techniques are being developed constantly. Other techniques used in biological psychology to investigate the interaction between the environment and the body are not quite as sophisticated as the neuroimaging techniques and were developed either in the nineteenth century or at the turn of the twentieth. Some of these measure responses (usually in the form of electrical activity) from parts of the body (other than the brain), such as the skin, the heart, the muscles and the immune system, as an organism undergoes a task or is provoked to behave in a particular way. Other techniques allow biological psychologists to investigate biological processes at the micro level (the level of the cell). These techniques help in outlining the structure and organisation of cells in the brain and its structures, and how these cells communicate with each other to allow us to behave. This chapter describes these and other techniques, and illustrates how they have been used to help the biological psychologist understand the psychobiological basis of behaviour. It begins with a description of the neuroimaging methods and with one of the earliest examples of these: Computer Axial Tomography (CAT) or Computer Tomography (CT).

2.2 COMPUTERISED TOMOGRAPHY (CT)

Computerised Axial Tomography (CAT), or Computerised Tomography (CT) as it is now known, is a technique that was developed independently by a South African physicist and a British engineer in the 1960s and 1970s. It provides what is, in effect, an x-ray of the brain and skull. Different tissues in the brain absorb different amounts of x-ray energy. CT measures the amount of radiation not absorbed by tissue when x-rays are passed through it. The resulting scan is usually a black and white image showing various parts of the brain in greyscale. At the time it was developed, this was an extremely useful tool – especially for clinicians – because it allowed observers to detect structural abnormalities in living tissue for the first time in a direct way. The CT technique is relatively non-invasive – that is, no object or process invades the body – but its spatial resolution is a little poor. This means that some of the structures cannot be seen with cut-glass clarity. CT is a measure of brain structure, not activity.

2.3 POSITRON EMISSION TOMOGRAPHY (PET)

Positron Emission Tomography (PET), unlike CT, is a measure of the living brain's activity, rather than its structure. A PET scanner measures blood flow/oxygen consumption in the brain – the more active cells are, the more blood will flow to them and the more oxygen they will need (provided by the blood). The procedure and rationale for a PET scan is roughly as follows: harmless radioactively labelled water or glucose is injected into the participant as he or she lies on a bed with their head just inside a doughnut-shaped hole in the scanner (this is the part of the equipment that will detect the brain activity). Once injected, it takes about a minute for the water to reach the brain via blood flow. This tracer substance, as it is called, decays, but when it does particles called positrons are emitted (hence, *Positron Emission* Tomography). When positrons are emitted and collide with electrons, they form gamma rays, which are detected by the scanner. Thus, as water containing oxygen moves to active cells that need oxygen, the labelled water emits positrons that are detected by the scanner. The scanner can then construct a 2D or 3D, colour-coded image of 'active' brain areas based on the emission of these positrons. The water takes about 10–15 minutes to decay fully and become non-radioactive. A similar pattern is seen when radioactive glucose (2-DG) is injected. Radioactive glucose is taken up by metabolically active cells; the glucose emits positrons – like the water – which are detected by the scanner. The areas that are most metabolically active are those emitting more positrons/gamma rays because they use up more glucose.

A characteristic of the PET procedure in psychological experiments is that trials are repeated, then averaged and then subtracted from each other. For example, baseline measures of activity may be taken in a language experiment where the participant is lying on the scanner bed doing nothing in particular at first (the control condition). The next condition may be reading words from a monitor silently; the third may be reading words aloud from a monitor; the fourth may be listening to words delivered via a speaker. The experimental conditions may be repeated two or three times. Activation during each of the conditions is then averaged. The next step is to subtract one condition from another. For example, subtracting the silent reading condition from the baseline condition will highlight those areas active during silent reading but not rest; subtracting the silent reading condition from the reading aloud condition will highlight those areas active during reading aloud but not silent reading, and so on. PET is capable of excellent spatial resolution – sometimes to within 3 mm of the area under study – but its temporal resolution is comparatively poor. Blood flow, for example, is much slower than neural transmission and averaging results means that scanners do not show representation of activity in 'real time'.

PET is used to study many psychological processes. Some of these include:
- memory processes such as encoding, recall and retrieval
- cognitive processes such as planning and decision-making
- language processes such as reading aloud and silently, making judgements about the meaning and shape of words and sentences
- disorders of language such as aphasia and developmental dyslexia (described in more detail in Chapter 9)
- perceptual processes such as object and face recognition
- movement processes such as reaching, intention to reach, fine finger movement, etc.
- movement disorders such as Parkinson's disease
- emotion processes such as identifying emotions from voices and facial expressions, and experiencing emotions elicited by stimuli in many modalities.

An example of a PET scan can be seen in Figure 2.1.

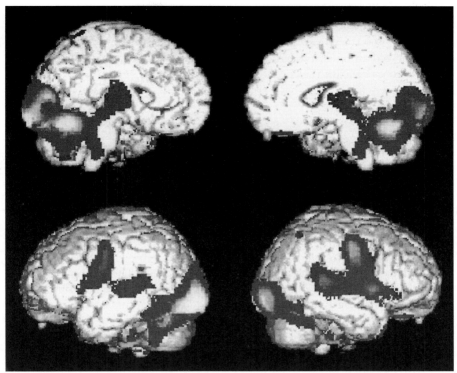

Fig 2.1 Areas of brain activation, measured using PET, seen when dyslexic and normal readers read aloud word and nonwords. From Brunswick, N., McCrory, E., Price, C.J., Frith, C.D. and Frith, U. (1999). *Brain*, 122, 1901-1917.

The greater the number of PET studies published, the clearer is the pattern of consistency in brain activation under specific conditions. The part of the brain responsible for the processing of the sounds of words (its phonology), for example, has been consistently localised in a part of the brain called the temporal cortex (see Cabeza and Nyberg, 2000, for a review). Retrieval of autobiographical information from memory appears to be closely associated with activity in the left-front part of the brain, whereas encoding (learning) material is associated with activity in the right.

There is also good evidence that PET measures functions consistently across such research centres. A Japanese study of verb generation using two different PET scanners, for example, found that both scanners showed the same or similar activation during the task (Tatsumi *et al.*, 1999) and showed activation in similar areas to those active during verb generation in English speakers. (Chapter 9 takes a more detailed look at how universal the brain response is to language.) A comparison of eight European and four non-European PET centres, found that a simple language task – silently generating verbs to a series of auditorily presented nouns – generated activity in the same regions (parts of the left temporal lobe, parts of the frontal cortex and other cortical regions) in over 90 per cent of the centres but generated less consistent activation in other brain areas such as other regions of the cortex and structures beneath the cortex (Poline *et al.*, 1996).

2.4 SINGLE PHOTON EMISSION COMPUTERISED TOMOGRAPHY (SPECT)

Single Photon Emission Computerised Tomography (SPECT) works according to a similar principle to that seen in PET. Radioactively labelled radiopharmaceuticals – these are just biochemicals that emit radiation – are injected into the blood stream and a scanner with sensitive sensors picks up the emission of gamma rays produced by the radioactively labelled blood. The scanner attached to the sensors then reviews the distribution of the radioactivity and reconstructs it in the form of a scan. The radioactive tracer currently used is 99m Tc-hexamethylpropyleneamine oxime (HMPAO). It is called *Single* Photon Emission Computerised Tomography because it captures activity at one given point in time, as if 'locking in' brain activity and relating it to a specific event.

2.5 fUNCTIONAL/MAGNETIC RESONANCE IMAGING (fMRI/MRI)

Magnetic Resonance Imaging (MRI) and functional Magnetic Resonance Imaging (fMRI) are two other neuroimaging techniques developed in the 1980s. Although the names are similar, each technique has a different function.

MRI measures the structure of living tissue. It is superior to a CT scan because its spatial resolution is much better. Like CT, it can provide a 'snapshot' of the brain but it works via different principles. Originally, it was called Nuclear Magnetic Resonance Imaging (NMRI) but the word 'nuclear' was dropped in favour of the less anxiety-provoking MRI.

The MRI scanner detects hydrogen nuclei (called protons) in the brain, which respond like compass needles in the presence of a magnetic field. When the brain is scanned, the individual rests on a bed with their full body inside the scanner (a body-length cylinder). The scanner has a magnet that keeps the protons upright. When radio waves are passed through the head, reverberations are produced by the resonance of the hydrogen nuclei. This resonance produces an energy signal and this is picked up by the scanner as the protons return to their original state. This produces very good spatial, anatomical images of the brain and can even detect brain abnormalities in foetuses (Schierlitz *et al.*, 2001). An example of an MRI scan is seen in Figure 2.2.

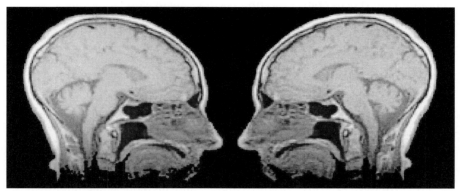

Fig 2.2 An example of an MRI scan

The technique was further developed in the 1990s to allow the functional imaging of the brain; functional MRI (fMRI) works by detecting the concentrations of oxygen that occur at cells receiving increased blood flow. As we have seen, when neurons are active, there is an increase in blood flow to them (this supplies the neuron with various materials, such as oxygen). However, not all active neurons make use of the oxygen carried by blood – they exhibit what is called anaerobic metabolism (active neurons receive more oxygen but they do not consume more than when at rest). fMRI thus measures the concentration in oxygen supplied by increased blood flow to active neurons. The oxygen concentration is found in nearby blood vessels. Changes in oxygen concentration can affect the magnetic properties of one of blood's constituents, haemoglobin, and fMRI detects these changes and those changes that are functionally induced.

Unlike PET, MRI and fMRI are non-invasive. They provide the best spatial resolution of any neuroimaging technique and can measure direct changes in brain tissue. They are also cheaper than PET. The disadvantages, however, are that their temporal resolution is quite poor – although better than PET – and that some brain areas may be more efficient at regulating blood supply than others. It is also noisy – the scanning produces a very loud buzzing, is susceptible to movement artifact and is not the ideal technique for claustrophobic individuals. No metal (ferromagnetic) objects are allowed into the MRI scanning environment (remember, the scanner is a magnet) and serious accidents – even death – can result from an individual bringing such objects into such an environment (Landrigan, 2001). Chairs with metal legs have been observed to fly violently from one side of the scanning room to the other, for example.

fMRI has been used to investigate similar behaviours to those explored with PET – face recognition, real and imagined movement, object perception, response to emotional stimuli, and even 'being in love' (Bartels and Zeki, 2000a). The 'Focus on...' section below gives you some idea of the behaviours that neuroscientists have recently studied using PET and fMRI, and shows you some of the recent findings from such endeavours.

Focus on ... neuroimaging and complex human behaviour

The first neuroimaging study of single-word processing, using Positron Emission Tomography (PET), involved measuring brain activation when people listened to or spoke single words. In the past 20 years, neuroscience has made enormous advances in the understanding of the role of the brain in 'complex' behaviour from planning, imagining and executing movement to perceiving different types of object.

For example, in 2001, Eraldo Paulesu and his colleagues published a PET study of English, French and Italian dyslexic readers (you'll find more on dyslexia in Chapter 9). They asked their participants to read aloud bisyllabic words, or non-words, or make judgements about the physical characteristics of words (Paulesu et al., 2001b). The aim was to discover whether the same brain areas were more or less active in poor readers across cultures; if they were, this would provide evidence for a universal brain mechanism that was impaired in dyslexia.

Paulesu et al. (2001b) found that activity in a region of the left side of the brain was reduced in all three cultures when participants read words (we know that specific regions of the left side – or hemisphere – of the brain mediate different aspects of language processing and tend to be active during tasks that involve these aspects) suggesting that the reading deficit was underpinned by a 'universal' brain dysfunction.

In contrast to the simplicity of Petersen et al.'s study (1988), which you read about in the table on milestones in neuroscience, Braun et al.'s (2001) PET study asked participants to converse as normally as they could while their brain activity was monitored. The study included participants who conversed orally and those who conversed via American Sign Language. They found that the areas in the left hemisphere typically activated during speech and production comprehension were more active during discourse, but also that other regions nearby were also active. In 20 years, neuroscience has gone from studying how the human brain utters a single word to seeing how it responds when its user is engaged in conversation. This example illustrates the 'evolution' of methods in neuroimaging. Early neuroimaging studies were of the Petersen et al. (1988) kind, where a conceptually simple behaviour was studied. Future studies developed the methodology of these studies and progressively embarked on the investigation of more and more complex behaviour.

Neuroimaging has also helped complement studies of brain damage. One current hypothesis in neuropsychology argues that specific brain regions are responsible for the recognition of faces because the recognition of faces requires or involves different mechanisms to object recognition depending on the face-recognition task undertaken. For example, recognising your own face or that of a very familiar other should be mediated by a slightly different mechanism to that involved in identifying the sex, colour or age of a face.

The theory was based on studies of brain damage in which individuals with normal vision could tell the sex of the face but could not identify it (even when the face was very well known). This disorder is called prosopagnosia. In the past five years, a large number of studies has shown that, in normal viewers with no brain damage, one specific region of the brain (called the fusiform face area, or FFA) is consistently activated during face perception (but not during general or visual object perception). A recent study, for example, asked participants to view two types of visual stimuli: buildings and faces (Gorno Tempini and Price, 2001). The study found that famous faces activated the FFA, as predicted, but that famous buildings activated different areas.

Do these studies mean that there are specific brain areas responsible for specific behaviours? 'Responsible' is probably stating the case too strongly. It may be more defensible to state that neuroimaging studies have highlighted regions involved in the execution and planning of these, and other, behaviours. Studies are continuing in their investigation of whether activation in brain regions is necessary or is sufficient for a behaviour to occur, and debates rage loudly and persuasively. The next few chapters will introduce you to the flavour of some of these debates and show you that, even though you are studying the most tangible part of psychology – the brain and the nervous system – neuroscientists can offer different interpretations of the findings they report. Science would not progress without contradiction.

2.6 MAGNETOENCEPHALOGRAPHY (MEG)

Magnetoencephalography (MEG) works by taking advantage of one of the properties of neurons: they generate magnetic fields when active. The magnetic fields generated by single neurons, however, are negligible but when they are combined they can be detected by a specialised piece of equipment called a SQUID machine (Superconducting Quantum Interference Device). This device is itself placed in liquid helium and has sensors that are placed along the surface of the head. The recording of the fields generated takes place in a magnetically shielded room. When the individual's neurons react to a specific stimulus, the magnetic fields generated by activity are detected by the SQUID machine and 'contour maps' of the brain's activity are produced, which show areas high and low in activity. For this reason, MEG is a good localising technique – it shows areas that are active under specific conditions.

2.7 PSYCHOPHYSIOLOGICAL TECHNIQUES

Although they measure the activity of the body – and, often, the brain – psychophysiological techniques are seen as separate from neuroimaging techniques. The principal reason for this is that psychophysiological techniques measure changes in electrical activity or potentials from specific parts of the body. Three of the most commonly used techniques in biological psychology measure muscle activity (EMG), heart activity (ECG) and brain electrical activity (EEG/ERP).

2.8 ELECTROMYOGRAPHY (EMG)

The body possesses three types of muscle: skeletal, smooth and cardiac. Skeletal muscles are those such as biceps, triceps and the flexor muscles of the upper arm and forearm. These are usually under voluntary control – they make up the voluntary motor system; we decide when to flex and tense our arms (such as when picking up a cup), legs (kicking a ball) or fingers (writing or typing at a keyboard). There are other muscles that are not under voluntary control. Smooth muscles are those over which we have little or no voluntary control – the constriction and dilation of blood vessels, for example. The third type of muscle is cardiac and, as the name suggests, this muscle makes up the heart and its valves. Smooth and cardiac muscles comprise about 10 per cent of total body weight; the skeletal muscles make up around 40 per cent of this weight.

When the muscles of the body contract, they generate electrical potentials. Often, muscles contract for psychological reasons – responding to stress, emotional stimuli, pictures, sounds, faces, and so on – and they sometimes contract in a way that is undetectable to the eye. The technique used for measuring skeletal muscles' electrical activity is Electromyography (EMG). EMG, or muscle activity, is recorded by electrodes – circular disks of around 10 mm in diameter – from the surface of the skin. The greater the muscle contraction and the closer the electrode is to the skin, the greater the electrical activity generated (in fact, EMG records activity from motor units just prior to muscle contraction).   Imagine a simple behaviour such as gripping an object like a hammer or handle. The harder you grip the object, the greater the electrical activity produced by musculature, and this activity can be picked up as EMG activity from the recording electrode.

Muscle activity recorded in a given period is summed to produce a signal representative of behaviour during this time-frame. Electrodes are usually bipolar – there are two of them placed over the body area of interest – and electrodes are placed according to a given system. The measurement of the frontalis muscle in the forehead, for example, involves placing the electrode at specific distances from parts of the brow. The major muscles of the face detected by EMG electrodes are illustrated in Figure 2.3.

Apart from using EMG to monitor normal muscle behaviour – or the lack of it – biological psychologists have also found the EMG to be a useful index of other types of behaviour such as feeling good or bad. Imagining pleasant thoughts, for example, results in increased muscle activity in the cheek area responsible for smiling (the zygomatic muscle). This may seem obvious on first reading but not when you consider that the muscle movement is not clearly visible to the human eye and would, therefore, go undetected during normal intercourse. A different set of muscles at the eyebrows – called corrugator muscles – are more active during the imagining of unpleasant thoughts (Schwartz *et al.*, 1980). Activity in the zygomatic muscles has also been found to increase when participants listen to stories with a sexual content, but that corrugator activity is greater when the stories are sexual and unpleasant (Sullivan and Brender, 1986). As you might predict from these results, seeing happy faces increases zygomatic muscle activity whereas seeing angry faces increases the activity of the corrugator muscle (Dimberg, 1982). This activity tells us much about how the person perceives a stimulus or thinks about a stimulus while their physical appearance may, to us, be superficially unchanged.

To show how such apparently invisible physical activity can change depending on what a person is doing, McHugo *et al.* (1985) exposed participants to videotape of Ronald Reagan (then President of the United States) and recorded their EMG. When Reagan was happy and reassuring, activity increased in the zygomatic muscle, especially among participants who were sympathetic to Reagan and the Republican Party. When Reagan was angry or appeared threatening or evasive, muscle activity characterising frowning was recorded from participants. The experimenters presented the Reagan video clip with sound present or absent; EMG was greater during the picture-only condition, perhaps reflecting how the processing of facial expressions may be more focused without the associated verbal clutter. Without the distraction of words, participants may have 'followed' the expressions of Reagan, perhaps (unconsciously) mimicking him.

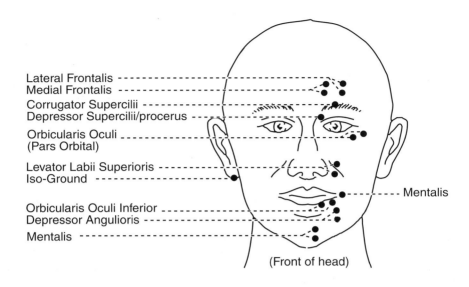

Lateral Frontalis
Medial Frontalis
Corrugator Supercilii
Depressor Supercilii/procerus
Orbicularis Oculi
(Pars Orbital)
Levator Labii Superioris
Iso-Ground
Orbicularis Oculi Inferior
Depressor Angulioris
Mentalis
Mentalis
(Front of head)

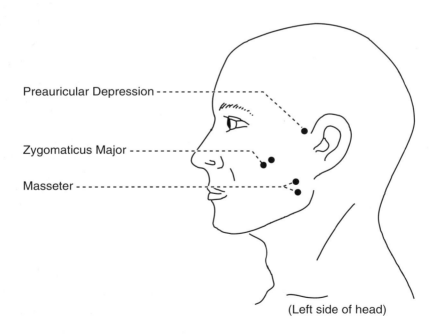

Preauricular Depression
Zygomaticus Major
Masseter
(Left side of head)

Fig 2.3 The regions and muscles of the face from which EMG electrodes can record muscle movement.

2.9 ELECTROCARDIOGRAPHY (ECG)

Cardiac muscle activity is recorded in a similar way to that of skeletal muscle but the differences between the recordings are greater than the similarities. Electrocardiography (ECG) refers to the study of the electrical potentials generated by the working of the heart. Before understanding how biological psychologists measure heart activity, it's useful to know a little about how the heart works.

When the heart contracts, it produces an electrical current (as do all other muscular contractions). By placing electrodes near the source of the current, scientists can measure the electrical activity of the heart. The contraction of the heart is the consequence of the organ's chief function – to pump blood around the body. The heart is made up of four chambers, which pump blood to the body's tissues. The two chambers at the top of the heart are the atria; the two at the bottom are the ventricles. The atria receive blood returned by the body's veins; the ventricles pump blood away from the heart via arteries (a useful way of remembering the direction in which the blood goes is to think of *a*rteries taking blood *a*way). When you feel – or record – your heartbeat, you are feeling or recording the contraction of the heart as it pumps blood. It beats, on average, 72 times a minute (72 bpm or beats per minute) and, therefore, about 100 000 times a day. The contraction phase of the heart's activity is called the systole; the relaxation phase is called the diastole.

The activity of the heart recorded by electrodes can be seen in a typical type of electrical wave. The wave is made up of various characteristic deflections (the direction of the wave characterises various points leading to and during the contraction) – these are the P, Q, R, S and T waves. The P wave is a small deflection produced by the current generated before contraction of the atria; the QRS complex of waves is produced by what is known as depolarisation (more on this in the next chapter) prior to the contraction of the ventricles. The R wave is the largest, most prominent wave. The T wave is the next, small blip-like, deflection after the large R wave and occurs as a result of relaxation activity in the ventricles. The P–Q interval lasts about 160 milliseconds; the Q–T interval lasts around 300 msecs. It takes around 370 msecs to go from the T wave to the next contraction. Figure 2.4 shows the important parts of the heart and the ECG.

Research update ... competitiveness and heart rate

Biological psychologists have been interested in how the heart responds to particular stimuli – especially emotionally arousing stimuli – because of the association between arousal, emotion and health. For example, heart rate can be affected by how we respond to stressors. There are also people who exhibit a series of personality characteristics called Type A personality – these people have increased heart rate and blood pressure, a risk factor for coronary heart disease. Type A personalities are those who are competitive, restless, aggressive, demanding and constantly need to achieve or succeed. The competitiveness component of Type A behaviour may be a key predictor of heart rate.

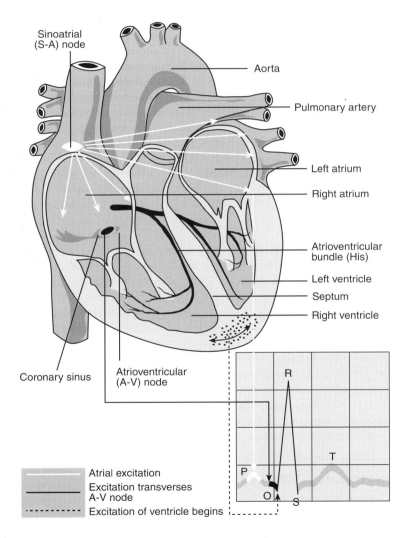

Fig 2.4 A schematic drawing of the heart and an illustration of the QRS complex

For example, Lesley Harrison and researchers from the University of Birmingham in the United Kingdom measured blood pressure and cardiovascular activity in 36 male and female undergraduates who took part in an experiment that involved playing a motorised racing game (Harrison, *et al.*, 2001). In one condition, participants played alone, in another they were in competition with the experimenter and, in a third, participants played with the experimenter but were instructed to cooperate to avoid collisions and to stay on the track.

The competitive condition was associated with significant increases in blood pressure and heart rate whereas the cooperative condition produced barely discernible changes in activity, a finding that echoes reports in the literature of reduced or stable cardiovascular activity in response to stress in the presence of a supportive person (what is known as social affiliation). For example, Karmarck *et al.* (1990) found that the heart rate of people doing a maths problem with a friend was lower than that recorded when they solved the problem alone.

The researchers also measured personality variables such as competitiveness and orientation to winning. Both factors were found to be associated with increased blood pressure and heart rate. The results suggest that heart rate increases in the Type A personality may be due to competitiveness or result from the greater physical activity exerted in tasks requiring competition. Heart rate changes have been seen in response to a number of psychological variables. The promise of financial reward for persuading others (Smith *et al.*, 1990), a fear of needles (Shapiro, 1975) and playing Space Invaders (Turner *et al.*, 1983) have all been found to increase heart rate.

2.10 ELECTRODERMAL RESPONSE (EDR)/GALVANIC SKIN RESPONSE (GSR)

The measurement of electrical activity of the skin – Electrodermal Response (EDR) – may seem to be completely irrelevant to the study of psychology. The technique, however, is surprisingly useful because skin conductance changes can be influenced by the experience of positive and negative emotion, the degree of thinking that goes into the processing of information, and in perceptual awareness. In fact, a French neurologist, Charles Fere, was the first to note in 1888 that changes in a person's mood and environment could lead to changes in the electrical activity recorded from the skin.

The recording of electrodermal activity is based on the properties of skin and what skin does. Human skin has two layers – the epidermis, the outer layer, which is about a millimetre thick, and the dermis, the inner layer, which varies in thickness depending on the part of the body; it is thinner in the eyelids than in the palms of the hand or soles of the foot, for example. The dermis contains blood vessels, hair follicles, sensory nerves and, importantly for EDR, the secretory part of sweat glands. It is sweat that allows conductance to occur on the skin. The electrode position for recording EDR is shown in Figure 2.5.

The body has two types of sweat gland – apocrine and eccrine. The larger of the two are the apocrine glands, which are found in especially hirsute regions such as the armpits and genitals. Sweat is odourless and the odour we associate with it is the result of the reaction between sweat and bacteria on the skin. The eccrine glands are distributed widely and cover most of the skin, with some exceptions (such as lips, outer ear and glans penis, among others). Sweat glands are most numerous on the palms of the hands and soles of the feet, with around one inch squared of skin having about 3000 glands (Fowles,

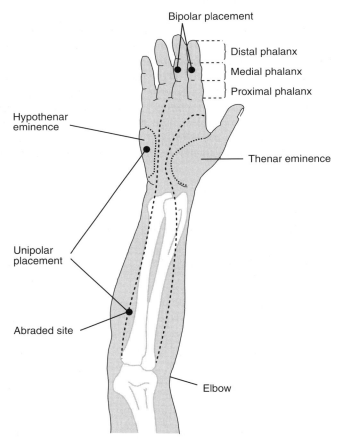

Fig 2.5 Placement of electrodes for skin conductance recording

1986). EDR recorded from fingers and palms responds more strongly to sensory stimulation than to physical stimuli such as heat; the opposite pattern is found for EDR recorded from the forehead, neck and back of the hands, which dictates the position of electrodes in EDR recording. Skin conductance increases with increased stress, arousal and cognitive activity, and reduces when the organism's level of activity is low. During states of anxiety, for example, there is a great deal of sweating, especially from the palms.

To show how the EDR measure can record changes in behaviour that are not immediately visible, some studies have reported increases in arousal to stimuli that are familiar. For example Tranel *et al.* (1985) found that when students viewed slides of familiar and unfamiliar faces, skin conductance response was higher when familiar faces were viewed (even when the participants themselves reported not having seen the face before; they had, in fact, viewed the faces in a previous slide show, which suggests that the body can reveal more than can self-reports).

Perhaps one of the more well-known, although poorly validated, uses of Galvanic Skin Response (GSR), is the polygraph, the so-called lie detector. While its ability to detect actual liars is abysmal, GSR has been found to be a very useful technique when measuring the responses of some criminals – specifically, psychopaths – to emotional stimuli. Psychopaths are people who are utterly remorseless, superficially charming, manipulative and socially deviant. Jailed psychopaths have been found to show little GSR in response to emotional stimulation, a finding that has also been found in studies of patients with damage to the front part of the brain (Raine, 1997). There is more on the relationship between GSR, personality, psychopathy and brain damage in Chapters 6 and 8.

2.11 ELECTROENCEPHALOGRAPHY (EEG)

Electroencephalography (EEG) uses electrodes to record the electrical activity of the brain; this activity could result from one neuron, as happens when you record activity from very small electrodes inserted into the brain, or millions of them, as happens when you record activity from the scalp. The first person to measure changes in electrical potentials from the brain was Richard Caton, from the University of Liverpool, in 1875.

When recording takes place from single neurons or small groups of neurons, electrodes are placed in (intracellular) or around (extracellular) the neuron(s). This can be an effective way of localising activity during behaviour; it can also help to identify malfunctioning cells in patients who experience seizures due to epilepsy. Such patients can also provide us with an understanding of the neurons that respond during particular tasks. Kreiman *et al.* (2000a), for example, recorded electrical activity from 276 neurons from the lateral (side) regions of the brain (called the medial temporal lobes) as participants imagined previously viewed faces, objects, spatial layouts and animals. The purpose of the experiment was to determine whether the same neurons would respond when viewing images as when imagining them. As predicted, the authors found that when neurons responded selectively to a stimulus (that is, responded to that stimulus but not to another, indicating that the response is stimulus-specific), the same neurons were active whether the person viewed or imagined the stimulus. There was a great deal of overlap between neural response during actual viewing and imagining what was viewed. This finding is not uncommon in neuroscience. There are neurons in the motor cortex, for example, that respond during actual and imagined movement (Sugishita *et al.*, 1996).

Most biological psychologists, however, record EEG from the human brain by using scalp electrodes. Recording takes place from at least three electrodes: two 'experimental' recording electrodes and one 'ground', which is placed on a relatively electrically inactive part of the body (such as the earlobe). Human EEG systems can record from as little as two to as many as 164 electrode leads. The signal produced by neurons underneath the electrodes is very weak and is, therefore, amplified by a piece of equipment called, logically enough, an amplifier. This amplifier is responsible for giving the experimenter the typical electroencephalographs (EEG; the initials EEG can be used to represent the technique or the actual wave) or 'brainwaves' (although avoid using the term 'brainwaves' – use EEG instead).

To obtain a signal that is as free from artifact and contamination as possible, the electrode must be securely attached – if you think about the pathway of the signal, the electrical potential has to make its way through many barriers before reaching the electrode, including the membranes that cover the brain, the fluid outside these membranes, the skull and the scalp. In our laboratory, when recording from a small number of electrodes, participants wear swimming caps to keep electrodes in place. If several electrodes are needed we can use an 'electrode cap', which has electrodes stitched into a stretchable cap. This cap is useful because there is an international placement system for electrodes that determines the precise positioning on the scalp for each electrode; if recording from an electrode called 'F3', for example, its position on the participant's skull will be the same if the recording takes place in Middlesex, Madagascar or Minnesota. The International Electrode Placement System is illustrated in Figure 2.6.

The EEG signal emerges as a single wave with deflections, but it can be (and usually is) decomposed into four different EEG frequencies. These frequencies are more commonly seen during some behaviours than others. These four frequencies are – from largest and slowest to smallest and fastest – delta (1–4 Hz, or one to four cycles per second), theta (4–7 Hz), alpha (8–13 Hz) and beta (14–30 Hz). The large, slow waves are characteristic of certain types of sleep such as deep sleep. Alpha is the adult resting EEG

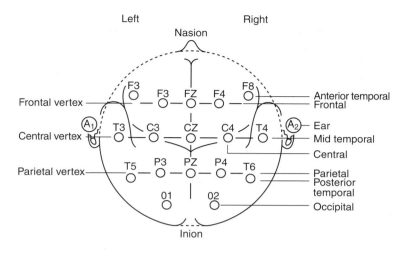

Fig 2.6 The international scalp electrode placement system

frequency. If you were sitting comfortably with your eyes closed, alpha would be the dominant rhythm produced by your brain. During states of alertness – opening your eyes after closing them, for example – alpha reduces and beta increases, a phenomenon called desynchronisation. Figure 2.7 shows the main EEG frequencies.

No one quite knows 'what' EEG frequencies mean or represent but psychologists have drawn conclusions about possible functions based on correlations between the appearance of certain frequencies and specific behaviour. Theta, for example, appears to increase during states of concentration and hard mental work. Experiments have shown that when people are given a series of words to learn, theta is greatest when recall is accurate (Klimesch *et al.*, 1997). In one of our experiments using the odour of

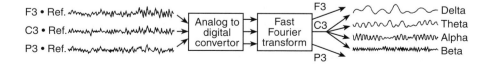

Fig 2.7 The four classical EEG frequencies

food as stimuli, we found that the odour of chocolate was consistently associated with a reduction in theta activity, when compared to other food odours including coffee, lemon, baked beans, rotting pork, cumin and almond (Martin, 1998b). Chocolate was rated as one of the more relaxing and pleasant of odours, and perhaps its effect was to 'relax' the brain. If the theta hypothesis is correct, the relaxed state induced by smelling chocolate resulted in reduced concentration, which produced the reduction in theta activity.

EEG is not a particularly effective localising technique but it is very effective at recording real-time brain electrical activity. The EEGs that the machine records represent brain activity 'as it happens'; even a blink can affect the shape of the EEG. The importance of the EEG to the biological psychologist lies in its good temporal resolution and its ability to change depending on the context. It can be used to measure brain response to a catalogue of psychological variables – thinking, feeling, recognition, perception, sensation, reading, selectively attending, sleeping, neurological disorders, mental illness and others.

2.12 EVENT-RELATED POTENTIALS (ERPS)/EVOKED POTENTIALS (EPS)

Event-Related Potentials (ERPs) or Evoked Potentials (EPs) are recordings of electrical signals – just like EEG – that have been averaged together to produce one waveform. Potentials are 'event-related' or 'evoked' because changes in electrical activity are related to/evoked by an event in the participant's internal or external environment. For example, a well-known paradigm in electroencephalography is called the auditory oddball paradigm. This involves delivering tones or 'beeps' of two different pitches through the participant's headphones. Around 75 per cent of the tones are low (frequent tones); around 25 per cent are high (infrequent tones) and the participant's task is to count the number of high tones as EEG is recorded. The EEG machine records electrical activity to the presentation of each beep, sums all the recorded EEGs and then averages them to produce one waveform. The advantage of this technique is that it eliminates a lot of background 'noise' (electrical activity that is randomly generated by the brain but that is not produced in response to a specific stimulus).

By averaging individual waveforms together, any clear deflection becomes more obvious and the background noise becomes 'quieter'. In the oddball example here, averaged waveforms are produced for the high and the low tones. Psychologists, however, are normally more interested in the ERP generated by the high tones because the participant had to consciously attend to these stimuli and add them together.

The ERP that is generated – called the Auditory Event-Related Potential

(AERP) – shows characteristic deflections. The first of these occurs at 100 msecs following the onset of the beeps and is downward pointing (N100; N=Negative, describing the direction of the wave). A second wave occurs at 200 msecs and is upward pointing (the P200; P=Positive). A third wave occurs at around 300 msecs after onset (the P300) and it is this wave that has roused greatest interest because it is thought to reflect context-updating or decision-making. In the experiment just described, the P300 is thought to reflect the participant's conscious attention to the high tones; because these tones had to be attended to (counted) but the low ones did not, this late 'cognitive' wave was generated. The earlier waves are thought to represent sensory processing and simple attention to the stimulus. If participants are not told to count the rarer tones (the less frequent ones) neither high nor low tones generate a P300, as Figure 2.8 shows.

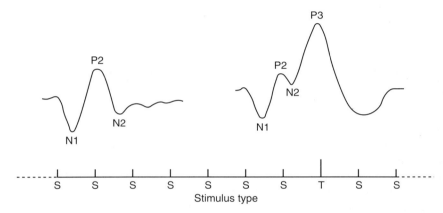

Fig 2.8 Two examples of an event-related potential

A number of variables have been found to influence the appearance of the P300, including food consumption, sex, attention, age, disease, and so on (Polich and Kok, 1995). A reduction of the P300, for example, may be a predictor of cognitive decline in Alzheimer's disease and other degenerative neurological conditions.

2.13 PSYCHONEUROIMMUNOLOGY

Biological psychologists sometimes study the secretions of substances associated with the body's immune system. These substances are important because they are correlated with specific behaviours such as the response to stressors. The role of the immune system is to protect the body from infection that can arise from invading bacteria, viruses and other foreign substances. Psychoneuroimmunology is the study of the interaction between the immune system and behaviour. For example, the body produces proteins called antibodies that attack other bacteria-laden proteins called antigens. The bacteria/antigen proteins tell the body that an invader is present and that it may need to do something about it if it is going to prevent its immune system from being compromised. The body learns to recognise such bacteria and develops a series of cells – a defence – which produces a protein that can kill invading bacteria. These proteins are the antibodies.

One type of antibody, the immunoglobulins, is produced by cells in bone marrow and kills invading bacteria either directly or by attracting other cells that do the killing. Another type of antibody is found in the mucus covering the nasal passages and the membrane in the stomach and intestine. This is called secretory immunoglobulin A (sIgA) and acts by creating a barrier between the invader and the defender. Because this can be sampled from saliva, it has been one of the most widely studied antibodies in psychology. Changes in its levels have been associated with behaviours from exam stress and lower quality of living (there is a decrease in sIgA (Evans *et al.*, 1997)) to humour and laughter (the effect is inconsistent (Martin, 2001)).

The other way in which the body can fight infection and invasion is via cells in the immune system called T lymphocytes. These also produce antibodies and defend the body from fungi, viruses and parasites. They either kill invading bacteria directly when antigens bind with the antibodies or attract other cells that do the killing. The relationship between stress and the immune system is described in more detail in Chapter 8.

2.14 HISTOLOGY

Histology is the study of individual nerve cells and their processes. Scientists take a sample of brain tissue, fix it in liquid, stain it, slice it thinly and then examine it under a microscope. Unlike the grosser techniques you have learned about so far, histological techniques are clearly focused on the micro- rather than macro-organism. By undertaking histological analysis, scientists can identify the organisation of neural tissue, identify specific parts of the nerve cell, observe abnormal nerve cell development and discover the effect of external agents – from visual stimulation to poisoning – on the structure and organisation of cells.

Histological analysis begins properly with fixing. Because nerve tissue decomposes quite rapidly (a process called autolysis) this dissolution needs to be halted. This is done by placing tissue in a fixative, such as formalin, which hardens the tissue and stops micro-organisms from destroying it.

Neural tissue is usually fixed in slices of around 10–80 micrometres in width. Slices are made with a microtome, a very precise cutter similar to a bacon slicer but smaller and a little more sophisticated. Slices are usually referred to as sections. These are then attached to microscopic slides, stained and covered with a mount – a liquid that keeps the section in place and attaches it to an upper glass slide.

The staining part of the process above is crucial because it is this that allows the scientist to observe different types of cell structure and organisation. Different stains allow the scientist to observe different processes in very sharp resolution and it is useful to know what these are.

Nissl stains are named after the German neurologist, Franz Nissl, who developed the technique in the nineteenth century. This stain highlights material in neurons called Nissl substance and allows us to observe the distribution of cell bodies. Nissl discovered that the dye, methylene blue, highlighted the cell bodies of neurons, not the processes extending from them. One of the commonest Nissl stains is called cresyl violet. There are other stains that highlight processes that send signals away from or towards the neuron. These processes are very important – and described in more detail in the next chapter – because they allow neurons to send electrical messages to each other (the way in which they communicate). A conceptually similar technique (called microdialysis) can show the types of chemical secreted by neurons in specific states or in response to specific stimulation (examples would include sleep and depression, and pain and movement, respectively). Other types of staining technique include Golgi silver staining, which highlights single cells well, and myelin stains, which highlight the coating of processes that extend from nerve cells.

2.15 EXPERIMENTAL LESIONING

In biological psychology and neuroscience, much of what we have learned about neural involvement in human and animal behaviour has derived from studies of accidental or experimental brain damage. Experimental brain damage – where a part of the organism's nervous system is selectively damaged – is called lesioning and the consequent damage, a lesion. It is also called experimental ablation. Experimental lesions can be made in two ways. The first approach involves anaesthetising an animal, inserting a glass pipette into the surface of the brain and sucking up the part of the brain to be removed; the second technique, especially effective at lesioning parts of the inner brain (the subcortex), involves inserting an electrode into the appropriate region and passing an electrical current to stimulate it. This technique can also be used for therapeutic purposes. One of the newer treatments for Parkinson's disease, a degenerative and fatal neurological disorder of the motor system, involves sending an electrical current to specific regions of the subcortex. The overstimulation from the tip of a heated electrode destroys the neural tissue responsible for producing Parkinsonian symptoms. You will find more about this in a special 'Focus on ...' section in Chapter 11.

The electrode is guided using a stereotaxic apparatus, which is operated according to co-ordinates provided by an atlas. The stereotaxic apparatus is a device that is placed on the skull, keeps it in place and allows the scientist to map, specifically, the region of the brain to be lesioned using a set of coordinates. There is some variability in the procedure – the location of brain regions will vary from individual to individual, but not greatly so. The coordinates allow the experimenter to start drilling into the skull and to lesion the organism. Once this is complete, the scalp is stitched and the organism allowed to recover. When using such a technique therapeutically in humans – as in the treatment of Parkinson's disease – extreme care is taken not to damage areas beyond those that require destruction. For this reason, a wire attached to the electrode allows an x-ray to be taken of its progress to the subcortex.

2.16 NEUROPSYCHOLOGY

Although we can, under very careful conditions, experimentally ablate (destroy) neural tissue from non-humans, we cannot experimentally ablate neural tissue in humans, for very obvious reasons. We have, therefore, relied on studies of accidental brain injury to help us build a picture of the role of damaged brain regions in causing specific functional impairments.

This approach usually utilises the single-case study design. Brain injury usually results from accident or disease, and because it is more difficult to obtain information of this kind, scientists have studied a small number of individuals intensively over a long period of time. The approach allows neuroscientists to observe how fairly localised brain damage can impair intellectual or emotional function. The brain injury in such patients has given rise to a large number of neuropsychological disorders that have informed theories of normal brain function. These disorders include an inability to produce or comprehend speech (aphasia), an inability to produce speech (fluent or Broca's aphasia), an inability to comprehend speech (Wernicke's aphasia), an inability to recognise objects (agnosia), an inability to follow motor commands (apraxia), reading impairment (acquired dyslexia), an inability to recognise familiar faces (prosopagnosia), an inability to attend to stimuli in one half of the visual field (spatial neglect), and a lack of awareness of visual objects, among many others. Other impairments have no specific name but involve an inability to perform a specific function, such as recognising emotional expression in faces, placing events in sequence, planning, learning new material or retrieving old material from memory. You can find good descriptions of the most significant case studies in neuropsychology in Code *et al.* (1996; 2001).

One of the most famous – if not *the* most famous – single-case study in neuropsychology is that of HM. You will find more about HM in the chapter on memory but, briefly, HM underwent surgery for intractable epilepsy in the late 1950s. The surgery involved removal of a part of the brain called the temporal lobe, which includes a structure called the hippocampus (this has been implicated in various memory functions). After the surgery and beyond, HM exhibited a form of memory impairment called anterograde amnesia – he was unable to learn new material. The intensive study of HM led to a neurobiological theory of human memory that involved the temporal lobe and the hippocampus, and the study has since been supplemented by other case studies and neuroimaging studies of memory in healthy participants.

Strong cognitive neuropsychology argues that the damaged region, if accompanied by functional impairment, is responsible for mediating the disrupted function. This is a strong form of what has been described as the fractionation hypothesis – the idea that brain damage results in selective impairments in function (Caramazza, 1992). Patients may show a dissociation – they perform well on tasks but fail on only one specific component – or they may show a double dissociation. A double dissociation is where Patient 1 may fail on Test A but do well on Test B, whereas Patient 2 may do well on Test A but poorly on Test B. Some patients with brain injury can understand speech but cannot produce it, for example, whereas some others – with damage to a different part of the brain – can produce it but not understand it.

Kosslyn and Van Kleek, however, have argued that there is 'no simple or direct relation between the nature of the behavioural dysfunction and the nature of the underlying (normal) components' (1990: 392). For example, there is a danger in interpreting the 'surface features' (the performance) of the brain-damaged individual as reflecting the activity (or lack of activity) of the processing mechanism that is responsible for the impaired performance. Although a specific brain region has been damaged, this region may project to an area that is responsible for the impaired function but because the connections between them have been damaged, the function is disrupted. There is evidence from brain injury and rehabilitation studies that function recovers over time due to neural reorganisation or the use of other regions of the brain, or to the use of different strategies to compensate for the 'lost' function. It is quite rare, however, for a single, specific, isolated structure or region to be discretely damaged. This makes precise interpretation of the role of the injured tissue very complicated. Finally, if there are dissociations seen in patients, these may not be evidence of two different systems but may reflect the fact that the two tasks differ in complexity – one may be more difficult than the other.

The brain is a dynamic organ and not composed of isolated, unconnected components. Because of this, damage may not only cause a disruption to the damaged tissue but also a disruption of connection to and from this region. This argument, however, does not apply to what Kosslyn and Intriligator (1992) call weak cognitive neuropsychology – the study of normal and brain-injured individuals to constrain theories of normal cognition. Studies of brain injury can inform theorising about cognitive processes and can show what happens when those cognitive systems fail.

While most neuropsychologists would argue that the strong version – in its strongest form – is unsupportable, for some of the reasons that Kosslyn and Van Kleek (1990) suggest, it is arguable that carefully described experiments of the effects of brain injury on function can result in the reasonable interpretation of brain function. The danger is that if a patient is given a test described as measuring a specific function, and this patient is impaired at the test, this person will be described as having an impairment in this specific function. If a patient can read verbs but not speak them while another cannot read them but can speak them, while both can speak and read nouns, is this evidence for the brain having two different representations for each type of verb processing – spoken and written (Caramazza and Hillis, 1990)? According to Kosslyn and Intriligator (1992), the answer would be no.

For example, a person who spends an abnormally long time reading or speaking a word has normal language because they can speak or write it (even though they show difficulty in doing so). Kosslyn and Intriligator (1992) suggest that if response time were measured for nouns in these patients, they may have spent an abnormally long time in reading/writing them, but they would eventually have read or written them. Thus, an entirely different interpretation of the data would be necessary. Measuring response times may show negative findings, but unless these times were taken, there would be other alternatives to the interpretation that different regions of the brain undertake verb writing and reading. As we will see, complementary evidence from brain imaging has helped provide some support for hypotheses generated from brain injury studies. Unlike brain injury studies, they explore healthy individuals' brain function, and the correlations between behaviour and brain activity.

There have been arguments for and against the single-case study approach in neuropsychology. As you have already seen, some researchers argue that damage to a brain region does not necessarily demonstrate that this region is responsible for any function that is disrupted following injury. There is also the need to specify exactly what function is being measured (this is a problem for psychology in general, rather than neuropsychology in particular). When we say that a region may be 'responsible' for phonological processing, what exactly is meant by phonological processing? Could the region be responsible for some other function that allows phonological processing, rather than being responsible for phonological processing itself?

There are also obvious methodological and practical problems with single-case studies such as the extent and locus of the lesion – because the brain injury is accidental or the result of a disease, the extent of the damage is uncontrollable. When brain injury occurs it is also unlikely to be limited to one specific region or structure; it may extend to more than one and so conclusions drawn about the significance of findings in studies such as these need to be done circumspectly. There is also great variation in regional brain structure between individuals. Amunts *et al.* (1999), for example, found that the size of Broca's area varied enormously in a group of ten individuals: there was a ten-fold difference between participants in some cases. There are also other factors, such as sex, personality, handedness and intellectual ability, which may need to be taken into account.

SOME USEFUL FURTHER READING

GENERAL READING ON METHODS

England, M.A. and Wakely, J. (1991) A *Colour Atlas of the Brain and Spinal Cord*. Aylesbury: Wolfe Publishing Ltd.

Martin, G.N. (1997) *Human Neuropsychology*. Hemel Hempstead: Prentice Hall.

Semenza, C. (1996) Methodological issues. In J.G. Beaumont, P.M. Kenealy and M.J.C. Rogers (eds), *The Blackwell Dictionary of Neuropsychology*. Oxford: Blackwell Publishers.

READINGS ON SPECIFIC METHODS AND APPROACHES – NEUROIMAGING

Beaulieu, A. (2002) A space for measuring mind and brain: interdisciplinarity and digital tools in the development of brain mapping and functional imaging, 1980–1990. *Brain and Cognition* 49, 13–33.

Cabeza, R. and Nyberg, L. (1997) Imaging cognition: an empirical review of PET studies with normal subjects. *Journal of Cognitive Neuroscience* 9(1), 1–26.

Cabeza, R. and Nyberg, L. (2000) Imaging cognition II: an empirical review of 275 PET and fMRI studies. *Journal of Cognitive Neuroscience* 12(1), 1–47.

Raichle, M.E. (1994) Images of the mind: studies with modern imaging techniques. *Annual Review of Psychology* 45, 333–56.

READINGS ON SPECIFIC METHODS AND APPROACHES – PSYCHOPHYSIOLOGICAL TECHNIQUES

Andreassi, J.L. (1995) *Psychophysiology: Human Behaviour and Physiological Response* (third edition). Hove, UK: Lawrence Erlbaum Associates.

Papanicolaou, M. (1995) An introduction to MEG with some applications. *Brain and Cognition* 27, 331–52.

Polich, J. and Kok, A. (1995) Cognitive and biological determinants of P300: an integrative overview. *Biological Psychology* 41, 103–46.

READINGS ON SPECIFIC METHODS AND APPROACHES – LESIONING/BRAIN DAMAGE

Beaumont, J.G. (1996) Neuropsychology. In J.G. Beaumont, P.M. Kenealy and M.J.C. Rogers (eds), *The Blackwell Dictionary of Neuropsychology*. Oxford: Blackwell Publishers.

Code, C., Wallesch, C.W., Joanette, Y. and Lecours, A.R. (1996) *Classic Cases in Neuropsychology*. Hove, UK: The Psychology Press.

Code, C., Wallesch, C.-W., Joanette, Y. and Lecours, A.R. (2001) *Classic Cases in Neuropsychology. Volume 2*. Hove, UK: The Psychology Press.

Robertson, L.C., Knight, R.T., Rafal, R. and Shimamura, A.P. (1993) Cognitive neuropsychology is more than single-case studies. *Journal of Experimental Psychology: Learning, Memory and Cognition*, 19(3), 710–17.

Shallice, T. (1988) *From Neuropsychology to Mental Structure*. Cambridge: Cambridge University Press.

READINGS ON SPECIFIC METHODS AND APPROACHES – PSYCHONEUROIMMUNOLOGY

Kiecolt-Glaser, J.K., McGuire, L., Robles, T.F. and Glaser, R. (2002) Psychoneuroimmunology: psychological influences on immune function and health. *Journal of Consulting and Clinical Psychology* 70(3), 537–47.

SOME USEFUL JOURNALS TO BROWSE

Biological Psychology
Brain
Cortex
International Journal of Psychophysiology
Journal of Cognitive Neuroscience
Journal of Neuroscience
Nature Neuroscience
Neuroimage
Neuropsychology
Physiology and Behavior
Psychoneuroimmunology
Psychophysiology
Trends in Cognitive Science
Trends in Neuroscience

3 The Nervous System and How it Works

WHAT YOU WILL FIND IN THIS CHAPTER
- a description of the nervous system and its two principal divisions
- a description of the cells in the central and peripheral nervous system, and what they do
- a description of neurotransmitters and neurotransmission

WHAT YOU SHOULD BE ABLE TO DO AFTER READING THE CHAPTER
- describe the major elements of the central nervous system and peripheral nervous system
- describe the various cells in the nervous system and what they do
- be aware of the importance of neurotransmitters and neurotransmission

3.1 THE BRAIN: AN INTRODUCTION

The Ancient Greek philosopher, Aristotle, had an interesting view of what part of the body controlled behaviour. According to Aristotle, the brain served a fairly minor role in sensation, perception and cognition. The organ of import for behaviour was, according to Aristotle and similar thinkers, the heart. The brain did little more than keep the heart happy by keeping it well heated. This view of the localisation of human function is known as the cardiocentric view.

The later, and now prevailing, view, which has dominated neural science for the last 2000 years is that the heart has little localisation significance and that the brain, and structures extending from it, is the structure that controls behaviour. This is known as the cephalocentric view and was one espoused by the Greek physicians Hippocrates (from whose writings we derive the Hippocratic oath) and Galen.

The brain weighs around 1400 g in the average adult, has the look of porridge, the consistency of blancmange, and contains an estimated 10 to 100 billion nerve cells, or neurons. It also has about as many more supporting cells, which supply neurons with nutrients and remove foreign bodies that might impair neurons' function. Cells work in groups and these groups communicate with each other. Cells come in various sizes, shapes and numbers, and the different layers and columns of the brain contain different types of cell. The brain itself is part of one of the two major divisions of the nervous system. These two divisions are the central nervous system and the peripheral nervous system.

3.2 THE CENTRAL NERVOUS SYSTEM (CNS)

The Central Nervous System (CNS) is made up of the brain and the spinal cord – a long, thin collection of nerve fibres attached to the brain's base and which makes its way to the end of the backbone, trailing off in what is called the horse's tail (*cauda equina*) because of its appearance. The spinal cord contains nerve cells that control simple reflexes – such as withdrawal from pain – and messages are sent via the spinal cord to the brain. The brain controls the activity of the body and responds to events outside it. It does this through communication with nerves – bundles of nerve fibres – attached to the spinal cord. This network of nerve fibres is called the peripheral nervous system.

The brain has three quite distinctive physical structures. From bottom to top, these are the brain stem, cerebellum and the cerebral hemispheres. The brain stem is attached to the top of the spinal cord and the base of the brain (hence, stem) and is the most primitive part of the brain. Its functions are basic – maintaining physiological processes and controlling automatic behaviours such as swallowing, breathing and sleeping. The cerebellum – attached to the base of the brain just to the side of the brain stem – looks like a miniature brain itself and the word literally means 'little brain'. The cerebral hemispheres are viewed as being the most sophisticated part of the brain; they contain the nerve cells that control the different forms of sensation, perception, cognition, memory and emotion, and these and the other structures are described in the next chapter. The main divisions of the CNS can be seen in Figure 3.1.

3.3 THE PERIPHERAL NERVOUS SYSTEM (PNS)

The Peripheral Nervous System (PNS) comprises the sets of well-protected nerves that connect the CNS with other nerves, from glands, sense organs and muscles. For example, the PNS receives information from the sense organs (such as information about temperature changes on the skin). This information is sent to the brain and signals are sent via the PNS from the brain to muscles (which may withdraw from a too-cold or too-hot surface).

PNS nerves are connected to various parts of the CNS. Spinal nerves, for example, are attached to the spinal cord, and transmit sensory and muscular

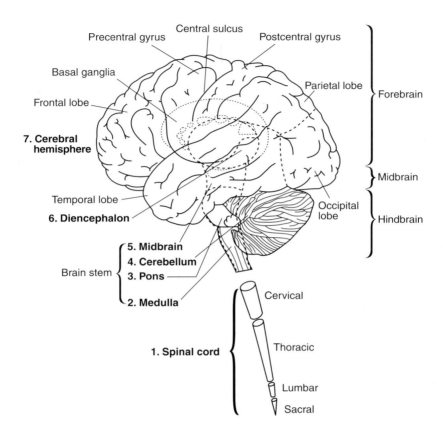

Fig 3.1 The principal divisions of the Central Nervous System

information from areas of the body below the neck. Another set of nerves, called cranial nerves, are attached to the brain, and serve muscles and sense receptors around the head and neck. There are 12 pairs of cranial nerves and each has specific functions. The oculomotor nerve (cranial nerve III), for example, is responsible for controlling extraocular movement such as moving the upper eyelid and moving the eye upwards and downwards; the trigeminal nerve (cranial nerve V) is the largest of the cranial nerves and is the sensory nerve of the face, detecting changes in the chemical environment – it responds to the vapours of peeled onions and to the respiratory assault of ammonia – and controlling muscles in the face that respond to sensory stimuli. A brief guide to the function of the cranial nerves can be found in Table 3.1.

Table 3.1 The functions of the 12 cranial nerves

Nerve	Function
12 Hypoglossal	Motor nerve of tongue; swallowing; vomiting
11 Access nerve	Sends fibres to two neck muscles; rotates shoulder blades
10 Vagus nerve	Sends fibres to neck, thorax, heart, stomach, liver and gall bladder; restricts heart rate and controls contractions in intestines
9 Glossopharyngeal nerve	Innervates the tongue, taste buds and saliva
8 Vestibulochoclear nerve	Maintains physical equilibrium; keeps eye stationary when it looks at moving objects
7 Facial nerve	Facial expression, and secretion of tears and saliva
6 Abducent nerve	Responsible for muscle that pulls eye so that the cornea is laterally facing
5 Trigeminal nerve	Sensory nerve of the face, which branches into three other facial nerves; mediates sneezing, sucking and stretching of masseter muscles
4 Trochlear nerve	Innervates muscle that directs gaze downwards and laterally
3 Oculomotor nerve	Innervates extraocular muscles such as those moving eyes upwards and downwards, and those lifting the upper eyelid
2 Optic nerve	Forms part of the visual pathway from the eye to the part of the brain where the nerves meet and cross
1 Olfactory nerve	Responsible for the sense of smell

3.4 CELLS IN THE NERVOUS SYSTEM

The CNS and PNS are made up of different types of cell. These cells are principally of two types: nerve cells, known as neurons, and supporting cells, known as glial cells. It has been estimated that between 10 and 100 billion (10 000 000 000) neurons exist in the NS, although the exact number can never be known, and that neurons make 13 trillion (13 000 000 000 000) connections with each other. There are different types of neuron and supporting cell, and some of these are summarised in Table 3.2.

Table 3.2 Types of neuron and glial cell

Type of neuron	Function
Projection neurons/ Golgi type 1 cells	Send impulses via long axons to other neurons across long distances
Interneuron/ Golgi type 2 cell	Neurons with short processes and that are close to the cell body; they communicate with only one group of nerve cells
Uni-polar neurons	Send one process that might bifurcate (divide into two) and are usually sensory in function (conveying information from the skin)
Multi-polar neurons	Have several processes such as one axon and many dendrites; the commonest type of neuron
Bi-polar neurons	Have one axon and one dendrite, which extend at opposite ends of the cell body; some sensory neurons are bipolar neurons, e.g. those found in the retina of the eye
Type of glial cell	**Function**
Astrocytes (astroglia)	The most common type of brain cell; star-shaped and gives physical support for cells; responsible for phagocytosis – the process where dead cells are engulfed and digested; can exchange substances with neurons and remove or break down the neurotransmitters released into the synaptic gap
Oligodendrocytes/ oligodendroglia	CNS cells whose principal function is the production of myelin
Microglial cells	Have phagocytic properties; sometimes called 'scavenger cells' – they destroy invading organisms, remove dangerous material and promote tissue repair by secreting growth factor; appear to have no clear-cut structural features
Schwann cells	Cells responsible for myelination in PNS; also give physical guidance to sprouting or damaged PNS axons
Terminal Schwann cells	PNS cells, which maintain and repair neurons

Glial, or supporting, cells are closely attached to neurons, and provide physical and mechanical support to them. Although glia means glue, supporting cells do not actually stick neurons together. Glial cells repair neuronal damage, shape the neuron and control how a neuron develops. There are more glial cells than neurons in the CNS.

Research update ... scientists should not underestimate the glial cell

Although around 90 per cent of the cells in the brain are supporting cells (glial cells) these have been thought, until relatively recently, to perform quite mundane functions such as serving the needs of neurons. Erik Ullian, Ben Barres and a research team at Stanford University School of Medicine have found that the glial cell may have a more vital role to play in the brain's development. Glial cells may determine the number of synapses – spaces between neurons where they communicate with each other – generated in the brain (Ullian *et al.*, 2001).

The finding followed an experiment in the same laboratory, which found that synapses of neurons grown with astrocytes (a type of glial cell) were ten times more active than those grown without. The mere proximity of glial cells to neurons made the neurons more responsive.

In their most recent experiment, neurons exposed to glial cells formed seven times as many synapses as those that were not exposed. This is important because it indicates that glial cells have a much greater role to play in synapse formation in the central nervous system than had previously been thought. The next step is to identify how the glial cells produce this increase.

3.5 THE NEURON

It used to be thought that we are born with all the neurons that we will get in life – hundreds of billions – and it has been estimated that we lose 100 000 of these a day from birth. Recent research, however, suggests that some neurons in some regions of the brain can regenerate, a phenomenon regarded as the holy grail of neuroscience because the accepted scientific view was that once a nerve cell died, it could not be revived or replaced. Researchers have now found that cells *can* be replaced in specific sites, such as the visual cortex and the hippocampus (Kempermann and Gage, 2002; Kaplan, 2001).

From birth onwards, however, we lose millions of neurons. Based on an estimated loss of 100 000 a day, we would lose about 36.5 million neurons in one year. This does not necessarily mean that we will be worse off, having to struggle with a few billion neurons. In fact, the neuronal loss is necessary because redundant neurons are shed and connections between the existing efficient neurons are increased.

The neuron comprises various elements; these are illustrated in Figure 3.2.

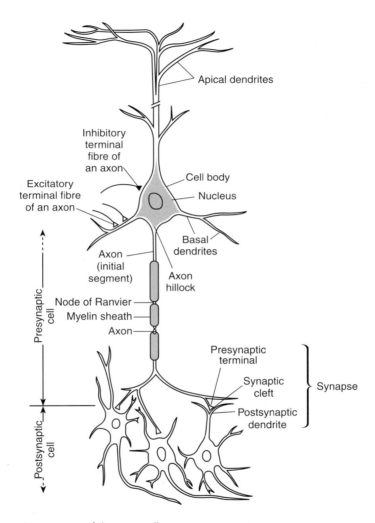

Fig 3.2 The major processes of the nerve cell

Some of the most important elements are:

- **The membrane:** this covers the neuron and separates it from others. It contains substances that detect material outside the cell and allows material to leave the cell. It can carry nerve impulses that enable neurons to communicate with each other.

- **The cell body:** this is the centre of the neuron and is also called the soma and perikaryon. Inside the cell body is a nucleus and inside the nucleus, a nucleolus. The nucleus is large and makes the neuron clearly distinguishable from other NS cells. The neuron is surrounded by extracellular fluid, so called because it exists outside the cell (this is also known as interstitial fluid). Fluid inside the cell is called intracellular fluid.
- **The nuclei:** this is the name given to collections of cell bodies in the CNS (they are called ganglions in the PNS). When groups of fibres extend from cell bodies, they form a tract (in the PNS, they form a nerve).
- **Axons and dendrites:** these are processes that extend from the cell body, which receive or send electrical signals. There are usually several dendrites extending from the cell body but only one axon. The dendrites might branch out to form a mass of dendritic processes and receive signals. The axon is responsible for sending the nerve impulse to other neurons. Axons vary in length. This allows them to send signals to neurons nearby or far away.
- **The synapse:** this represents the part of the NS where one neuron sends information to another. More specifically, an axon leaves the cell body at a point called the axon hillock or initial segment. At the end of the axon, there is a slight, knob-like enlargement called a terminal (it is also called a *bouton termineau*, terminal button or synaptic knob). The point of contact between the terminal button and the other neuron is called the synapse. In the PNS, terminal buttons may form synapses with muscle cells.

3.6 COMMUNICATION AT THE SYNAPSE

Communication at the synapse occurs via the release of chemical substances known as neurotransmitters. These are stored in parts of the terminal button in protective packages called synaptic vesicles. Although there are many neurotransmitters, they are fairly hard to identify. They are triggered by the nerve impulse that prompts the neurotransmitter to leave the terminal button and enter the space between the button and the receiving neuron. This space is called the synaptic cleft and is approximately 20 nm wide (about $^2/_{100\,000}$ of a millimetre). Those neurons situated before the cleft are called presynaptic neurons, whereas those receiving the neurotransmitter are called postsynaptic neurons. Synapses can occur almost anywhere on the neuron and there are hundreds, often thousands, of synapses made on each neuron.

3.7 INSIDE THE NEURON

The neuron contains various processes and substances that allow it to function. Inside, there is a fluid called cytoplasm, which contains various important materials:

- mitochondria – this uses the body's energy source, glucose
- chromosomes – (strands of deoxyribonucleic acid or DNA; more on this in Chapter 6) – these produce proteins that build cells and give each neuron its structure
- neurofibrils – these give the neuron its overall structure (cytoskeleton) and allow material to be transported by the neuron's processes
- microtubules – these allow the transport of materials within the neuron.

Anterograde axonal transport describes the transport of material from the cell body toward the axon's terminal buttons; retrograde axonal transport describes the transport of materials to the cell body. The former is useful because it can transport materials that can only be synthesised in the cell body (e.g. mitochondria). The latter helps bring substances to the cell body that could alter its function (such as changing the amount of neurotransmitter produced). It also brings back axonal debris that needs to be broken down.

3.8 MYELINATION

The axon is covered in a membrane called the axonal membrane (or axolemma) and almost all axons in the CNS are surrounded by a whiteish myelin sheath. This sheath is made up of layers of lipids (fats) and proteins, called myelin. This insulates the axon from its surroundings and other neurons, and helps the rapid conduction of nerve impulses. The myelin sheath is cylindrical in shape and is produced by the glial cells, oligodendrocytes/ oligodendroglia, in the CNS and by Schwann cells in the PNS.

Myelin helps conduction by reducing the loss of the flow of current from the axon to the surrounding fluid. Axons covered in myelin are called myelinated axons; those not covered are called unmyelinated axons. The thicker the sheath the more rapid the speed of signal conduction. One way of estimating conduction velocity (the speed of the nerve impulse) is to multiply the diameter of the axon (in micrometres) by six. Thus, an axon with a diameter of 20 micrometres (the maximum diameter) conducts at approximately 120 metres per second. A thinner axon with half that diameter would conduct at 60 metres per second. An unmyelinated axon with a diameter of 1 micrometre would conduct extremely slowly, at one metre or less per second. In some diseases, axons can become demyelinated (e.g. in multiple sclerosis). As a result, impulse conduction is either slowed down considerably or is stopped completely. If the disease progresses, even the axon itself (as well as its myelin sheaths) may degenerate.

At intervals, the axonal membrane is unmyelinated, exposing it to the surrounding fluid. These unmyelinated points of the axon are called the nodes of Ranvier (these are about 1–2 micrometres in length; the myelinated segment is about 1 mm). These nodes assist in the speed of conduction by making the nerve impulse jump from one node to the next, a process called saltatory conduction.

3.9 THE ACTION POTENTIAL

Neurons communicate with each other by sending electrical impulses called action potentials which release neurotransmitters at a synapse. Potential refers to a source of electrical activity – the neuron's method of communication is thus electrical. This communication depends on the neuron's excitability – its capacity to react to a stimulus with an electrical discharge (or current or impulse – all of these words refer to the same thing).

The action potential is produced by charged particles called ions that pass through the cell membrane. The extracellular and intracellular fluids both contain ions. These ions are either positively charged (cations) or negatively charged (anions). The familiar phrase saying that 'opposites attract' has its origin in electrolyte chemistry because while similarly charged ions repel (a + and a + or a – and a –), differently charged ions attract (+ and –). The force produced by this repulsion and attraction is called electrostatic pressure. There are many different ions unevenly distributed inside and outside the cell membrane (intracellularly and extracellularly). It is this distribution that gives the membrane its electrical potential and is, therefore, called the membrane potential. It has an electrical charge because there are positive and negative ions both inside and outside the cell membrane.

The membrane is selectively permeable to ions. That is, it only allows certain ions in. Perhaps the most significant ions are Na^+ (sodium), K^+ (potassium), Ca^{2+} (calcium) and Cl^- (chloride). Potassium, sodium and chloride ions are found in extracellular and intracellular fluid, although there is more potassium in intracellular fluid and more sodium and chloride in extracellular fluid. Chloride is the more prominent extracellular anion.

The type of channel opening that is governed by neurotransmitters is called transmitter, or ligand, gated. Some channels are regulated by the magnitude of the membrane potential. These channels are called voltage gated and it is these that are responsible for producing the action potential. The permeability of the membrane – that is, its ability to allow K^+ to enter or exit – is dependent not only on how many channels there are, how they are distributed and how much they open, but also on the concentration gradient of the ion. The steeper this is, the greater the flow of ions.

3.10 THE MEMBRANE POTENTIAL

If the inside of the membrane is negatively charged relative to the outside, positive ions will be attracted inside. As a result, positive ions will be forced out because, as you will recall, similarly charged ions repel. The degree of attraction or repulsion is determined by the membrane potential. For most neurons, the charge across this membrane is about 60–70 millivolts when it receives no stimulation. This charge is called the resting potential. Because there are more negative ions inside the cell, this resting potential has been arbitrarily defined as negative, i.e. –60/70 millivolts.

The action potential is produced by the membrane's selective permeability to ions and the different concentrations of ions inside and outside the cell. The unequal distribution of ions is maintained by 'pumps' in the cell membrane. Potassium, for example, flows through the membrane quite easily when the cell is at rest, whereas sodium passes through with difficulty. Thus the expulsion of potassium results in the inside of the cell losing positive ions, producing a negative charge on the inside. Potassium does not leave the inside of the cell endlessly because at a certain point the membrane will force potassium to flow back into the cell. At –70 millivolts, the strength of the outward and inward flow of potassium are similar, a status that represents potassium's equilibrium potential.

The resting potential is slightly lower than potassium's equilibrium potential because the membrane is also permeable (but only slightly) to positively charged sodium ions. Thus, as potassium ions flow out, a small number of sodium ions enter the membrane making the inside negative charge slightly less negative. The mechanism regulating the influx and efflux of sodium and potassium is the sodium-potassium pump. This forces out sodium ions in exchange for potassium ions. For every three sodium ions expelled, two potassium ions are pushed in.

3.11 DEPOLARISATION AND HYPERPOLARISATION

When sodium channels are opened, the cell becomes more permeable to sodium and the resting potential becomes more like the equilibrium potential for sodium (55 millivolts). The increased permeability and influx of sodium is called depolarisation: the positive ions make the membrane potential less negative. If this continues and positive ions continue to flow into the cell, the intracellular charge reverses from negative to positive. Eventually, the resting potential is reached but is first overshot. When this happens the membrane is described as hyperpolarised and the process is called hyperpolarisation. The time taken from depolarisation to hyperpolarisation is approximately two to three milliseconds.

This is the action potential: the depolarisation and hyperpolarisation of the cell membrane produced by an increase in the cell's permeability to sodium ions. To allow an action potential to occur, the membrane must reach the threshold of excitation – that is, it must be excited to a certain threshold before an action potential is fired. The number of action potentials can reach 100 per second. Although this process might seem to require a large exchange of ions, the actual quantity of ions flowing in and out of the cell is small (one for every 3000 ions in the case of potassium, for example). There is a period of relative calm before another action potential is fired. This resting state is called the cell's refractory period. Figure 3.3 illustrates the flow of potassium into the cell.

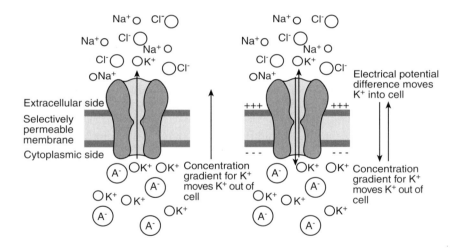

Fig 3.3 The flow of potassium across the cell membrane

The strength of an action potential is the same regardless of the strength of the stimulation. So, although a weak and a strong stimulus can both trigger off an action potential, the strength of the action potential is the same. However, there are factors that influence the appearance of the action potential. These are the frequency and the pattern of the stimulation.

Sometimes, one stimulus is not enough to precipitate an action potential; several bouts of stimulation are needed.

Calcium is an ion that appears not to be as important as sodium and potassium but extracellularly regulates the excitability of the cell membrane. The membrane does contain voltage-gated calcium channels. Calcium enters the cell during the action potential (actually, through sodium as well as calcium channels). Perhaps its most important role is intracellular. Its presence in the terminal buttons of axons is necessary for the release of neurotransmitters.

3.12 HOW A NERVE IMPULSE IS TRANSMITTED

Once an action potential starts, it does not stop. As it makes its way along the axon having unmyelinated nodes, it is repropagated (or recharged). Whereas the passage of the action potential in unmyelinated axons is smooth, the course of the action potential in myelinated axons is slightly more 'jumpy' because of the repropagation at each node where the membrane has to open channels to allow the flow of ions in and out.

The simplest pathway – an axon from one neuron sending an action potential to only one other neuron – does not exist in the CNS. Usually, neurons contact many other neurons. Two neurons can also send an action potential in parallel to another neuron and there are intricate feedback loops. For example, a neuron could fire an action potential to another by a neuron that, in turn, sends a message back to the sender. This return message can tell the neuron whether its effect was weak or strong.

3.13 NEUROTRANSMISSION

The synapse

When depolarisation occurs at the terminal button, calcium channels open, allowing this ion to enter the cell. The increased permeability to calcium and its presence in the cell is responsible for the secretion of a neurotransmitter. The neurotransmitter is released into the synaptic gap by a process called exocytosis. This means that the transmitter-containing vesicle moves up to the cell membrane of the presynaptic terminal button, pushes up against it and fuses with it. The vesicle releases the neurotransmitter, which moves in to the extracellular fluid of the synaptic gap where it binds to the postsynaptic, or receiving, terminal button of another neuron.

Neurotransmitters can alter the membrane potential and its permeability. Because of these effects, the neurotransmitter produces a synaptic potential that is slower than the action potential. If this potential is a depolarising one, then the postsynaptic neuron may fire an action potential. When this happens, the effect of the neurotransmitter is excitatory: it excites a cell into producing an action potential, and results from sodium and calcium ions going in and potassium ions being pushed out. This type of potential is called an excitatory postsynaptic potential (EPSP).

It takes more than just one EPSP to produce an action potential in the receiving cell. Normally, repeated stimulation (many EPSPs) are needed before this can happen. There is a certain threshold value that these potentials must reach before the depolarisation triggers off an action potential. The process of repeated stimulation which produces an action potential is called summation because the effect of one EPSP is added to the next, which is added to the next, and so on, until the threshold for depolarisation is reached.

If the postsynaptic button and the membrane become hyperpolarised, the firing of an action potential by the postsynaptic button is prevented. When this occurs, the neurotransmitter's effect is called inhibitory, and the potential produced by these transmitters, the inhibitory postsynaptic potential (IPSP). Here, potassium ions leave the membrane and negative chloride ions might be pumped in leaving the inside of the cell negatively charged. The point of inhibition is that it prevents the neuron from becoming overexcited, a result that could result in cell damage or death. Epileptic seizures result from an uncontrolled firing of impulses, which is why many drugs to combat epilepsy help the inhibition of impulses. Because of the two different effects neurotransmitters have, they are referred to as either excitatory or inhibitory neurotransmitters. The process of neurotransmission is illustrated in Figure 3.4.

Neurotransmitters and neuromodulators

So far, we have described the effects of chemicals released by presynaptic buttons at the synapse on the activity of postsynaptic neurons. These chemicals send a signal to the postsynaptic button and can be inhibitory or excitatory. The probability of a postsynaptic neuron firing an action potential depends on the total amount of stimulation it receives. The stimulation could be both inhibitory and excitatory. If stimulation is predominantly excitatory, an action potential is likely. If it is predominantly inhibitory, no action potential is likely. Furthermore there may be neurons that excite strongly and others that excite weakly. If the stimulus is excited, depolarisation lasts from a few seconds to a few minutes.

There are slow synaptic potentials and there are fast ones. Slow potentials tend to result not from effects of the neurotransmitter on ion channels but

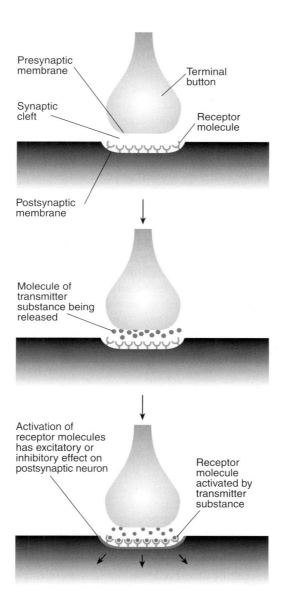

Fig 3.4 The process of neurotransmission

from the binding of the transmitter to receptor sites, which then triggers off intracellular changes. These effects are called modulatory synaptic effects, and the transmitters that produce them are called modulatory neurotransmitters (or neuromodulators) because they modulate the activity of the membrane they come into contact with but do not change it directly. They make the membrane more susceptible to producing an action potential. At some synapses, transmitters will be modulatory; at others they will be excitatory.

Most of the more prominent neurotransmitters are protein-based. Neurotransmitters can be made up of small or large protein molecules. All small molecule neurotransmitters, except acetylcholine, are amino acids or a type of amino acid called amines. Larger molecules are made up of peptides (proteins that are composed of a small number of amino acids). Because of this they are called neuropeptides and their function is not as clear as that of the small molecule transmitters. There are probably about 30–40 identifiable neuropeptides in the CNS.

The function of all neurotransmitters is not clear because the type of effect they produce depends on the type of receptor they bind to or communicate with. Neurotransmitters are made in the cell body and stored in the vesicles, as you saw in the section above. Usually, a terminal button contains one neurotransmitter and one or more neuropeptide. This complicates any understanding of the specific effects of each type of transmitter because the transmitters are released together. Some of the known major neurotransmitters and the functions they appear to perform are described in Table 3.3.

Table 3.3. The types of neurotransmitter and their putative function

Neurotransmitter	Important features
Acetylcholine	A small-molecule neurotransmitter that is synthesised by binding choline to acetyl coenzyme A
	Mostly found in the motor system, especially in brain stem and spinal cord motor neurons that innervate muscles of the skeleton
	Neurons that contain acetylcholine or chAT are called cholinergic neurons
	Acetylcholine receptors are also known as nicotinic receptors because nicotine seems to produce the same effects on muscles as acetylcholine does; the receptors can be blocked, which sometimes results in motor impairments; curare is one acetylcholine blocker – another is atropine; atropine acts by blocking the stimulation of a particular acetylcholine receptor – called a muscarinic receptor – by muscarine; these types of receptor are usually only found in smooth muscles and are slower to respond than are nicotinic receptors

Monoamines (biogenic amines)

Norepinephine/ noradrenaline	A catecholamine involved in most important behaviours such as movement, mood and cognition; stimulates the sympathetic nerves of the mammalian heart
Epinephrine/ adrenaline	A catecholamine involved in most important behaviours such as movement, mood and cognition
Dopamine	A catecholamine involved in most important behaviours such as movement, mood and cognition
Serotonin/5-HT (5-Hydroxytryptamine)	A catecholamine involved in the regulation of mood, especially depression.
Glutamate/ glutamic acid	Excitatory amino acid, served by three receptor types; two are responsible for fast depolarisation; a subtype, N-methyl-D-aspartate, is involved in learning and memory formation

Gamma-aminobutyric acid (GABA)

	The most common of the inhibitory amino acid CNS neurotransmitters; this transmitter produces hyperpolarisation by either opening chloride channels or potassium channels GABA has two types of receptor: GABA$_A$ and GABA$_B$. The $_A$ receptor is responsible for inhibition before the synapse and mediates the membrane permeability of chloride; the $_B$ receptor mediates potassium permeability
Glycine	An inhibiting neurotransmitter found in the brain stem and interneurons of the spinal cord; inhibits motor neurons – for example, the glycine-receptor blocker, strychnine, causes muscle spasms

---

The effects that these neurotransmitters have on postsynaptic neurons are complex. For example, each neurotransmitter has different types of receptor. For dopamine, there are so-called D1 and D2 receptors, which are different in function and distribution. Norepinephrine and epinephrine have alpha and beta receptors, which sometimes produce completely different effects. Serotonin has several types of receptor. All of this receptor divergence means that a monoamine can inhibit or excite depending on the type of receptor it contacts.

If there is surplus neurotransmitter in the extracellular fluid (i.e. substance that does not bind to the postsynaptic membrane) this can be cleaned away by reuptake mechanisms. Reuptake refers to the process whereby a neurotransmitter is taken back into the presynaptic button and either stored and reused or broken down. Some neurotransmitters, such as acetylcholine and 5HT, also have enzymes in the synaptic gap that can enhance reuptake. Some chemicals, such as cocaine and amphetamine, can prevent reuptake – this potentiates the excitatory effect of the neurotransmitter.

Focus on ... dopamine

Dopamine is one of the brain's most studied neurotransmitters and, like all of the major neurotransmitters, exerts different effects on behaviour depending on which parts of the brain it acts. It has been implicated in behaviours as diverse as memory, depression, schizophrenia, movement disorders and emotion. Dopamine is a type of neurotransmitter that belongs to the catecholamine family (as does norepinephrine). Dopamine's pathways to the brain arise from the brain stem and there are three of them. The first pathway leads from the hypothalamus to the pituitary gland; the second from the substantia nigra (an area near the brainstem) and basal ganglia (a collection of structures found beneath the cortex) and a third from the midbrain (specifically, the ventral tegmental area) to the cortex, specifically the frontal cortex and the limbic system (a collection of regions found subcortically that includes the amygdala and nucleus accumbens; more on these in the next chapter). You'll find more detail on these structures in the next chapter.

Parkinson's disease

Perhaps dopamine's best-known effect is seen in Parkinson's disease (PD). PD, as you will see in more detail in the final chapter, is a degenerative brain disorder characterised by slow or absent movement, poor gait, falling down, muscle rigidity and tremor in limbs when the body is at rest. The key neurophysiological symptom of PD is a loss of dopamine. The gold standard treatment of PD, however, involves not replacing dopamine directly but giving a drug that can be converted into dopamine. This is because dopamine does not cross the barrier between blood and the CNS. Dopamine's precursor, l-DOPA (or levodopa), however, does and when this happens it is converted by the CNS into dopamine. The drug appears to act by replacing the dopamine loss seen in the basal ganglia. Interestingly, drugs used to treat some mental illnesses (such as schizophrenia) produce Parkinsonian side-effects because they block the activity of certain dopamine receptors. Conversely, levodopa can produce symptoms of schizophrenia.

Schizophrenia

Schizophrenia is a disorder of thought and emotion characterised by positive symptoms (delusions, hallucinations), negative symptoms (apathy, social withdrawal) and cognitive impairment (lack of attention, short-term memory problems). The dominant biological theory of schizophrenia is that there is a dysfunction of the dopamine system (Lidow *et al.*, 1998). Drugs used to treat schizophrenia, anti-psychotic drugs, act by blocking dopamine at two receptors, D2 and D3. Cocaine, which potentiates the effects of dopamine at these receptors, can produce schizophrenia-type symptoms. However, the drugs only seem to combat the positive symptoms of the disorder. It may be that other dopamine receptor types may be responsible for negative symptoms, possibly D1 receptors.

Attention deficit hyperactivity disorder (ADHD)

Another disorder that implicates dopamine is ADHD, the most common childhood disorder of this type, which is characterised by attention and learning difficulties, lack of impulse control and hyperactivity. Around 1.29 million children receive some type of medication, such as methylphenidate (Ritalin), to alleviate the symptoms of the disorder (O'Toole *et al.*, 1997). Animal models of the disorder implicate dopamine system dyfunction in the front of the brain (specifically, a region called the nucleus accumbens). Dopamine also seems to play an important role in attention and in inhibiting impulses (two functions of the frontal cortex). The disorder seems to involve a disinhibition of attention and control through a decrease in the activity of dopamine.

Emotion and reward

In recent years, emotion researchers interested in the neurochemical basis of emotion have focused on dopamine because periods of positive emotion appear to be accompanied by releases of the neurotransmitter. This increase in dopamine during periods of positive mood are thought to be responsible for the well-documented improvements in performance on cognitive tasks when positive mood has been induced (see Carlson *et al.*, 2000, for a review of the evidence for this). Also, drugs that have similar effects to dopamine (such as amphetamines and morphine, discussed in the chapter on consciousness) also produce an elevation or an enhancement in mood. The pathways involved appear to be the second and third described above. The pathways between the substantia nigra and the striatum, and between the ventral tegmental area and the cortex become active during periods of good mood.

What the example of dopamine shows is that the same neurotransmitter can be implicated in different types of behaviour depending on the specific dopamine receptor and the dopaminergic projection system involved.

As you will see in the following chapters, neurotransmitters are implicated in various ways in the execution of specific behaviours. Much of what we know of the effects of neurotransmitter release on behaviour has been derived from animal studies or studies of the psychopharmacology of mental illness. Chapters 10 and 11 look at the contribution of the neurotransmitter systems to behaviour in most detail. The next chapter introduces you to the various important parts of the CNS subserved by neurotransmitters, and the roles they undertake in executing and maintaining behaviour.

SOME USEFUL FURTHER READING

GENERAL NEUROTRANSMISSION AND NEUROPHYSIOLOGY
Brodal, P. (1998) *The Central Nervous System: Structure and Function* (second edition). New York: Oxford University Press.
Kandel, E.R., Schwartz, J.H. and Jessell, T.M. (1995) *Essentials of Neural Science and Behaviour.* New Jersey: Prentice Hall International.

NEURONS AND SYNAPSES
Atwood, H.L. and Lnenicka, G.A. (1986) Structure and function in synapses: emerging correlations. *Trends in Neurosciences* 9, 248–50.
Levitan, I.B. and Kaczmarek, L.K. (1991) *The Neuron.* Oxford: Oxford University Press.
Shepard, G.M. (1998) *The Synaptic Organisation of the Brain.* Oxford: Oxford University Press.

NEUROTRANSMITTERS AND NEUROTRANSMISSION
Bellen, H. (1999) *Neurotransmitter Release.* Oxford: Oxford University Press.
Katz, P. (1999) *Beyond Neurotransmission.* Oxford: Oxford University Press.
Valenstein, E.S. (2002) The discovery of chemical neurotransmitters. *Brain and Cognition* 49, 73–95.

SOME USEFUL JOURNALS TO BROWSE

Brain
Cell
Current Opinion in Neurobiology
Journal of Neuroscience
Nature
Nature Neuroscience
Neuron
Science
Trends in Neurosciences

4 The Brain: its Structures, Regions and Functions

WHAT YOU WILL FIND IN THIS CHAPTER
- a description of the major structures and regions of the central nervous system and their role in behaviour

WHAT YOU SHOULD BE ABLE TO DO AFTER READING THE CHAPTER
- identify regions of the central nervous system that control or mediate specific behaviours

4.1 DEVELOPMENT OF THE CNS

A human embryo begins life as a hollow tube called a neural tube. As the embryo develops, the tube elongates and folds, and its tissue thickens. The wall's tube is made up of cells that will later become the glial cells and the neurons of the nervous system. At this stage, these cells are called neuroepithelial cells: the prospective glial cells are called spongioblasts and the prospective neurons are called neuroblasts. The inside of the tube forms a canal, which contains cerebrospinal fluid (CSF), a clear, watery liquid that serves a number of functions in the CNS. The head of the embryo develops into the brain; the remainder straightens and becomes the spinal cord.

The canal develops four protuberances, which later develop into the brain's four ventricles – chambers deep inside the brain – which contain CSF. The spinal cord end of the canal becomes one long fluid-filled canal that connects the four ventricles of the brain. The ventricles help divide the brain into various general regions called the forebrain, midbrain and hindbrain. The rostral ventricles are called the lateral and third ventricles. The region surrounding the third ventricle is called the endbrain or telencephalon and represents the most recently developed and most sophisticated part of the CNS, the cerebral cortex. The area surrounding the third ventricle becomes the diencephalon, or interbrain.

4.2 THE CEREBRAL HEMISPHERES

The most prominent and distinctive parts of the brain are the cerebral hemispheres. These make up the two 'halves' of the brain and comprise grey matter and white matter, two types of collection of nerve cells. Grey matter is so called because it contains nerve cells' blood capillaries. White matter is made up of processes called axons, which are covered with a milk-coloured membrane. The cerebral hemispheres are responsible for all the major, important sophisticated behaviour we – and other primates – engage in: sensation, perception, remembering, feeling emotion, planning, and so on. Much of the data in this and the next chapters derive from our study of healthy or damaged cerebral hemispheres.

4.3 FISSURES AND GYRI

The cerebral hemispheres are covered with cerebral cortex (literally, bark or rind) and this has a convoluted appearance as if you had taken a grey sheet of membrane and crumpled it up. The convolutions are made up of gyri (the raised parts of the cortex) sulci and fissures (the 'cracks' or valleys in between the gyri fissure are the deepest). The cortex is a layer of nerve tissue, about 3 mm thick, and the more sophisticated organisms tend to have the most wrinkled cortices. The structure is illustrated, from various angles, in Figure 4.1.

Fissures describe very deep grooves; sulci describe more superficial ones. Each hemisphere contains one large fissure called the lateral, or Sylvian, fissure. This, as its name suggests, extends laterally and medially down each hemisphere.

There is much variation in the appearance and length of fissures and sulci, but some are well described, such as the large groove in the middle of the brain – the central sulcus or Rolandic fissure. In front of this is the precentral gyrus. Together these two features form the cortical area responsible for motor movement. Damage to these gyri can result in paralysis in the contralateral (opposite) side of the body. The gyrus appearing after the central sulcus is called the postcentral gyrus and is the region responsible for receiving sensory information from the skin and muscles.

As well as being convoluted, the cortex is also made up of six parallel layers, or laminae, found perpendicular to the surface. The division of the cortex into six layers is made on the basis of cytoarchitecture: the number, size and density of cell bodies in the cortex. Neurons are not arranged randomly across the whole cortex but in some orderly fashion. Some layers send projections to other brain regions while others receive projections.

A well-known and widely used example of a cytoarchitectonic map – a

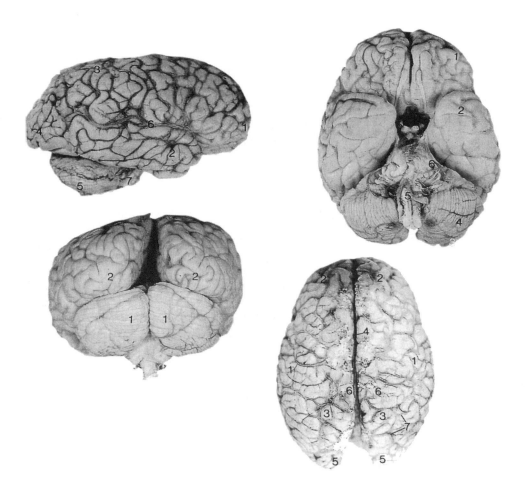

Fig 4.1 External features of the brain from four different angles

map of the cortex that divides the brain according to cell size, type and density – is that of Korbinian Brodmann (1909). Brodmann's map assigns numbers to various areas of the brain based on the cellular arrangement in those areas. If you see in this book and others areas of the brain being described as Area 44 or BA 44, the descriptors refer to Brodmann's original demarcation. There is a very close relationship between Brodmann's areas and their functional significance. The area identified as 44, for example, corresponds exactly to Broca's area, the region of the cortex involved in speech production. Brodmann's map is seen in Figure 4.2.

The cortex is also arranged in another way: it manifests distinct columns within these cortical layers. Each of these columns has a function that is not normally shared with immediate, neighbouring columns. The existence of the columnar arrangement in the cortex was demonstrated by early electrophysiological studies in which electrodes were placed into the cortex perpendicularly. The neurons – regardless of the depth of the cortex reached – had the same receptive field. However, when the electrode was placed into the cortex at an angle, different receptive fields were recorded at each level.

4.4 PROTECTION OF THE CNS

The central nervous system, containing as its does some of the body's most sensitive parts, is well protected. The spinal cord is surrounded by a long bone structure called the vertebral column (this is made up of interconnecting bones called vertebrae). The brain is also encased by a bone – the skull – but it and the spinal cord has other protective mechanisms. For example, their immediate surface is covered by layers of membrane of varying thickness. These are called meninges (the plural of the Greek for membrane) and there are three of them. Working from the brain outward, these are the pia mater, arachnoid mater and dura mater.

The dura mater is the toughest layer; it covers the inside of the skull and goes right to and around the very tip of the spinal cord. At the bottom of the spinal cord – the cauda equina – the mater forms a sac called the dural sac. It is here where a clinician might perform a lumbar puncture, which involves extracting a small amount of liquid (CSF) that may give a clue to brain dysfunction. CSF is found between the meninges and the skull/vertebrae and helps cushion the movement of the brain. Neither the brain nor the spinal cord make direct contact with these bones but are suspended in this liquid. The suspension prevents the brain and spinal cord from becoming bruised. There are instances when bruising does happen such as during closed-head injury where there is no penetration of the skull; the most deliberate example of this is boxing.

CSF is also found in the brain's four ventricles and protects the brain from

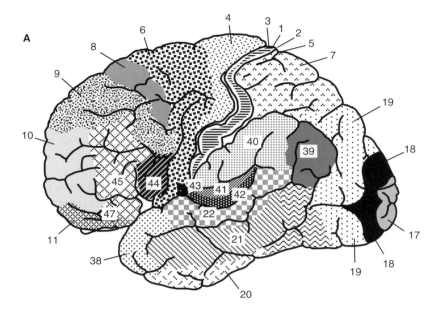

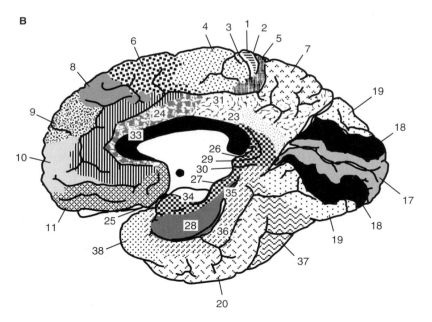

Fig 4.2 Brodmann's cytoarchitectonic map

extreme pressure such as that caused by a blow to the head. Effectively, it makes the head 1300 grammes lighter. When impact is made, fluid has to be moved aside before the brain hits the skull.

The most important liquid in the brain is blood. The brain's blood supply is provided by the internal carotid artery – which supplies the cortex – and the vertebral artery – which supplies the brainstem and cerebellum. The carotid artery enters the cavity of the skull and branches off to make three more arteries (which supply the motor and sensory areas of the brain). The vertebral artery (or arteries; there are two of them) also branches into other arteries, which supply blood to the visual cortex and the sides of the cortex. The spinal cord has its own arteries, the posterior and anterior spinal arteries, which run along its side and midline, respectively.

4.5 DAMAGE TO THE CNS

With such protection, damage is rare but does occur, whether through accident or deliberate harm. Closed-head injury, as you have seen, describes an insult to the head that does not penetrate the skull or meninges. The brain can bleed or swell as a result of impact. A penetrating brain injury does, as the name suggests, penetrate the skull. Some of the types of specific condition arising from these injuries, and other causes, include:

- swelling of part of the brain (oedema)
- presence of dead tissue resulting from a loss of blood supply (infarction)
- loss of blood flow due to the narrowing or blockage of an artery (ischemia)
- blockage of a blood vessel caused by coagulated blood (thrombosis)
- coagulated blood travelling down narrow arteries, thereby blocking them (embolism)
- a sudden loss of blood supply to the brain (cardiovascular accident or stroke; one type of stroke results from a reduction in blood supply leading to a lack of oxygen; another results from a bleed into the brain, called a haemorrhage)
- the ballooning of an artery wall (aneurysm)
- a collection of abnormal blood vessels providing an abnormal blood supply (arteriovenous malformation or angioma)
- bleeding into the space between the meninge and the second membrane (subarachnoid haemorrhage)
- a space-occupying lesion and surrounding tissue (intracranial tumour)
- loss of oxygen in the blood supply to the brain (anoxia)
- partial loss of oxygen in the blood supply to the brain (hypoxia)
- inflammation of the brain (encephalitis)
- increased ventricular volume (hydrocephalus).

4.6 THE BRAINSTEM

The brainstem is actually a continuation of the spinal cord. It comprises, from bottom to top, the medulla oblongata, the pons and the mesencephalon. Neurons in the medulla oblongata control fairly basic, sometimes involuntary, 'internal' behaviour such as heart rate, blood pressure and respiration. The medulla oblongata extends into the pons (meaning 'bridge'), a structure that contains cells that send projections to the cerebellum. The pons is an important structure because several of the cranial nerves exit here and its neurons control some stages of sleep. The mesencephalon is the next clear region up from the pons and is quite short. It contains four small, rounded 'bumps' called colliculi. There are two pairs – inferior colliculi and superior colliculi – and these are involved in the relay of auditory and visual information, respectively. The mesencephalon contains the substantia nigra ('black substance'), an area that is involved in the regulation of movement and is often referred to as part of the basal ganglia.

In the core of the brainstem, there is a mass of neurons called the reticular formation, an interesting collection of fibres. Some parts of it are involved in sleep, others in respiration. Its activity has also been thought to provide a biological basis of the personality dimensions extroversion and neuroticism.

4.7 THE THALAMUS

The next region up from the mesencephalon is the diencephalon, which comprises two principal structures called the thalamus and hypothalamus. The thalamus resides on either side of the third ventricle and has a flattened, egg-shaped appearance. It plays a vital, important role as a relay station for almost all information coming from the lower brainstem and CNS on its way to the cortex. To its side is a thick covering of white matter, which extends into another fibre structure, the corpus callosum, a thick band of fibres that connects the two cerebral hemispheres.

The thalamus can be divided into different regions of nuclei, all of which are described by their position (e.g. anterior, lateral, etc.). These nuclei can themselves be subdvided into smaller nuclei. One large set of nuclei in the posterior part, called the pulvinar, partly covers two other nuclei: the lateral geniculate body and the medial geniculate body. The first of these acts as a relay station for visual information, the second as a relay station for auditory information. The importance of the diencephalon to vision does not end here. The optic nerves themselves, which deliver information from each retina, course under the diencephalon and meet, forming a chasm. Here, there is a partial crossing over of fibres so that some axons cross over to the contralateral hemisphere. Fibres leaving this chasm form an optic tract. The visual pathway is described in more detail in the next chapter.

4.8 THE HYPOTHALAMUS

Beneath and anterior to the thalamus lies the hypothalamus ('hypo' means 'less than' or 'beneath'). It is about 1 cubic centimetre in size (i.e. no bigger than a grape) but its functional importance is enormous. The hypothalamus, along with other areas of the brainstem, are responsible for mediating or maintaining homeostasis. Homeostasis ('homoios' – similar; 'stasis' – fixed, or staying put) refers to the process whereby physiological variables such as temperature, fluid regulation and nutrient storage are maintained. The hypothalamus is also involved in species-typical behaviours that are either involuntary or semi-involuntary, such as aggressing, feeding (eating and drinking), and mating.

It receives sensory information from receptors inside the organs of the body and controls a small structure called the pituitary gland, which secretes hormones into the blood supply (according to Descartes, this is where our soul eventually reached). Hormones are chemicals produced by the endocrine glands. Hormones act in a similar way to neurotransmitters – they stimulate receptor molecules – but, unlike neurotransmitters, their reach is wider. The molecules are located on particular cells (called target cells because hormones cause physiological changes in them). Almost all cells, even neurons, have receptor molecules susceptible to hormones.

4.9 THE AUTONOMIC NERVOUS SYSTEM (ANS)

The pituitary gland has been described as a 'master gland' because it can also affect the activity of other endocrine glands. As the pituitary gland is controlled by the hypothalamus, the significance of the hypothalamus becomes very clear: it controls the entire endocrine system. The nerves that control the functions of glands and internal organs form the autonomic nervous system (ANS). The ANS is responsible for controlling behaviours such as sweating, salivating, secreting gastric juices and crying, among others. It has two branches: the sympathetic branch, which directs activities that involve the expenditure of energy; and the parasympathetic branch, which controls activities that do not require a great expenditure of energy. An example of the former's effects is increased blood flow to muscles in preparation for fighting; an example of the latter is digestion of food. A number of the techniques described in the psychophysiological techniques section in Chapter 2 measures changes in the ANS (heart rate and blood pressure, for example). Table 4.1 shows the glands that are affected by the activity of the two branches of the ANS and the internal behaviour the branches control.

Table 4.1 The glands directed by the sympathetic and parasympathetic branches of the autonomic nervous system (ANS), and the behaviour controlled by these branches

Gland	Sympathetic branch	Parasympathetic branch
Lachrymal gland (eye)	Secretion of tears; pupil dilation	Pupil constriction
Blood vessels	Constriction of abdomen and skin; muscle dilation	Abdomen and muscle constriction; skin dilation
Stomach	Inhibition of contraction and secretion of stomach acid	Production of contraction and secretion of stomach acid
Intestine	Decrease of activity	Increase of activity
Bladder	Inhibition of contraction	Contraction
Salivary gland	Secretion of thick saliva	Secretion of thin saliva
Sweat gland	Sweating; pilorection (goosebumps)	
Heart	Increase in speed of contraction	Decrease in speed of contraction
Adrenal gland	Secretion of adrenalin	
External genitalia	Ejaculation; orgasm	Erection and vaginal lubrication

Near the hypothalamus are two structures that appear to play a special role in memory and learning: these are the mamillary bodies and the fornix, and more on their function appears in the chapter on memory (Chapter 7).

4.10 THE CEREBELLUM

The cerebellum (literally, 'little brain') extends from the pons and is responsible for the execution of movement and maintaining balance of posture. The cerebellum is located beneath the cortex and posterior of the brainstem. Its name, little brain, nicely describes the structure because it does look like a small brain attached to the back of the brainstem. The cerebellum contains white matter, which has a distinctive appearance: like a mature, leafy tree. Because of this, it is called the arbor vitae (literally, 'the tree of life'). Recent studies have implicated the cerebellum in more sophisticated, complex behaviour such as cognition, especially language (more on this in Chapter 9).

4.11 THE LIMBIC SYSTEM

Another collection of structures important for behaviour is called the limbic system (see Figure 4.3), a name given by the neuroanatomist Paul Maclean to a collection of subcortical structures that includes the hippocampus, the septal nuclei, the amygdala, the cingulate gyrus, the mamillary bodies and the hypothalamus, although there is still argument over whether these structures actually do constitute a system.

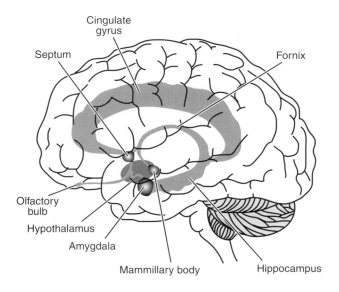

Fig 4.3 The structures of the limbic system

The hypothalamus, for example, appears to be involved in the regulation of eating and drinking via connections with the amygdala. The amygdala has been thought to play a role in a number of behaviours including face recognition, emotion, responding to painful events and aggression. In laboratory animals whose amygdala has been destroyed, normal aggressive behaviour is abolished. The role of the amygdala in emotion is described and discussed in Chapter 8.

The hippocampus (or hippocampal formation) is a collection of structures found just behind the amygdala. Lesions to the hippocampus result in an inability to learn or remember new material. Patient HM, for example, whom you came across in Chapter 1, had his hippocampus removed and suffered severe anterograde amnesia. We'll discover more about the role of the hippocampus in memory in Chapter 7. The structure also seems to play a role in spatial navigation – it appears to allow us to navigate our way in familiar and unfamiliar environments (Maguire *et al.*, 1997; Maguire *et al.*, 1998a; 1998b), and we will return to this role in the chapter on memory.

4.12 THE BASAL GANGLIA

Inside the cortex, there are several small structures integral to the functioning of the human brain and behaviour. The basal ganglia, for example, are involved in certain aspects of movement. They receive connections from parts of the cortex and send axons to the motor cortex. The basal ganglia have two main parts. The smallest is found in front of the thalamus, has a long, curved tail and is called the caudate nucleus. The caudate has a large part (called the caput) and a tail-end (the cauda), which points upwards then backwards into the temporal lobe. The largest part of the basal ganglia, found lateral to the internal capsule, is called the lentiform nucleus. The lateral and external part of this is called the putamen. The medial and internal part is called the globus pallidus. These regions are affected in Parkinson's disease, which is considered in detail in Chapter 11.

4.13 LOBES OF THE BRAIN

The fissures and sulci of the cortex appear to divide the brain into geographically distinct regions called lobes. There are four of them: frontal, temporal, parietal and occipital but there is no underlying psychological logic to their names. The areas are named after the bone that covers them. However, specific functions do seem to 'reside' in specific lobes (e.g. the primary visual cortex is found in the occipital lobe, for example, and the auditory cortex is found in the temporal lobe). Table 4.2 summarises some of the main functions of the four lobes. Although functions have been placed under specific lobes, there is often overlap in activation. The lobes and important regions of the brain are seen in photographic and schematic form in Figures 4.4a, 4.4b and 4.4c.

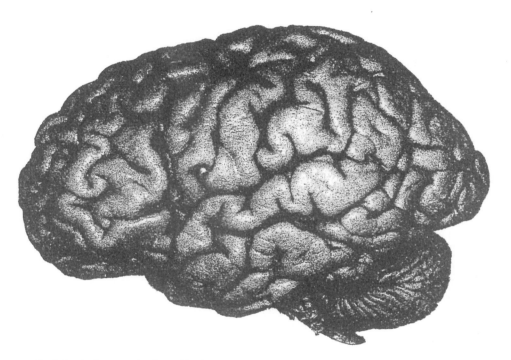

Fig 4.4a A photograph of a real brain

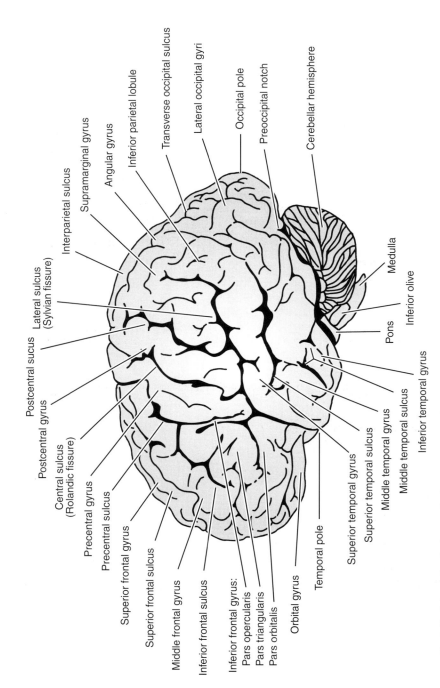

Fig 4.4b Schematic of a human brain

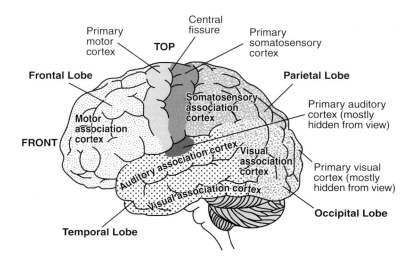

Figs 4.4a, b & c A lateral photograph of a real brain (4.4a), a labelled schematic drawing of the surface features of the brain (4.4b) and a drawing of the association areas of the brain (4.4c)

Table 4.2 Some of the principal functions associated with the lobes of the brain

Occipital lobe
Perception and manipulation of visual information
Perception of objects and faces
Mental imagery

Temporal lobe
Spoken-word recognition
Language comprehension
Verbal and non-verbal retrieval of general knowledge
Encoding of autobiographical memory
Memory formation (hippocampus)
Processing of sounds and music
Braille reading

Parietal lobe
Attention
Spatial perception
Imagery
Working memory

Skill learning
Reaching
Memory retrieval
Arithmetical ability
Somatosensation (sense of touch)

Frontal lobe
Working memory
Memory retrieval
Speech production and written-word recognition
Sustained attention
Planning
Social behaviour
Emotional inhibition
Initiating and planning movements
Ongoing monitoring of behaviour
Olfactory detection and discrimination
Temporal sequencing of events

There are quite specific connections made between certain brain regions. Perhaps the most important are between the thalamus and the cortex (thalamocortical connections), between one region of the cortex and another (cortico–cortical connections) and between large areas of cortex and another (commissures). Cortico–cortical connections are usually reciprocal (i.e. the sending area receives fibres from the region it sends to, thereby providing 'feedback loops').

Many of the connections made within the cortex are made via association cortices. These cortices do not directly receive inputs from sensory or motor receptors but do receive projections from the primary sensory and motor cortices. The role of the association cortices appears to be to integrate information and to send back information to other parts of the cortex.

4.14 THE OCCIPITAL LOBE

The occipital lobe (ob – 'in the back of'; caput – head) is found at the back of the brain and forms a boundary with two other lobes (parietal and temporal). The primary visual cortex – the part of the brain that receives sensory information from the eyes – is located here, and the area is often known by the abbreviation V1. Thus, the occipital lobe's principal role involves the control of vision and perception. Damage to V1, for example, produces cortical blindness where individuals report being unable to see particular aspects of the world (this is different from 'normal' blindness).

The information from the primary visual cortex projects to the visual association cortex which, like V1, is located in the occipital lobe. Damage to the visual association cortex results in an unusual condition called visual agnosia. Although the individual may be able to see normally – visual acuity is intact – he or she may not be able to recognise objects visually. When given an object to palpate, however, they are able to name the object (using the sense of touch). This suggests that there is no verbal deficit – the individual can name the object by touch – but that the area that allows the visual representation of the object is impaired. We will return to agnosia in more detail in the next chapter.

4.15 THE TEMPORAL LOBE

The temporal lobes are primarily responsible for audition (hearing), language comprehension, memory and learning. The temporal lobes have been divided into four distinct regions: the lateral, medial, posterior and polar regions. These lobes are particularly important for hearing because they contain both the primary auditory cortex and the auditory association areas. Bilateral damage to a region called Area 41 (Heschl's gyrus), for example, can lead to cortical deafness. Unilateral lesions to this area result in less severe auditory consequences, such as a reduction in the threshold for auditory sensation.

Damage to other regions of the auditory cortex can lead to musical deficits such as tone deafness or poor pitch/melody perception (musical agnosia), or an inability to comprehend non-verbal sounds (sound agnosia). Language comprehension is most affected by damage to unilateral lesions to Area 22/39 or Wernicke's area, a region important for the recognition of spoken words. There may also be a multi-modal language area in these lobes which undertakes language processing (not necessarily orally). This area is in the posterior part of the left temporal lobe and becomes active when people read text or when people read Braille (Buchel et al., 1998). The area (Area 37) seems to be specialised for written-word recognition, rather than spoken-word recognition.

The medial part of the temporal lobes seems to be important for encoding episodic memory and for recalling non-verbal autobiographical memories (Schachter and Wagner, 1999). Episodic memory is the memory for personally meaningful information and is often referred to as autobiographical memory.

The hippocampus, as you saw in Chapter 1, is located in these lobes and appears to be important for spatially navigating environments and remembering contexts in which information was learned (Gerlai, 2001). The medial temporal lobe is also active during the processing of spatial information (Maguire et al., 1998a; 1998b), a topic returned to in Chapter 7.

Finally, damage to the right temporal (and orbitofrontal cortex) has been associated with deficits in odour recognition memory (Jones-Gotman and Zatorre, 1993).

4.16 THE PARIETAL LOBE

The parietal lobe contains the primary and association cortices for somatosensation – our sense of touch. Damage to the parietal cortex, therefore, can produce deficits in behaviours such as tactile perception and touch discrimination. As the parietal lobe also contains the motor cortex, damage to the motor area can result in impairments in gross limb movement.

The parietal lobe becomes active during attention, spatial perception, imagery, the learning of skills and encoding spatial information. Conducting a search of visual information – finding a letter in an array of letters, for example – seems to produce increased activity in this area (Corbetta *et al.*, 1995). Perception of spatial locations is also associated with increases in parietal lobe activity (Aguirre and D'Esposito, 1997), and mentally rotating visual stimuli and map/route finding also elicit responses in this region (Kosslyn *et al.*, 1998). One part seems to be involved in retrieving episodic memories whereas another is involved in paying attention to stimuli and in perceiving spatial relations. The region also appears to be activated during working memory tasks – those that require a person to hold information in short-term memory for immediate use. The posterior part of the parietal cortex (PPC) may be the region that is specialised for storing representations of motor actions (Milner, 1998) and for controlling our intention to move. There may also be vision-specific neurons in this area, which control visually guided movement (Sakata, *et al.*, 1995).

Parietal cortex damage is often associated with deficits in spatial representation such as spatial neglect, where the patient is unable to 'see' objects in one half of the visual field or to copy a drawing in the absence of a neurological motor impairment (Halligan and Marshall, 1994). There is more on spatial neglect in the next chapter. Finally, the parietal cortex also seems to play a role in mathematics, a point taken up in the 'Focus on ...' section below.

Focus on ... mathematics and the developing brain

Studies suggest that the frontal and parietal cortices are more involved than others in the process of mental arithmetic (Menon *et al.*, 2000). Menon *et al.* (2000) found that the left and right angular gyri (parts of the cortex located in the parietal lobe) were selectively active during mental calculation, and other researchers have found activation in the same area (Cowell *et al.*, 2000). A neuroanatomical study has recently found that this region is smaller in children with mathematical operations deficits when compared with children with normal maths performance (Isaacs *et al.*, 2001).

Children of low birth weight are known to develop deficits in cognitive ability later in life. Isaacs *et al.* (2001) investigated whether there would be a neural correlate of mental arithmetic deficits in adolescent children who had been born at 30 weeks' gestation. The children were given mental arithmetic tests (addition, subtraction, multiplication and division; problem-solving, statistics and understanding of graphs), basic reading, spelling and comprehension tests and a standing intelligence test. One group of children had specific arithmetic deficits; another (control) group had scores within the normal range; a third group had deficient mathematical reasoning skills; a fourth group was able to reason mathematically.

While there was no significant difference in scores between groups for the reading and intelligence tests, there were differences on the mathematics tests. Those children with numerical operations problems performed more poorly than a control group on tests of numerical operations such as division and addition. When the researchers correlated the performance of the group with brain volume, they found that the low birth weight children with good numerical operations ability had greater grey matter in the left parietal lobe than did the low birth weight children. No such difference in regional mass was found between children with deficient mathematical reasoning ability and those with good ability, suggesting that this specific region may be involved in mediating aspects of mental calculation. The results are compatible with a reported single-case study of developmental dyscalculia (the development of mathematical impairment), which showed decreased activation in the left temporo-parietal cortex (Levy *et al.*, 1999).

4.17 THE FRONTAL LOBE

The frontal lobe comprises around a third of the cortex and is the most recently developed part of the brain. Because of its size, it contains many regions with distinct roles. The premotor cortex, for example, is found in the frontal lobe. Damage to the primary motor cortex results in a paralysis in the contralateral side of the body. The prefrontal cortex – the tip of the frontal lobe – seems to be important for inhibiting inappropriate emotional and social responses, and for organising and planning behaviour. The prefrontal cortex represents the association area of the frontal lobes. It is an important association area because it receives projections from all sensory modalities and also has connections with areas responsible for mediating emotion. For this reason, the frontal lobes have been described as the brain's 'orchestra leader'.

Two generally accepted subdivisions of the frontal cortex are the dorsolateral and orbitofrontal areas. Damage to the dorsolateral cortex has been associated with planning or ordering deficits; people will have difficulty in changing strategies, for example, or be able to place a series of pictures in the correct order to form a logical sequence (Sirigu *et al.*, 1995). Damage to the orbitofrontal cortex has been associated with the inability to inhibit emotionally and socially inappropriate behaviours. Patients will report being franker, more aggressive and less emotionally sensitive than they were prior to the injury, for example (Hornak *et al.*, 1996). These patients may show no intellectual impairment but will show impairments in emotional expression and social behaviour (Eslinger and Damasio, 1985).

Curiously, individuals diagnosed with anti-social personality disorder show an 11 per cent reduction in prefrontal cortex volume compared with a control group (Raine *et al.*, 2000) and there are reports of individuals with damage to this region subsequently developing an anti-social way of behaving (Blair and Cipolotti, 2000).

The prefrontal cortex is also involved in working memory, encoding and retrieval, and sustained attention (Cabeza and Nyberg, 2000; Fletcher and Henson, 2001). For example, in neuroimaging studies, the prefrontal cortex is consistently activated by working memory tasks. Working memory tasks require participants to hold information in mind over a very short period of time. These tasks either involve simple maintenance or manipulation of material. Maintenance tasks, for example, might require participants to decide whether a single item had been included in a previously presented series of four to nine items. Participants have to hold the information about the previously presented items in working memory in order to decide on whether the single item was one of those they had just seen (or heard). Manipulation tasks involve the reorganisation of the material that is held in mind for a brief time. Stimuli used in working memory tasks can be verbal or non-verbal and each stimulus type appears to recruit different sides of the frontal cortex: left for verbal and right for non-verbal.

The left side has also been found to be active during the retrieval of semantic memory – knowledge of the meaning of words, objects and facts (Martin *et al.*, 1996) – the encoding and retrieval of episodic memory (Nolde *et al.*, 1998) and during tasks that require divided attention (Benedict *et al.*, 1998). Broca's area is also located in the frontal lobe and this region is important to word production.

There are some inconsistent findings, however. Not all studies report exclusive activation of these areas during working memory and the specific activation of frontal regions. This is especially true when researchers have studied the retrieval of information from long-term memory (see Fletcher and Henson, 2001).

In later chapters, you will see how the four lobes have been implicated in behaviours from emotion and personality to language and reasoning. The next chapter explores in more detail the role of the lobes, and parts of the cortex and subcortex, in the sensory and motor systems.

SOME USEFUL FURTHER READING

GENERAL NEUROANATOMY

Brodal, P. (1998) *The Central Nervous System: Structure and Function* (second edition). New York: Oxford University Press.
England, M.A. and Wakely, J. (1991) *A Colour Atlas of the Brain and Spinal Cord.* Aylesbury: Wolfe Publishing Ltd.
Greenfield, S. (1997) *The Human Brain: A Guided Tour.* London: Weidenfeld and Nicholson.

NERVOUS SYSTEM DEVELOPMENT

Brown, M., Keynes, R. and Lumsden, A. (2001) *The Developing Brain.* Oxford: Oxford University Press.

THE LOBES OF THE BRAIN AND FUNCTIONAL LOCALISATION

Cabeza, R. and Nyberg, L. (2000) Imaging cognition II: an empirical review of 275 PET and fMRI studies. *Journal of Cognitive Neuroscience* 12(1), 1–47.
Culham, J.C. and Kanwisher, N.G. (2001) Neuroimaging of cognitive functions in human parietal cortex. *Current Opinion in Neurobiology* 11, 157–63.
Duncan, J. and Owen, A.M. (2000) Common regions of the human frontal lobe recruited by diverse cognitive demands. *Trends in Neurosciences* 23(10), 475–83.
Funahashi, S. (2001) Neuronal mechanisms of executive control by the prefrontal cortex. *Neuroscience Research* 39, 147–65.

SOME USEFUL JOURNALS TO BROWSE

Archives of General Psychiatry
Brain
Cognitive Neuropsychology
Cortex
Hippocampus
Journal of Cognitive Neuroscience
Journal of Neuroscience
Nature Neuroscience
Neuropsychologia
Neuropsychology
NeuroReport
Psychophysiology
Science
Trends in Cognitive Sciences
Trends in Neurosciences

5

The Sensory and Motor Systems

WHAT YOU WILL FIND IN THIS CHAPTER
- a description of the visual, auditory, somatosensory, gustatory, olfactory and motor systems
- discussion of the consequences of damage to these systems for sensory and motor behaviour
- discussion of the localisation of sensory, perceptual and motor functions

WHAT YOU SHOULD BE ABLE TO DO AFTER READING THE CHAPTER
- be aware of the basic neural machinery of the sensory and motor systems
- be aware of the consequences of damage to parts of these systems
- be able to outline the evidence for (and against) localisation of sensory, perceptual and motor function

5.1 INTRODUCTION

As you are reading this sentence, your brain is engaged in a fantastically complex series of activities. It is allowing you to hold and position your book, to position your head toward the right page and your eyes toward the right sentences, to use your hands to turn the page and to reach for the page accurately. It is allowing you to translate the little black marks on a white background (and before that, to perceive black marks on a white background) into meaningful symbols; a part of it may be helping you to understand or remember the collective meaning of those symbols. At the same time, your brain is helping you ignore other information on the page until you need to come to it. It is also allowing you to shut out extraneous noise or alerting you to loud or personally meaningful noises surrounding you (the sound of a television programme, or your friend shouting to find out your dinner preference). This chapter explores some of the neural mechanisms behind what allows you to engage in these behaviours; it also explores how brain injury can affect the execution of these behaviours.

5.2 THE VISUAL SYSTEM

The sense on which we rely and prize the most is vision. In evolutionary terms, this sense has become our dominant means of perceiving the world following our ancestors' development in raising themselves from the ground and walking on their hind legs. Given its importance, it is not surprising that studies of the neuropsychology of the senses have been dominated by vision research.

5.3 WHAT THE EYE DOES

The initial structure for sensing the visual environment is the eye. The eye contains the retina, which itself contains certain cells important for the relaying of visual information. These cells are called ganglion cells and are made up of X, Y or W cells. These cells are categorised by size, the areas they project to and the function they serve. W cells have small cell bodies and comprise about 10 per cent of retinal cells; X cells have medium-sized cell bodies and comprise 80 per cent of retinal cells, and Y cells have large cell bodies and comprise the final 10 per cent of cells. Y cells appear to respond to large, moving objects in the visual environment, and seem to be involved in the analysis of crude forms and in directing attention to moving objects. X cells, in contrast, respond better to small targets and appear to be involved in the analysis of detailed, high-resolution and colour images. This arrangement illustrates one principle of visual system functioning: that it is involved in the parallel processing of stimuli; one type of cell responds to moving images, another responds to colour, another responds to size, and so on, simultaneously.

The cells of the retina have a specific property called a receptive field. A receptive field is an area in which stimulation causes excitation or inhibition. Different parts of the eye have cells with differently sized receptive fields. For example, the receptive fields are larger in the peripheral parts of the retina than in the fovea. The fields also have two types of cell. The on-centre cells have a central excitatory area and an inhibitory surround, whereas the off-centre cells have an excitatory surround and an inhibitory centre. These cells are important because they can detect and appreciate contrasts in the visual environment.

All retinal cells project to the optic disk at the back of the eye where they become myelinated and join other axons to form the optic nerve (this has over one million fibres; compare this with the auditory nerve, which has 30 000). The optic disk lies medial to the fovea and is insensitive to light. An intriguing phenomenon in vision is the blindspot: light from the area that reaches both eyes does not hit both optic disks. Eventually, the optic nerve of each eye converges at a point called the optic chiasm.

When we see, we see from two visual fields: the right and the left visual fields. Visual fields are the area in which the external world is viewed by the eye without the head moving. The right visual field contains light that is sensed predominantly by the right eye; conversely, the light in the left visual field is sensed primarily by the left eye. Light that goes directly to both eyes (from the middle of the visual fields) occupies the binocular zone; light reaching only one eye occupies the monocular zone. A term used with regard to visual fields is hemiretina. The part of the retina that is medial to the fovea is called the nasal hemiretina; the hemiretina lateral to the fovea is called the temporal hemiretina. Each half of the hemiretina is divided into dorsal and ventral parts.

The superior half of the visual field projects to the inferior half of the retina; similarly, the inferior half of the visual field projects to the superior half of the retina. This arrangement allows the brain to help us to see normally. Light that occupies the binocular zones goes to both retinas: light falls on the temporal hemiretina of the left eye and the nasal hemiretina of the right eye. Only the fibres from the nasal hemiretina of each retina cross at the optic chiasm; the fibres from the temporal hemiretina do not. Fibres that exit the optic tract project to the lateral geniculate nucleus of the thalamus, an important relay station in the visual system. From here, axons are sent to the visual cortex.

Light that occupies monocular zones projects to the nasal hemiretina on the same side as the light (the nose prevents light from reaching the other eye). The monocular area of the visual field is called the temporal crescent. Light from this region can not be sensed binocularly.

5.4 THE NEXT STAGE: THE LATERAL GENICULATE NUCLEUS

The lateral geniculate nucleus (LGN) is found in the posterior thalamus and is important for a number of reasons, not least because the optic tract fibres terminate here and because different axons terminate in specific areas of the LGN. In the primate, the LGN has six layers of neurons separated by axons and dendrites. Each layer receives information from one eye only: the contralateral nasal hemiretina projects to the sixth, fourth and first layers; the ipsilateral temporal hemiretina projects to the fifth, third and second layers.

Layers I and II (the most ventral layers) are called magnocellular layers because they contain large cells. Layers III to VI (the most dorsal layers) are called parvocellular layers. Y cells project to the magnocellular layer; X cells to the parvocellular layer. Because of this projection pattern, the pathways are called X-parvocellular and Y-magnocellular pathways, and may have an important role to play in reading disorders.

All thalamic layers project to the visual cortex. Retina cells, however, also project to the superior colliculus, a structure that is important for the control of eye movement. The types of ganglion cells found in these structures differ. X cells project only to the LGN; Y cells project to those layers of the LGN not receiving X axons, and the superior colliculus; W cells project primarily to the superior colliculus. Figure 5.1 illustrates these pathways.

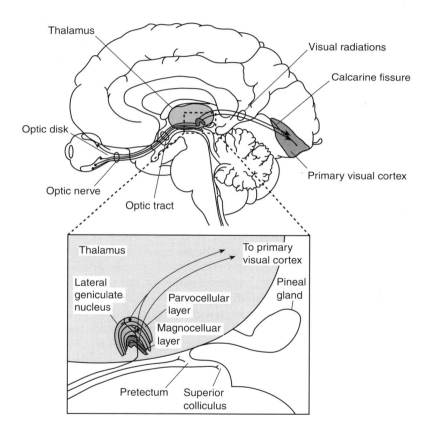

Fig 5.1 The parvocellular and magnocellular visual pathways

5.5 THE SUPERIOR COLLICULUS

Like the LGN, the superior colliculus also has several layers and receives visual input from the retina. Its superficial layers receive visual input; its deepest layers receive somatic, sensory and auditory input. The primary function of the superior colliculus, however, appears to be the orienting of head and eyes towards a visual stimulus and the control of rapid eye movements (called saccades). The guidance of the head is done in association with the frontal eye fields of the frontal cortex, which receives information from the visual cortex via X cells. The superior colliculus, via the Y cells, is also concerned with movement, visual attention and identifying broad visual outlines.

5.6 DAMAGE TO THE VISUAL PATHWAY

Damage to any point from the retina to the visual cortex, can produce blindness, although about half of all cases of blindness results from damage to the retina (Krumpazsky and Klauss, 1996). If the optic nerve is lesioned, vision functions only in the intact eye (monocular blindness). Damage to the optic nerve can also result in blindness in the temporal crescent on the lesioned side. Damage to the fibres crossing the optic chiasm results in a bilateral hemianopia: a loss of vision in the temporal parts of both visual fields. A complete homonymous hemianopia can result from a lesion to one optic tract. When this ocurrs, there is a complete loss of vision in the contralateral visual field. Quadrantic anopia occurs when there is partial loss of vision in one visual field. Sometimes, individuals develop 'blindspots' (scotomas), which result from isolated lesions of the primary visual cortex. Individuals are aware of what they see and are capable of responding to stimuli because involuntary eye movements are made that cover these blind spots (this is called nystagmus). When the eyes move about, the scotoma also moves about. More information in the visual fields thus reaches the brain. If, however, the patient stays still and an object is placed directly in front of the scotoma, the object cannot be seen.

5.7 ORGANISATION OF THE PRIMARY VISUAL CORTEX

As you saw in Chapter 4, the primary visual cortex (PVC) is located in the occipital lobe. It is also referred to as the striate cortex (Brodmann's Area 17). It was given the name striate because it contains a distinctive stripe of white matter called the stria of Genari, resulting from the termination of myelinated axons from the LGN in layer IV. Like much of the visual cortex, layer IV consists of further subdivisions. In a series of innovative experiments, Hubel and Wiesel (see Hubel and Wiesel, 1979) discovered that layer IV was made up of three separate layers (IVa, b and c; IVc can be further subdivided into IVc alpha and IVc beta). Layer IVc receives input from one or other eye from different layers of the LGN; the output from layer IVc goes to the larger layers above and below it. Layer IVc neurons also send axons to layers II and III, which in turn connect to layer V. Layer V itself projects to layer VI. Each layer projects to different parts of the cortex. For example, axons from layer II and layer III project to the medial temporal lobe of Area 18 (the area of higher visual function); layer V projects to the superior colliculus. Layer VI projects back to the LGN thus providing the visual system with a feedback loop. To further illustrate the interconnectedness of the visual system, neurons in layer IV project axons to layers II and III, to the superior colliculus via layer V and back to the LGN via layer VI.

The cells above and below layer IVc have receptive fields that respond to stimuli with linear properties (such as lines or bars). These cells are either simple or complex. The simple cells, the smaller of the two, are excited by parallel, perpendicular lines. The complex cells are larger and respond to the position and movement of a stimulus. A simplified diagram of the visual system of the brain can be seen in Figure 5.2.

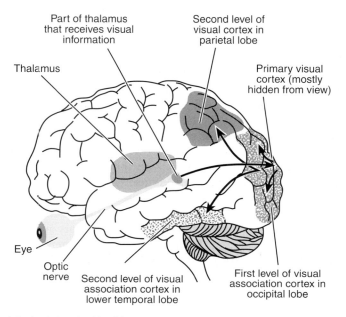

Fig 5.2 Parts of the brain involved in vision

5.8 ROLES OF THE PRIMARY VISUAL CORTEX

Like the rest of the neocortex, the visual system's arrangement is both laminar (layered) and columnar. Columns are about 2 mm deep and 30–100 micrometres wide. The columns appear to represent a shift in orientation and alternate, representing left and right eye movement, for binocular and depth perception. We know that the visual cortex comprises different areas that undertake different functions (Zeki and Bartels, 1999; Zeki, 2001).

Research with laboratory animals and data from individuals with brain damage have shown that certain areas of the visual cortex, the lingual and fusiform gyri, are important for discriminating between colours (Davidoff, 1997; Bartels and Zeki, 2000b). Damage to an area of the visual cortex called V4, for example, causes achromatopsia, a form of colour blindness in which the world is seen in shades of grey. The retina and pathways to V1 are intact, and patients with V4 damage can detect changes in lightness but are unable to discriminate between colours (Zeki, 1990). Neuroimaging studies also illustrate that these areas are active in healthy individuals during a simple task where participants perceive colours (McKeefry and Zeki, 1997).

Damage to V5 results in akinetopsia: the patient cannot see or understand the world in motion. Curiously, when objects are still, they can be seen clearly; when they are moved, they appear to disappear. This occurs even when motion is actually illusory. Because of this V5 is considered the brain's motion centre, which allows visual perception of movement. The consequences of damage to V4 and V5 highlight another example of the brain's double dissociations – damage to one results in an impairment that is not seen when the other is damaged.

These areas allow the parallel processing of different types of visual information and are distributed within a circumscribed region of the brain. Zeki (1978) had suggested that parallel visual systems were specialised for specific visual functions and cited evidence from the neurology literature showing that people with a deficit in one type of visual function were relatively unimpaired in another. The idea was given further support by studies showing that we perceive some visual attributes before others. Colour, for example, is perceived before motion (Montoussis and Zeki, 1997), and this led to the notion that different systems reached an end-point faster than others. Colour, orientation, motion, depth, faces, facial expressions and other types of object are all perceived at different times, although we may not show awareness of this (Zeki and Bartels, 1999). Yet other features of visual perception appear to be perceived at the same time – depth and orientation, for example, and upward and downward, and left-to-right motion (Zeki, 2001). Whether the paired functions are undertaken by the same or different areas is not known.

The PVC only receives information from the contralateral hemifield.

Information can also be sent to the higher visual function areas, or extrastriate cortex (Area 18), which can send information to the medial temporal cortex (Area 19), inferotemporal cortex (Areas 20 and 21) and posterior parietal cortex (Area 7). In a series of pioneering studies involving primates, Zeki (1993) has argued that Area 17 sends four separate projections to Area 18. These four parallel systems represent colour, motion and form (two systems). One X pathway projects from the PVC (V1) to area V2, then V3 and V3a, V4 and the inferotemporal cortex. This system is involved in the perception of form and colour. Y cells project from the PVC to V2 and V3, and then to V5 and the posterior parietal cortex.

The massive complexity of this arrangement has to accommodate the lowest-level visual response (e.g. the retina's response to brightness) to the highest level (e.g. abstracting information and ascribing meaning to the visual images perceived as well as being able to act on what is seen).

5.9 ARE THERE TWO DIFFERENT VISUAL PATHWAYS?

Damage to different parts of the visual system can result in different types of impairment in visual perception. This suggests that some visual system pathways carry one type of information whereas others carry different types of information (Schneider, 1969).

Ungerleider and Mishkin (1982), for example, proposed that different parts of the brain are involved in object identification and object location: the appreciation of an object's qualities is the role of the inferior temporal cortex; the ability to locate an object is the role of the posterior parietal cortex. Primates with posterior parietal cortex lesions make consistent errors in accurately reaching out for or grasping objects, although their ability to discriminate between objects is intact. Similar damage in humans also results in difficulties performing visuospatial tasks such as estimating length and distance (von Cramon and Kerkhoff, 1993).

Importantly, Ungerleider and Mishkin distinguished between a ventral and dorsal pathway, or stream, which projected from the primary visual cortex to these areas. Thus, although originating in the PVC, the two pathways were independent and projected to different areas of the brain (to the temporal and posterior parietal cortices, respectively).

Goodale and Milner (1992; Milner and Goodale, 1995) argue that the most important questions are not 'what' and 'where' but 'what' and 'how'. In Ungerleider and Mishkin's model, the ventral stream processes the 'what' component of visual perception (identification of an object) whereas the dorsal stream processes the 'where' component (the spatial location of an object and the attention paid to objects in space). Goodale and Milner's research has focused on the 'what' and 'how' areas. Both of these areas are represented cortically, although there are subcortical analogues of these pathways called the magnocellular (M) and parvocellular (P) streams. The M stream can process transient visual information, has little affinity for processing fine detail and processes colour poorly whereas the P stream is slower, can process fine detail and does respond to colour. This ability to respond to colour also helps it to guide attention to objects distinguished by colour (Snowden, 2002).

Goodale and Milner have made an extensive study of DF, a woman with substantial bilateral damage to the occipital cortex (but sparing the PVC) resulting from carbon monoxide poisoning (Goodale and Milner, 1992; Milner and Goodale, 1995). DF is unable to discriminate between geometric shapes and is unable to recognise or identify objects, despite having normal language and an intact visual sensory system. That is, she exhibits a perceptual disorder called visual form agnosia (agnosia is described in more detail in a later section). But while DF is able to respond to objects (she can place her hand into a slot of varying orientations, or grasp blocks), she is unable to estimate the orientation of the slot or the width of the box by verbally reporting or by gesturing.

Goodale and Milner suggest that DF is using the intact visuomotor processing system in the parietal cortex to perform the grasping and orientation tasks. The guidance of motor behaviour relies on a primitive dorsal stream in the parietal cortex and this has been spared, hence the accurate execution of DF's motor behaviour. When asked to indicate which of two boxes is a rectangle and which is a square, she can respond correctly when holding the boxes but less correctly when making a verbal response (Murphy et al., 1996). The experimenters noticed that DF would make partial movements towards one of the boxes before correcting herself. When these initial reaches were analysed, they showed the same level of accuracy as if she had verbally reported which box was which.

On the basis of DF's behaviour, research from neuroimaging studies of motor movement and vision, and animal lesions to parietal and occipital areas, Milner and Goodale (1995) propose that the dorsal stream sends information about object characteristics and orientation that is related to movement from the primary visual cortex to the parietal cortex. Damage to the ventral stream, which projects to the inferior temporal cortex, is what is responsible for DF's inability to access perceptual information.

A recent study of a unique patient has provided further evidence for the role of the dorsal stream in visual perception (Le et al., 2002). Le et al. studied a 30-year-old man (SB) who had developed visual agnosia at the age of three, after suffering brain inflammation at that time. This resulted in damage to the right and left ventral streams and right dorsal pathway (leaving the primary visual cortex and left dorsal pathway intact). Following the damage, SB showed a severe inability to identify objects, words and faces visually, although his ability to detect movement and perceive space was relatively spared. He could move from outdoors to indoors with little difficulty (poor lighting seemed to be no real obstacle), although he preferred low levels of luminance and moved more often at dawn or dusk. While his ability to perceive colour was poor, his mental imagery performance was excellent, as was his ability to rotate objects mentally. According to Le *et al.*, 'Observing S.B. in his daily life is a surprising experience since one is confronted by a person who alternately seems blind or visually normal, depending on the behaviour required.' (2002: 70). The study suggests that the dorsal stream can process at least rudimentary elements of visual analysis up until the point when a person decides to act. However, this case study also suggests that the pathway is involved in perception as well as the visual control of skilled movement.

5.10 BRAIN DAMAGE AND VISUAL PERCEPTION

When the brain is damaged and visual perception is impaired, the patient, like DF, is said to exhibit a perceptual disorder. There are several perceptual disorders and each is associated with damage to different parts of the visual system. Perceptual disorders are just that, perceptual – there is no underlying impairment in vision and patients still show visual acuity and can tell light from dark, and so on. Three of the most interesting perceptual disorders are blindsight, agnosia and spatial neglect.

Blindsight

When the primary visual cortex is damaged, a person becomes blind in some portion of the visual field. Some individuals, however, can lose substantial areas of the PVC and yet show evidence of perceiving objects despite being 'cortically blind'. This phenomenon is called blindsight (Weiskrantz, 1986) because although patients are unable to see properties of objects, they are aware of other aspects such as the movement of objects. (There are equivalent phenomena in the auditory and somatosensory systems called deaf hearing and blindtouch.) The earliest case was reported towards the beginning of the last century (Riddoch, 1917). Riddoch was an army medical officer who had made a study of soldiers whose primary visual cortex had been damaged by gunshot wounds. Although none of the patients could directly describe objects placed in front of them (neither shape, form nor colour), they were conscious of the movement of the objects, despite the movement being 'vague and shadowy'. This suggested to Riddoch that there was some residual visual ability in the PVC that allowed the perception of object motion but no other aspect of visual perception.

Since Riddoch's study, several other cases of blindsight have been reported, notably Larry Weiskrantz's famous patient, DB (Weiskrantz, 1986). DB had undergone surgery for a brain tumour, which necessitated removal of the area of the visual cortex in the right occipital lobe. This surgery resulted in a scotoma – an area of complete blindness in the visual field. DB could indicate whether a stick was horizontal or vertical, could point to the location of an object when instructed, and could detect whether an object was present or absent. Other tasks presented greater difficulty: DB could not distinguish a triangle from a cross or a curved triangle from a normal one. The most intriguing feature of DB's behaviour, however, was a lack of awareness of the stimuli presented. According to DB, he 'couldn't see anything' when test stimuli were seen. Why could DB, and patients like DB, make perceptual decisions despite being unaware of visual stimuli?

One hypothesis suggests that blindsight patients have degraded normal vision. The normal vision is degraded because some of the visual areas remain but are clearly not working at an optimal level. So, the residual visual cortex is capable of providing a primitive perceptual service to its user. However, evidence from animal studies in which the striate cortex is completely removed suggests that this hypothesis is not correct because these animals exhibit blindsight (Stoerig and Cowey, 1997).

A more plausible alternative to the above account is that there are areas outside the PVC that allow perception to take place in the absence of awareness. For example, neuroimaging studies show that when the brain activity of blindsight patients is measured, areas outside V1/PVC are activated (Zeki and ffytche, 1998). In fact, Zeki and ffytche propose that the processes of awareness and visual discrimination are independent but closely coupled in normal individuals. The result of damage to the PVC is to uncouple these functions; this can lead to awareness without discrimination (AWD) and discrimination without awareness (DWA). Activity in a visual association area called V5 has been found to be greater during DWA than AWD; this area may, therefore, mediate the functions seen in blindsight patients.

Zeki and ffytche (1998) base much of their thesis on the behaviour of patient GY who has a long-standing lesion to V1. GY's visual capacity is basic – he is conscious of contrasts and of fast-moving stimuli that reach V5 but without being processed via V1. However, he is not capable of conscious awareness of slow-moving objects. When brain activation is measured during perceptual tasks, activity is limited to area V5. These and other findings suggest that conscious vision can occur without an intact V1. They also present other interesting possibilities. For example, a patient with damage to V5 but with an intact V1 showed an impairment in the awareness of fast-moving objects but a good awareness of slow-moving objects (Hess *et al.*, 1989). It is possible that different pathways from the pulvinar/the thalamus project to different parts of the primary visual cortex, and that the perception of fast- and slow-moving objects uses different pathways to reach the cortex and, therefore, 'conscious awareness'.

Visual agnosia

Patients with posterior lesions to the left or right hemisphere sometimes have considerable difficulty in recognising objects, despite having intact sensory systems (patient DF, for example). This disorder is called agnosia (literally, 'without knowledge'), a term coined by Sigmund Freud. Agnosia can occur in any sense (tactile agnosia refers to the inability to recognise objects by touch, for example), but visual agnosia is the most common type (Farah, 1990).

The existence of specific types of agnosia is a controversial topic in perception and neuropsychology. A distinction is usually made between two types of visual agnosia: associative and apperceptive. Apperceptive agnosia is the inability to recognise objects, whereas associative agnosia is the inability to make meaningful associations to objects that are visually presented. Some neuropsychologists have argued that the boundaries between these two types are 'fuzzy' (DeRenzi and Lucchelli, 1993) and other subtypes of visual agnosia have been suggested (Humphreys and Riddoch, 1987a; 1987b). Apperceptive agnosics have a severe impairment in their ability to copy drawings, as patient DF did. Associative agnosics, conversely, can copy accurately but are unable to identify their drawings. For example, Humphreys and Riddoch's patient, HJA, spent six hours completing an accurate drawing but was unable to identify it when he had finished (see Figure 5.3).

Prosopagnosia: deficits in face perception

A more category-specific form of agnosia is prosopagnosia. Some individuals with damage to specific areas of the posterior right hemisphere (and sometimes left and right hemispheres) show an impairment in the ability to recognise familiar faces. This condition is known as prosopagnosia ('loss of knowledge for faces'). Some patients are unable to recognise famous faces, familiar people such as spouses or even themselves. One patient, studied by Tippett et al. (2000), was unable to recognise hospital staff or some members of his family after surgery to the right temporal lobe. The patient was a man of average to high intelligence who, at the age of 22, had been in a motorcycle accident that resulted in brain injury leading to epileptic seizures. Six years later, the temporal cortex was removed to alleviate the epilepsy. It became apparent after the surgery that he was unable to identify hospital staff or even his daughter, and could identify his wife only by her hair or gait. However, he was able to identify some members of his family and some famous faces. He also appeared to show selective deficits in the ability to learn new faces. When given a test involving the identification of famous faces prior to 1982 (the year of the accident) and those faces famous after that year, he could identify

Fig 5.3 A drawing of an agnosic patient. The patient could copy a building and the objects well but was unable to identify them. From Humphreys and Riddoch (1987b). To see but not to see. Lawrence Erlbaum Associates: Hove, UK

20 out of 23 of faces that were famous before 1982 but only 8 out of 17 of those post-1982. His learning of other visual stimuli was preserved after injury, suggesting that the damage affected the learning of face stimuli only.

Research update ... how face recognition develops after brain injury

Another case study has highlighted how early brain damage can permanently affect the perception of faces (Farah *et al.*, 2000). Farah *et al.*'s patient was a 16-year-old boy called Adam who had a normal birth but developed streptococcal meningitis at one day old. A CT scan at the age of six, showed lesions in the occipital and temporal cortices in both hemispheres. Although he showed no object agnosia, he did show prosopagnosic symptoms. At meetings with doctors and nurses he waited until he was spoken to because he could recognise voices but not faces. He could identify features of faces well (a typical prosopagnosic symptom).

But putting these features together to form a meaningful label was almost impossible. When he was asked to identify 10 photographs of people from the TV show *Baywatch*, 10 famous people he knew of and 20 photographs of people he did not know, he was unable to identify one of them. Yet, he was able to match faces when given a task that required him to match a face with the same face presented in a series of faces, so long as the angle of the face and the lighting conditions were adequate.

The significance of the lesions in prosopagnosic patients, however, is complicated by the extent of the damage and the occurrence of other symptoms. Even prosopagnosic patients show deficits in the ability to name living and non-living objects, especially the latter. And there is some evidence to suggest that prosopagnosics do show an awareness of faces, despite being unable to identify them. Studies have shown, for example, that if a prosopagnosic patient's GSR is measured during the presentation of faces that have either been seen or not seen before, there is an increase in skin conductance during the viewing of previously seen faces, although the patient claims not to have seen them before and not to recognise them (Tranel and Damasio, 1985). Whether there might be a specific region in the brain responsible for face perception is discussed in a section below.

Spatial neglect

Patients with lesions in the right parietotemporal cortex sometimes have difficulty in perceiving objects to their left (Vallar, 1998). In fact, in 80 per cent of patients with right hemisphere stroke, patients are unable to attend automatically to any stimuli in left space (Halligan and Marshall, 1994). This is called spatial neglect (or unilateral spatial hemineglect) and occurs on the side of the body that is contralateral to the side of the brain damage. Neglect for the left side is more common than right neglect (which would be caused by damage to the left hemisphere). Typical examples of the symptoms seen in neglect patients include orienting to the side of the lesion when their name is called, and ignoring objects and people in the side of the visual world opposite to that of the brain lesion.

Patients exhibiting spatial neglect behave as if half of the world does not exist. They may forget to attend to their clothing on the left-hand side, neglect food on the left side of their plate or ignore the left-hand side of their newspaper (Halligan and Marshall, 1994). Spatial neglect patients show a characteristic pattern of behaviour on visuospatial tests. For example, if they are required to bisect lines of varying length, they will err to the right. If they are presented with an array of stimuli (such as small lines) and asked to mark off as many as possible, they mark off those on the right-hand side but fail to mark off those on the left.

Similarly, neglect patients, when asked to draw (or mentally imagine a scene) fail to draw or report details from the left side of the object or image (Halligan and Marshall, 1994). Sometimes, patients will transfer details from the left- to the right-hand side, as Figure 5.4 shows.

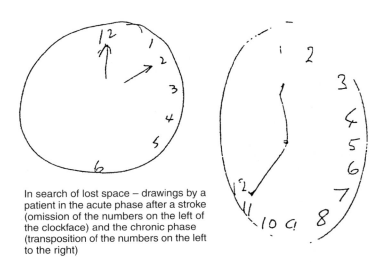

In search of lost space – drawings by a patient in the acute phase after a stroke (omission of the numbers on the left of the clockface) and the chronic phase (transposition of the numbers on the left to the right)

Fig 5.4 The drawing of a clock by a patient with spatial neglect. Note how the numbers on the left have been crammed into the space on the right

Halligan and Marshall (1997) reported a case study of a 75-year-old artist and sculptor who had suffered a right hemisphere stroke. Six months after the stroke, his drawings were poorer and less elaborate than they were before the stroke. His family also noted that he seemed to concentrate on the right-hand side of the drawings. In fact, on all the standard tests of neglect, he showed impairment. Figure 5.5 illustrates some of his difficulties.

The reasons for spatial neglect are unclear; models suggest that there may either be a deficit in the representation of objects or that neglect patients cannot spontaneously attend to the neglected side, deficits that are viewed as the responsibility of the right temporo-parietal cortex. The deficit may also arise with damage to some subcortical structures: the right putamen, one of three structures that makes up the basal ganglia; the right pulvinar of the thalamus; and the right side of another structure in the basal ganglia, the caudate nucleus (Karnath *et al.*, 2002). In fact, Karnath *et al.* suggest that patients showing occipito-parietal cortical deficits show symptoms other than spatial neglect. In patients who show only neglect symptoms, damage is to the superior temporal gyrus (Karnath *et al.*, 2001), an area that, in monkeys, has connections to the subcortical structures identified by Karnath *et al.* (2002).

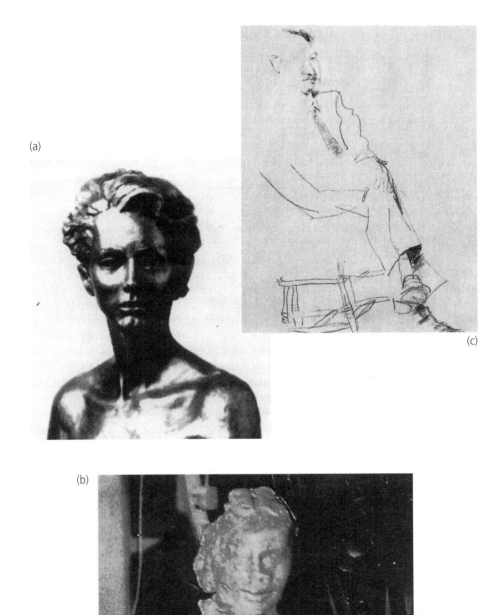

(a)

(c)

(b)

Fig 5.5 Some of the practical consequences of spatial neglect for a patient who was an artist

5.11 HOW THE HEALTHY BRAIN PERCEIVES VISUAL STIMULI

Much of our knowledge about the neuropsychology of vision and perception was originally derived from lesion work in animals. This was supplemented by the study of the effect of brain damage on human visual system function. Then, in the past 20 years, functional neuroimaging allowed us to see how the brain responded when it was exposed to visual images. These studies sparked a controversy of a specific kind that has, in reality, been present in neuropsychology and neuroscience since its genesis. Downing *et al.* (2001) state the controversy succinctly: 'One of the most fundamental questions about visual object recognition in humans is whether all kinds of objects are processed by the same neural mechanisms, or whether instead some object classes are handled by distinct processing modules' (2001: 2470).

This evidence has been reviewed by Martha Farah and Geoffrey Aguirre of the University of Pennsylvania in an attempt to reconcile what we know about vision from animal/human brain damage work with that from neuroimaging work (Farah and Aguirre, 1999). They have asked which parts of the human brain are involved in visual recognition and whether faces, words and objects require different neuroanatomical systems to process them.

The recognition of objects appears to activate the ventral pathway described above. The processing of information about an object activates the ventral occipital/temporal areas, whereas processing spatial information about an object (such as its location) activates more dorsal areas. However, recent neuroimaging has gone beyond these generalities and has appeared to show specific types of activation that are linked to particular tasks. For example, the process of recognising faces, as you will see in a later section, is thought to activate selectively a part of the extrastriate cortex near the junction of the temporal and occipital lobe (Kanwisher, 2000). The processing of faces is thought to recruit different brain areas to those involved in object perception although there continues to be debate over whether parts of the cortex are so specialised for function (Tarr and Gauthier, 2000). The perception of different shapes appears to activate selectively the lateral part of the occipital cortex and similar areas become active when people judge the appearance, rather than imagine the rotation, of objects (Grill-Spector *et al.*, 1998).

As you will see in the chapter on memory, the perception of the spatial location of an object appears to rely on dorsal regions of the parietal cortex. For example, Aguirre and D'Esposito (1997) found that when people were asked to make judgements about the appearance of an object or about its spatial location, the latter task was associated with selective activation in the superior parietal lobe and premotor cortex (the last finding perhaps reflects the brain's readiness to approach and reach for the object). Spatial location, however, involves more than the activation of the cortex.

5.12 FACE PROCESSING

As you saw in the discussion of prosopagnosia (in Section 5.9), faces have always occupied a special place in psychology. Part of the reason for this is that they are considered to be 'special' stimuli (Farah *et al.*, 1998). Some brain-injured individuals are unable to recognise familiar faces yet recognise familiar bodies or voices while the neurons of some primates selectively fire to face stimuli only. Even babies 30 minutes old are adept at orienting towards faces. Some authors argue that an infant's visual system is set up to process stimuli with low spatial frequency – their visual acuity is low – and that more specialised visual processing such as configural processing (perceiving the relationship between the features of an object) follows. This development continues until around the age of ten (LeGrand *et al.*, 2001). LeGrand *et al.* showed that if the system is dysfunctional even at two months of age – it cannot process certain types of information – this can lead to permanent deficits in the ability to make judgements about the configuration of features in faces.

Face recognition is important to us. It helps us to identify friends, family and acquaintances, and it can make us attracted to others. The face can carry significant social information; signals from it can cue responses from us and change our behaviour. We might comfort someone who looks sad and is crying; we may smile when another person smiles; we may avoid or confront those who look angry; we may be offended at another's rolling of the eyes or help those with a furrowed brow. All of these signals are social ones, helping us to interpret how another person is behaving or feeling. Much of the recent neuropsychological work on face recognition has exploited neuroimaging techniques in order to determine whether different regions of the human brain respond to faces selectively. One controversy in the area surrounds whether such selective activation is specific to faces or to some other perceptual aspect of faces such as whether they appear in greyscale or two-tone.

In one fMRI experiment, participants observed inverted or upright faces in greyscale; in a second experiment, participants observed upright or inverted two-tone faces (Kanwisher *et al.*, 1998). One specific brain region – the human fusiform face area (HFFA) – was singled out for analysis. Both the upright and inverted greyscale faces activated the HFFA but the inverted faces produced less activation. Inverted two-tone faces, however, were associated with significantly reduced brain activation. The results suggest that the HFFA does not respond specifically to low-level features of faces (or the inverted and upright two-tone faces would have produced similar activation) but does respond to face stimuli. The authors acknowledge, however, that this may not be the only brain region specialised for face processing.

Current neuroimaging data, however, make it a strong contender. The HFFA is activated selectively by the perceptual analysis of faces whereas different regions are implicated in famous name processing, relative to common names. (Gorno Tempini *et al.*, 1998). The right HFFA is also active during the memorisation (rather than passive watching) of unfamiliar faces, which suggests the region's involvement in remembering faces, as well as processing them (Kuskowski and Pardo, 1999).

To determine whether the HFFA really did just respond to faces and not animate objects in general, Kanwisher *et al.* (1999) asked participants to view various pictorial stimuli, such as human heads, animal heads, human bodies and animal bodies, in an fMRI study. The strongest response in the HFFA was found during face perception, followed by whole humans and animal heads, which suggests that the area is more involved in face, than other object, perception.

5.13 PLACE PERCEPTION

Some researchers claim that the face-processing region of the brain, highlighted in those studies reviewed in the previous section, has a building or place analogue. That is, there is a part of the extrastriate cortex that is selectively activated during the perception of places or buildings, an area called the parahippocampal place area (so called because these stimuli seem to activate (selectively) the parahippocampal gyrus). The evidence for the specialisation of this region is growing. It began when studies of brain injury showed that some patients with damage to the occipital lobe had difficulty in using features of the environment to find their way along a route (Whiteley and Warrington, 1978). The disorder, called 'landmark agnosia', was characterised by an impairment in the perception or recognition of street scenes, landscapes, monuments and buildings (Hecaen *et al.*, 1980). What is interesting is that agnosia for faces and objects can occur without agnosia for landmarks (Tohgi *et al.*, 1994), suggesting that the functions are dissociable and may be mediated by a different part of the brain.

Aguirre *et al.* (1998) found that buildings and faces activated different brain regions fairly consistently. When people viewed buildings, a region near the right lingual gyrus was observed; when people viewed faces, the fusiform gyrus region residing near to the 'building area' was observed. To see whether the building effect was due to featural rather than categorical reasons (i.e. to investigate whether the lingual gyrus responded to features of objects in general or to buildings in particular), the researchers asked participants to view two-tone images of buildings and scrambled versions of these, and then compared their brain activation with responses to images of another, different object – cars. They found that the right lingual gyrus's response was twice as large when participants viewed buildings as when viewing cars.

Although the findings do not demonstrate that this area is necessary for the perception of buildings, they do suggest that this area might play an important role in the perception of building or building-type objects. The question then is: if these findings can be replicated, what is the special quality of buildings that makes brain regions selectively activated during their perception? The question is currently unanswered. Aguirre *et al.* suggest that this region may be involved in representing stimuli that are used for orientation; using landmarks such as buildings, for example, helps us to orient ourselves, determine where we are and where we need to go to. A further question then arises: what exactly is a landmark?

5.14 IMAGERY

One of the intriguing questions in cognitive and neuro-psychology is whether the events you mentally imagine use the same brain areas as those used in the perception of those events (Kaski, 2002). Does visual imagery, for example, use the same brain areas as those involved in visual perception? Additionally, does the imagining of different types of 'mental' content activate different brain areas and, if so, are they areas that would normally be activated by the actual perception of such content (so that imaging faces activates the same area as that activated by the viewing of actual faces)? There is some evidence that they are.

The mental manipulation of objects – such as rotating objects in the mind in order to reach a target position – is associated with activity in the temporal and parietal cortices (Kosslyn *et al.*, 1998). Other studies show considerable overlap between imagination and actual perception of objects. The brain areas activated by mentally imagining faces are different to those activated by imaging places (O'Craven and Kanwisher, 2000). The fusiform face area is also significantly more active during the mental imagining of faces than places. Imagining places activates the parahippocampal place area (PPA) to a much greater extent than does imagining faces.

The results are similar to those found by Goebel *et al.* (1998) who reported that the brain region activated during visual motion was also activated by mental imagery of that motion. There is also a great similarity between the areas that respond during the act of writing and those at work during the mental imagery of the writing (Sugishita *et al.*, 1996).

These studies suggest that the mechanisms responsible for visual perception of images and those responsible for the mental imagining of the same images may be similar. The mechanisms may be shared – the results from O'Craven and Kanwisher's study, for example, suggest that the difference in activation between the two types of condition (imagery vs viewing) was one of degree.

5.15 CATEGORY-SPECIFIC DEFICITS

The evidence above suggests that different brain regions might respond differentially to different categories of object. In the earliest such studies, Elizabeth Warrington and her colleagues noted specific perceptual deficits in patients with temporal and parietal lobe lesions (Warrington, 1975; McKenna and Warrington, 1978; Warrington and McCarthy, 1987). These patients seemed able to name some classes of object but not others. Some patients could name concrete nouns but not abstract ones. The most interesting dissociation concerned the naming of animate and inanimate objects.

Warrington's studies showed that patients with specific brain injury showed severe and consistent impairment in the naming of living things (Warrington and Shallice, 1984). This dissociation was found whether the stimuli were verbal or non-verbal. On the basis of these findings Warrington and Shallice argued that the distinction could be explained in terms of the perception of different features of these objects. Living things would be perceived in terms of their individual attributes, such as shape, colour, size, and so on, whereas non-living things are perceived in terms of the function they seem to carry out. The living-thing impairment, therefore, was a problem in perceiving individual sensory attributes.

Warrington and Shallice's study was based on four patients with herpes simplex encephalitis, a degenerative brain disease that obviously warrants a degree of caution in interpreting their results. Some psychologists, however, have argued that brain injury studies do not show differences between the categories of object but between the ways in which these two different types of stimulus are presented. Parkin and Stewart (1993), for example, have suggested that it is more difficult to recognise drawings of animate than inanimate objects. An inanimate object such as a cup is a lot less detailed than an animate object such as a fly. The dissociation seen in agnosic patients, therefore, may be due to the complexity and/or familiarity of the perceived stimulus. Stewart et al. (1992) have suggested that when these artifacts are limited, these dissociations disappear. However, the issue continues to be controversial. Sheridan and Humphreys (1993), for example, have shown that patients show such dissociations even under well-controlled conditions.

Neuroimaging data generally support the proposition that certain brain regions are specifically activated by specific stimuli, but leave open the explanation for such specificity. Tools have been found to generate more brain activity in the left parietal and premotor cortex than do pictures of animals and objects (Martin et al., 1996); the fusiform gyrus, as you have seen, appears to be selectively activated during face perception; and other stimuli, such as buildings and houses, seem to activate selectively certain brain regions (Epstein and Kanwisher, 1998).

At a more cellular level, Kreiman et al. (2000b) recorded activity in various regions of the temporal lobe in 11 epileptic patients as the participants viewed images of unknown faces depicting emotion, objects, spatial layouts, drawings and photographs of famous people, foods and abstract shapes. They found that the three regions they studied fired selectively to specific categories of object: the entorhinal cortex responded selectively to pictures of animals, the anterior hippocampus to images of famous people (but not emotional faces) and the hippocampus in general to layouts, houses and interiors (a finding consistent with the proposed, classical role of the hippocampus in spatial navigation).

The visual features vs function interpretation has been challenged. Caramazza and Shelton (1998), for example, suggest a much stronger specificity model of brain function arguing that different regions of the brain mediate different 'domains of knowledge'. Others have drawn attention to the interconnectedness of features in living stimuli (Moss et al., 1998). For example, an animal may have features such as eyes, ears and legs, indicating that it can see, hear and walk, and that these features are processed in an interconnected way when we see them; non-living things have fewer interconnected features. Current evidence suggests that brain regions may mediate specific semantic categories, rather than the interconnectedness of features of stimuli or the visual or functional nature of stimuli (Gainotti, 2000). The brain imaging studies described here provide strong support for such a view. One reason for this may be the heterogeneity of objects that fall into the categories of living and non-living things. When you examine brain injury studies more closely, the naming deficit is specific to a certain type of living or non-living thing, such as plants and animals. The naming deficit for living things can also extend to non-living things such as food or musical instruments (Gainotti, 2000).

5.16 THE AUDITORY SYSTEM

Audition, like vision, makes use of a number of distinct structures and neural pathways. A person with 'normal' hearing will be able to detect a soundwave that is between 20 and 20 000 Hz although he or she will be most sensitive to sounds that are between 1000 and 4000 Hz. These soundwaves travel through the air, reach the ear and stimulate a structure called the tympanic membrane (more commonly known as the eardrum). From this point, the signal is transmitted via three ossicles (or bones), called the malleus, incus and stapes, to an important auditory apparatus, the cochlea (Nobili et al., 1998). The cochlea is part of a labyrinth of membranes; the membraneous part of the cochlea is called the cochlear duct. This is about 3 cm long and forms a spiral-shaped structure. The lowest part of this duct is made up of the basilar membrane on which rests the organ of Corti (see below). The top end is made up of the vestibular membrane. Outside the duct are two parallel canals: the scala tympani, situated below the basilar membrane, and the scala vestibuli, situated above the vestibular membrane. These tympani have windows or openings called fenestra vestibuli and fenestra cochleae, which are closed by different mechanisms. At the end of the scala vestibuli, there lies the oval window; at the end of the scala tympani lies the fenestra cochleae or round window. The basic structures of the auditory system are seen in Figure 5.6.

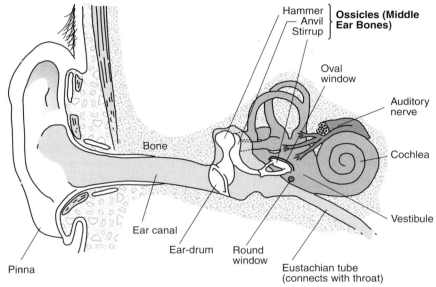

Fig 5.6 The auditory system

So how does a 'sound' recruit all of these structures? Audition begins when a soundwave reaches the external ear (the external auditory meatus). The wave also reaches the middle ear and tympanic membrane, found at the lower end of the auditory meatus. Connecting the eardrum with the oval windows are the ossicles. The malleus (or hammer) connects to the incus (or anvil) and the incus is connected to the stapes (or stirrup). These bones are important because they are sensitive to soundwaves; the waves make them vibrate and thus transmit an impulse to the fluid in the cochlea.

When the stapes are pressed into the oval window, the scala vestibuli are closed and the fluid in them (called perilymph) is stimulated by movement from the soundwave that stimulated the stapes. The movement caused by the vibration is then transmitted to the fluid in the auditory canal; the movement travels on to the basilar membrane, which transmits an impulse to the fluid in the scala tympani. The movement of the basilar membrane stimulates receptors in the cochlea that contain sensory hairs. The inner hair cells and outer hair cells are separated by large supporting cells called pillar cells. Together, these form the tunnel of Corti, which is part of the organ of Corti, the region where receptors are organised. One of the most interesting features of the basilar membrane is that different frequencies are required to stimulate it at different points along its length. The highest pitches are sensed by hair cells near the oval window (the bottom of the basilar membrane); the lowest pitches are sensed at the anterior part of the cochlea.

From the cochlea, the sound impulse is sent via the eighth cranial nerve (the cochlear nerve) to a collection of structures called the superior olivary complex in the medulla of the brainstem. From here, projections are sent to the inferior colliculi and fibres from here are sent to the medial geniculate body of the thalamus. Almost at the end of this process, signals are sent from the thalamus, which terminate in a specific part of the cortex – called the auditory cortex, or AI – in the temporal lobe. As in the visual system, there is some crossing of the pathways in the auditory system (with information from the right ear going to the left side of the brain and information from the left ear going to the right side). Unlike the visual system, however, there is a considerable number of uncrossed fibres. This means that damage to the auditory pathway in one hemisphere may not result in obvious hearing impairment because there are uncrossed fibres that still allow auditory information to be processed. Damage to the cochlear nerve, however, does result in deafness in the ear ipsilateral to the lesion.

The auditory pathways contain many inhibitory interneurons. Given the amount of auditory information this system receives, this inhibition is understandable. Imagine how difficult it would be to attend to a single conversation in a crowded room of several noisy, chattering individuals. Of course, the system not only allows selective attention to auditory information but also mediates startle reflexes (sudden, involuntary, behavioural responses prompted by unexpected or loud auditory stimuli), which occurs via the reticular formation's links with the association auditory pathways.

5.17 HIERARCHICAL ORGANISATION OF THE AUDITORY SYSTEM

One of the key features of the visual system is that it is organised hierarchically at the neural level. That is, sensory input is broken down and then put together to form complex stimuli in various regions of the brain. This means that different regions of neurons are responsible for processing different types of visual stimuli. Does the auditory system have the same property? Do certain types of stimuli activate 'core' auditory areas and others activate a region outside this core area?

Wessinger *et al.* (2001) presented pure tones and complex auditory stimuli to 12 healthy right-handed men and women, and used functional Magnetic Resonance Imaging (fMRI) to monitor changes in brain activation. They found that the pure tones activated a core area – one that surrounded Heschl's gyrus – but that more complex stimuli activated areas outside this core (the pure tones did not). The results suggest that this hierarchical system of sound analysis participates in the early processing of many sounds, including those for speech.

Focus on ... music and the auditory cortex

The region of the brain that processes the sound of music is found, perhaps logically, in the primary auditory cortex. Our ability to perceive and discriminate between melodies, and our ability to distinguish between speech sounds and musical tones, seems to be undertaken by this part of the brain (Zatorre *et al.*, 2002). People with damage to both sides of the temporal cortex sometimes develop a disorder called amusia in which participants are unable to perform simple tone processing such as recognising familiar tunes. The right primary auditory cortex appears to be important for musical processes such as melody and harmony processing, pitch perception, and discriminating between tones of different pitch (Zatorre, 1988), whereas the left primary auditory cortex appears to be able to detect changes in the timing or duration of tones. The actual process of singing recruits the expected motor areas, as well as the cerebellum, and also the right primary auditory cortex (Perry *et al.*, 1999).

In an ingenious experiment, Halpern and Zatorre (1999) asked people to imagine the rest of a musical excerpt after being cued with the first few notes. Blood flow was measured during the imagining of the music. In the recruiting session, and prior to the scanning, the tune was played. The tune was the theme to the TV series *Dallas*. During scanning the first five notes were played and participants were asked to imagine the rest of the sequence. The control group listened to a random arrangement of five notes. The researchers found that when people imagined the rest of the tune, the right auditory association cortex and supplementary motor area were activated.

The current view of the auditory cortex contribution to music processing sees it as a region that is made up of a core, surrounded by a belt of cortex and, beyond that, a parabelt (Zattore *et al.*, 2002; Tramo, 2001). The core area extracts and analyses information about the pitch of tones (Zatorre *et al.*, 2002). The belt and the parabelt in the right hemisphere appear to be areas that detect changes in the duration of notes and in the patterns of music; the parabelt in both hemispheres may be involved in grouping sounds by meter (Tramo, 2001). An area beyond the auditory cortex, the frontal cortex, may be involved in organising sounds in time and keeping them 'in mind'.

5.18 THE SOMATOSENSORY SYSTEM

The system that allows us to sense touch, feel pain, experience changes in temperature, and ascertain the position of limbs and other parts of the body (proprioception) is the somatosensory system, and all of these phenomena are described by the term somatosensation. In addition to sensing all the somatosensory input described above, this system also allows us to detect differences in pressure placed on the skin, the usual receptor site of the somatosensory system.

There are four types of afferent fibres in the human skin. Two of these respond to indentations in the skin very rapidly; two other types adapt to the indentation very slowly; each type of response is associated with an anatomical connection to specific types of skin receptor. Information from these receptors is sent to the CNS where the body can prepare to respond to the stimulation.

Tactile sensation for most somatosensory functions, except proprioception of the lower extremities and basic forms of tactile stimulation, is undertaken by the dorsal column-medial lemniscal system. Pain and crude tactile sensation, on the other hand, is mediated by the anterolateral system. Receptors in the skin and subcutaneous tissue send afferents to the spinal cord via the dorsal roots. An axon branch ascends into the dorsal column and synapses in the medulla. Those axons of sensory cells in the dorsal column nuclei then project in the opposite direction. At the midline of the medulla, they cross and pass through the brainstem contralaterally, making synapses with cells in the ventral posterior lateral nucleus of the thalamus.

From here, thalamic projections are sent to the cerebral cortex. This pathway is called the thalamocortical projection, or radiation, and runs through the internal capsule, terminating in the primary somatic sensory cortex (S I), or somatosensory cortex, which is found in the precentral gyrus of the parietal lobe. S I can be subdivided into distinct but interconnected areas, based on Brodmann's classification: Areas 1, 2, 3a and 3b. This arrangement appears to be important because the thalamic axons terminate primarily in Areas 3a and 3b. These areas then send projections to Areas 1 and 2. Thalamic fibres also project to nearby cortex called the secondary somatic sensory cortex (S II). S I and S II are distinctive in that S I receives primarily contralateral input, whereas S II receives bilateral input. The next projection stage sees axons being sent from S I to the posterior parietal cortex (Areas 5 and 7) and it has been suggested that, in a similar way to vision processing, the flow of information from the somatosensory cortex to other cortical areas continues in two streams: a dorsal stream goes via the posterior parietal cortex and projects to the premotor and primary motor cortex; a ventral stream goes via lateral somatosensory areas to the lateral premotor cortex and prefrontal cortex. The roles of the two streams are unclear but might reflect the ability to initiate somatosensation-related voluntary movement or to respond to stimuli that provoke voluntary movement (dorsal stream), and the ability to make fine discriminations between somatosensory stimuli and to recognise these stimuli (Romo and Salinas, 2001).

It has been suggested that there are neurons in S I that correspond to the receptor types found under the skin: so slowly adapting receptors have corresponding slowly responding neurons in S I (Mountcastle *et al.*, 1969). There is also evidence showing that neurons in S I respond to movement on the skin (Romo *et al.*, 1996). Romo *et al.* found that two groups of neurons responded to motion on the skin. One type responded to touch regardless of the speed of the touch; the other responded to the speed of the touch.

If lesions are made to different parts of the primary somatosensory cortex in animals, different deficits in somatosensation are observed. If S I is removed, for example, there is an impairment in the ability to discriminate between different types of touch and in proprioception. Deficits in appreciating the texture of stimuli are observed following lesions to Area 3b. Lesions to Area 2 are associated with impairments in the ability to discriminate shapes and sizes in the tactile modality. Damage to S II, however, results in the inability to learn to discriminate between objects of different shapes.

5.19 SOMATOSENSORY CORTEX AND BODY PARTS

There is further differentiation at the cortical level in relation to the body parts subserved by the somatosensory cortex. For example, electrical stimulation studies have shown that parts of the somatosensory cortex are more devoted to certain parts of the body than others. The area responsible for the hand (especially the index finger) and face (especially the lips), for example, is larger than that responsible for the big toe. The reason for this is because body parts such as the hand and face are involved in finer, more complicated and sophisticated movements than are other parts of the body, and require more cortical 'power' to enable them to function at this level.

5.20 HOW DOES THE BRAIN DECIDE TO RESPOND TO TOUCH?

There is also evidence that parts of the cortex can become more or less active when it anticipates that we are about to be touched. Carlsson *et al.* (2000) found that activity in the primary sensory motor cortex increased and activity in the sensorimotor cortex decreased when people anticipated being tickled.

The most likely candidate for the brain's 'decision-making' region when responding to touch appears to be the motor area of the frontal cortex. The motor system is described in more detail in a later section, but, for now, a simple description of how it responds to touch is adequate. There is general agreement that the motor area needs to receive projections from the somatosensory system in order to make a decision about what to do in response to stimulation. When it receives this information, the motor area can then generate the appropriate action (Schall and Thompson, 1999).

Research update ... how the brain distinguishes between a pleasant and a neutral touch

Edmund Rolls and his colleagues at the University of Oxford have compared those brain regions that are activated during perception of a pleasant or neutral touch, smell and taste (Francis, Rolls *et al.*, 1999). In their first experiment, participants had their hands stroked by either a velvet glove or a piece of wood as their brain activity was monitored. The pleasant touch (velvet) was associated with significantly greater activation in the orbitofrontal cortex than was the neutral touch (wood). The more intense touch (the neutral wood) was associated with activation in the part of the brain that represents touch. The taste of pleasant glucose and the smell of pleasant vanillin were associated with similar but different activation in the oribitofrontal cortex and in other parts of the brain. Given that all stimuli activated areas in or around this region, the researchers concluded that their findings point to yet more evidence for the role of the orbitofrontal cortex in the regulation of emotion (evidence reviewed in Chapter 8).

5.21 THE GUSTATORY SYSTEM

The gustatory system is one of the two most important senses for the perception of food flavour. Its receptors allow us to distinguish between at least four classes of taste: sourness, bitterness, sweetness and saltiness. There is also a commonly agreed fifth taste, called umami, which represents a savoury taste similar to monosodium glutamate. The external receptors for taste are the taste buds found on the tongue; these contain epithelial cells that are specialised in taste reception. Each taste bud contains about 50–100 cells and they are found principally on the tongue, although some are also found in the pharynx and palate. Although the tongue detects thermal stimulation and is capable of allowing the sensation of a limited number of tastes, there is evidence that direct stimulation of the tongue with heat between 20 and 35°C can lead to the experience of sweet sensations, whereas stimulation by cooling the tongue can lead to sensations of sourness or saltiness (Cruz and Green, 2000). This suggests an interesting interaction between the taste receptors and the heat of the food they detect.

The taste buds are innervated by three cranial nerves (the seventh, ninth and tenth), each of which innervates a different collection of taste buds. In primates, these cranial projections terminate in the rostral region of the nucleus of the solitary tract in the medulla (Scott *et al.*, 1986). Second-order neurons are then projected to the parvocellular division of the ventroposteromedial thalamic nucleus, or the taste thalamus. Fibres from the taste thalamus project to the cortex, specifically the rostral frontal operculum and insula. These regions comprise the primary taste cortex (Rolls, 1989).

There may also be a secondary taste cortex in the caudolateral orbitofrontal cortex, which lies anterior to the primary taste cortex (Rolls *et al.*, 1989). A part of the orbitofrontal cortex may act as a form of convergence zone for chemosensation because olfactory stimulation produces responses in its medial part, visual stimulation activates an area between the secondary taste cortex and the medial orbitofrontal cortex and, as we have already seen, gustatory inputs stimulate the secondary taste cortex (Rolls and Baylis, 1994). This study found that some neurons were activated by taste and visual stimuli, others by both taste and olfactory stimuli, and still others by one type of sensory stimulus. All were in very close proximity to each other, suggesting that this region of the brain might be the first cortical stage of integrating food-related information.

5.22 HOW THE BRAIN PROCESSES AVERSIVE TASTES

The part of the brain described as the primary taste (gustatory) area is found near the front of the brain in regions called the insula or frontal operculum, and further back in part of the parietal cortex. The location of the secondary taste cortex is not as well documented but may be in the orbitofontal cortex where flavour is thought to be processed.

Other brain structures, such as the amygdala, contain cells that are responsive to taste and these cells may responsible for determining the hedonic quality of taste (whether food is palatable). The amygdala forms part of an area that Small *et al.* (1997) describe as the anteromedial temporal lobe (AMTL). In patients who have had this area removed or damaged, there has been a reported increased sensitivity to bitter tastes and an elevated ability to recognise, but not detect, citric acid. Small *et al.* (2001a) have proposed that this region may play an important role in perceiving the intensity of tastes, especially aversive taste. Bitter aversive taste is considered important because this is the one gustatory category that we may be genetically programmed to detect; almost all natural poisons are bitter so an ability to detect them would be evolutionarily advantageous.

Small *et al.* (2001) asked 18 patients with either left or right AMTL lesions, and a healthy control group, to rate the intensity of taste stimuli representing the qualities of sweet, sour, bitter and salty. Taste solutions were placed on either the left or right papillae of the tongue. Patients who had right AMTL lesions rated the bitter taste as significantly more intense than did the control group. The side of the tongue stimulated had no effect on the results. The researchers suggest that one reason for the increase in intensity may be that the damage to the AMTL disinhibited cells in the cortex that are sensitive to taste concentration or palatability.

5.23 THE OLFACTORY SYSTEM

Like the gustatory system, the olfactory system is important (if not more important) for the perception of food flavour. Unlike the sense of taste, the number of classes of stimuli the olfactory system can perceive is apparently limitless. We can perceive thousands of different odours but only very few tastes. This is why, when individuals have a cold or the 'flu, they fail to identify the food they eat, claiming it has lost its taste. What they actually mean is that the food has lost its smell. About 80 per cent of food flavour is olfactory. Influenza or a cold can impair gustation but the primary deficit, in terms of food flavour, is olfactory. We can still identify classes of taste; what we cannot seem to do is identify food because the olfactory receptors are impaired.

Initial perception in the olfactory system occurs at the back of the nasal cavities in a region called the olfactory neuroepithelium. This contains specialised receptors and three types of cell: olfactory sensory neurons, supporting cells and basal cells. Unlike the neurons in other parts of the central nervous system, the cells of the olfactory system are the only ones that can regenerate. The olfactory neuron extends a dendrite whose cilia extends into a layer of mucus; an axon from each receptor is sent to a structure called the olfactory bulb. There are two of these located, in humans and non-human primates, beneath the frontal lobes (Buck *et al.*, 1994). The olfactory bulbs are made up of six layers of different types of neuron. One layer is the superficial olfactory nerve layer, which terminates in regions called glomeruli. The projection pathway of the olfactory bulbs is ipsilateral and fairly extensive, reaching the primary olfactory cortex (principally, the piriform cortex), parts of the amygdaloid nucleus and the lateral part of the entorhinal cortex. All of these regions send connections back to the olfactory bulb.

Some research suggests that women are, on average, better at identifying, recognising and detecting odours than are men (Doty *et al.*, 1985). This sex difference may have important implications for any study of the neural basis of olfactory perception. If individual differences exist at the behavioural level (detecting, recognising, identifying), then the brains of men and women may respond differently when they both smell the same odours.

To test this hypothesis, David Yousem and his colleagues from the University of Pennsylvania carried out an fMRI study of the brain activation of eight right-handed men and eight right-handed women as they smelled pleasant, neutral and unpleasant odours – eugenol, ethyl alcohol and hydrogen sulphide (Yousem *et al.*, 1999). These odours were chosen because they were thought to stimulate the olfactory nerve only (unlike other odours that also stimulate the touch nerve, 'the trigeminal' nerve, which responds to chemical stimulation). The authors found that not only was activation greater in women, it was also greater in specific parts of the brain, namely the frontal and perisylvian regions. Activation was greater in both left and right frontal hemispheres in women.

The brain also appears to respond to 'psychological' properties of odour, rather than to the odour *per se*. An EEG study in which participants smelled the real or artificial aroma of food, including chocolate, coffee, garlic, cumin and peppermint, for example, found that one odour – chocolate – was consistently associated with decreased EEG theta activity (Martin, 1998b). Chocolate was also the odour rated most relaxing and one of the most pleasant. Given that increased theta is seen when people concentrate on perceptual and geometric tasks, and work hard to remember words, the relaxing effect of the chocolate might have led to the reduction in an EEG frequency you normally see under conditions of high cognitive demand. The aroma of bergamot appears to have a similar effect on visual vigilance: it makes us less vigilant (Gould and Martin, 2001).

The effect of odour on the CNS has led some to argue that this supports its use in clinical, therapeutic settings. However, the evidence for pure aromatherapy – the beneficial effect of smelling aroma on ill-health – is poor: the methodology is often flawed, samples are small, there is no rationale for the odours used and results do not reach statistical significance (Martin, 1996). Odour may help enhance quality of life or distract from the experience of pain (although no study has demonstrated this systematically) and may even smell rather nice, but there is no evidence that it is useful in the treatment of mental illness or physical ailments.

5.24 THE MOTOR SYSTEM

The general motor system is subserved by two distinct motor systems: one involving the peripheral motor neurons and another involving central motor neurons. Both of these systems are responsible for mediating the responses from muscles to motor centres, such as the initiation of movement. Other important structures play a part in these systems, such as the basal ganglia and the cerebellum. These are involved in the execution and maintenance of motor behaviour rather than in its initiation.

The types of behaviour governed by the motor system can be crudely described as automatic and voluntary. Basic, reflexive motor movements, such as withdrawing your hand from fire, are automatic and these rely on responses from receptors in the spinal cord. Motor behaviour such as precision grip or reaching for an object, is voluntary and requires control at the cortical level. Walking, however, is neither fully one nor the other, being under the control of the brainstem or the cortex's input to the brainstem.

Peripheral motor system

Peripheral motor neurons send axons to skeletal muscles. Lower motor neurons are found in the ventral horn of the spinal cord and are of two types: alpha and gamma motorneurons. The axons of these neurons leave the spinal cord, and innervate muscle at the trunk and extremities. When axons are damaged, muscle paralysis can result. As we saw in the section on cranial nerves, several of these nerves also innervate various muscles in the body.

Central motor system

The central motor system contains the upper motor neurons important for voluntary movement and found in the brainstem and cortex. The system is roughly divided into neurons of the pyramidal tract (also called the corticospinal tract) and the rest (the extrapyramidal system). The pyramidal tract is important for the execution of precise, voluntary movement. Most fibres cross over to the opposite side of the body at the point of the medulla; the pyramidal tract is the only pathway making its way directly from the cortex to the spinal cord. Most motor neurons in this system are found in the fifth cortical layer, which contains pyramidal cells; many, the thickest, are found in the precentral gyrus (the primary motor area or M1). Electrically stimulating M1 produces muscle contraction.

Other tracts also pass impulses from higher cortical areas to the motorneurons in the spinal cord. The rubrospinal tract sends fibres from the red nucleus to the spinal cord and influences the activity of the cerebellum. The reticulospinal tract is composed of the reticular formation, which can influence motor neurons and appears to be involved in maintaining posture, orienting to external stimuli and executing stereotypical movements. The tectospinal tract represents fibres found in the superior colliculus and is important for controlling the movement of the head and eyes in response to movement in the visual field. Finally, the vestibulospinal tract is important for maintaining balance and posture.

The cortex and movement

The higher brain areas responsible for the maintenance of voluntary movement are the primary motor cortex (PMC or M1), the premotor area (A6) and the supplementary motor area (SMA). There are other regions, such as the cerebellum, that are responsible for coordinating or learning sequential movement (Ito, 1984). From the kicking of a ball to using a pen, to playing the piano, to opening a specific page in a book, the motor cortex and its interaction with other sensory systems allows us to engage in behaviours many of us take for granted.

Region M1 responds with involuntary movement when electrically stimulated, and lesions to the area cause paralysis (damage to any part of the motor system, from motor cortex to motor neuron, can cause paralysis or partial paralysis). Areas 5, 7 and the prefrontal cortex are also important cortical areas for movement. M1 becomes active when people are executing a movement or even when they are preparing to move (Tanji and Evarts, 1976). It also seems to be responsive when people have to execute a sequence of movements (Catalan *et al.*, 1998). Recent evidence suggests that it is important for the consolidation of motor skill – that is, it is needed for more proficient execution of movement (Muellbacher *et al.*, 2002). Muellbacher *et al.* found that when people learned a motor skill that involved making rapid finger movements, the movements became more rapid as the participants practised (not surprisingly). However, if M1 was disrupted during practice, the improvement in execution did not occur, suggesting that the primary motor cortex has a role to play in early motor skill learning.

The PMC receives afferent axons from a variety of areas including Areas 1, 2, 3, 5 and 6 and the ventrolateral nucleus of the thalamus. A large part of the PMC is devoted to hand movement (especially the finger and thumb), probably due to the cortical requirements necessary to make precision movements. Stimulation of the PMC also elicits movement in other muscles, such as the abdomen and back muscles. Unilateral or bilateral stimulation will result in movement of these muscles. However, unilateral stimulation of the 'hand area' of the cortex will produce movement in the contralateral hand, because pyramidal tract fibres are crossed.

The premotor cortex, as you saw in the section on somatosensation, is involved in motoric decision-making. Neurons in this area are also active during the preparation for sequential movement (Kettner *et al.*, 1996).

The SMA appears to subserve a different type of motor behaviour.

Whereas movement of the hand will activate the PMC, sequences of movement will activate the SMA. Some of the earliest evidence for this role was reported in the 1970s. Laplane and colleagues, for example, found that if the SMA was lesioned, there was a significant impairment in the ability to make serial, alternating hand movements (Laplane *et al.*, 1977).

More recent studies have highlighted a role for the region in the temporal control of motor movement, such as the timing of finger movement (Halsband *et al.*, 1993) and the ordering of complex finger movement in time (Gerloff *et al.*, 1997). If the region is lesioned, then impairment in these movements is observed. Data from other sources also support these findings. If the region is made inactive by the injection of a chemical (muscimol), the ability to make simple motor movements is not impaired: the monkeys in this experiment, for example, could reach for a single target with their arms quite easily (Shima and Tanji, 1998). However, the primates' ability to make three separate movements that had been previously learned, was impaired. The ability to imagine also activates this part of the motor cortex, and it appears to be involved in motor planning and organisation. The execution of novel, recently learned sequences of actions is also more susceptible to SMA and pre-SMA lesions than is the execution of well-learned single movements. Together, these findings suggest that this region is important for the execution of sequences of voluntary movement and is involved in the learning of new sequences: if the area is damaged near to the learning of new sequential movements, motor behaviour is impaired.

Subcortical regions

Finally, some structures beneath the cortex are considered vital for the control of motor behaviour. A collection of structures called the basal ganglia, for example, also shares responsibility for sequential motor movement. When the region is inhibited in monkeys, by the administration of a neurotoxin to two parts of the basal ganglia (the putamen and caudate nucleus), the learning and execution of movement is impaired (Matsumoto *et al.*, 1999). This specific neurotoxin, MPTP, attacks what is called the nigrostriatal dopamine system. This is a neurotransmitter pathway that leads from the basal ganglia to the striatum and is important because it is the key neurotransmitter affected in movement disorders such as Parkinson's disease (Bergman *et al.*, 1998). The lesion studies are complemented by neuroimaging in healthy adults: there is evidence from this method, too, showing the importance of the basal ganglia in sequential motor behaviour (Jueptner and Weiller, 1998).

Disorders of movement and the motor system, such as Huntington's chorea and Parkinson's disease are described and discussed in the final chapter.

SOME USEFUL FURTHER READING

THE VISUAL SYSTEM AND DISORDERS OF VISUAL PERCEPTION
Bruce, V. and Young, A.W. (1998) *In the Eye of the Beholder: The Science of Face Perception*. Oxford: Oxford University Press.
Farah, M.J. (2001) *The Cognitive Neuroscience of Vision*. Oxford: Oxford University Press.
Logothetis, N.K. (1999) Vision: a window on consciousness. *Scientific American, November*, 44–51.
Milner, A.D. (1998) Streams of consciousness: visual awareness and the brain. *Trends in Cognitive Sciences* 2(1), 25–30.
Rees, G. (2001) Neuroimaging of visual awareness in patients and normal subjects. *Current Opinion in Neurobiology* 11, 150–6.
Zeki, S. (2001) Localization and globalization in conscious vision. *Annual Review of Neuroscience* 24, 57–86.

THE AUDITORY SYSTEM
Geisler, C.D. (1998) *From Sound to Synapse*. Oxford: Oxford University Press.
Zattore, R.J., Belin, P. and Penhune, V.B. (2002) Structure and function of auditory cortex: music and speech. *Trends in Cognitive Sciences* 6(1), 37–46.

THE GUSTATORY AND OLFACTORY SYSTEMS
Doty, R. (1995) *Handbook of Olfaction and Gustation*. New York: Marcel Dekker.

THE MOTOR SYSTEM
Jeannerod, M. (1997) *The Cognitive Neuroscience of Action*. Oxford: Blackwell.

SOME USEFUL JOURNALS TO BROWSE

Brain
Chemical Senses
Cortex
Journal of Cognitive Neuroscience
Journal of Neurology, Neurosurgery and Neuroanatomy
Journal of Neuroscience
Nature Neuroscience
Neuroimage
Neuropsychologia
Neuroreport
Trends in Cognitive Sciences
Trends in Neurosciences
Vision Science

6
Motivation: Genes, Thirst, Hunger, Sex and Aggression

WHAT YOU WILL FIND IN THIS CHAPTER

- a definition of motivation and an outline of models that try to explain what propels us to action
- a review of the main features of Darwin's theory of evolution
- a review of genetics and the consequences of defective genes
- a description of the biological basis of thirst
- a description of the biological basis of hunger and satiety, and the models that may account for these behaviours
- an evaluation of the role of biology in eating disorders
- a review of the biological basis of sexual activity and orientation
- a review of the biological correlates of aggressive behaviour

WHAT YOU SHOULD BE ABLE TO DO AFTER READING THE CHAPTER

- define the term motivation
- outline the main principles of Darwin's theory of evolution
- have a basic understanding of genetics
- have an awareness of the biological basis of thirst and hunger
- have an awareness of the biological basis of sexual behaviour
- outline the role of hormones and the brain in aggression

6.1 MOTIVATION

What motivates us to behave in the way that we do? What makes us hungry for food, want sex with other people, thirsty for a drink, or hate others to such an extent that we want to harm them? Motivation is a term used to describe what drives us to engage in a particular action and the likelihood of repeating that action in future. We are motivated to approach (or avoid) events, objects or people that we have learned, through previous experience, to like (or dislike). We are also motivated to behave in ways that may not involve reinforcement – we search for food or drink when hungry or thirsty (although the types of food and drink depend on previously established preferences). We are also motivated to relax and take a break from work when this becomes too onerous or boring.

The motivation to drink is an example of a biological need; our bodies tell us that we need to behave in a particular way to meet its needs. Behaviours – called regulatory behaviours – are then observed, which help meet the physiological demands of the body and bring its internal state back into equilibrium. The process of ensuring that physical systems are working at optimum level is called homeostasis ('stable state'). When our stable state is imbalanced, or deficient in some way, we are motivated to correct the imbalance. Why?

6.2 DRIVE REDUCTION HYPOTHESIS

According to the drive reduction hypothesis, the imbalances in our physiology are generally unpleasant – we feel hunger if the body experiences a loss of nutrients or energy, for example – and we are thus motivated to reduce these unpleasant feelings. Hunger, in this example, is seen as a drive that needs to be reduced to keep the body's physiology happy. We search for food, which if eaten, reduces the hunger 'drive'. Consequently, the drive reduction becomes reinforcing – we learn that eating food reduces hunger and makes us feel positive – and therefore will be pursued again whenever we feel hungry. Drives need not be necessary for survival; the drive to have sex with a person, for example, does not affect your ability to survive but sexual intercourse is rewarding and reinforcing. If put in a featureless environment, we will be motivated to explore it but our physical survival would not depend on it.

There are problems with the drive hypothesis, however. The first is that it is almost impossible to measure a 'drive'. We could measure the body's level of glucose, correlate this with hunger and satiety, and observe whether eating takes place when the amount of glucose in the blood falls, but how would we measure the drive that leads us to play a specific piece of music, watch a particular film, read a particular book or visit a particular country. We can describe reasons for engaging in all of these behaviours but whether we are driven to them is doubtful. Because we have no operational definition of a drive, its existence is impossible to test experimentally. A second criticism is that we often engage in behaviour not to reduce a 'drive' but to increase it. If we engage in conversation, we don't want to end up falling asleep; if we take a trip on a rollercoaster, we don't want our arousal to be reduced, we want it to be increased. These behaviours are reinforcing because we find them pleasant, arousing and, consequently, we perform them again and again.

6.3 WHAT CAUSES REINFORCEMENT?

What makes a behaviour reinforcing? Well, one obvious answer is that we like behaving in that way because it arouses us, makes us feel good and is generally pleasant. That is one, superficial, answer. What might explain this arousal and positive effect that accompanies reinforcing behaviours? At the physiological level, one candidate may be the neurotransmitter dopamine. There are neurons and systems of neurons in the brain that respond to natural reinforcers such as food, drink and sexual contact. This electrical stimulation is also seen when people take arousing drugs, such as cocaine (of which more in Chapter 10). The key chemical feature of this stimulation is the release of dopamine; reinforcing behaviours are invariably accompanied by the release of this neurotransmitter.

6.4 OPTIMUM LEVEL HYPOTHESIS

To account for the arousing and assuaging effects of reinforcing stimuli, Berlyne (1966) suggested that when we are understimulated or bored, we explore our environment discursively and search for objects or events that will stimulate us. However, when we are overstimulated, our search is much more specific. If we need food or water, we will need to search for a reinforcer to reduce this overstimulation. This is a form of optimum level hypothesis, which states that we and, in fact, any organism, will seek an optimum level of arousal. When we are overstimulated, we need less reinforcement; when we are understimulated, we seek stimulation to maintain a certain level of arousal. The hypothesis, however, suffers from the same shortcoming as the drive reduction hypothesis in that it is almost impossible to define arousal or measure it experimentally.

6.5 HUNGER, THIRST, SEX AND VIOLENCE

The two models in the previous sections were valiant and logical attempts to explain why we are motivated to behave in particular ways. While the concepts they suggested were often vaguely defined and difficult to test experimentally, they highlighted the role of reinforcement in the persistence of our behaviour. Hunger and thirst are good examples of motivating behaviours or 'states' because we can measure their reduction biologically. We know a great deal about the nature of hunger (although not necessarily how it occurs) and the next sections will look at some of the possible causes of the most prominent motivating and motivated behaviours: hunger, thirst, sex and violence. As genetics play an important part in some of these behaviours (and those mentioned elsewhere in this book), the first section below describes some of the basic tenets of genetics and our physical evolution.

6.6 EVOLUTION AND BEHAVIOUR

According to Darwin's theory of evolution, generations of species can either adapt effectively or ineffectively to changes in their environment – a concept called adaptation. Some variations in species will be transferred from one generation to the next, a feature of the theory called natural selection. The world is not a static place but a dynamic one that requires our responses to it to change during our interaction with it. Of course, the way of ensuring that variations are transferred from one generation to the next is to reproduce; reproductive success is measured as the number of viable offspring produced by an individual relative to the number of offspring produced by other members of the same species. But all offspring are slightly different from their parents, and living things will encounter changing environments that will require them to adapt. It is these variations and the ability to adapt to changes in the environment that fuel the evolution of species (Jacob, 1977).

Variation and competition

Two determinants of natural selection are variation – physical and behavioural differences among members of a species – and competition – where organisms compete for limited resources in the environment. We differ, genetically, from all members of our species (unless we are identical twins). Our genetic make-up is called our genotype. The physical difference we see between ourselves and others, and which arises from our genetic make-up and its interaction with the environment, is called our phenotype. Having an identical genotype, for example, does not mean that the phenype will also be identical. If identical twins are separated at birth and one is exposed to a good diet and the other to a poor diet, there would be physical differences between them. Our genetic make-up, therefore, interacts significantly with changes in our environment. On the other hand, if the twins lack the gene for tallness or physical strength, no environmental change will alter this status significantly.

The interaction was observed by Darwin when he discovered 13 species of finches in the Galapagos Islands. Some had small, thin beaks (good for picking up small seeds); others had large, thick beaks that could pick larger seeds and break shells. Grant (1986) observed that when a drought occurred on one island (and small seeds were, therefore, rare), the incidence of finches with the small, thin beak phenotype dropped and, during the next few years of the drought, the finches with the large, thick beak phenotype increased. When rainfall came, the number of small-beaked birds increased again, thus illustrating Darwin's concept of natural selection. If all of the finches were of the short, thin-beaked variety, all would probably have died during the drought – they would not have been able to feed and their declining numbers would have reduced the likelihood of reproduction. In other words, they would have become extinct. As there was genetically determined variation in beak size on the island, this ensured that the large-beaked birds continued to flourish.

In the example of the finches, each type of bird sought different types of food. Some species, however, share the same food and territory and are, therefore, in competition with each other for these resources. If there is a limited supply of fish, one fish caught by one species is one less available to feed another. Species develop strategies to secure such resources in a competitive environment. The species with the most adaptable phenotype, the theory argues, is the one most likely to survive and reproduce.

Darwin's theory applied to animals but natural scientists at the time argued that the theory could extend to all animals and humans (others disagreed, arguing that natural selection could explain the evolution of animals but not humans). However, fossil records and evidence from (the admittedly questionable study of) paleoanthropology, suggest that our evolution, although lengthy, followed this principle. In recent years, psychologists have proposed that the mechanism could also explain our social behaviour, such as our ability to commit infidelity or to remain monogamous or to aggress towards kin who are not related to us by blood (Buss, 1995). If you would like to learn more see Chapter 3 of Carlson et al. (2000).

Genetics and heredity

While Darwin knew that individual differences were passed on from generation to generation, he did not know how the process of inheritance occurred. Genetics is the study of how genes are passed from one generation to the next. Heredity refers to the sum total of the traits and tendencies passed on from one generation to another.

Genes are bits of genetic material made of DNA (deoxyribonucleic acid). DNA is made up of strands of sugar and phosphate connected by molecules of adenine, thymine, guanine and cytosine. Each molecule is paired with another, but guanine always pairs with cytosine and adenine with thymine. The pairs of nucleotides form rungs on a ladder where the arms of the ladder are represented by the sugar and phosphate. This ladder-shaped organisation is actually more like a spiral staircase because it is twisted. These nucleotides, the so-called building blocks of life, form the basis of our development and do so by influencing protein synthesis. Each sequence of rungs on the genetic ladder is specific to a certain amino acid. Proteins are made up of strings of amino acids, and the combination of sequences of nucleotides allows the creation and development of physical structures.

It is easy to get carried away with the psychology of genetics by attributing a behaviour to a gene sequence – describing an intelligence gene or a homosexuality gene, for example – but while there may be a genetic contribution to each of these characteristics, the genetic contribution is at a physical, molecular level. That is, if we invoke a gene for intelligence, we are simply stating that this gene is responsible for synthesising particular proteins, which gives rise to the development of specific physiological processes that contribute to intelligent thinking. Of course, there could be more than one gene (and we also need to be aware of the lack of general agreement among psychologists over the precise definition of intelligence). Finally, genes also control the synthesis of enzymes (proteins that occur in every cell in the body, and control cells' structure and function).

Genes and sex

Genes are located on chromosomes, rod-like structures found within the nuclei of cells. We inherit 46 chromosomes from our parents – 23 from each – and these are paired. The 23rd pair represents the sex chromosomes (i.e. it contains the instructions for the development of male or female sexual characteristics). The sex chromosomes are of two different types: X and Y. Females have a pair of X chromosomes (XX); males have one of each type (XY). Men's sperm contains X and Y chromosomes, whereas women's ova contain only X chromosomes. Because half of a man's sperm contains X chromosomes and the other half, Y, it is the man's sperm that determines the sex of the offspring. If an X chromosome fertilises a woman's ovum, the offspring will be female; if a Y chromosome fertilises the ovum, the offspring will be male.

Alleles

The individual genes in each pair of chromosomes can be the same or different. Alternative forms of genes are called alleles, and these can be dominant or recessive. For example, the allele for brown eyes is dominant. If each parent contributes the same allele for eye colour, then the child will show the phenotype for that colour. If the alleles contributed by each parent are different (the combination of genes is called homozygous), then the phenotype is controlled by the dominant allele (so called because, not surprisingly, it has the greater influence over the phenotype exhibited). If one parent contributed a blue eye allele and the other a brown eye allele, the child would have brown eyes. In this example, the blue eye allele is called recessive because it has a weaker effect on the expression of the phenotype. Following this logic, if both parents contribute a recessive blue eye allele, what would the child's eye colour be? The correct answer is blue. Of course, some people have black or hazel eyes. These variations are produced by the influence exerted by the dominant brown allele.

Sex-related effects on heredity

We are not genetically equal and the sexes are not genetically equal either. There are some genes that are thought to be sex-linked: they reside on the sex chromosomes. Haemophilia is a good example. This is a condition where serious bleeding can occur with even minor cuts; in the most extreme circumstances, a person with the condition can bleed to death. The condition results from the blood's inability to clot (and, therefore, prevent bleeding) and is caused by a recessive gene on the X chromosome that fails to produce the protein necessary for blood clotting. Because females have two X chromosomes, if one allele is that for haemophilia and the other isn't, they will not develop the disorder. Because males only have one X chromosome, if this is affected (the gene for blood clotting is faulty) then the condition will occur.

A different group of genes is that of the sex-influenced genes. These genes express themselves in both sexes but the phenotype is more common in one sex than the other. Pattern baldness – a thinning of the hair across the scalp – is caused by the inheritance of one or both alleles for baldness. The condition, however, develops in men but not women, even if women inherit both alleles. Findings suggest that the phenotype is expressed in men because of the interaction with sex hormones.

6.7 BEHAVIOURAL GENETICS

Perhaps the greatest interest in the contribution of genetics to understanding the biological basis of behaviour has been in the area of intelligence. Is it inherited and, if it is, how can it be modified? If genes do code for intelligence, which ones are they? Heritability refers to the amount of variation in a trait that is due to genetic differences among people in the population. The scientific study of heritability is called behavioural genetics (Plomin and Colledge, 2001) and the discipline strives to explain why people differ.

In a recent study of the attitudes of 195 pairs of monozygotic twins and 141 pairs of dizygotic twins, James Olson and researchers at the Universities of Western Ontario and British Columbia distributed questionnaires asking participants for their views on 30 diverse topics such as how favourably they viewed crossword puzzles, the death penalty for murder, sweets, immigration, loud music, making racial discrimination illegal, exercising and so on (Olson *et al.*, 2001). Participants also rated themselves according to 20 personality traits and were asked how athletic, strong and physically attractive they thought they were, and whether people considered them to be good-looking. A total of 26 out of the 30 attitude items showed strong genetic effects, with identical twins more likely to share views.

6.8 MUTATIONS AND ABERRATIONS

In the comic book and film, *The X Men*, much is made of genetic modification, or mutation, that results in otherwise normal human beings possessing strange, novel but uncontrollable behaviour – such as the ability to act as a magnet, create electrical storms or breathe ice. These are inventive and fanciful ideas but there are serious genetic mutations and aberrations that can have stark effects on phenotype and behaviour. When genetic material changes, the change is caused by mutation or chromosomal aberration. Mutations are accidental alterations in the DNA code within a single gene and an example of the phenotype expressed from such a mutation is haemophilia. Chromosomal aberration, however, refers to changes in parts of the chromosome or to a change in the number of chromosomes. Children with a partial deletion of chromosome 5, for example, develop gastrointestinal and cardiac problems, become mentally retarded and make crying sounds resembling those of a cat (the condition is called *cri-du-chat* syndrome).

Another condition caused by chromosomal aberration is Down's syndrome where an extra 25th chromosome results in a phenotype characterised by short stature, broad skulls, round faces, and impaired motor and cognitive development. Around one in a thousand births will be Down's syndrome births, and 15 per cent of children born with the condition die before their first birthday. Although the condition is caused by a chromosomal aberration, it is not heritable.

The expression of a dominant gene on the arm of chromosome 4 results in a condition called Huntington's chorea. This is a movement disorder characterised by dance-like, jerky actions, and although the phenotype may be dormant for many years into adulthood, when it is expressed there is serious mental and physical deterioration. The prevalence is rare (two to seven individuals per thousand) but because it is autosomal-dominant, a child of a parent contributing the gene will have a 50 per cent chance of developing the disorder. There is no current cure and people can be genetically tested for the presence of the gene, which presents a potentially devastating dilemma. Chapter 11 looks at Huntington's chorea in more detail.

6.9 INGESTION: HUNGER AND THIRST

The two factors that motivate us most are hunger and thirst: without satisfying our craving for food and drink, we would not survive. We need nutrients to provide the body with energy. At a superficial level, answering the question 'why do we eat when we do?' is simple: we are hungry. But what does being hungry and thirsty mean? What causes that craving for a particular food or drink? And how does hunger or thirst subside?

Why do we feel thirsty?

A popular theory at the turn of the twentieth century argued that thirst was caused by a dry mouth, and that it was this dryness that regulated how much water we ingested. When the salivary glands reduced the amount of fluid they secreted, this made the mouth dry and was the cue for drinking. While plausible, the theory was not supported because even if water was made available to the mouth but was prevented from reaching the stomach, drinking would still continue: the mouth was being kept wet, not dry, and yet drinking continued because the fluid did not reach the stomach. Why?

Osmometric thirst

A later theory suggested that thirst was caused by dehydration within cells (Gilman, 1937). The fluid in cells is called intracellular fluid, and contains a little sodium but large amounts of potassium and other metabolites. The other source of fluid in the body is extracellular fluid and this is found in two places. Interstitial fluid surrounds the cell body and is salty; blood plasma is found in the capillaries, arteries and veins, and allows living cells and blood to be suspended within it. Extracellular fluid comprises about 20 per cent of the body's weight; intraceleular fluid comprises about 40 per cent of body weight. Gilman administered solutions of sodium chloride to animals. The membranes surrounding cells are not very permeable to sodium and so water is drawn from the intracellular fluid to the extracellular fluid by a process called osmosis, the process whereby water moves through a semipermeable membrane from a region where there is a low concentration of solutes to one where there is a high concentration. This reduces the concentration of sodium available across the membrane and the movement of water by osmosis dehydrates and shrinks the body's cells. This is what Gilman found and the type of thirst is called osmometric thirst. Because the organism needs to be aware of this thirst, there must be cells in the body that serve to inform the CNS that dehydration is occurring. These cells are called osmoreceptors and are located in the brain. When salt solutions are injected into the brain, drinking increases, but if sodium chloride is injected into the general blood supply, no such increase is observed (Wood *et al.*, 1977).

The precise locus of the osmoreceptors seems to be the lateral preoptic area. If even small lesions are made to this region, the typical increase in drinking seen in response to dehydration is reduced (Mason, 1980). When neurons are exposed to urea, salt and sucrose (neurons are impermeable to salt and sucrose but not urea) those neurons stimulated by salt and sucrose, and that caused increased drinking, were located in the later preoptic area (Peck and Novin, 1971).

Volumetric thirst

Osmometric thirst is caused by dehydration within cells. There is another type of thirst that results from dehydration outside cells – that is, a reduction in the level of blood plasma – this is called volumetric thirst, because the thirst is provoked by a reduction in the volume of blood plasma. One obvious way in which volumetric thirst can occur is through bleeding – a loss of blood leads to a great loss of extracellular fluid with all the substances that the fluid contains. People who suffer from haemophilia experience thirst during a bleeding episode, which is alleviated by an infusion of blood.

Volumetric thirst can also result from low levels of salt in the diet. The loss of extracellular fluid produces the movement of water from the extracellular fluid and into cell bodies, by the process of osmosis described earlier. This process leads to drinking.

Given that blood plasma is lost as a result of extracellular/volumetric thirst, you might reasonably hypothesise that receptors detecting this loss are located in the vascular or circulatory system. One important structure in this system is the kidney. If blood flow to the kidney is reduced, the total volume of blood in the body does not change, but there is an increase in thirst and drinking (often excessive). The kidney responds to this inhibition (effectively, a decrease in blood pressure) by releasing an enzyme, renin, which produces two hormones called angiotensin I and II. Rolls and colleagues found that when animals were injected with angiotensin II, they strived to complete a task that gave them water (Rolls *et al.*, 1972). The animals gave priority to searching for water and stopped eating, even when they had been deprived of food. The kidney's secretions, therefore, appear to be play an important part in regulating the body's awareness of volumetric thirst.

One further way in which the body experiences volumetric thirst is via baroreceptors. Baroreceptors are receptors on the walls of blood vessels that detect changes in the blood pressure of the cardiovascular system. If blood pressure drops, these baroreceptors can detect this drop and initiate volumetric thirst via the brain.

Why do we feel hungry?

Like the ingestion of fluid, there are some social and cultural conventions that dictate the ingestion of food; we may sit at the dining table three times a day for our meals or we may set aside a specific time of day for a meal. But whereas these conventions may explain *when* we start eating, they do not explain *why*. Of course, we could learn by association that these times are set aside for meals and therefore anticipate them with a sense of hunger, but what is the cause of this feeling of hunger?

One, now discredited, theory of hunger argued that we felt hungry because we had an empty stomach (Cannon and Washburn, 1912). The hunger pangs experienced were due to the walls of the stomach rubbing against each other. Cannon and Washburn argued that thirst arose from a dry mouth and, together, these two views of ingestion became known as the 'spit and rumble' theory of ingestion. The rumble theory was soon challenged, however, when it was found that people with no stomach still felt hunger pangs (Inglefinger, 1944). These people had had their stomach removed due to cancer/ulceration and their oesophagus – the gullet – was attached directly to their small intestine. They felt hunger and satiety in the same way as those with stomachs.

Ingestion and digestion

Food is the body's fuel but the food we eat needs to be broken down before the body extracts what it needs from it. When food enters our mouth, it is chewed and combined with saliva. The chewed food (called a bolus) is broken down by saliva, a process controlled by the brainstem. Specifically an enzyme in saliva, salivary amylase, breaks down starches in food in preparation for digestion. The mouth is the first part of the gastrointestinal tract, which describes the physical pathway from mouth to stomach, intestine, liver and rectum.

When food reaches the stomach, it is further broken down by hydrochloric acid and pepsinogen. The acid helps the process of digestion and the elimination of bacteria; the pepsinogen breaks down peptide bonds in the food. Digestion continues in the next stage of the tract, the small intestine, which is 6 m long, and where bile and pancreatic juice further break down the remaining material. Bile is important because it is responsible for emulsification – the process by which fats are broken down (fats are difficult to break down). The small intestine is made up of the duodenum, jejenum and ileum, and the contents of the ileum are passed on to the next part of the digestive system, the large intestine. Food material makes its way through the intestine by peristalsis – muscular contractions that force the food along in stages. After the material leaves the large intestine, it goes to the rectum and then, eventually, is expelled.

The role of glucose

The most likely factor to cause hunger and the desire to eat is the depletion of the body's nutrients. The body derives most of its energy from a simple sugar called glucose and from fatty acids (the chemicals produced when fats are broken down). It also receives more glucose than it needs and, therefore, needs to store the excess energy. Carbohydrates will give the body glucose, proteins will give the body amino acids and animal starch will give the body fats or glycogen. Of these, glucose appears to be the most important.

Absorption and fasting

When the body has received its nutrients, it goes about utilising the energy it needs but also stores what it doesn't. This part of the digestive process is called the absorptive phase because nutrients are being absorbed by the body and converted into energy. Excess glucose is converted into glycogen in the liver and the muscles; glucose, and the excess amino acids from proteins, can also be converted into fats. The liver itself cannot store fat but sends the converted material to adipose tissue.

During the fasting phase, where no food is ingested, the body makes use of its newly derived energy in order to function. Most organs, apart from the brain, can use fatty tissue, and the muscle tissue uses its own stored glycogen.

The key to the utilisation of glucose by the body is the hormone insulin. Insulin facilitates the entry of glucose into cells and allows cells to receive the energy they need. It prepares the body for the absorptive phase. If insulin is not produced by the body, then the excess glucose cannot be used by cells; this gives rise to the condition diabetes mellitus and sufferers need to self-administer the hormone to prevent damage to tissue.

During the fasting phase, the body is using up the glucose it needs to function. It is at the end of this process that hunger occurs. The glucostatic hypothesis of hunger argues that low levels of glucose in the body at this point provoke feelings of hunger (Mayer, 1955). Liver glycogen levels drop, the levels of glucose in the blood fall and we will be motivated to search for food. If the body does not receive additional nutrients, it will try to derive energy from its stored energy sources (this is how we can survive fasting over long periods). However, energy is derived from the most easily utilisable stores first (these are not usually the fatty tissue). Figure 6.1 provides a summary of the process of food metabolism.

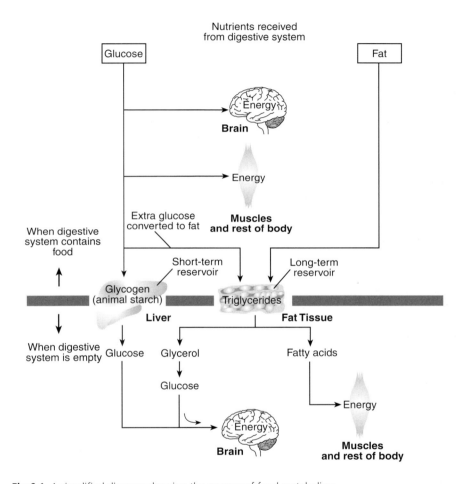

Fig 6.1 A simplified diagram showing the process of food metabolism

What stops us eating?

There comes a point when the body will reject too much food if it is surplus to its requirements. The initial ingestion of food is enjoyed, and this enjoyment continues throughout the meal until it wanes and we feel sated. Satiety refers to the feeling of fullness we experience after having eaten a meal.

It is interesting to observe that we will ingest more of a specific food, depending on its nutritional properties. People who ingest drinks containing simple sugars, for example, ingest less than do those who receive drinks with no calories (Birch *et al.*, 1989). If carbohydrates are added to food this also reduces feeding, compared to unsupplemented foods or foods with a sweetener added (Blundell *et al.*, 1994). Ingesting fats, however, seems to have little effect on subsequent ingestion. People will spontaneously eat more snacks containing fats than they would those containing carbohydrates, and this does not affect their intake of a subsequent meal (Green *et al.*, 1994).

The oral intake of food is important for our feelings of hunger and satiety. When participants ingested a high-fat soup, they experienced a greater reduction in feelings of hunger compared to when the food was directly infused into the stomach (Cecil *et al.*, 1998). Both methods of intake, however, were more successful in reducing hunger than was infusion into the small intestine, although direct infusion into the small intestine does reduce subsequent intake (French *et al.*, 2000). If the intake of fat and carbohydrate is oral, then appetite and food intake is more reduced than it would be by direct infusion (Cecil *et al.*, 1999). The rate of gastric emptying is also faster. These findings suggest that 'mouth feel' or oral intake is important for our rate of ingestion.

Sensory-specific satiety (SSS)

Some well-known studies in psychology have demonstrated how changing the sensory properties of food can lead to increases or decreases in intake and in the perceived pleasantness of food. For example, if a food is eaten to satiety and a second course of the same food is presented, subsequent intake is reduced by around 50 per cent (Rolls *et al.*, 1981). However, if people are given either a single food to eat or a selection of four foods, people eat more of the varied, than the single, meal.

In one experiment, participants ate either a four-course meal of sausages, bread and butter, chocolate dessert and bananas, or ate only one of these foods to satiety. The researchers found that consumption was 60 per cent higher when foods were presented together than when presented as separate courses (Rolls *et al.*, 1986). At a post-satiety tasting session, those foods presented singly were also rated as less pleasant than those eaten as part of a four-course meal (Rolls *et al.*, 1984). Even colour and shape influenced the amount of food eaten.

In Rolls's experiments, when a variety of pasta shapes were presented for consumption, more was eaten than when only one pasta shape was presented; similarly, more was eaten of a food that varied in colour than when the food was of just one colour (Rolls *et al.*, 1982), as Figure 6.2 shows.

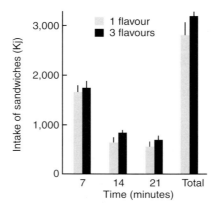

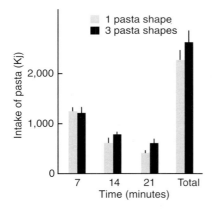

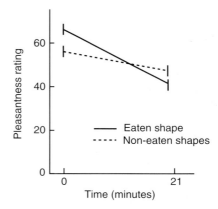

Fig 6.2 Some examples of sensory specific satiety. The graphs show how people eat more of a meal that is varied and that foods not eaten to satiety can still be perceived as pleasant

These experiences are examples of sensory-specific satiety (SSS) – the decrease in the pleasantness and consumption of specific food after eating it to satiety. The satiety is sensory-specific because individuals may become sated eating foods of specific tastes, shapes, sizes and textures, but not foods of different tastes, shapes, sizes and textures (Rolls et al., 1986). This phenomenon explains why, if we eat a meal composed of a variety of specific foods, we eat more of it because there is greater sensory stimulation available from a varied meal (say, a bowl of soup, sausages, egg and bacon, and chocolate mousse versus simply a big plate of sausages). SSS also has survival value because if we become bored with eating one food but not another, this increases the likelihood of a variety of foods being eaten.

Is the smell of a food eaten to satiety rated less pleasant than the odour of a food that is not eaten? O'Doherty *et al.* (2000) required five healthy participants to smell the odour of banana and vanilla and rate their pleasantness. They were asked to eat banana to satiety and were then asked to rate the two odours for pleasantness again. fMRI was used to explore changes in brain response to satiety.

A part of the frontal lobe (the orbitofrontal cortex or OFC) showed a decrease in activation during the smelling of the odour of the food eaten to satiety (there was no such decrease found when smelling vanilla). The authors relate these changes to the role of the orbitofrontal cortex in mediating emotional responses such as reacting favourably or unfavourably towards stimuli. A similar finding was reported by Small *et al.* (2001b) who measured brain activity during satiety induced by eating chocolate. The researchers found that when participants ate chocolate, which they found pleasant, there was increased blood flow in a collection of regions including areas beneath the corpus callosum, a part of the OFC (called the caudomedial OFC), the insula, striatum and midbrain. When participants were sated, blood flow increased in the parahippocampal gyrus and a different part of the OFC (the caudolateral OFC) activated during initial eating.

Research update ... psychonutrition

Can what you eat affect the way in which you think? Clearly, we need food to provide the body with the energy it needs to function and this includes energy needed to allow the brain to work. The area in which the interaction between food ingestion and psychological performance is studied is sometimes referred to as psychonutrition. Several studies in the 1980s and 1990s suggested that taking vitamin supplements improved non-verbal IQ in schoolchildren (see Chapter 11 of Carlson *et al.*, 2000, for a review). More recent studies have shown how meals can influence cognitive function such as memory in adults. Breakfast is sometimes the meal that researchers have attached some importance to.

Research into children's behaviour after breakfast ingestion, for example, has suggested that memory is adversely affected by missing breakfast (Benton and Parker, 1998), and that mental and physical performance is enhanced if breakfast is eaten (Owens *et al.*, 1997; Wyon *et al.*, 1997). In Wyon *et al.*'s study, 10-year-old Swedish girls who ate larger breakfasts exercised for longer during a morning gym session and scored better on tests of verbal fluency than those who did not eat breakfast. This is one of several studies to show a breakfast-related benefit. Vaisman *et al.* (1996), for example, found that 11–13-year-old Israeli children showed better memory half an hour after breakfast but not one and a half to two hours after eating.

During mid-morning and afternoon, an afternoon dip is experienced where people feel tired, listless and less motivated. Eating food high in glucose seems to reduce this feeling of tiredness and feelings of irritability in children (Thayer, 1987; Benton *et al.*, 1987) although cognitive performance only seems to improve in people with low levels of glucose; it does not improve performance in and of itself.

A recent study reported that a stress-prone group of people who received a meal rich in carbohydrate but low in protein expressed significantly lower feelings of stress, regardless of the controllability of the stress they experienced (Markus *et al.*, 2000). Benton *et al.* (2001) asked 150 women to fast or eat 10/50 g of carbohydrate (cornflakes) for breakfast. Half of the eaters received an additional 25 g of food an hour and a half later. Although there was no difference between the groups in terms of their memory recall performance, there were differences in behaviour and mood. Snack consumers were more agreeable, confident and energetic later in the day and spent longer trying to recall the words presented in the memory test. However, the mood of the group that received the 50 g deteriorated later in the morning but this mood change was reversed with the additional 25 g given later in the morning. The results suggest that the association between food, mood and thought is still a complex one.

6.10 THE BIOLOGICAL BASIS OF EATING DISORDERS

Most of us eat a moderate amount of food. Others, however, either eat too little or too much, with serious psychological and physical consequences. The three most debilitating eating disorders encountered by psychologists, psychiatrists and physicians are anorexia nervosa, bulimia nervosa and obesity. Several models have tried to explain why these disorders occur and many of them focus on the family or mental health of the sufferer. These are important models but this chapter will focus, primarily, on the possible biological bases of the disorders.

Anorexia nervosa

Anorexia nervosa – literally, yet ironically – means lack of appetite although the people who suffer from it do not experience a lack of appetite. The disorder is characterised by a pathological fear of weight gain, an obsession with being fat, despite the alarming weight loss, and a preoccupation with food and food-based rituals. Although it has been in the public eye to a great extent in the past two decades, there are references to it dating back to the nineteenth century (Treasure and Campbell, 1994).

Some researchers have identified two types of the disorder (Garner *et al.*, 1985). The restrictor type has a subnormal body weight and is malnourished; the bulimic subtype also shows these features but also engages in periodic binge eating, which is usually followed by taking laxatives or vomiting. Most sufferers, however, are characterised by a personality that is perfectionist, conforming, obsessive, and emotionally and socially inhibited. (Casper, 1990).

The disorder emerges during adolescence but is also seen in young children. Recovery tends to be drawn out, if it occurs at all, and the prognosis is unstable with 50 per cent recovering fairly completely, 30 per cent showing residual symptoms, 10 per cent not recovering at all and 10 per cent dying of the disorder (Kaye and Strober, 1999).

The biological causes or correlates of the disorder have included genetics, neurotransmitter and neuropeptide disturbance, and hormonal dysfunction. There is evidence, for example, that anorexia (and bulimia) clusters in families and that there is a small risk (4 per cent) that mothers and sisters of sufferers will also exhibit symptoms of the disorder (Lilenfeld *et al.*, 1997). The precise role of genetics in the disorder, however, is unclear.

What is slightly clearer is the role of neurotransmitters, neuropeptides and hormones, and the focus of research has been on the neuropeptides – neuropeptide Y and peptide YY, opioid peptides, cholecystokinin and the hormone leptin. There is evidence that the neuroendochrine system is abnormal in patients with anorexia and bulimia. Animal studies, for example, show that disruption of neuropeptide Y, which regulates the rate, duration and size of meals (Morley and Blundell, 1988), results in anorexia-type symptoms in these animals. Levels of neuropeptide Y are high in anorexics, and injections of the peptide in animals leads to anorexic symptoms.

Cholecystokinin (CCK) is a peptide secreted by the gastric system during food intake and is thought to play a role in chemically regulating satiety. When the hormone is administered to animals and humans, food intake is significantly reduced (Baile *et al.*, 1986). In anorexia, high levels of CCK have been found after eating but evidence for its role in causing the disorder is mixed.

Leptin is a hormone secreted by adipose tissue cells and is associated with obesity (as you will see later). Reduced levels of the hormone have been found in malnourished and underweight anorexics (Ferron *et al.*, 1997). Some researchers have suggested that leptin is responsible for triggering the body's response to starvation: when the body is underweight, concentrations of leptin are lower than would be expected given the loss of actual fat (Boden *et al.*, 1996). Leptin, therefore, might be a warning signal indicating that the body is losing too much weight (rather than being a cause of the weight loss).

All of the above factors have been implicated in anorexia nervosa, but none has been found to be causally related to the disorder. Some researchers have suggested that neurotransmitter imbalance may be involved because treatment with certain anti-depressants (such as fluoxetine – Prozac) leads to improved prognosis and relapse prevention (Kaye *et al.*, 1991). Fluoxetine acts by increasing the amount of the neurotransmitter, serotonin, available to cells at synapses. Other monoamines – the class of neurotransmitter to which serotonin belongs – such as norepinephrine are reduced in underweight people with anorexia nervosa (Pirke, 1996). When serotonin is administered to animals and humans, food intake increases. This might suggest that anorexics have reduced serotonin metabolism but, like the causal candidates described above, this is one of many alternatives.

Bulimia nervosa

Unlike anorexia nervosa, bulimia may not necessarily be associated with weight loss although dieting does occur. In fact, abnormally low weight rules out a diagnosis of bulimia. The disorder is characterised by binge eating, which is followed by some behaviour designed to remove the food from the body such as vomiting, taking laxatives or engaging in excessive exercise. There is a pathological concern with body weight and shape – patients have a distorted body image and seriously fear weight gain – and sufferers have low self-esteem, frequently showing episodes of anxiety and depression. DSM-IV, the diagnostic manual that contains the criteria for the disorder, identifies two types of bulimic: those who binge and purge (vomiting/taking laxatives) and those who do not purge (and fast or exercise instead).

Age of onset is unclear but can occur between mid- to late adolescence to the mid-twenties. Some 50 per cent of sufferers recover, with 20 per cent showing no recovery (Keel and Mitchell, 1997). Anti-depressants are associated with a good outcome, with initial complete suppression of symptoms in a minority of patients. With behavioural therapy, between 60 and 70 per cent show good prognosis but 30 to 50 per cent will remit.

Unlike anorexia nervosa, levels of peptide YY are normal in bulimic individuals, and levels of leptin are also comparable to normal women within the same weight range. Bulimics tend to show lower than average baselines levels of CCK (Lydiard *et al.*, 1993), however, and the serotonin system may be dysfunctional. For example, when a precursor to serotonin is low in bulimics, women experience severe bad moods and a drive to overeat. The reduction in the precursor in control women does not cause similar effects. If this precursor is low in bulimic women, the overeating might restore the levels of the precursor, which will themselves affect the release of serotonin. As with anorexia, however, these causes are speculative and may simply be correlational.

Obesity

Obesity refers to a pathological gain in weight, and results from an imbalance between food intake and the energy the body expends. If a person has a high-fat diet, engages in little or no physical exercise and may have genes predisposing him or her to develop in a particular way, then he or she will become obese. Obesity is usually defined as being 20 per cent above the normal weight for a person of your height and build. It is a difficult condition to combat, with short-term treatments showing no real success. People who begin a treatment regime involving appetite suppressants or drugs that inhibit fat absorption do not lose weight easily and neither do they tolerate these drugs well (Chiesi *et al.*, 2001). Although some early intervention programmes suggested that weight loss was not sustainable, some recent research suggests that if obese individuals monitor their weight and weight loss, this could lead to some long-term success (Boutelle *et al.*, 1999).

Physiological correlates of obesity

Although the disparity between intake and energy expenditure is a general cause of obesity, the possible specific causes are many. Why is there a disparity between intake and energy expenditure, for example? Is it due to genetics, lack of motivation, lack of self-esteem, failure of a neurotransmitter system? All have been suggested but the actual cause is still unclear. One promising candidate is leptin, which you read about in the section on anorexia ('leptin' comes from the Greek, meaning thin). Leptin is a protein produced by a specific gene discovered in the mid-1990s. Researchers had studied a strain of genetically obese mouse, called the ob mouse, which had low metabolism and overate monstrously. It is about twice the size of other mice without the gene and like many obese people, develops diabetes in adulthood. It was found that the fat cells of ob mice were unable to secrete leptin due to a mutation in the ob gene responsible for producing it (Campfield *et al.*, 1995; Halaas *et al.*, 1995; Pelleymounter, *et al.*, 1995). If the obese mice were given doses of leptin, their metabolism increased, their body temperature rose, they became more active and ate less. Consequently, their weight returned to normal levels.

Intriguingly, leptin is also found in humans, as is its genetic mutation, and its presence in blood is correlated with obesity (Maffei *et al.*, 1995; Strosberg and Issad, 1999). Even when leptin is adminstered to obese individuals, high doses are associated with variable weight loss (Farooqi *et al.*, 1999). Although the fat cells of most obese people do secrete leptin, these people continue to overeat. So if levels of leptin are not the answer, what contribution, if any, does this protein make to human obesity?

One group has suggested that in order for leptin to reduce weight, the brain must contain leptin receptors (Tartaglia *et al.*, 1995). The Tartaglia group discovered this leptin receptor in the brain. It was suggested, therefore, that leptin receptors did not detect the presence of leptin in the blood of obese people properly. There are also other receptor candidates that may be involved in obesity. The receptor melanocortin MC4, for example, which is found in many brain regions including the hypothalamus, appears to respond to agonists by decreasing appetite in rats and mice; antagonists have the opposite effect (Benoit *et al.*, 2000). Research with the receptor is at an early stage but the evidence suggests that it may be involved in the regulation of human body weight.

6.11 SEX

Unlike eating, the motivation to engage in sexual behaviour is not an automatic one born of a physiological need. Clearly, however, physiological processes help the process along. The body's sex hormones cause the production of sperm, create the lining of the uterus, stimulate milk production and trigger ovulation; they also affect the nerve cells of the brain, but they do not control behaviour. Sexual behaviour in humans is voluntary but sex hormones influence its direction.

As Masters and Johnson observed in their pioneering studies of the 1960s, humans undergo various stages of sexual arousal leading to orgasm. These stages follow a similar pattern in men and women, and appeared in this order: excitement, plateau, orgasm and satiety (Masters and Johnson, 1970). There is an initial period of great arousal, followed by sustained sexual activity where arousal does not increase further. This leads to orgasm and, then, physical relief and psychological relaxation. Both sexes report engaging in sexual imagery and both show vasocongestion during arousal (i.e. the sexual organs and parts of the skin, such as the chest, experience a rush of blood).

Androgens

The androgen testosterone plays an important role in male sexual development. During prenatal development, the secretion of testosterone by the foetus's testes causes the male sexual organs to develop. This effect of testosterone is called an organisational effect because it organises the development of sex organs. If these organisational effects are inhibited during development, typical male mating behaviour does not occur.

The other effect testosterone has on sexual development is activational: it activates sex organs and brain regions. Having an erection and having sex, for example, is not possible without the activational effect of testosterone. In men whose testes produce very low levels of androgens, the administration of testosterone significantly increases the number of attempts at sexual intercourse and the number of erections (Davidson *et al.*, 1979). Similarly, if men are castrated, the ability to ejaculate declines, as does the ability to achieve erection (Bermant and Davidson, 1974), but this can be reversed with injections of testosterone. Testosterone appears to influence the sex drive, regardless of sexual orientation: increases in the androgen in homosexual men, for example, will not make the man more heterosexual but will increase his interest in having sex with other men. It also influences the woman's sex drive. Couples are more likely to have sex when the woman's level of testosterone is at its peak; women also report that sex is more enjoyable during this period (Persky *et al.*, 1978).

Progesterone and oestrogen

Two important hormones that exert influences over female sexual behaviour are progesterone and oestrogen. These hormones fluctuate during a primate's menstrual cycle: in primates, the lining of the uterus builds up in the first part of the cycle and is removed in the second part. In non-primates, oestrogen and progesterone significantly influence the ability to mate. Therefore, when levels of these hormones are high, female mammals will engage in sexually seductive behaviour, enticing their male partners to mate with them. The hormones do not exert these effects in primates.

Focus on ... pheromones and sex

Can the scent of another human being automatically stimulate your sex drive? According to some of the more lurid adverts in even more lurid magazines, it can. But the evidence for so-called pheromones in humans is questionable. Pheromones are chemicals secreted by the body that provoke stereotypical responses in a recipient organism. The animal world is replete with examples of pheromonal effects. The most important pheromone in the animal kindgom is the steroid androstenone. Androstenone is an interesting chemical because it can induce a sow to adopt the mating position, and farmers and vets can buy the steroid in cans ready for spraying on their livestock (truffle hunters use sows to detect the delicacy because it contains androstenone). Androstenone is also present in men's sweat glands and in the urine of men and women, although at stronger concentrations in men (Brooksbank *et al.*, 1974), which has led to the possibility that it may play a role in influencing humans' sexual behaviour.

Much of this work has focused on examining whether certain of the body's chemicals alter the length of the menstrual cycle and whether they increase sexual attractiveness in a person of the opposite sex. One of the earliest studies of the pheromone effect in humans found that 17–22-year-old women students who lived and slept in the same halls of residence reported menstrual synchrony (McClintock, 1971). That is, their menstrual cycles began on, or about, the same time. The effect was unrelated to food intake, lifestyle pattern or stress. The result is difficult to explain because no mechanism that we know of can account for the finding. McClintock suggested that the mechanism might be pheromonal or mediated by an awareness of another's menstrual cycle.

In a similar experiment, Stern and McClintock (1998) examined whether such a pheromone could affect the length of ovulation. The experimenters took the odourless compounds from the armpits of women in the late (follicular) or ovulatory stages of their menstrual cycle and applied them to the top lips of 29 healthy young women aged between 20 and 35 years old. The length of the recipients' menstrual cycle was then measured. The experimenters found that women reported shorter cycles when receiving follicular compounds and longer cycles when receiving ovulatory compounds. There was a significant difference between the baseline cycle length and the cycle length reported when carriers 'wore' the compounds. A total of 68 per cent of women responded to the compounds of both kinds.

Jacob and McClintock (2000) measured baseline mood in women before exposure to androstenone and had them undertake a very monotonous two-hour period of study. This time, the steroid was associated with an elevation in mood, whereas exposure to a control odour (clove oil) was associated with a deterioration in mood. The results suggest that rather than affecting mood directly, the odour modulates mood: it modulates affective reactions to other stimuli (in this example, the tedious study session).

Whether androstenone directly influences the desire to have sex, however, is questionable. The majority of experiments, for example, have tended to expose subjects to volatile chemicals in contexts that are not generally appropriate. For example, participants have rated imaginary verbal descriptions of people, or pictures and slides of buildings, people and animals. When Black and Biron (1982) required participants to interact with a confederate of the opposite sex who wore either androstenone or a control odour, and asked the participant to rate the confederate for attractiveness, the experimenters found no effect of these chemicals on the rated attractiveness of the confederate. The negative finding may be attributable to humans' lack of a vomeronasal organ. This structure is present in animals who do respond to pheromones in a stereotypical way, but it appears to be absent in humans.

Odours themselves might enhance sexual desire, however, although the effect is not pheromonal. A study of the effect of male and female fragrances on women's genital arousal as participants watched a hardcore video or sexually fantasised at two points in the menstrual cycle (the follicular stage and the periovulatory stage) found that while no effect of the male fragrance was found at any stage when the women watched the film, there was a significant effect of fragrance when women engaged in sexual fantasy (Graham *et al.*, 2000). During the follicular stage only, genital arousal was greater during exposure to male fragrance when women were fantasising. The message from this research is that daubing yourself with an attractive scent may be a better mate-attracting strategy than annointing yourself with a pheromone.

6.12 SEX AND THE BRAIN

Our intentions, desires, wants and needs are the result of an interaction between our biochemistry and our neuroanatomy. We can think about sex – an act that needs the brain – and we can engage in sex – also an act that requires the brain. The two aspects of sexual desire are different and we might expect our neural circuitry to mediate both differently. There is evidence that this is the case (Everitt, 1990).

At the neuroanatomical level, regions involved in thinking about and executing sexual behaviour include the preoptic area, hypothalamus and amygdala. These regions, as you saw in Chapter 4, are interconnected and form part of the limbic system. Each of these regions contains receptors sensitive to sex hormones.

If lesions are made to the medial preoptic area in male rats and monkeys, sexual behaviour is inhibited; stimulating this area electrically, however, elicits sexual behaviour, indicating that this area may be important to sexual motivation. Removing the hypothalamus also inhibits sexual aggression (Schmidt and Schorsch, 1981). In men who have suffered strokes affecting these areas, there is a reduction in libido and sexual performance but evidence is mixed with other studies reporting that patients become sexually very active (Miller *et al.*, 1986). Furthermore, still other studies report decreased sexual activity in both men and women with damage to the preoptic area and hypothalamus (Lechtenberg and Ohl, 1994).

The locus of sexual initiation in females is less clear but may involve a part of the hypothalamus called the ventromedial nucleus of the thalamus. In rats, lesions to this area inhibit the animals from adopting the mating position (Pfaff *et al.*, 1994) but whether similar damage would result in the same effect in women is unknown.

The amygdala, as you will see in the chapter on emotion (Chapter 8), has been described as the 'gateway to the emotions' and its role in sexual behaviour may not, therefore, be unexpected. The amygdala comprises two general sets of nuclei – one has steroid receptors and links to the hypothalamus; the second connects to the prefrontal cortex and the autonomic nervous system, and responds to emotional events in the environment. In rats, if the first set of nuclei is damaged, there is reduced desire to copulate but the act of copulation itself can be achieved (Everitt *et al.*, 1989).

In humans, damage specifically to each set of nuclei is rare. Patients who have had their temporal lobe removed (and, therefore, their amydala too) show evidence of excessive sexual behaviour (Monga *et al.*, 1986). This increased inappropriate sexual behaviour suggests that the amygdala may be responsible for inhibiting such behaviours because, when damaged, it cannot perform this function (the role of the amygdala in inhibiting socially inappropriate responses is described in Chapter 8, on emotion and stress).

The amygdala is connected to the orbitofrontal cortex, an area which, when damaged, can produce significantly increased or decreased sexual activity. In a PET study of sexual arousal in men, Tiihonen *et al.* (1994) found an increase in the right prefrontal cortex during orgasm. Bruce Arnow and colleagues from Stanford University Medical School used functional Magnetic Resonance Imaging (fMRI) to determine which regions of the brain were recruited when men watched 'explicitly erotic' video material, or relaxing or sports-related material (Arnow *et al.*, 2002). During viewing, penile turgidity was measured using a custom-built device. The aim of the study was to identify those regions associated with sexual arousal in men.

The right hemisphere showed the most consistent activation during arousal. Various regions, including the premotor region, subcortical parts of the motor system, and the occipital and temporal cortex, were activated during tumescence (much more so than during non-tumescence). The authors suggest that the results are consistent with those of other, differently designed studies. However, they cite a study showing that there is little overlap between the areas activated in men and those in women. 'Further studies will be needed,' the authors say, 'to determine if such discrepancies reflect gender or paradigm differences in sexual arousal related brain activation.'

6.13 SEX AND NEUROCHEMISTRY

There seem to be a few key neurotransmitters involved in sexual behaviour and those that are involved in the CNS tend to be those involved in genital arousal in the PNS (Meisel and Sachs, 1994). The monoamines, especially dopamine, are associated with the promotion of sexual desire and performance. There is neurotransmitter release in the preoptic area and nucleus accumbens during mating in male rats (Pfaus and Everitt, 1995) and administering amphetamine, which is a dopamine agonist, to the nucleus accumbens reverses the decline in sexual activity that accompanies lesions to the amygdala (Everitt *et al.*, 1989). However, while drugs that enhance dopamine release, such as cocaine and amphetamines, increase the desire to have sex, they eventually lead to a decline in sexual performance (Lechtenberg and Ohl, 1994).

The other monoamine of interest, serotonin, promotes sexual activity at low levels but inhibits it at high levels, hence the sexually inhibiting effects of anti-depressants, which tend to increase the amount of serotonin available to brain receptors.

6.14 SEXUAL ORIENTATION

Homosexuality refers to the engagement in sexual activity with members of the same sex (from the Greek homos, meaning 'the same') and is seen in male and female animals of many different species. Is there evidence of what the biological causes of homosexuality may be? Homosexuals have the same levels of testosterone as do heterosexuals so the presence of this hormone is not likely to be a candidate (Tourney, 1980).

One clue may lie in the limbic system – specifically, the hypothalamus. Three laboratories have studied the brains of deceased heterosexual and homosexual men, and have found differences in the size of two different sub-regions of the hypothalamus and in a bundle of axons that connects the right and left temporal lobes (Swaab and Hofman, 1990; LeVay, 1991; Allen and Gorski, 1992).

When the organisational effects of androgens are blocked in male laboratory animals, the animals fail to develop normal male sex behaviour. A similar effect is found in people with androgen insensitivity syndrome, a disorder caused by a genetic mutation that prevents the formation of androgen receptors (Ris-Stalpers *et al.*, 1990). Because the cells of the body cannot respond to the androgens, a genetic male with this syndrome develops female external genitalia instead of a penis and scrotum. The person does not develop ovaries or a uterus.

Although little research has been done on the origins of female homosexuality, Money *et al.* (1984) found that the incidence of homosexuality was several times higher in women who had been exposed to high levels of androgens prenatally. The cause of the exposure was an abnormality of the adrenal glands, which usually secrete very low levels of these hormones. Thus, sexual orientation in females may be affected by biological factors and, as the following 'Focus on ...' section shows, nicotine and stress.

Focus on ... sexual orientation: does prenatal stress play a role?

One of the more controversial topics in biology and human sexuality is the issue of what 'causes' a person to express one type of sexual orientation over another. Some social psychologists point to the role of socialisation and the encouragement of specific sex roles as a cause; some biologists argue that certain brain regions are larger in homosexual men than heterosexual men. While all of these views have been debated with no clear conclusions drawn, one of the strongest lines of evidence in support of a biological contribution to sexual orientation concerns the role of stress in the development and function of the organism's hormone system and its effect on later sexual development.

Prenatal stress in male rats, for example, has been found to lead to increased mounting of members of the same sex, a sensitivity to alcohol (a typically female rat characteristic), and decreased levels of aggression (Ward, 1984; Kinsley and Svare, 1986; De Turk and Pohorecky, 1987). One explanation for these findings holds that stress in the mother causes her adrenal glands to release increased levels of stress-related hormones, which circulate in the blood, cross the placenta and interfere with the foetus's own hormone-producing system, especially that producing testosterone (Ward and Weisz, 1984). The affected hormone system influences the degree of masculinisation or feminisation of the brain.

According to Ellis and Cole-Harding (2001), the evidence for this theory is strong in rodents, but more equivocal in humans. They draw attention to five studies that have examined the effects of stress on sexual orientation. Two German studies found that mothers who recalled experiencing stress during pregnancy produced offspring with a higher than average degree of homosexuality (Dorner et al., 1980; Dorner et al., 1983). An American study found a similar relationship but only when stress was experienced during the second trimester (weeks 13–26) of pregnancy (Ellis et al., 1988). Two other studies, one German, one American, have failed to replicate these findings, although the American study noted a higher degree of effeminacy in boys whose mothers had experienced high and repeated levels of stress (Schmidt and Clement, 1990; Bailey et al., 1991).

Ellis and Cole-Harding (2001) suggest that while these studies are informative, they draw their conclusions on the basis of small samples. They also criticise the studies for being largely retrospective (the mothers were asked to recall events from 20 years previously) and note that the two German studies reporting positive results assumed the mothers experienced stress because they lived in frequently bombed areas in Germany during the Second World War. As well as prenatal stress, Ellis and Cole-Harding (2001) review evidence that other external factors – such as alcohol – reduce testosterone levels in rats (Kakihana *et al.*, 1980) and lead to mothers producing male offspring who adopt what they call 'feminine' postures at puberty (Ward *et al.*, 1994; Ward *et al.*, 1996). Also, nicotine delivered prenatally leads to female-typical behaviour and reduced mounting behaviour (Lichtensteiger and Schlumpf, 1985; Segarra and Strand, 1989).

Given these findings, Ellis and Cole-Harding (2001) retested the hypothesis that prenatal stress in mothers leads to an increase in homosexuality in offspring and addressed the additional hypothesis that alcohol and nicotine exert the same type of influence. Masculinisation of offspring, they predicted, would be greatest in mothers experiencing high levels of stress and who also drink and smoke.

A total of 12 152 undergraduates from American and Canadian universities were asked to complete questionnaires asking them about their sexual orientation. The mothers of these students (7605 of them) were also contacted and asked about their experiences before, during and after pregnancy. Additional data were obtained from 227 mothers who were members of the group Parents and Friends of Gays and Lesbians. The total sample contained 209 homosexual men, 39 bisexual men, 2486 heterosexual men, 123 lesbians, 48 bisexual women and 4987 heterosexual women.

Prenatal stress was significantly associated with mothers' stress, especially when this stress was experienced in the first trimester. No effect of alcohol was found. Prenatal levels of nicotine showed an unusual relationship with sexual orientation. Exposure to nicotine during pregnancy significantly increased the likelihood of female offspring becoming lesbian. The likelihood was further increased if exposure to nicotine occurred in the first trimester and prenatal stress was experienced in the second. Other research has found that smoking mothers and their female offspring have greater amounts of circulating testosterone than do non-smokers (Kandel and Udry, 1999). Of course, these mothers may have been those with already high circulating levels of testosterone (which led to smoking).

As with all previous studies of prenatal stress and sexual orientation, this study relied on retrospective reports of stress. The researchers suggest that the relationship between stress, nicotine use and sexual orientation could be made clearer by monitoring the frequency and degree of stress 18 months prior to pregnancy and then prenatally until three months post-partum.

6.15 HUMAN AGGRESSION

What makes one human being commit an act of physical violence towards another human being? The most obvious answer is the most simple one: when we are angered by another person we may feel such ill-will towards them that we want to hurt them. In extreme cases, however, humans can aggress without such provocation; in the most extreme of these cases, one human being might kill another.

Aggression appears to be common in most species; in some, if not most, it is used in order to maintain a particular position in the social hierarchy. Among humans, it may be used to the same effect, often on a grander scale. War, for example, is an act of instrumental aggression that – theoretically – has specific, clearly stated outcomes such as the removal of a state or the reclaiming of invaded land. Defending oneself against the violence of another is also an example of aggression having a clear objective.

Evolutionary psychologists have referred to the aggression that occurs between members of species as intraspecific aggression. They argue that such aggression has advantages to certain species: it forces members of a population to disperse into other territories and ensures that the healthier males, who compete for the attention of the available females, are those that witness the continuation of their genes. These outcomes, however, seem inappropriate for human species. We have laws that are designed to prevent and punish such aggression; it is not seen as socially or intellectually desirable to commit acts of aggression. While monkeys, lions or stags may engage in paw-to-paw, tooth-to-tooth or antler-to-antler combat, humans have moved beyond hand-to-hand combat and have developed more creative ways of harming and destroying each other. Ultimately, we have the power to eliminate large sections of the human population.

Biological psychology has studied a number of the chemical and neural bases of aggression, especially the unprovoked type because this is socially the most vexed kind (we may disagree with wars but the democracies that wage them usually have some purpose, even if one disagrees with that purpose). Unprovoked aggression is anti-social, dangerous and damaging to the quality of our lives. If there is a biological basis to this aggression, we may be in a better position to understand it and, possibly, limit it. Biological explanations are not the only explanations for violent behaviour, however. Social psychology, while recognising our potentially innate disposition to aggress, has proposed social and/or environmental interpretations of the causes that encourage (as well as inhibit) violent behaviour, from the frustration of our goals, to the learning of aggressive behaviour from others (Bandura, 1977), to the potentiation of aggression in people already having a tendency to respond to events aggressively. The focus in the next sections, however, will be limited to the evident biological correlates of (principally) human violence. Studies of non-human species are also important and these will be used to speculate on their importance to human species.

According to Linnoila and Charney (1999), aggression can be characterised in three ways: competitive, premeditated and impulsive. Competitive aggression is socially sanctioned where violence occurs in acceptable circumstances. Sport is an obvious example. The primary aim of rugby is not to aggress but it is an unavoidable consequence of playing the game. Boxing and wrestling, however, are (at least to some) socially acceptable sports in which aggression is central. Few studies have explored the biological correlates of competitive aggression, but there are studies that do show hormonal changes in people who observe competitive sports (and we'll return to these in a later section).

Premeditated physical aggression refers to acts that are not impulsive: the behaviour of the police, the armed forces and certain criminals can be described as premeditated in this sense.

The most common form of violence, in terms of frequency, is impulsive aggression. These acts of physical violence are invariably associated with alcohol and other substance use and are usually inexplicable to the observer. The acts are usually repeated and are unprovoked; even when they are provoked, the retribution is dispropportionate to the initial provocation. The victim may be unknown to the perpetrator and, if the violence involves a weapon, the consequences can be fatal.

This type of aggression has interested psychologists because it appears to lack control and reason. The violence, although appearing to be an example of lack of control, may be an abnormal attempt to control events outside the perpetrator's control. What interests biological psychologists is the possibility that biological events may either precede these events or make perpetrators predisposed to act violently. The most promising line of research has focused on three lines of investigation: neuroanatomy, neurochemistry and endocrinology.

Neuroanatomical substrates of aggression

The search for regions of the brain that are selectively implicated in violence has led researchers to identify two areas: the hypothalamus and the orbitofrontal cortex. Lesions to the hypothalamus have been associated with extreme rage in laboratory animals; these animals physically aggress at the slightest provocation (Schubert and Siegel, 1994).

The second region, the orbitofrontal cortex, is (as you saw in Chapter 4) responsible for monitoring and organising behaviour and sensory input; this area of the brain appears to mediate the inhibition of inappropriate behaviour (among other things). Some studies report that patients with frontal cortex damage appear to 'feel' less for other human beings; they appear to be more callous than they once were – laughing at others' tears, for example, or feeling no pity for others (Hornak *et al.*, 1996). Historically, demolition of the frontal lobes was seen as a surgical cure for violent behaviour in patients, although the treatment was not entirely successful and side-effects soon became apparent.

The direct involvement of the orbitofrontal cortex in aggression is suggestive. While there is behavioural evidence that patients with lesions to this area have difficulty in inhibiting socially and emotionally incorrect behaviour, evidence from neuroimaging suggests that this region is dysfunctional in violent individuals. Adrian Raine and his colleagues at the University of California at Santa Barbara, for example, have published a number of studies generally concluding that violent individuals show a smaller volume of frontal cortex than do non-violent offenders (Raine *et al.*, 1997).

Anti-social behaviour and the frontal cortex

A recent study by Raine's group found evidence for a structural brain deficit in anti-social personality disorder (APD; Raine *et al.*, 2000). They compared the brain volume of 21 community volunteers with the DSM-IV ratified APD, with control groups. The experimental sample was derived from five temporary employment agencies in Los Angeles known to have clients that had commited high levels of violence. The control groups comprised psychiatric controls, healthy individuals and substance abusers. In addition to the brain scanning, participants also had their behaviour videotaped as they talked about their faults (a social stressor). During this task, their skin conductance and heart rate was recorded.

The prefrontal brain volume of the APD group was 11 per cent less compared to the other groups. The APD sample also showed little autonomic response when undertaking the social stressor task. Both of these findings are consistent with evidence from brain-damaged individuals, showing that frontal patients have social problems and are unresponsive to threatening or risky behaviour when this response is measured autonomically.

A complementary study looked at a case of acquired sociopathy, meaning that the anti-social behaviour resulted from brain damage (Blair and Cipolotti, 2000). The patient (JS), was a 56-year-old electrical engineer who had collapsed with trauma to the orbitofrontal cortex. After this episode, he began behaving very bizarrely: he would be uncooperative with hospital staff, aggressive and would ride around on hospital trolleys. His performance on typical frontal lobe tests was impaired. He had difficulty in recognising emotional expression, especially expressions of anger and disgust. He failed to attribute appropriate emotions (such as fear, anger and embarrassment) to characters in stories and also failed to identify anti-social behaviour when presented with it.

Ruling out most of the existing explanations of behaviour change following frontal lobe damage (such as the inability to inhibit behaviour or engage in abstract thinking), Blair and Cipolotti suggest that we normally have a system that is activated by someone's anger. This system gets rid of current behaviour and switches one response for another. This system is activated by representations of situations in which other people have expressed anger or where we have experienced embarrassment. Such a system is damaged in JS, the authors argue: he could not retrieve representations in which another's anger is anticipated. So he failed to attribute negative emotions to characters in stories because he was unable to summon up similar experiences or representations of such experiences. This aspect of emotion is taken up in Chapter 8.

Neurochemical substrates of aggression

Perhaps the most successful attempts at pinning down the biological correlates of aggression have been those seeking to identify changes in neurotransmitter release or in the number or types of neurotransmitter receptors in violent individuals. The specific focus of this approach has been on the neurotransmitter serotonin (or 5-hydroxytryptamine, 5-HT) and the 5-hydroxyindoleacetic acid (5-HIAA)-to-serotonin ratio.

There is evidence that a decrease in 5-HT is a predisposition to aggression or impulsive behaviour, whereas an increase has the opposite effect (Higley and Linnoila, 1997). One interpretation of the finding that suicides' brains have depleted serotonin, is that the depletion is associated with the self-immolation because suicide is a violent act against the self (Linnoila and Charney, 1999). Given that suicides are likely to have low levels of serotonin in the first place – decreased serotonin is the key neurochemical feature of depression – this finding more probably reflects individuals' depressed state rather than violent intention.

Early evidence linking 5-HIAA with aggression was based on animal studies. Rats who were disposed to kill or harm mice were found to have lower concentrations of 5-HIAA than their non-aggressing counterparts (Valzelli, 1971). Human research has demonstrated various links between the chemical and aggression. Scores on aggression scales and on personality measures tapping psychopathic and deviant behaviour have been found to correlate with 5-HIAA concentrations: the higher the score, the lower the concentration (Brown *et al.*, 1982). In Brown *et al.*'s study, navy recruits were being assessed for discharge because their behaviour was disruptive and violent.

Similarly violent personality dispositions have been associated with low 5-HIAA concentrations in women who had made suicide attempts (Gardner *et al.*, 1990). Not surprisingly, researchers have focused their attention not only on clinical samples but on criminal populations also.

For example, studies of violent offenders show an association between low 5-HIAA and violence. A Finnish study of offenders who had committed acts of extreme violence found that this link obtained, but only in prisoners categorised as impulsive. Patients who were impulsively violent had lower 5-HIAA concentrations than did prisoners whose violence was premeditated (Linnoila *et al.*, 1983). Those prisoners with the longest history of suicide attempts were those with the lowest concentrations. Similarly, low concentrations of the chemical have been reported in murderers who killed their children or their lovers (Lidberg *et al.*, 1985).

Two other studies seem to support the role of low 5-HIAA concentrations in aggressive behaviour. Virkkunen *et al.* (1989) studied the rate of recidivism in 58 violent prisoners and arsonists three years after their release from prison and found that the 13 individuals who had re-offended had lower 5-HIAA levels than non-re-offenders. 5-HIAA concentrations predicted 84.2 per cent of individuals correctly. Second, low concentrations of 5-HIAA have predicted later violent behaviour in a group of adolescents (Kruesi *et al.*, 1992).

Neuroendocrinal substrates of aggression

The most widely studied hormone in the field of aggression is testosterone. Testosterone is secreted by the testes and when circulated can be found in cerebrospinal fluid (a better measure of the general levels of testosterone in the body) and blood plasma. A trait associated with high testosterone levels is dominance. Correlations have been reported between CSF levels of testosterone and dominance in rhesus monkeys but only when they were maintaining their role in the social hierarchy, rather than when seriously aggressing against other group members.

Some controversial research, for example, suggested that dominant women were more likely to give birth to boys than were less dominant women (Grant, 1994). More recent research has found that the way in which women view themselves is directly related to the degree of testosterone they secrete (Grant and France, 2001). Women with higher levels of testosterone were more likely to describe themselves using more dominant adjectives than were those with lower levels. The study provides additional evidence for the link between testosterone and dominance. However, the authors admit that hormone levels might fluctuate due to social and environmental factors. Stress, for example, may be a key moderator, as might personality.

The link between testosterone and dominance has perhaps been most dramatically highlighted in studies of violent offenders. Violent crimes are significantly more likely to have been committed by prisoners with high than low testosterone (Dabbs *et al.*, 1995). Dabbs *et al.* studied 230 male prisoners who had been convicted of crimes from theft to violent crime. Violent crimes included murder, voluntary manslaughter, robbery, assault, rape and child molestation. They took records from ten inmates who secreted high levels of testosterone and ten who secreted low levels, to determine whether the criminal knew the victim, whether the crime was planned, whether the consequences were intended, whether the act was especially violent and whether the act was especially cold-hearted.

Prisoners who secreted high levels of testosterone were more likely than those with low levels to have known their victims and to have planned the actions that killed them. There was no significant relationship between the cold-heartedness of the crime and testosterone. The authors suggest that the link between intent and familiarity and testosterone levels may also be connected to other research showing that testosterone was associated with increased competitiveness and dominance as well as persistence and focused attention.

This focused attention was revealed in experiments where people showing comparatively high and low levels of testosterone reacted differently in even simple social settings (Dabbs *et al.*, 2001). Dabbs *et al.* set up four correlational experiments in which people were either videotaped entering a room or conversing with another person. In the first experiment, they asked 40 male and 59 female undergraduates to enter a room and talk directly to a video camera for about 45 seconds. Participants with low testosterone looked around the room more on entering (to the left and the exit) and focused less frequently on the camera than did high testosterone participants. There was no difference between high and low-testosterone participants in the directness of the walk to the camera or their tone of voice. The results suggested to the authors that high testosterone individuals appeared less tentative and more focused than their low testosterone counterparts.

In a second study, 21 male and 57 female undergraduates entered a room and stood and spoke briefly to a female confederate, answering questions about themselves; 26 independent raters judged how cautious, poised, happy, friendly, aggressive or charming the participants were. Few differences were found between high and low testosterone participants; the only significant correlation was for overall forwardness, suggesting that high testosterone individuals were more forward and 'businesslike'.

The third and fourth experiments required participants to talk to a female confederate for about five to ten minutes while seated (experiment 3) and to talk to a peer who was either high or low in testosterone so that a low testosterone individual would speak to a high testosterone individual and vice versa (experiment 4). In the third study, high testosterone participants moved more quickly to be seated than did the low testosterone individuals, approaching the interviewer more quickly. In the fourth study, raters were asked to attribute characteristics to the conversationalists. Few assigned the expected characteristics to the talking pairs but when the experimenter informed them that one of the pair was 'independent' and the other was 'responsive', 10 of the 13 judges identified the high testosterone participants as 'independent' and the low testosterone participants as 'responsive'.

The results suggest that comparatively high levels of testosterone are associated with a more assertive, confident and direct manner. Specifically, they suggest that such characteristics are fleetingly apparent in the very early stages of social interaction. Whether dominance is the link between biology and aggression, however, is open to debate.

SOME USEFUL FURTHER READING

Lask, B., and Bryant-Waugh, R. (1999) *Anorexia Nervosa and Related Eating Disorders in Childhood and Adolescence*. London: The Psychology Press.

Mazur, A. and Booth, A. (1998) Testosterone and dominance in men. *Behavioural and Brain Sciences* 21, 353–97.

Plomin, R. and Colledge, E. (2001) Genetics and psychology: beyond heritability. *European Psychologist* 6(4), 229–40.

Smith, G.P. (1998) *Satiation: From Gut to Brain*. Oxford: Oxford University Press.

Toates, F.M. and Jensen, P. (1991) Ethological and psychological models of motivation – towards a synthesis. In J.A. Meyer and S. Wilson (eds) *From Animals to Animats*. Cambridge: MIT Press.

Wadden, T.A., Brownell, K.D. and Foster, G.D. (2002) Obesity: responding to the global epidemic. *Journal of Consulting and Clinical Psychology* 70(3), 510–25.

SOME USEFUL JOURNALS TO BROWSE

Appetite
Biological Psychology
Brain
Brain and Cognition
British Journal of Clinical Psychology
Cell
Ethology and Sociobiology
European Eating Disorders Review
Human Reproduction
International Journal of Eating Disorders
Journal of Neuroscience
Nature Neuroscience
Neuroimage
Personality and Individual Differences
Physiology and Behavior
Psychological Bulletin
Trends in Cognitive Science
Trends in Neuroscience
Science

7 Learning and Memory

WHAT YOU WILL FIND IN THIS CHAPTER
- a description of the basic types of learning
- a description of the biology underlying some of these types of learning
- an evaluation of the role of neurotransmitters and synapses in the formation of memory
- a definition of memory and of the different types of memory process
- an evaluation of the role of the hippocampus and the cortex in memory

WHAT YOU SHOULD BE ABLE TO DO AFTER READING THE CHAPTER
- be aware of what psychologists describe as learning
- be aware of the different types of learning
- outline the changes in the synapse that reflect the formation of memory
- understand that there are different types of memory, and that each may be the responsibility of different brain regions or processes
- be aware of the consequences of hippocampus and diencephalon damage on memory
- describe the brain regions highlighted by neuroimaging studies as being active during specific memory tasks

7.1 LEARNING AND MEMORY DEFINED

What is memory? This is a simple question that probably invites a simple answer, but the more you think about it, the more complex the answer becomes. Humans show evidence of memory, as do animals. Even organisms with a primitive nervous system – such as the sea slug, *Aplysia* – can learn and show evidence of 'memory'.

Memory is a process, rather than a thing or an entity, and refers to the cognitive process involved in acquiring and retrieving material. This material could be verbal or pictorial such as the words on the page of this book or pictures from a manual showing you how to install your DVD or video recorder; it could be event-related (the circumstances of an accident or a recent trip to the cinema); or it could be skill-based (riding a bike, driving a car or typing on a computer keyboard). All of these different types of memory suggest that memory is not a unitary process, and it is not. The type of memory involved in recalling personally meaningful events, for example, seems to be different to that which involves recalling the names of capital cities or previous British prime ministers. The type of memory involved in learning to use a computer is different to that involved in temporarily holding a telephone number in mind as you dial it.

As a consequence, if these processes are distinct and separable, you might expect different regions of the brain to be recruited during their execution. The evidence from studies of brain injury and from neuroimaging supports this dissociation hypothesis. We'll explore this evidence and the behavioural evidence for distinguishing between different types of memory in the next section. Before that let us take a look at the earliest stage in the process of long-term memory: learning.

7.2 THE DIFFERENT TYPES OF LEARNING

Much of what we know of the psychology of learning and the principles of learning has been derived from the observation of animal behaviour. Learning involves three basic processes: the acquisition of material, its consolidation and its retrieval. Two basic types of learning have been identified: instrumental learning and classical conditioning. In instrumental learning, the organism identifies a link between the stimulus and the response; it learns that by making a certain number of behavioural responses or by making these responses at certain intervals, they will be rewarded (or reinforced; the reward reinforces the behaviour and encourages it to be repeated to achieve the same outcome). In instrumental learning, the organism acts or operates on the environment and learns by interacting with it. This is also called operant conditioning.

Classical conditioning, in contrast, involves little direct action on the organism's part. In classical conditioning, an organism learns that two previously unassociated stimuli become associated so that exposure to one generates the same response as does exposure to the other. In a typical classical conditioning experiment, a participant may receive a small puff of air to the eye, which causes the person to blink. This blinking is an involuntary reflexive response: few people can inhibit the urge to blink if their eyeball receives a puff of air. In the next stage of the experiment, a tone is sounded just before the puff of air and this process is repeated a number of times. Finally, the tones alone are presented (there is no accompanying puff of air). When this happens, the tone itself is sufficient to produce an eye blink even though it had not produced blinking prior to being paired with the puff and the tone does not 'cause' the blinking. It is as if the person has learned to associate the tone with the puff of air, which produces the blinking.

In classical conditioning terms, the puff of air is the unconditioned stimulus (because it produces blinking without learning), the tone is the conditioned stimulus (because this is the stimulus the person learns to associate with blinking), blinking to the puff of air is the unconditioned response and blinking to the tones is the conditioned response (because the person has learned to respond in this way to a stimulus that was previously unconnected with the response). The learning of the association between two previously unrelated events/stimuli is thought to be accompanied by changes in the structure of the synapse, specifically, strengthening of connections between neurons.

7.3 THE NEURAL BASIS OF LEARNING

This theory was first proposed by Hebb (1949) in his famous book *Organisation of Behaviour*. Hebb argued that each psychologically important event is conceived of as the flow of activity in a neuronal loop. This loop is made up of the interconnections between dendrite, cell body and the synapses on these structures. The synapses in a particular path become functionally connected to form what Hebb called a cell assembly. The assumption he made was that if two neurons are excited together they fire together. If the synapse between two neurons is repeatedly activated as the postsynaptic neuron fires, then the structure or chemistry of the synapse changes. This change strengthens the connection between neurons.

Hebb proposed that short-term memory resulted from reverberation of the closed loops of the cell assembly; long-term memory is the more structural, lasting change in synaptic connections. This long-term change in structure is thought to reflect long-term potentiation (LTP), a term that describes the strengthening of neuronal connections via repeated stimulation (Lomo, 1966). Lomo found that if the axonal pathway from two regions of the brain (the entorhinal cortex to the dendate gyrus) was repeatedly electrically stimulated, then there was a long-term increase in the size of potentials generated by the postsynaptic neurons. LTP, therefore, seemed to be produced by the activation of synapses and the depolarisation of postsynaptic neurons. Psychologists agree that long-term memory involves more or less permanent changes in the structure of the brain. But where and, exactly, how?

Where are long-term memories formed?

Long-term potentiation seems to predominate in the hippocampus. Long-term physical changes are observed in the hippocampus if it is stimulated (Bliss and Gardner-Medwin, 1973). However, the hippocampal formation itself is composed of two distinct structures: Ammon's horn (often referred to as the hippocampus) and the dendate gyrus. Ammon's horn comprises the substructures CA1, CA2 and CA3. CA1 is sometimes referred to as 'Sommer's sector'. There is also significant hippocampal output to the mammillary body via a tract called the fornix. Damage to each of these structures is sometimes associated with memory loss although the evidence for the involvement of the fornix is mixed (Calabrese *et al.*, 1995).

Translating this process into the behaviour seen in classical conditioning, the unconditioned stimulus (the puff of air) makes strong synaptic connections with the neurons that produce the unconditioned response (the blink). Presenting the conditioned stimulus (the tone) alone, generates weak synapses. But pairing the tone with the unconditioned stimulus, leads to the conditioned stimulus forming very strong synaptic connections. The more often the pairing is made, the stronger the connection becomes. For this type of classical conditioning to occur, a functioning hippocampus appears to be necessary and the structure appears to be necessary for the acquisition of conscious knowledge of the relationship between the conditioned and unconditioned stimulus. The hippocampus is also involved in learning the relationship between the unconditioned and conditioned stimulus when there is a delay between the presentation of each – a process called trace conditioning (Clark and Squire, 1998).

The consolidation of memory seems to be time-dependent. For example, the initial period of learning and the few hours after the learning of UCS and CS pairings appears to be the moment when memory is consolidated. Therefore, interruption of the process at these times will impede consolidation (Bourtchouladze *et al.*, 1998). The first period of consolidation may be dependent on a different neurotransmitter system to that involved in the second. These are the NMDA and dopaminergic systems, respectively.

Chemical modulation of LTP

The most important excitatory neurotransmitter in the Nervous System is glutamic acid, or glutamate. One sub-type of glutamate, N-methyl-D-aspartate (NMDA) appears to be important for producing long-term potentiation (Abel and Lattal, 2001). NMDA receptors are found within the CA1 sector of the hippocampus and blocking the activity of NMDA receptors prevents long-term potentiation in CA1 and the dendate gyrus. Blocking activity does not prevent or reverse LTP that has already occurred however. The key process is the entry of calcium ions through ion channels, a phenomenon mediated by NMDA receptors.

When calcium enters an ion channel, changes in the structure of the neuron are produced by an enzyme, called a calcium-dependent enzyme (CDE) (Lynch *et al.*, 1988). One CDE is called calpain; this breaks down proteins in the spines of dendrites. Without this entry of calcium, LTP does not occur. Weak synapses, resulting from weak activation, do not lead to depolarisation that allows calcium ions to enter ion channels. Strong synapses that are activated do lead to this polarisation, suggesting that the NMDA receptor is vital for the process of learning acquisition (Steele and Morris, 1999).

However, LTP can occur in other parts of the brain, apart from the hippocampus, and not all forms of LTP involve the NMDA receptors. So, although the hippocampus and the NMDA receptors seem to be prime mechanisms for LTP, they may not be the only ones. There are structures such as the amygdala, for example, that are involved in the conditioning of fear. Temporarily inactivating part of the amygdala can impair an organism's ability to learn to be afraid, whereas inactivating the same area after conditioning has taken place still results in a fear response in the organism (Wilensky *et al.*, 1999). The finding suggests that this part of the amygdala may be involved in the acquisition, but not consolidation, of memory. The topic of fear conditioning is returned to in more detail in the chapter on emotion (Chapter 8).

7.4 THE DIFFERENT TYPES OF MEMORY

Once something has been learned, it enters long-term memory. At the beginning of this chapter, you saw how memory was not viewed as a unitary phenomenon but as a multiple system: there are different types of memory. William James (1890), one of the founding fathers of modern psychology, was one of the earliest scientists to suggest that memory was made up of different systems. He proposed that memory comprised different elements called primary memory (memory for short-term processing) and secondary memory (long-term processing and storage). Over 60 years later, Broadbent (1958) specifically postulated short-term (STM) and long-term memory (LTM) processes in which items from STM would, via specific mechanisms, make their way into LTM. This was a significant dissociation at the time but, like most models in psychology, was later seen to be insufficient in explaining the range of human memory fully although these terms are still used today.

The current literature is dominated by dichotomies of memory processes. One dichotomy is represented by declarative memory (Cohen and Squire, 1980), which refers to facts that are accessible to conscious recollection (the facts from this book, for example) and procedural memory, which refers to the skills and automatic operations needed to perform a certain function (e.g. the motor skills required for word processing or riding a bike). Another is between explicit and implicit memory, where explicit memory refers to the process of recalling material that is deliberately learned and retrieved, whereas implicit memory refers to the recall of material that may not be deliberately encoded or retrieved.

Declarative memory is similar to explicit memory because it represents the conscious learning or memorisation of material. According to Squire (1994), declarative memory, 'refers to a biologically meaningful category of memory dependent on a specific brain system'. Some forms of memory, however, clearly do not fit the declarative memory description but, simultaneously, do not fit the definition of procedural memory particularly well either. A broader term, 'non-declarative memory', has been used to describe those abilities not fitting the other description (Squire and Zola-Morgan, 1988). This is similar to Schacter's (1987) implicit memory: memory that involves no explicit or conscious intention to learn or memorise (the learning is incidental and another name for this type of memory is incidental memory).

A further psychological distinction is seen between episodic (autobiographical) and semantic memory. Episodic memory represents memories that are personally meaningful, such as meeting your favourite actor or remembering your summer break at Gleneagles, whereas semantic memory refers to memories based on knowledge of events, people or places, such as knowing that John Major was prime minister of the United Kingdom but William Hague was not.

In addition to episodic and semantic memory, another type of memory process is working memory. Working memory is not short-term memory but describes what we do with the material in short-term memory. Working memory, as you saw in Chapter 4, is what allows us to undertake one task while keeping another in our mind – for example, reading aloud sentences and verifying how truthful they are while, at the same time, remembering the last word of each sentence (Daneman and Carpenter, 1980). This task, like many others of working memory, requires a person to maintain some information in memory (storage) while simultaneously manipulating other information (processing).

There is evidence that this is a distinct memory system, recruiting specific parts of the brain to subserve it. It is thought to be made up of three parts: the phonological loop, which briefly stores verbal information; the visuospatial scratchpad, which stores visuospatial information; and a central executive which co-ordinates the activity of the two (Baddeley and Hitch, 1974; Baddeley and Logie, 1992). People have likened the central executive to the function of the frontal lobes that coordinate our ability to sequence and plan behaviour. We will return to this relationship in the later section on the biological basis of working memory.

With this plethora of dissociations and distinctions, is any of them valid? The distinction between episodic and semantic memory appears to be real; the distinction between implicit and explicit memory has been challenged (Buchner and Wippich, 2000).

7.5 BRAIN INJURY AND MEMORY: AMNESIA

Much of the evidence implicating particular regions of the brain in memory is derived from studies of pathological memory loss, or amnesia. Amnesia refers to the partial or total loss of memory but two sub-types have been identified that appear to be dissociable: that is, a patient may show symptoms of one while showing none of the other. Retrograde amnesia refers to an inability or difficulty in recalling events prior to the onset of the injury; anterograde amnesia refers to an inability or difficulty in remembering events subsequent to injury. Although anterograde patients can talk about events experienced before the onset of their amnesia, they cannot remember what has happened since. The names of people they meet after the injury are hardly ever remembered, even several years after the injury occurred.

The injury giving rise to amnesia can be caused by many factors, including head trauma, surgery involving the lesioning or removal of parts of the cortex or structures found subcortically, cardiovascular disorders (such as stroke), infection, malnutrition and degeneration of the brain (such as that seen in Alzheimer's disease, which is described in more detail in Chapter 11).

Amnesia is not an all-or-nothing phenomenon. Even people with severe amnesia can recognise familiar faces, learn complex hand-to-eye movement, and acquire knowledge of the meaning of words (Squire, 1987). The fact that some amnesic patients can remember facts and describe experiences that occurred before the brain injury indicates that their ability to recall explicit memories acquired prior to the injury is not severely disrupted. Of those parts of the brain necessary for establishing new explicit memories, the most important part seems to be the hippocampus; others are the diencephalon and the frontal lobes.

7.6 THE TEMPORAL LOBES: HM

The hippocampus, like many structures of the brain, is not fully mature at birth. In fact, it is not until a child is two to three years old that the structure is fully developed. As a result, many cognitive activities, such as the formation of semantic memories, are not well developed until this age. One reason that few people remember events that occurred during infancy may be the immaturity of the hippocampus. The hippocampus receives information from all association areas of the brain and sends information back to them.

The most famous example of memory impairment following brain damage is patient HM (Scoville and Milner, 1957; Milner *et al.*, 1968). HM was a young man who had experienced epileptic seizures that did not respond to medication. On 23 August 1953, when HM was 27 years old, William

Scoville surgically removed the medial temporal lobe on both sides of the brain in an attempt to stop the seizures. The surgery involved the removal of the hippocampus and was successful in alleviating the symptoms of epilepsy. However, it did produce symptoms of severe anterograde memory impairment. Following the surgery, HM could carry on a conversation quite adequately and could also talk about his life prior to the surgery, but could not talk about anything that had happened since 1953.

Demonstrating a typical anterograde amnesia symptom, HM was unable to store new information in long-term memory, but his short-term memory was good. If he was given a series of numbers to repeat backwards and forwards, for example, he could do this well. It seems as if HM's damage disrupted his ability to form explicit memory rather than disrupting the ability to consolidate memories. HM has been described as having a pure memory deficit, one that affects acquisition or recall of information but leaves other cognitive abilities, such as the production and comprehension of language, intact.

The explicit memory impairment associated with HM's amnesia was demonstrated in a classic study by Graf *et al.* (1984). This study appeared to demonstrate that different types of memory were dissociable. They presented a series of six-letter words to a group of amnesic and non-amnesic participants, and asked them to indicate how much they liked them. They then presented the participants with two memory tasks. In the first, participants were asked to recall as many words they had seen as they could: a test of explicit memory. In the second task, participants were asked to complete a word using the first three letters. They were not instructed to think about the words they had previously seen (this was a test of implicit memory). Amnesic patients were poorer than controls at remembering words explicitly, but there was no significant difference between the groups on the implicit memory task. This suggested that the locus of the damage in amnesic patients was associated with explicit memory impairment.

Later studies showed that selective damage to parts of the temporal lobe resulted in specific memory impairments. Lesions to the anterior temporal lobe which spared the hippocampus, for example, resulted in memory impairments, but not of the global kind seen in HM. Lesions to the right temporal lobe produced impairment in non-verbal memory (such as the recall of complex geometric figures, paired-associate learning of nonsense figures and recognition of nonsense figures, tunes and photographs); left temporal lobe lesions produced impairments in verbal memory (recall of previously presented stories, pairs of words, recognition of words, numbers and nonsense syllables). Verbal memory impairments are common following temporal lobe lesions (Ivnik *et al.*, 1987).

7.7 THE DIENCEPHALON: KORSAKOFF'S SYNDROME

The major structures of the diencephalon are the hypothalamus and the thalamus, and damage to either can cause amnesia. These regions become degenerated to some extent in chronic alcoholics who exhibit Korsakoff's syndrome. Korsakoff's syndrome is a condition in which memory impairments result from long-term alcoholism. It was first described in 1889 by Sergei Korsakoff, a Russian physician, who noted a syndrome of memory impairment following chronic alcoholism. The most marked feature of Korsakoff's syndrome is severe anterograde amnesia. The disorder is caused by a thiamine (vitamin B1) deficiency that results from the excessive alcohol intake. Because their diet is primarily made up of alcohol, drinkers get their calories from alcohol and, therefore, ingest fewer vitamins. Alcohol also appears to interfere with the intestinal absorption of thiamine. Prognosis is poor, with only about 20 per cent of patients showing much recovery over a year on a B1-enriched diet. The location of brain damage in Korsakoff's is unclear since all cases are accompanied by damage to many regions. Current thinking, however, suggests specific damage to the medial thalamus, and possibly the mammillary bodies of the hypothalamus.

The importance of parts of the thalamus to memory is highlighted by another of psychology's famous case studies. Squire and Moore's (1979) patient, NA, had suffered a lesion in the dorsal medial nucleus of the thalamus. The lesion resulted from an accident in which a fencing foil entered the right nostril and punctured the base of the brain. Severe amnesia followed. PET scans show little activation in NA's right medial temporal lobe, and this was correlated with poor memory performance, which suggests the importance of this structure to memory. However, the relative contribution of other damaged parts of NA's brain to amnesia is unclear.

7.8 HIPPOCAMPAL LESIONS AND SPATIAL AWARENESS

As well as its importance to memory, the hippocampus is also important for navigating or exploring the spatial environment and in forming representations of the locations of objects (O'Keefe and Nadel, 1978). This was clearly seen in a very famous experiment by Morris et al. (1982). The experimenters placed rats in a pool of milky water that contained a platform just beneath the water. In order to avoid swimming constantly, the rats had to find the platform hidden beneath the milky water and stay there.

Eventually, through trial and error, the rats would find the platform when released from different locations in the pool. Then the researchers performed a series of experimental ablations. One group of rats received lesions to the hippocampus, another received lesions to the cerebral cortex and another received no lesion. The rats were then allowed into the pool. Rats with the hippocampal lesions showed extremely poor navigation compared with the cortex lesion and control group: they were unable to find the platform. When rats had learned that there was a platform underwater and were then allowed to explore the water with the platform removed, those with an intact hippocampus would spend longer in the part of the maze where the platform had previously been positioned. The rats with hippocampal lesions, however, did not engage in this 'dwell time' in the quadrant where the platform once was (Gerlai, 2001). (Figure 7.1 illustrates this pattern.) This suggested an important role for the hippocampus in spatial learning.

Fig 7.1 The pathways of rats who try to find a hidden platform under three conditions: no lesions, cortical lesions or hippocampal lesions

The hippocampus is also implicated in a different type of learning: context-dependent fear conditioning (Gerlai, 2001). Damage to the hippocampus in rats causes the animals to forget the place in which they received an electric shock. But, if they were presented with a stimulus, a tone, that was paired with the pain during the initial conditioning, they still responded in the same way as they did during conditioning: the tone alone would lead to a fear response (Phillips and LeDoux, 1994). These findings suggest that the hippocampus is important to the learning of a sense of place, findings that have been confirmed by those of human studies.

7.9 HIPPOCAMPAL LESIONS AND SPATIAL MEMORY IN HUMANS

The role of the hippocampus in aspects of spatial memory (the ability to encode and retrieve information about locations and routes) has been well documented in animals, but O'Keefe and Nadel's (1978) view of hippocampal function has not gone unchallenged. Olton *et al.* (1979), for example, argued that the hippocampus was not exclusively responsible for spatial memory but was more involved in working memory. Tests used in spatial memory tasks were, according to the theory, tests of short-term or working memory rather than spatial memory: all required the organism to keep information in mind while it engaged in another behaviour that used such information, and this is the feature that was disrupted by damage.

To test whether the hippocampus played more of a role in working memory or spatial memory, Kessels *et al.* (2001) conducted a meta-analysis of 27 studies that reviewed the consequences of hippocampal dysfunction. The researchers examined the effects of damage on the ability of a person to (i) learn to navigate their way through a maze, a task that requires spatial and temporal ordering; (ii) hold information about spatial layouts in mind for a short space of time, a measure of spatial working memory; (iii) remember positions of objects and locations; and (iv) bind or integrate information about an object and its location.

The researchers found that there was impairment on all tasks but that some tasks were performed more badly than others. Whereas mild or moderate impairments were found on tasks requiring integration of information or navigation around a maze, there was little effect of hippocampal damage on spatial working memory. There was, however, a large impairment on tests of positional memory such as locating Xs in an array of letters. The lesions in patients showing mild to severe impairment were invariably to the right hippocampus, a finding that is consistent with O'Keefe and Nadel's (1978) hypothesis that the right hippocampus is specialised for mapping spatial information.

Kessels *et al.*'s results (2001) support the hypothesis that the hippocampus is important to our understanding of relations between objects and their positioning but not the hypothesis that it is primarily involved in working memory. You will see in the section below that this last finding may not be surprising in view of neuroimaging data from healthy people showing involvement of the prefrontal cortex, rather than the hippocampus, during the execution of working memory tasks.

7.10 MEMORY AND THE HEALTHY BRAIN

Although much of our knowledge about the brain mechanisms that underlie memory has been derived from animal studies or from studies of individuals with brain injury, the development of neuroimaging has provided evidence from healthy individuals suggesting that different regions of the brain are more involved than others in performing different types of memory task (Cabeza and Nyberg, 2000; Fletcher and Henson, 2001).

Spatial navigation

Maguire and her colleagues set up a novel and unusual experiment to see whether the hippocampus was active during spatial navigation (Maguire *et al.*, 1997). In their study, 11 London taxi drivers with 14 years' experience of driving described the shortest legal route between two locations in London as a Positron Emission Tomography (PET) scanner observed their brain activity.

The taxi drivers were also asked to recall famous London landmarks (an examination of topographical memory). The activation during these tasks was compared with that during the recall of sequences from famous films. When the drivers described the route from one location to another, significant activation of the right hippocampus was found (but was not found with the landmark or film conditions).

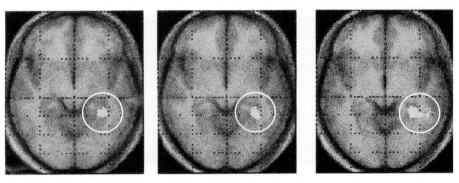

Fig 7.2 Areas of the hippocampus which become active during London cabbies' recall of routes

This finding suggests that the right part of the hippocampus is involved in the retrieval of information that involves recall of movement in complex environments. In another PET experiment, participants were asked to navigate their way around a familiar but complex virtual town, using a pair of virtual reality goggles (Maguire *et al.*, 1998a). Activation of the right hippocampus was again associated with knowing accurately where places were located and with navigating between them. The speed with which individuals navigated their environment was associated with right caudate nucleus activity. Also activated, however, were the right inferior parietal and bilateral medial cortex, which suggests, as many imaging studies do, that memory performance is not exclusively dependent on one region or structure.

Working memory

The ability to manipulate information in memory over a short space of time seems to be the primary responsibility of the frontal lobes (Fletcher and Henson, 2001), regions that, apparently contrarily, also become active during the retrieval of material that has been retained over long periods. Fletcher and Henson (2001) distinguish between two types of measure in working memory tasks: maintenance and manipulation. Working memory maintenance tasks involve measuring the process of keeping information in mind; working memory manipulation tasks involve measuring the reorganisation of material that is kept in mind.

A typical maintenance task involves presenting a participant with three to nine stimuli and then asking him or her to indicate whether a single stimulus presented subsequently formed part of the original stimulus array. The letter-based version of this task is usually associated with significant increases in activation in the left hemisphere, especially the ventrolateral frontal cortex, parietal lobe and premotor area (Awh *et al.*, 1996). When the task involves spatial or object information, right hemisphere activity is usually seen. Often, the same regions activated by letters or words in the left hemisphere are also activated in the right by spatial/object stimuli (Smith *et al.*, 1996).

A manipulation task in working memory might involve presenting the participant with a series of five letters and then asking them to recite the letters forwards, backwards or in alphabetical order, in the mind. After a delay, the participant is asked to match the number order of a given letter, according to the mental manipulation (e.g. forwards, backwards or alphabetical). So, if the letters B, M, T, E, I were presented and the participant was asked to alphabetise them, the digit probe 4 should elicit the correct answer, M (because M is the fourth letter in the alphabetised string, B, E, I, M, T). During the delay, there is usually activation seen in the ventrolateral and dorsolateral frontal cortex; during the re-ordering part of the task, activation is seen more in the dorsolateral part.

In tasks that involve the generation of words, left dorsolateral activation is observed but not if words simply have to be repeated (Frith *et al.*, 1991). Word generation is a common 'frontal lobe' test: people with frontal lobe injury are poor at generating words from a given first-letter, for example. The link between frontal lobe activity and working memory may be biochemical. The 'Research update …' section below reviews some evidence for this proposition.

Research update … the neurochemical basis of working memory

Neurons projecting to the prefrontal cortex contain a specific neurotransmitter, acetylcholine, which is delivered by a specific type of neurotransmitter pathway, the cholinergic pathway. Recently, it has been hypothesised that an increase in acetylcholine to the frontal cortex might lead to an improvement in working memory (Furey *et al.*, 2000). Furey *et al.* administered the drug physostigmine (which increases the amount of acetylcholine available) to a small group of men and women who completed a working memory task as a functional Magnetic Resonance Imaging (fMRI) scanner monitored their brain activity. Participants completed the same task the following day but received a placebo (saline). The task involved watching a human face for three seconds, and then after a nine-second delay when the face was removed, identifying which of two or more subsequently presented faces was that originally seen.

Participants who received the physostigmine showed increased activation in the visual cortex during the encoding of the face, activation that was significantly lower in the saline condition. The physostigmine condition also produced better face recognition when participants had to decide which of the faces had previously been presented. The finding suggests that the improvement in working memory may be due to enhanced visual processing in the earliest stages of encoding. One practical application of this may be to administer such drugs to patients with stark memory deficits, such as patients with Alzheimer's disease (Robbins *et al.*, 2000).

7.11 ENCODING AND RETRIEVAL IN EPISODIC AND SEMANTIC MEMORY

The encoding of episodic memory, memory for personally meaningful events, people and objects, is associated with activity in regions including the prefrontal and medial-temporal cortex and the cerebellum (Cabeza and Nyberg, 2000). Studies have usually found left-sided activation during episodic memory encoding, especially during the encoding of verbal material. The encoding of non-verbal material tends to be associated with bilateral activity in the frontal cortex. The role of the left prefrontal cortex in memory may be that of organising information: this part of the brain is responsible for our ability to group items on the basis of some characteristic or attribute.

To test this hypothesis, Fletcher *et al.* (1998) conducted a PET study in which participants listened to words that were either semantically organised or disorganised but had to be put into categories. As expected, the condition in which the list was already organised produced the least amount of left prefrontal cortex activation, whereas the task requiring the participant to generate an organisational structure resulted in greatest activation. A distractor task reduced activation during the organisation task but not during any other encoding task, suggesting that the organisational, executive role of the left prefrontal cortex can be disrupted.

7.12 REMEMBERING AND LONG-TERM MEMORY

Neuroimaging studies of long-term memory typically involve presenting participants with several items that they are told to memorise (or they may be given no memorisation instructions), and asking them to recall the presented material sometime later. Usually, the participant is asked to recognise the presented stimulus from a range of target and distractor stimuli. The process involves encoding and retrieval, and neuroimaging research has highlighted the different brain regions involved in each type of process. If encoding is intentional or incidental, it is associated with left frontal cortex activation, as we have already seen.

If encoding and retrieval is successful, would greater brain activation be seen during encoding for those stimuli that were successfully encoded or for all stimuli regardless of how well they were retrieved? In a recent neuroimaging study, Brewer *et al.* (1998) found that greater right frontal cortex activity was associated with successful encoding. Individuals were asked to view a series of indoor or outdoor scenes and to decide whether each scene depicted outdoors or indoors; 30 minutes later, they were given a recognition test and asked to indicate whether they remembered the scene, thought the scene was familiar but not well remembered or was forgotten. Memory for the scenes was predicted by frontal and parahippocampal activation with greater activation found for the remembered images.

Focus on ... lateralisation of memory processes

A model called the HERA model has been proposed to account for the differences in brain activation seen during memory encoding and retrieval. HERA stands for Hemispheric Encoding-Retrieval Asymmetry and the model argues that greater left than right frontal cortex activation is seen during episodic encoding, whereas greater right than left frontal cortex activation is seen during episodic retrieval (Tulving *et al.*, 1994). The evidence reviewed in this chapter and more extensively in Fletcher and Henson (2001) and Cabeza and Nyberg (2000) suggests very strong support for the model. In general, verbal encoding is associated with left frontal activation whereas right activation is more common during retrieval but, as we have seen, such areas as well as others can be bilaterally active during encoding and retrieval. Why?

Fletcher and Henson (2001) put forward some interesting possibilities. Two are statistical and methodological and hinge on (i) the type of statistical parameters a study sets for statistical significance in neuroimaging research (different studies may set different parameters so that more liberal criteria make it easier to find areas of activation) and (ii) the small number of samples used in neuroimaging research. A further reason may be the lack of clarity over the precise definition of cognitive processes in memory studies. Setting aside questions regarding what is verbal and what is non-verbal (and whether these two categories could be considered unitary), there are also questions regarding the nature of encoding and retrieval. Not all studies use the same measures of encoding or retrieval; perhaps the inconsistencies in findings can, therefore, be attributed to these different methodological approaches.

7.13 IS THERE A PART OF THE BRAIN THAT REPRESENTS A MEMORY?

A question often asked by people unfamiliar with the evidence above is whether our memory for meeting a person and falling in love, or our memory of a good holiday or a good restaurant is represented by the activity of specific neurons. This concept is called an engram – the neural equivalent of a memory. It is similar, conceptually, to the notion of the grandmother cell – the proposition that there are specific cells that encode our ability to recognise our grandmothers and not any other human being. The short answer to the question is, no. Current evidence suggests that various brain regions are involved in evoking an autobiographical memory but no technique is sophisticated enough to allow us to observe neural behaviour that can be identified with specific memories. This may change. There are current data showing that different regions of the brain respond to places and buildings, and that people respond differently to the faces of those they love than to friends. Whether these changes in brain activity represent something 'psychological' rather than a response to the physical features of objects is open to debate. It is the key to the enigma surrounding the relationship between neural activity and experience: how does the latter produce the former? The later chapter, on consciousness (Chapter 10), considers this enigma further.

SOME USEFUL FURTHER READING

LEARNING AND MEMORY, GENERAL
Anderson, J.R. (1999) *Learning and memory* (second edition). Chichester: John Wiley.
Tulving, E. and Craik, F.M. (2000) *The Oxford Handbook of Memory*. Oxford: Oxford University Press.

MOLECULAR MECHANISMS OF MEMORY AND LEARNING
Abel, T. and Lattal, K.M. (2001) Molecular mechanisms of memory acquisition, consolidation and retrieval. *Current Opinion in Neurobiology* 11, 180–7.

NEUROIMAGING AND MEMORY
Fletcher, P.C. and Henson, R.N.A. (2001) Frontal lobes and human memory. *Brain*, 849–81.
Gabrieli, J.D.E. (1998) Cognitive neuroscience of human memory. *Annual Review of Psychology* 49, 87–115.
Wagner, A.D., Kovstaal, W. and Schacter, D.L. (1999) When encoding yields remembering: insights from event-related neuroimaging. *Philosophical Transactions of the Royal Society of London B*, (354), 1307–24.

AMNESIA, MEMORY AND BRAIN INJURY
Baddeley, A.D., Kopelman, M. and Wilson, B.A. (2002) *Handbook of Memory Disorders*. Chichester: John Wiley.
Parkin, A.J. (1996) *Memory and Amnesia: An Introduction*. Oxford: Blackwell.
Parkin, A.J. (1997) *Case Studies in the Neuropsychology of Memory*. Hove, UK: The Psychology Press.

SOME USEFUL JOURNALS TO BROWSE

Behavioural Brain Reviews
Brain
Brain and Cognition
Cortex
Hippocampus
Journal of Cognitive Neuroscience
Journal of Neuroscience
Learning and Memory
Nature Neuroscience
Neurobiology of Learning
Neuroimage
Science
Trends in Cognitive Sciences
Trends in Neurosciences

8 Emotion and Stress

WHAT YOU WILL FIND IN THIS CHAPTER
- a discussion of the term emotion and whether basic emotions exist
- a description of the roles of the amygdala and the frontal cortex in the recognition and expression of emotion
- a description and evaluation of biological models of emotion, and the approach–withdrawal model of EEG asymmetry and emotion in particular
- a definition of the term stress and a description of the factors that can give rise to stress
- a description of the immune system and an evaluation of the effect of stressors on the immune system

WHAT YOU SHOULD BE ABLE TO DO AFTER READING THE CHAPTER
- be aware of the difficulty in defining emotion scientifically and of the controversies surrounding the scientific study of emotion
- be aware of how the classical conditioning of fear can occur in animals
- describe the contribution of the amygdala and frontal cortex to our understanding of the neural basis of emotional expression and recognition
- describe the effect of emotional experience on EEG frontal asymmetry and be aware of explanations for this asymmetry
- define stress and stressors, and outline some of the factors that can give rise to stress
- have a basic understanding of how the immune system works and how stressors can impair its functioning

8.1 WHAT IS AN EMOTION?

The previous chapter, on memory began with what seemed like a simple question (but with a complex answer): 'What is memory?' Defining memory, however, pales before attempts at defining emotion. One study found that when students were asked to generate as many different synonyms for the word emotion as they could, they came up with 556 different terms (Davitz, 1970). Kleinginna and Kleinginna (1981, cited in Plutchik, 1994) reviewed a series of dictionaries, textbooks and other relevant materials, and found that emotion and emotions were defined in 92 different ways. According to LeDoux (1995a), emotion has 'proved to be a slippery concept for both psychologists and neuroscientists', a conclusion that underlies this plethora of definitions for emotion. If emotion is this slippery a concept, how can biological psychologists get to grips with it?

The word emotion is closely associated with words such as 'feelings', 'sadness', 'joy', 'fear', 'disgust', and so on. While we may not be able to provide an operational definition of the term, like Art, we know it when we see it. Psychologists have defined emotions in various ways. According to William James, emotion is the feeling we get when we note bodily changes that arise from perceiving some fact or event (James, 1884). The fright at being chased by a bear is due to our perception of changes in the body, which result from our being aware that we are being chased by a bear. Later psychologists argued that emotions involve behaviour that results from the appraisal or perception of subjectively experienced but evocative events or objects (Borod, 1992) or that they 'can be usefully defined as states produced by instrumental reinforcing stimuli' (Rolls, 1990). This last view suggests that our experience of emotion is attributable to activation between cortical and subcortical regions in response to reward or punishment. The literal Latin translation of the word 'emotion' is 'to move' or 'to stir up'.

8.2 DOES EMOTION NEED COGNITION?

One of the controversies tied to the definition of emotion is whether it can exist without cognition. Is cognition a precursor to emotion? Some theorists have argued that the process of experiencing emotion relies to a great extent on appraising our environment. According to Lazarus (1966), emotions arise from 'how a person construes the outcome, actual or anticipated, of a transaction or a bit of commerce with the environment'. In order to experience anxiety, for example, we need to attribute anxiety-provoking properties to an object, event or person in the environment. We need, in short, to think about the object/event/person, and this leads to the emotion. Seeing a spider, for example, involves first being able to identify the creature as a spider, a cognitive process. Based on this attribution, and then some combination of evolution or learned behaviour, people (arachnophobes) become frightened. At the core of the response is a person's cognitive operations – attributions and appraisals – but not all theorists agree that the precursor model explains all emotion. Zajonc (1980), for example, provided some evidence to show that we can respond emotionally to events that we were not capable of consciously perceiving. The solution to this conundrum probably lies in how we define cognition. If cognition is the act of perception, then it is almost unarguable that cognition does not precede emotion. If perception is not regarded as a cognitive operation, then the view that emotions are not preceded by cognition is justified.

8.3 ARE EMOTIONS UNIVERSAL?

If defining emotion is problematic, perhaps an alternative approach to studying the topic is to cite examples of what we think emotions are, and to work backwards. We may not have a universally agreed definition of emotion but we almost universally agree that sadness and joy are two examples of it. According to Ekman (1973), there are six basic emotions and all other emotional reactions are variants or combinations of these. The six are: happiness, anger, fear, sadness, disgust and surprise, and are thought to be universal. Ekman's is probably the best-known taxonomy of emotion, but his is not the only one. Others have posited six, seven, eight and even ten basic emotions.

Ekman drew his conclusions from a series of cross-cultural studies in which fairly primitive tribes (by western standards) were able to distinguish between categories of emotion. One tribe lived in an isolated area of remote New Guinea, and comprised 319 adults and children who had not been exposed to western culture. If the members of the tribe identified the emotional expressions of westerners as well as their own, and if their facial expressions of emotions were the same as those of westerners, this would suggest that emotions were not culturally determined but universal.

Ekman and Friesen (1969; Ekman *et al.*, 1972) read stories representing an emotion to the tribe members who were then asked to select which of three photographs representing facial expressions by westerners reflected the emotion in the story. In a second experiment, the tribespeople were asked to make facial expressions associated with emotions; photographs of these were then presented to westerners who were asked to identify them. The results showed that members of the tribe were able to identify emotion correctly in westerners' faces and that westerners had no difficulty in correctly identifying the emotion in the tribespeople's faces.

Critics, however, have argued that while facial expressions may be universal, the significance of these expressions is open to question. Some psychologists have argued that a facial expression may not reflect actual emotion but a need to communicate some social signal to others, an important function of facial expression. A smile, for example, may be a genuine expression of joy or a reflection of sarcasm or threat. Facial expressions may, therefore, not reflect the emotion but the social signalling of emotion.

8.4 A BIOLOGICAL ESCAPE ROUTE?

If the cognitive aspects of emotion are problematic, with disagreement over what constitutes the behavioural analogues of basic emotions and disagreement over what the 'basic' in basic emotions means, perhaps there may be a solution that biological psychology could provide. If, for example, there is a neural pathway or brain region that is active during the experience of one emotion and not another, this suggests that the two emotions are distinct because they are subserved by different brain machinery. Like most cognitive studies, biological studies of emotion in psychology have focused on a select group of emotions and they tend to be those described by Ekman. However, there is evidence that there are distinct structures and regions implicated in specific emotions and in the valence of emotions – whether they are positive or negative. The two most important regions are the orbitofrontal cortex and the amygdala.

8.5 THE AMYGDALA

According to Aggleton and Mishkin (1986), the amygdala serves as the sensory gateway to the emotions, but recent studies suggest that its role in emotion is not so general. The amygdala is a collection of subnuclei in the anterior temporal lobe thought to be heavily involved in the learning and maintenance of fear, anxiety and other emotions. Together with the hippocampus, septum, fornix and olfactory bulb, it is considered part of the limbic system (the collective name for subcortical structures near the thalamus). It was thought that emotional expression was the result of the activity of these interconnecting structures, the so-called Papez circuit.

If the anterior temporal lobes were damaged or removed in monkeys (which means that the amygdala is removed or damaged also), inappropriate emotional behaviour was elicited. For example, the animal might indiscriminately consume anything that is edible, become highly sexually active and mount sexually inappropriate objects, repeatedly explore familiar objects, and exhibit tameness and lack of fear. This has been termed Kluver-Bucy syndrome (Kluver and Bucy, 1939). In humans, however, the same behaviours are not elicited.

The structure has connections with the neocortex, hypothalamus, the septum, the thalamus, the hippocampus and the reticular formation. Inputs from the sensory systems normally arrive in the amygdala. The amygdala and hippocampal system also project to regions controlling endocrine, autonomic and motor activity. LeDoux (1995a) has described some of the pathways to and from various brain structures, but especially the amygdala and thalamus, that are involved in the conditioning of fear. Fear is a 'good' emotion to study in a laboratory because procedures for eliciting fear within a classical conditioning framework are relatively easy to control and undertake with animal subjects.

Fear conditioning and the amygdala in animals

In animal studies, the conditioning of fear involves exposing the organism to a tone or flash of light (the conditioned stimulus, CS), followed by a brief electric shock (the unconditioned stimulus, US). If the US is intense enough, then pairing the CS with the US will result in rapid conditioning of the fear response, a process similar to the classical conditioning of eye blinking you read about in the previous chapter. This conditioning is measured by freezing responses, endocrine activity, autonomic activity, reflexes (eye blink) or the degree to which the CS interferes with the organism's routine behaviour.

Using neuroanatomical staining and lesioning techniques, the pathway of an acoustic stimulus, for example (the CS), can be traced from the auditory system outwards after conditioning has taken place. In fact, lesions to the midbrain and thalamus along this pathway prevent conditioning, but lesioning the auditory cortex does not (LeDoux *et al.*, 1984). Furthermore, the auditory thalamus projects to the auditory cortex and the amygdala. Lesioning the connections between the auditory thalamus and the amygdala interferes with conditioning. LeDoux and his colleagues observed that the lateral nucleus of the amygdala was the region responsible for receiving information about the auditory stimulus (LeDoux *et al.*, 1990). Cells in this area were particularly responsive to stimuli similar to auditory CS stimuli.

The direct thalamic pathway to the amygdala is direct and fast but carries few auditory impulses; the link to the amygdala from the thalamic pathway via cortico-cortical connections is slower but carries greater auditory impulses. Thus, emotional responses associated with simple stimuli might be mediated by the first route; responses associated with complex sets of stimuli may be mediated via the second route. It is thought that the lateral nucleus acts as the place where these two systems meet and possibly integrates information from the two parallel systems (LeDoux, 1995b).

To illustrate the extent of the amygdala's involvement in the acquisition and maintenance of fear learning, lesioning of the structure, even after extensive training, produces deficits in fear conditioning (Kim and Davis, 1993). The origin of the US's pathway to the amygdala, however, is unknown.

As LeDoux notes (1995b), whether the mechanisms of fear conditioning outlined from these studies are the same ones that mediate other forms of fear specific to humans (e.g. fear of authority, heights, social situations) is unclear. LeDoux's protocol is also highly experimental and based on animal data. There is some evidence from the human literature, however, that the amygdala plays a role in the perception of fearful or fear-related stimuli.

Fear and the amygdala in humans

A recent case study of a 30-year-old woman who had sustained complete bilateral destruction of the amygdala (sparing the hippocampus and cortex) showed how important this structure appeared to be for the recognition and expression of fear. The patient was unable to recognise fear in facial expressions but could recognise happiness, surprise, anger, disgust and sadness. She also had difficulty in recognising multiple emotions in a single facial expression (Adolphs et al., 1994). Adolphs et al. (1995) have also reported data showing that unilateral but not bilateral damage to the amygdala impairs the recognition of fearful facial expressions. A patient with almost complete bilateral amygdala damage, for example, was unable to draw fearful facial expression from memory but was able to draw other types of emotional facial expression (see Figure 8.1).

Adolphs et al. have also reported a case study; theirs was of a 31-year-old woman who sustained bilateral amygdala damage (Adolphs et al., 1999). They asked her to rate facial expressions, words and sentences along two dimensions: how arousing they were and how pleasant they were. While she was able to distinguish pleasant from unpleasant emotions, she was unable to recognise emotional arousal in those expressions conveying negative emotions, specifically fear and anger. The authors argue that these results support a role for the amygdala in responding to highly negative, threat-related stimuli that require quick responses.

The data from brain injury studies are supported by the findings from studies of healthy brains. Morris and his colleagues recently observed that the left side of the amygdala became active in five individuals who viewed photographs of individuals with fearful facial expressions; as the intensity of the facial expression increased, so did activation in the amygdala (Morris et al., 1996).

The amygdala and positive emotion

The role of the amygdala in responding to fear-type stimuli has been fairly well documented. Its involvement in the perception of positive stimuli is not so clear and the data are mixed. However, a recent study reports that the structure can be activated by both negative and positive stimulation (Hamann et al., 2002).

Hamann et al. asked ten right-handed men to view a series of photographs of various types as a PET scanner monitored their brain activity. These photographs included nude or semi-nude women, appealing animals and infants, and appetising food (a pleasant condition); mutilated or diseased bodies, frightening animals and graphic violence (an aversive condition); chess players, plants and household scenes (a low-interest, neutral condition); and a

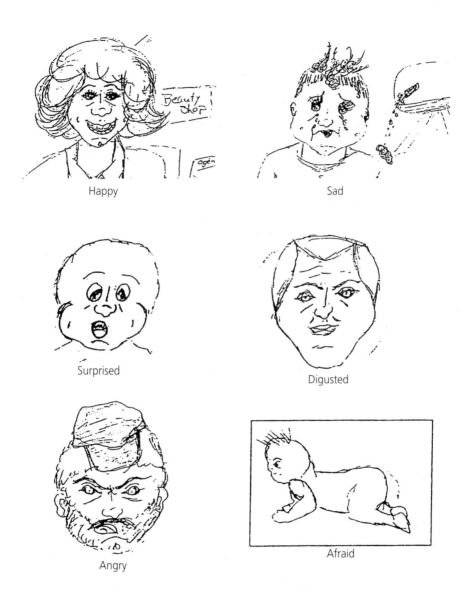

Happy

Sad

Surprised

Digusted

Angry

Afraid

Fig 8.1 The drawings of a patient with damage to the amygdala. Her drawing of most emotions is good but she appears unable to draw the emotion of fear

chrome rhinoceros, scenes from a surrealistic film and an exotic religious parade (a high-interest, unusual condition).

Watching the positive stimuli resulted in a significant increase in activation in the left side of the amygdala; this activation also extended to other brain areas known to be involved in drug addiction and reward (the ventral striatum); watching diseased and mutilated bodies stimulated both sides of the amygdala (but little beyond it). The left side was also active while people viewed the high-interest pictures.

The authors suggest that there could be various explanations for the findings. The most interesting hinges on previous studies showing that the amygdala is active when encoding and retrieving positive memories. While the amygdala has been thought to be a structure that might process and interpret ambiguity – or at least become active during those states – its role here may be due to its role in remembering positive events. That said, the amygdala has many parts (and parts that PET was not sensitive enough to measure) and the authors suggest that different parts may play different roles.

Research update ... anger and the amygdala

While the study of fear has always been a fruitful vineyard of discovery for neuroscientists, the study of other emotions (such as anger) has not generally been as productive. R.J.R. Blair and colleagues at University College London and St Andrews University studied the brain activity of 13 healthy young men as they decided whether facial expressions belonged to men or women (Blair *et al.*, 1999). Each face expressed either sadness or anger, and the expressions were of varying intensity. They found that as the intensity of the sad expression increased, so did activity in the left amygdala and right temporal lobe. As the intensity of the angry expression increased, so did activity in the right oribitofrontal cortex and a part of the brain called the anterior cingulate gyrus (which previous studies have linked with the intensity of emotional facial expression). There was no significant increase in amygdala activity during exposure to angry expressions.

The authors propose that the results signify a clear model: there is no unitary system that responds to negative stimuli, but two systems. One system mediates responses to negative stimuli involved in social aversive conditioning (sadness, fear); the other mediates responses to negative stimuli (anger and related stimuli) that curtail behaviour (the emotion is thought to suppress behaviour).

The frontal lobes

Another region thought to play an important role in emotion is the frontal cortex. In one early study, for example, Kolodny (1929) described two consequences of frontal lobe lesion: mood alteration (exaltation or depression) and changes in the social aspects of personality. This study was not unique, with Holmes (1931) later arguing that frontal brain damage could result in increased indifference, depression or exuberance/euphoria. It is the peculiar and striking change in personality that partly informed the movement in the 1940s and 1950s toward lobectomy for the removal of psychotic symptoms.

The orbitofrontal cortex is located at the base of the frontal lobes. It covers the part of the brain just above the orbits – the bones that form the eye sockets – hence the term orbitofrontal. Damage to this region is often associated with euphoria and deviant behaviour (Stuss and Benson, 1986). Rolls (1990) has argued that the orbitofrontal cortex is an important structure for making associations between a stimulus and reinforcement; the association, Rolls argues, makes up our experience of emotions. The amygdala, Rolls suggests, may elicit learned emotional responses while the orbitofrontal cortex may be involved in the correction 'or adjustment of these emotional responses as the reinforcing value of environmental stimuli alters'. Much of Rolls' evidence is derived from animal work; human data, however, appear to confirm the frontal cortex's involvement in the perception and expression of emotion. More interestingly, these data indicate that the left and right frontal cortices may have different parts to play in emotion.

8.6 THE ORBITOFRONTAL CORTEX

The role of the orbitofrontal cortex in emotional behaviour was illustrated dramatically by the case of Phineas Gage. Phineas Gage was a dynamite worker who, one day in September 1848, was flattening rocky terrain for the laying of train tracks. He removed large rocks and boulders by ramming dynamite into a hole drilled in the rock. The dynamite was rammed by a tamping iron and to prevent the iron making contact with the gunpowder, a cloth was placed around the end of the rod. On this occasion, however, Gage forgot the cloth, the charge exploded and the rod shot into his cheek, through his brain and out the top of his head. He survived, but he was a different man.

Before his injury, he was serious, industrious and energetic. Afterwards, he became childish, irresponsible, boorish and thoughtless of others (Harlow, 1848; 1868). He was unable to make or carry out plans, and his actions appeared to be capricious and whimsical. According to those who knew him well, he was 'no longer Gage'. His accident had destroyed a significant part of the orbitofrontal cortex, as Figure 8.2 shows (Harlow, 1848; Damasio et al., 1994).

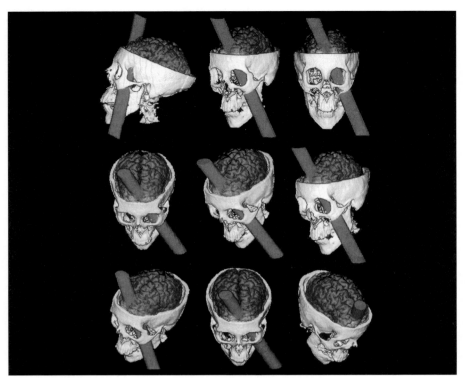

Fig 8.2 The trajectory of the tamping iron through Phineas Gage's head

Although scientists and physicians at the time were slow to seize upon the relationship between this behaviour change and the associated damage, studies since have demonstrated similar personality and social behaviour changes in patients with orbitofrontal cortex damage. Cicerone and Tanenbaum (1997), for example, described the case of a 38-year-old woman with orbitofrontal damage who made a good recovery from the injury but who showed disturbed social and emotional perception. She appeared to have severe difficulty in integrating or appreciating subtle social and emotional cues.

Hornak *et al.* (1996) have also reported 12 cases of ventral frontal lobe damage, which was associated with an impairment in identifying facial and vocal expressions of emotion. Some of the comments made by orbitofrontal lobe patients on their disorder can help to illuminate the phenomenology of the social impairment – they illustrate in personal terms how brain damage has affected that person's behaviour.

According to one patient, 'Emotion, tears, that's all gone out of the window. If I saw somebody cry I'd just laugh – people look really silly getting upset'; according to another, 'I ain't scared of nobody. I'm not frightened of opening my mouth and speaking my mind. If I think someone's in the wrong, I'll tell them and not give a monkey's what they think of me.' One explanation for this behaviour is that the orbitofrontal cortex is involved in assessing the personal significance of what is currently happening to the individual and that this is impaired with damage; an alternative view is that these patients cannot inhibit socially inappropriate responses because the frontal connections responsible for such inhibition have been damaged.

EVR

However, a person whose orbitofrontal cortex has been damaged by disease or accident is still able to assess accurately the significance of particular situations, but only in a theoretical sense. For example, Eslinger and Damasio (1985) found that their patient, EVR, although sustaining bilateral damage of the orbitofrontal cortex, displayed excellent social judgement and intellectual ability. His personal life, in contrast, was disastrous.

Prior to surgery, EVR was a well-liked, well-respected accountant with a family and strong connections with his community. Three months after the operation, he became an accountant for a small home construction business. Against the advice of his friends and family, he invested all his savings in setting up a home-building partnership with a former co-worker described by Eslinger and Damasio as having a 'questionable reputation'. The business failed and EVR became a bankrupt. Following this incident, he attempted, and failed, to hold down a number of other jobs including warehouse labourer, a buildings manager, and accountant for a car spares company. He was described by his employers as tardy and disorganised, although his skills, manners and temperament were acceptable. His marriage broke up (after 17 years) and, unable to keep a job or a family, EVR moved in with his parents.

Two years after the operation, EVR's difficulties continued. He worked, for a while, as a tax returns officer but his employment was terminated. He was fired from another job, which he had to drive 100 miles to get to (he was fired for lack of punctuality). He remarried after his divorce but this marriage ended after two years. He would take an inappropriately long time to make the simplest of decisions, taking two hours to get ready for work, and spending an inordinately long time shaving and grooming. He would spend hours deciding on a restaurant in which to dine, poring over the restaurant's seating arrangements, the menu plan and the atmosphere. He would drive to restaurants to see how busy they were, but could not decide which one to choose. Even buying the most insignificant of items was tortuous: he would need to know the exact price of the item, make a comparison of prices and ponder the best method of purchase. He also began to hoard, refusing to part with dead houseplants, old phone books, six broken fans, three empty orange juice cartons and 15 cigarette lighters, among other detritus.

At two and six years after the operation, his cognitive ability was evaluated using a range of tests. Two years after the injury, his verbal IQ was superior, his performance IQ average, his memory IQ above average and his personality showed no deviation from the norm. Six years after surgery, his IQ still placed him in the average to superior category.

Damasio proposed that our ability to make social and emotional decisions depends on our being able to make sense of the somatic information the body generates in response to specific events. If we are making a risky decision, this risk will be associated with a physiological response that will reflect our uncertainty about the decision we have made. In frontal lobe patients, Damasio argues, these connections between somatic states and an appreciation of them, are missing. We will return to this in the next chapter.

8.7 HEMISPHERIC ASYMMETRY AND EMOTION: RECOGNITION

Early studies of emotion and the brain in humans focused on emotional disturbances following head injury. A common finding in these and later studies was that left-sided lesions were associated with depressive symptoms (such as crying, low self-esteem, misery) whereas lesions to the right hemisphere were associated with increased elevation and euphoria (Robinson and Benson, 1981; Sackheim *et al.*, 1982). These studies showed that the common right-for-emotion hypothesis – emotion was the sole responsibility of the right cerebral hemisphere – was a partial truism at best and a bland caricature at worst because it failed to distinguish between the perception of affect and the experience of it. This distinction is an important one because the functions recruit not only different sides but different regions of the cortex.

The ability to perceive or recognise emotions is thought to be a right-hemisphere function. If participants are asked (1) whether two emotionally toned sentences are the same or different, (2) to identify or discriminate between emotional facial expressions, or (3) to process non-emotional and emotional words, there is usually a left-ear and left-visual-field advantage in these tasks, indicating the involvement of the right hemisphere (Bryden and Ley, 1983).

8.8 HEMISPHERIC ASYMMETRY AND EMOTION: EXPERIENCE

Evidence collected over the last 25 years suggests that left-sided increases in

EEG alpha activity are seen during the experience of positive emotion and relative right-sided increases during the experience of negative emotion. The presence of increased left frontal alpha activation led some researchers to suggest that this may be an index of baseline emotional response. Wheeler *et al.* (1993), for example, reported that increased left frontal activation and decreased right frontal alpha activation predicted greater affective response to positive films. Those participants showing increased left frontal hemisphere activity responded most emotionally to assorted video clips designed to evoke intense emotion. Tomarken *et al.* (1990) reported that baseline frontal asymmetry significantly predicted global negative affect so that participants with decreased left frontal activity and increased right frontal activity responded more negatively to unpleasant visual stimuli. Taken together with the reports of decreased left frontal activation in depressed subjects, these findings suggest a diathesis model of affective response. As Davidson (1988) puts it: 'right frontal activation may be necessary but not sufficient for the experience of negative emotion. Its presence may mark a vulnerability for negative affect, given an appropriate elicitor.'

8.9 APPROACH-WITHDRAWAL BEHAVIOUR

Other studies by Davidson and his colleagues have demonstrated similar asymmetries to positive and negative emotional stimuli, primarily in the alpha frequency of the EEG and in response to visual stimuli. According to Davidson (1992), these changes reflect differences in motivational behaviour – whether we want to approach or withdraw from a stimulus. This hypothesis – the approach–withdrawal hypothesis – argues that differences between the two sides of the brain during the experience of emotion reflect different motivational tendencies (Ehrlichman, 1987). We approach stimuli we like (these generate positive emotion) and withdraw from those we do not (these generate negative emotion).

Several other studies have provided support for the asymmetry model (Harmon-Jones and Allen, 1998; Sutton and Davidson, 2000; Schmidt and Trainor, 2001). For example, Sutton and Davidson (2000) measured resting EEG in men and women at two sessions separated by six weeks. At the second session, participants were given a word-pair judgement task. Participants were required to indicate which of two word pairs went together the best. The words were manipulated for emotional tone so that some word pairs were pleasant and some were unpleasant (although the associative strength between words in all pairs was the same).

Participants with greater relative left-sided activation were more likely to select the pleasant word pairs as being the two that went best together. The results, the authors suggest, show an attentional bias towards positive stimuli in healthy individuals who show frontal left-sided baseline EEG.

While some studies have supported the frontal asymmetry model, recent evidence has suggested that the type of asymmetry seen depends on the methods of analysis and EEG recording one uses (Hagemann *et al.*, 1998), although the criticism of these studies has not gone unchallenged (Davidson, 1998). A recent study however has shown that the left-based frontal asymmetry may reflect a genuine latent trait rather than a state (Hagemann *et al.*, 2002).

Focus on ... resting brain activity and the development of sociability

Studies of distressed infants have highlighted similar asymmetries in EEG to those found in adults experiencing negative emotion. Davidson and Fox (1989) measured EEG from infants they characterised as criers and non-criers (criers were those who became distressed when separated from their mothers) and found that the criers were distinguished from the non-criers by greater right-sided frontal EEG activation. Dawson *et al.* (1997) reported that the infants of depressed mothers (as well as the mothers themselves) showed reduced left frontal EEG activity. These asymmetries have also been found in studies comparing four-year-old infants who are either happy and sociable or unhappy and unsociable. The sociable children showed greater left frontal activation (Fox *et al.*, 1995).

Fox and his team at the University of Maryland also investigated whether resting frontal brain activity predicted later behavioural inhibition in children assessed at 9, 14, 24 and 48 months of age (Fox *et al.*, 2001). Behavioural inhibition is a temperamental pattern characterised by increased vigilance and decreased motor behaviour when confronted with a novel stimulus. Children are likely to avoid unfamiliar adults, show little spontaneous behaviour in the presence of unfamiliar peers, and are regarded by their parents and peers as anxious and fearful. Fox *et al.* found that the temperament of infants at four months predicted the development of behavioural inhibition two years later. The study also found that those children who displayed a consistent pattern of right frontal EEG activity were more likely to be behaviourally inhibited. Children who were initially assessed as inhibited but who later became non-inhibited did not show this characteristic pattern of right-sided EEG activity. The researchers interpret these findings to mean that infants showing an increase in left-sided activity used approach (positive) behaviour to modulate negative affect; those infants who show right-sided activity were less likely to do this.

Finally, using the approach–withdrawal model as his starting point, Schmidt (1999) examined whether the resting brain activity would predict levels of adult shyness and sociability. He predicted that the more sociable the participant, the greater the left hemisphere activation; the more withdrawn and shy the participant, the greater the right frontal activation observed. This is the pattern that Schmidt found.

What seems unclear in these EEG studies of sociability, however, is the nature of cause and effect. Does the distress cause the EEG asymmetry or does the EEG asymmetry cause the distress? Does the asymmetry predispose the infant to distress? Is the resting frontal asymmetry produced by some other factor not yet considered? These are some of the interesting questions that EEG studies provoke.

8.10 STRESS

Stress is a word that is commonly and routinely used in the press, television and radio, but its use isn't usually the correct one. A simple definition of stress is that the term denotes 'a pattern of physiological, behavioural, emotional and cognitive responses to real or imagined stimuli that are perceived as preventing a goal or endangering or threatening well-being' (Carlson *et al.*, 2000). The consequence of stress, however, is usually accurately portrayed. It is a response to a threat from the environment and makes us engage in 'fight' or 'flight': we either confront what causes the stress or we avoid or escape it.

The triggers of stress are called stressors and there are many examples, major and minor. Being mugged, burgled or raped are major stressors; failing to receive an important letter or getting stuck in a broken-down train on your way to an important interview are comparatively minor. Not all stressors are negatively perceived. Performing in front of an audience if you are an actor, meeting a publication deadline if you are an author or sitting an exam if you are a student, are all stressors but these can have positive effects on performance. Long-term stressors, however, can potentially be harmful to health.

The biology of stress

The biological response to stress is governed by our autonomic nervous system (ANS), a part of the CNS that is partly under the control of the hypothalamus. When the individual is aroused – experiences a stressor – the hypothalamus stimulates the ANS and a structure in the subcortex called the pituitary gland which, in turn, signal the organs of the body to react in a specific way. Because the stressor can either affect us positively or negatively – causing fright or exhilaration – these organs react differently. Some of the biological features that characterise the response to almost all stressors, are described in Table 8.1.

Table 8.1 The major physiological changes that occur in response to a stressor

Heart rate increases
Blood pressure increases
Blood vessel constriction
Blood sugar levels increase
Blood flow is directed to major organs
Breathing is deeper and faster
Perspiration increases
Digestion stops
Adrenaline (epinephrine) is secreted by adrenal glands

The changes listed in Table 8.1 help the organism to cope with a stressor; they ready the organism for action, and heighten psychological and physical awareness. In this sense, they are adaptive because they help us to cope with unexpected or arousing events. However, they become maladaptive if they generate anxiety and are prolonged in nature. If people experience extreme stress on a regular basis, this will affect their psychological and physical health. Much of the current work on the psychology of stress and prolonged stress is based on a model proposed by the Canadian endocrinologist Hans Selye.

Selye's general adaptation syndrome

In a series of experiments in which animals were presented with a series of stressors, Selye found a pattern of response that was consistent and regular. He found that the animals would first show signs of alarm, followed by resistance and then exhaustion. He called this staged process of response the 'general adaptation syndrome' (Selye, 1956).

The first stage – alarm – occurs when the animal first encounters and experiences the stressor. Resistance to it is deflated a little and the animal may experience a sense of shock. The ANS is aroused at this stage but produces a temporary lack of resistance. Further exposure to the stressor leads to an increase in resistance. It is as if the organism is reorienting itself or adapting its behaviour after exposure to an unexpected/unwanted stimulus. This resistance levels out until, eventually, with continued exposure to the stressor, the animal becomes exhausted. At this stage, resistance is minimal, the animal loses the ability to adapt and becomes ill.

However, not all animals, and not all humans, will behave in this way. Our experience of a stressor affects the way in which we respond to it. You might be inclined to run away from a man with a gun, but a soldier might view the event less emotionally. Each person's response is a way of coping with a stressor. Most of us are not soldiers and might either run away from a gunman or might freeze. A soldier, by means of his or her training, would confront the gunman. These two examples of response to stress have been described as fight or flight: we either flee a stressor or confront it. In the short term these coping mechanisms work: they return the body to its normal physiological state after an intense period of change. But if the stressor is continuous, this could have serious consequences and lead to potentially fatal illness such as a stroke or cardiac arrest, or other serious illnesses, and exacerbate other physical symptoms such as stomach ulcers.

Hormonal control of the stress response

One of the most important hormonal contributions to the body's response to stress involves adrenaline (also called epinephrine), which is secreted by the adrenal glands. These glands also release other chemicals in response to stressors such as norepinephrine and steroids. Why? Our response to stress involves expending energy: the body is readying itself for a fight or for escape, both of which need energy. Adrenaline helps release glucose that is stored in muscles (remember from Chapter 6 that glucose is the body's most important source of energy) and, therefore, helps provide the body with energy. The associated release of norepinephrine helps direct blood flow to the muscles which, again, readies the body for action.

The other important hormonal contributor to stress is cortisol. Cortisol is a steroid that is secreted, like adrenaline, by the adrenal glands. The technical term for it is a glucocorticoid because, again like adrenaline, it affects glucose metabolism. Glucocorticoids also serve the purpose of breaking down protein to provide energy, increasing blood flow and converting fats into an energy source. Receptors for these hormones are found in almost every cell in the body.

According to Selye (1976), an excess or prolonged secretion of glucocorticoids is responsible for the negative effects of stress. These effects include high blood pressure, damage to muscle tissue, immune system dysfunction, a form of diabetes, the slowing of wound healing, and infertility. All of these can have fairly harmful effects. The production of cortisol is also associated with severe memory dysfunction (De Kloet et al., 1999).

8.11 COPING WITH STRESS

Not all of us respond negatively to stress, although most of us probably do. There are events like rape, exposure to bank robberies, being involved in a motor vehicle accident, and so on, that can have severe consequences for mental health. People who have experienced these events show symptoms of post-traumatic stress disorder, a psychiatric condition characterised by persistent anxiety following a traumatic event. But our responses to less traumatic events, however (such as attending a job interview or sitting an exam) can, to some extent, be moderated by how we respond emotionally to them. This psychological component was missing from Selye's model but is one that explains individual differences in response to stressors.

One of the more important moderators of coping is the controllability of the stimulus. If the stressor, or its effects, can be controlled, its effect is lessened. An experiment in which rats were taught to minimise the effects of an electric shock, found that the animals developed fewer stomach ulcers than did those given no such control (Weiss, 1968). Having control over an unpleasant stimulus, such as a malodour, results in a greater feeling of dominance than if we had no control (Rotton, 1983). Our appraisal of a stressor as a stressor is also important. As you saw earlier in this chapter, Lazarus proposed that we respond emotionally to a stimulus or an event only after we have appraised it as being stressful. This process of cognition affects the levels of stress the person experiences.

In Lazarus and Folkman's (1984) model, cognitive appraisal entails the following two stages. The first involves evaluating the environment for threat and determining whether the environment contains a stimulus likely to be a stressor. The second involves assessing our ability to cope with that stressor if it is identified as a threat. If we perceive a threat but do not believe we have the resources to cope with it, we will experience high levels of stress; if the threat is extremely dangerous and we feel we are unable to cope, this will lead to the greatest level of stress. From snakes to exams, our interpretation of the stressor as threatening will determine how stressed we feel; for the ophidianaphobe, seeing a snake will be highly stressful; for those indifferent to snakes, the stress will be lower, if experienced at all. Similarly, some people will not react badly to stressors at work, although some will. A study of business people by Kobasa (1979), found that those who experienced less work-related stress were more likely to view stressors as challenging (rather than threatening) and as factors not to be avoided or become anxious about. These 'hardy' types also reported being able to exert control over these stressors. The way in which the stressor was perceived or appraised, therefore, determined its psychological impact (a point returned to a little later).

Stress and the immune system: psychoneuroimmunology

Glucocorticoids are not the only physical cause of stress. Stressors can also cause an impairment in the function of the immune system, the body's means of protecting us against infection from viruses, microbes and other parasites. As you saw in Chapters 1 and 2, psychoneuroimmunology is the study of the interaction between the immune system and behaviour, and stressors have been found to affect the production of chemicals by the immune system. By reducing the body's capacity to fight infection, stress becomes a harmful and potentially dangerous process.

Our immune system is a collection of organs and white blood cells that develop in the thymus gland and in bone marrow. Although the immune system's job is to protect us from invasion by foreign bodies, these foreign bodies have developed ways of circumventing parts of the system. The system, in turn, has evolved in other ways to prevent these foreign bodies infecting our body. The immune system is not constant but a constantly evolving protective mechanism.

The immune system responds in two ways to invasion: it recruits cells to fight the infection or it produces chemicals to do the same. These are called cell-mediated and chemically mediated reactions. Chemically mediated reactions involve the production of proteins called antibodies in response to an invading organism. Bacteria have proteins on their surface called antigens: these proteins help the immune system identify the material as an invader. The body has developed a way of identifying these antigens and responding to them by producing antibodies that kill invading micro-organisms. One type of antibody is called immunoglobulin, which is released into the body by B lymphocytes that develop in bone marrow. There are five basic types of immunoglobulin and all are similar except that they have a unique type of receptor at one end. This receptor binds with specific types of antigen so that when the bacterium is recognised, these antibodies are released and kill the bacteria or attract other white blood cells to the bacteria to help fight the invasion.

One widely studied antibody in biological psychology is secretory immunoglobulin A (sIgA), which is secreted by mucosal membranes in the body such as those covering parts of the respiratory tract and the gastrointestinal system. It appears to work by providing a barrier against infection and can be usefully measured from samples of saliva.

The second type of defence mechanism involves T lymphocytes, which are developed in the thymus gland. These cells help the body protect itself from fungi, viruses and complex parasites. When antigens bind with the antibodies on the surface of these cells, the cells either kill them or attract other white cells to do the job. Another type of cell that helps fight infection is the 'natural killer cell' which constantly roams around cell tissue. When these cells find an infected or cancerous cell, they surround and destroy it.

The immune system, however, can cause us harm though its activity. Allergies are a common example of this. Allergies result when antigens cause the immune system to overact; the overaction takes the form of the production of an immunoglobulin, which causes an inflammatory response.

Why the immune system behaves in this way to often apparently harmless substances, such as peanuts, is largely unknown.

The immune system can also harm us in a second way: it can attack its own cells. Autoimmune diseases, as they are called, attack tissue that contains specific proteins although why they should do this is unclear. Such responses often occur after a viral or bacterial infection. Perhaps having learned to identify the invading antigen, the immune system develops a line of defence that attacks one of it own (harmless) proteins and treats it as a foreign body. Examples of autoimmune diseases include rheumatoid arthritis, AIDS and multiple sclerosis.

8.12 WHAT CONTROLS THE IMMUNE SYSTEM?

If stress is associated with a reduction in immune system function, what controls the body's reduction? The key factor appears to be the glucocorticoids, which suppress the function of the immune system. All white blood cells contain glucocorticoid receptors, but glucocorticoid secretion itself is controlled by the brain. One region that appears to contain more corticosteroid receptors than others is the hippocampus (De Kloet *et al.*, 1999).

Stress and the immune system

Different stressors appear to affect the function of the immune system differently. Acute short-term stressors, for example, are associated with an increase in natural killer cells and sIgA levels (Delahanty *et al.*, 1996) but chronic stressors such as bereavement are associated with reduced immune system function. In one study of the ability of wounds to heal in people who looked after relatives with Alzheimer's disease – a stressful occupation – caregivers' wounds took nine days longer to heal than did those in a stress-free control group (Kiecolt-Glaser *et al.*, 1995).

Exams and oral presentations also seem to have different effects on the immune system. When students were asked to present their work orally to their fellow students, an increase in sIgA was found. But during examination periods, however, sIgA levels decreased (Evans, *et al.*, 1993; Evans *et al.*, 1994), suggesting that the long-term and short-term stressors exert different immune system effects. Some of the other factors that can produce stress or can be associated with it are described next.

Infectious disease

The Kiecolt-Glaser study described in the last section highlighted the very real, physical effect of experiencing a chronic stressor. Similar studies have reported that people experiencing stressors can develop diseases or infections. For example, medical students were more likely to contract infectious diseases during the examination period than before this period (Glaser *et al.*, 1987).

Reasoning that stress would produce an increase in respiratory infection, Stone *et al.* (1987) asked people to keep a diary of daily hassles and symptoms of illness over a 12-week period, and monitored whether exposure to stressors would be associated with respiratory illness. Exposure to an infectious agent leads to the body incubating the foreign body so that symptoms are seen several days after the infection has entered the body. As predicted, there was a significant correlation between stressful events and respiratory infection occurring three to five days later. The researchers hypothesised that the stress-related illness was brought about by decreased production of immunoglobulin.

Stone *et al.*'s (1987) study, however, was correlational and based on self-reports of illness and stressors. In an ingenious experiment, Cohen *et al.* (1998), exposed individuals to one of two common cold viruses, measured various personality and behavioural variables (such as sex, alcohol consumption and sleep pattern), and monitored which individuals developed a respiratory infection that led to the cold. A total of 84 per cent became infected, but only 40 per cent developed a cold. Those who did were reported to have endured chronic life stressors for at least a month. Participants who had endured little stress or experienced the effect of stressors for less than a month were less likely to develop the cold. Other factors positively related to developing a cold were smoking, fewer than three exercise sessions per week, poor sleep, drinking fewer than two alcoholic drinks a day, ingesting less than 85 mg of vitamin C and being introverted. Cohen *et al.*'s (1998) study is informative because it directly manipulated the infection and observed the effects of stressors and other relevant factors on the development of these infections.

Bereavement

The loss of a close relative or a loved one can have devastating psychological consequences. There is also evidence that the death of a partner is associated with impaired immune system function, and that the incidence of illness increases in people who are widowed, compared to those whose partners are alive and well. To test the hypothesis that bereavement is a stressor with significant consequences for immune system functioning, Schleifer *et al.* (1983) took blood samples from men whose wives were dying of cancer. They compared the levels of blood lymphocytes before the death of the spouse and then two months after the death. The researchers found that the level of blood lymphocytes was lower after the death than before, suggesting that the bereavement led to a susceptibility to infection.

Personality

In the late 1950s, two researchers proposed that our susceptibility to illness and to stress may be determined by personality type. Friedman and Rosenman (1959) identified a personality type that was specifically susceptible to coronary heart disease (CHD). CHD results from a lack of oxygen to the heart (cardiac arrest) or the brain (stroke or cerebrovascular accident), and two risk factors for these are high blood pressure and high levels of blood cholesterol. The type of personality prone to develop CHD was termed Type A and the pattern of behaviour in these people was characterised by excessive competition, intensiveness, impatience, hostility, fast movement and rapid speech. As you saw in Chapter 2, those who showed the Type A behaviour of competitiveness showed increased heart rate during a competitive racing game (Harrison *et al.*, 2001). The other personality type Friedman and Rosenman identified was Type B, a pattern of behaviour characterised by a more easy-going style. Type B people were less competitive, more patient and tolerant, and moved and spoke more slowly.

The connection between Type A behaviour and CHD is strong. A study of 3154 healthy men who were observed over a period of eight and a half years found that those exhibiting Type A behaviour were twice as likely to develop CHD than were those not exhibiting this pattern (Rosenman *et al.*, 1975). However, the picture is more complex than this. Studies have found, for example, that although Type A personalities are more susceptible to CHD, their recovery rates after the illness are faster than for Type B people (Ragland and Brand, 1988). Other studies have found no difference between the two types in the occurrence of CHD (Dimsdale, 1988).

There are other personality characteristics, however, that seem to be risk factors or protective factors for CHD. Submissiveness, for example, is one characteristic that has recently been observed to be associated with reduced likelihood of CHD (Whiteman *et al.*, 1997). Submissive people let others dominate, prefer to stay in the background and have low self-confidence. This behaviour is different to Type B behaviour, however, because it is not characterised by the Type B person's sense of security.

Williams *et al.* (1980) suggested that one aspect of the Type A personality – hostility – is of particular importance in CHD. Several studies carried out in the early to mid-1980s confirmed that hostility was an important risk factor for CHD, but more recent studies have not.

Work, unemployment and stress

Occupational stress refers to the degree of stress experienced by members of different professions. This area of research is a popular one in organisational psychology and the Whitehall study of CHD in British civil servants is a good example of the type of work carried out in this area. This study has shown that the lower the grade of employment in the civil service, the higher the mortality rate from CHD. A subsequent study found that CHD-related mortality could also be predicted by high psychosocial pressure and low control over the work environment (Marmot *et al.*, 1997).

There appears to be a significant relationship between the number of hours worked and the symptoms of physical and mental ill-health an employee experiences. The extent of this relationship, however, is unclear: most conclude that there is a significant relationship between these factors but that this relationship is not particularly strong (Sparks *et al.*, 1997). Recent studies from Japan, however, suggest that individuals who work in excess of 11 hours a day are more at risk of myocardial infarction than are those who work a moderate number of hours (Sokejima and Kagamimori, 1998). In Japan, it is thought that long working hours can cause sudden fatal heart attacks, called 'karoshi' (Uehata, 1991; cited in Kageyama *et al.*, 1997). Kageyama *et al.*'s study of working commuters suggests that those with the longest commuting times and who work the most overtime, show greater variability in heart rate than do those who commute and work less.

The converse to heavy workloads – having none or having lost them: unemployment – is also associated with an increase in ill-health and psychological disturbance (Warr, 1987). Employment allows us to earn money, and gives structure and meaning to our lives. Unemployment, however, takes away these positive benefits and can result in stress. One consequence of unemployment, for example, is increased isolation and loss of social context (Donovan and Oddy, 1982). A longitudinal study of 1060 young people who were monitored over five years following their final term at school in northern Sweden found that unemployment was correlated significantly with increases in depressive symptoms, even when initial health was accounted for (Hammarstrom and Janlert, 1997).

SOME USEFUL FURTHER READING

EMOTION
Dalgleish, T. and Power, M. (1999) *Handbook of Cognition and Emotion.* Chichester: John Wiley.

Davidson, R.J. and Irwin, W. (1999) The functional neuroanatomy of emotion and affective style. *Trends in Cognitive Science*, 44–54.

LeDoux, J. (1998) *The Emotional Brain.* London: Weidenfeld and Nicolson.

LeDoux, J. (2002) Emotion, memory and the brain. *Scientific American* 12(1), 62–71.

Power, M. and Dalgleish, T. (1997) *Cognition and Emotion*. Hove: The Psychology Press.

STRESS
Kiecolt-Glaser, J.K., McGuire, L., Robles, T.F. and Glaser, R. (2002) Psychoneuroimmunology: psychological influences on immune function and health. *Journal of Consulting and Clinical Psychology* 70(3), 537–47.
Sarafino, E.P. (2001) *Health Psychology: Biopsychosocial Interactions* (fourth edition). Chichester: John Wiley.
Smith, T.W. and Ruiz, J.M. (2002) Psychosocial influences on the development and course of coronary heart disease: current status and implications for research and practice. *Journal of Consulting and Clinical Psychology* 70(3), 548–68.
Sternberg, E. and Gold, P.W. (2002) The mind–body interaction in disease. *Scientific American* 12(1), 82–9.

SOME USEFUL JOURNALS TO BROWSE

Biological Psychology
Brain
British Journal of Health Psychology
British Medical Journal
Cognition and Emotion
Health Psychology
International Journal of Stress
Journal of Abnormal Psychology
Journal of Occupational Health Psychology
Journal of Occupational Medicine
Journal of Personality and Social Psychology
Nature Neuroscience
Personality and Individual Differences
Physiology and Behaviour
Psychological Science
Psychology, Health and Medicine
Psychosomatic Medicine
Social Science and Medicine
Stress and Health
Stress Medicine
The Lancet
Trends in Cognitive Sciences
Work and Stress

Language and Other Higher Functions

WHAT YOU WILL FIND IN THIS CHAPTER
- a definition of language
- a description of brain development and language
- a description of language disorders arising from brain injury, such as aphasia and acquired dyslexia
- a review of the symptoms and possible biological causes of developmental dyslexia
- a review of neuroimaging studies of language production and comprehension
- a review of the biological basis of intelligence and reasoning

WHAT YOU SHOULD BE ABLE TO DO AFTER READING THE CHAPTER
- understand how the development of the brain affects the localisation of language processes
- describe the major features of the main aphasias and the dyslexias
- outline some of the possible biological causes of developmental dyslexia, including visual system impairment, cerebellar dysfunction and lateralisation failure
- be aware of the major findings of neuroimaging studies of language and how these highlight regions of the brain involved in specific language tasks
- be aware of the neurobiological basis of intelligence and reasoning

9.1 LANGUAGE AND COMMUNICATION

Words are the means by which most humans communicate. Words make up language but they are not the only means we have of communicating with other human beings. Congenitally deaf people use gestures to communicate with others; hearing individuals also gesture to make a point; facial expression, as you saw in the chapter on emotion (Chapter 8), is often used as a social tool to signal an emotion or a feeling. There is no clear definition of what makes a language but a rough description would be that it is a system of visual and/or vocal symbols that have meaning to the user and the recipient.

Reading is probably our most sophisticated use of language; it is a very artificial activity, unlike vocalising, and it has to be learned. A child learns to read after it has learned to speak. The development of language appears to be dependent on the development of the cerebral hemispheres. What is called our 'language centre' (but it really is not) is usually described as being localised in the left hemisphere, but a more accurate way of phrasing this concept would be to say that the regions responsible for specific aspects of language processing are localised, in the majority of right-handed people, in the left hemisphere. However, even the right hemisphere can undertake some language functions such as appreciating metaphors (Bottini *et al.*, 1994), the processing of prosody and the affective tone of speech (Pell and Baum, 1997) and it may even undertake the majority of these functions if the left hemisphere is damaged at an early age.

9.2 THE DEVELOPMENT OF LANGUAGE

In 1967, Lenneberg, in his book *The Biological Foundations of Language*, argued that the functional lateralisation of language – one hemisphere's superiority for processing language – begins at the same time as the child begins to acquire language and is complete at puberty. This conclusion was based on studies showing that in half a sample of children with lesions to the right or left sides of the brain, language was delayed if the lesion occurred in the first two years of life. The other half developed language normally (Basser, 1962). In adults and adolescents, however, language difficulties were associated with left hemisphere lesions whereas mild language difficulties were associated with right hemisphere lesions. Lenneberg thus argued that there was a sensitive period during which language should be acquired and lateralisation would develop.

These lateralisation milestones were challenged by Krashen (1973), who argued that the hemispheres of the brain were equipotential at birth – that is, each hemisphere was capable of undertaking the function for which the other becomes specialised. According to Krashen, the critical period for lateralisation was complete by the age of five or six years. If lesions to the right hemisphere occurred before the age of five, the child would show symptoms of aphasia, a disorder involving the inability to produce or comprehend speech. If damage occurred after the age of five, no deficits in speech would arise, suggesting that the normal left-for-language functional asymmetry had developed and was relatively complete. Krashen was involved in the study of an unusual case in which a young girl had been deprived of auditory stimulation and had failed to develop normal language. This case study appeared to illustrate how important linguistic stimulation was during early language development.

The case of Genie

Genie was a 13-year-old girl who had been chronically abused since infancy. The girl's father had harnessed her to a potty in a room in the back of the family house since she was at least 20 months old, and deprived her of any linguistic stimulation. She slept in a crib covered with wire mesh. Her father was intolerant of noise and would beat her whenever she made any sound. Her mother fed her a diet of baby food, cereals and, occasionally, boiled eggs. When eventually spotted by social workers, the girl was four and a half feet tall and weighed four stone. She could not eat solid food and had nearly two complete sets of teeth. She was 13 years and 9 months old.

Her most remarkable psychological feature was her almost complete lack of language. She could not talk and had a vocabulary of about 20 words (she could understand concepts such as 'red', 'blue', 'green'). Her speech production was limited to 'nomore', 'stopit' and other negatives. Following her discovery, she was admitted to the Children's Hospital in Los Angeles for treatment. Researchers were interested in how handicapped Genie's language had become and what possible recovery could be made from such gross linguistic impairment (Fromkin et al., 1972/3; Curtiss, 1977). There had been isolated instances of 'accidental' cases of language deprivation before. Victor, the 'wild boy of Aveyron', for example, who had been found in 1800 lurking naked in front of a cottage in the Languedoc region of France. He had spent his 12 years from infancy living in the woods, surviving on a diet of acorns and potatoes. He had had his throat cut as a toddler and had been left to die. Victor had no language and, while he never learned to speak, he achieved a rudimentary ability to spell.

A year after she was discovered, Genie's language ability underwent marked improvement. Her ability to structure according to rules was the equivalent of a 20 year old's and her spatial ability placed her in the adult ability category. She could tell the difference between singular and plural words and positive and negative sentences, and could understand some prepositions. Her speech was limited to one- or two-word sentences, however, eventually becoming very descriptive and concrete ('big rectangular pillow', 'very, very, very dark-green box'). The 'explosion' of language, normally expected after such dramatic improvements, never materialised.

It became clear that Genie could develop new but basic language skills. She made a dramatic recovery from the time of her discovery to the time when the scientists had to abandon their studies. Yet, her language never fully recovered, remaining steadfastly descriptive, almost at the level one would expect primates to achieve with intensive language training. Her study showed, however, the remarkable, devastating effects of linguistic and auditory deprivation on the development of language ability.

9.3 PLASTICITY AND LANGUAGE DEVELOPMENT

In a series of famous experiments, Dennis and Whitaker (1976) and Woods (1980) found that the incidence of aphasia following right hemisphere lesions was greater during infancy than if the lesions had occurred later in life.

Similar findings were reported by other researchers who found that left hemisphere lesions produced the greatest deficits in language and speech if they occurred after the age of five or six years (Vargha-Khadem *et al.*, 1985).

Another source of data suggesting a critical period for the development of functional asymmetry is found in studies of hemispherectomy, where one hemisphere is removed for medical reasons, usually because of the growth of a large tumour or because of intractable epilepsy. In adults, left hemispherectomies result in fairly severe aphasia; left hemispherectomies in children, however, are associated with almost complete recovery of language function (Searleman, 1977).

What these data suggest is that the brain has a degree of plasticity when it is developing. That is, specialised functions have not developed in any sophisticated way in one or other hemisphere during early growth. After a specific age, however, this specialisation has begun but one or other hemisphere can undertake the functions of the other if the other is damaged.

Studies have shown that early brain lesions in children between 13 and 36 months are associated with a delay in the development of expressive vocabulary, especially if damage is to the left side. However, there seems to be little effect on the next stage of language development: sentence production (Vicari *et al.*, 2000). If the damage occurs later, in adulthood, then it is hypothesised that the right hemisphere undertakes the language functions of the left.

Is half a brain enough?

In a novel experiment to explore the nature of plasticity, Hertz-Pannier *et al.* (2002) studied six children who underwent left hemispherectomy for intractable epilepsy and monitored their brain activity during language tasks before and after the surgery. They hypothesised that if the brain shows evidence of plasticity, then we might expect the right hemisphere to take over the language function of the left. They used fMRI to study the children at age six years and 10 months, and found the typical left lateralisation for language tasks such as word generation; there was little right hemisphere activity.

Following surgery, receptive language recovered quickly but expressive language and reading were slower to recover. When fMRI scanning was undertaken again at ten years 6 months, there was a shift in activity to the right hemisphere during expressive and receptive language tasks. The regions that were activated – the inferior frontal temporal and parietal cortices – were analogous to those in the left hemisphere prior to the surgery.

This activation in the right hemisphere is also seen in adults recovering from aphasia. For example, Cappa *et al.* (1997) found that activation in the right temporoparietal region during the acute phase of recovery predicted improvement in auditory comprehension later on. More recently, a group of researchers has found that a period of intensive training in a group of patients who had suffered a stroke, destroying parts of the left frontal cortex, and who had difficulty in comprehending speech, led to increased activation in a bilateral network of regions associated with language. There were also increases in right hemisphere regions.

A recent case study highlights how successful language development could be following radical surgery (Battro, 2000). Nico was an Italian boy who was born with left hemiplegia (loss of voluntary motor control). He managed to walk by age one and a half but developed intractable epilepsy at 22 months. Drugs and selective lesioning of the brain failed to halt the epilepsy and so, as a last resort and with the permission of Nico's parents, surgeons performed a right hemidecortication (removal of the right cerebral cortex) when the boy was three years and seven months.

Nico recovered well and did not lose his speech. His IQ was 107 and he learned to develop the basics of spelling and grammar at the same age as normal children through the use of a computer. He is still behind other children in his ability to draw and has difficulty forming the letters of the alphabet and numbers with his right hand. The outcome of Nico's surgery suggests that the right hemisphere may be what Popper and Eccles (1977) have described as a 'minor brain'. Without it, Nico learned to develop the important function of language although his 'right hemisphere' functions such as drawing are impaired.

9.4 LANGUAGE DISORDERS

Normal language processing is the result of a complex interaction of sensory, motor and memory processes. Impairments in any of these processes can lead to language disorders such as aphasia (a disturbance in the comprehension or production of speech), dysgraphia (impairment in writing) or dyslexia (disorder of reading). One of the most important of these disorders is aphasia because it can accompany cerebrovascular disorders (stroke) and much of the rehabilitation after stroke is designed to help the patient recover some aspect of language. Aphasia is also important because it can help us understand which regions of the brain may be sufficient for a specific language function to occur. Attempts to localise aphasic symptoms to particular regions of the brain are, however, problematic. As Jackson noted in 1874, 'to locate the damage which destroys speech, and to localize speech, are two different things'.

Aphasia

The term aphasia literally means 'complete loss of language', but a more accurate description of the language difficulties arising from brain injury would be dysphasia (meaning a 'partial lack of language') because patients with aphasia retain some degree of linguistic ability. The term aphasia, however, is the one that is commonly used to describe a specific disturbance in the comprehension or production of spoken, written or signed language. Its diagnosis is made only in the absence of sensory impairments (poor vision or hearing), perceptual impairments (agnosia), impaired movement (apraxia) or thought disturbances (autism, dementia or schizophrenia, for example).

Various sub-types of aphasia have been described, each with its own specific cluster of symptoms, and each associated with damage to a particular region of the cortex. These regions are generally found in the left hemisphere, near the Sylvian fissure. Structures including Broca's area, Wernicke's area, Heschl's gyrus, the planum temporale, the supramarginal, angular and temporal gyri, and the frontal gyri are the key regions which, if damaged, produce disruptions to language. As you will see in a later section, these regions are also involved in language processing in undamaged brains. Some of the symptoms and regions of damage of the various types of aphasia (sensory, production, conduction, deep, transcortical sensory, transcortical motor and global) are summarised in Table 9.1 and the major brain regions involved in aphasia can be seen in Figure 9.1.

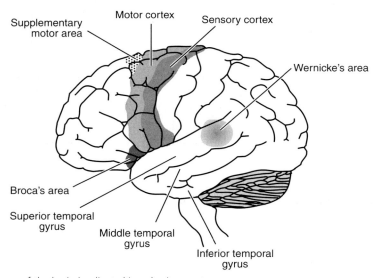

Fig 9.1 Areas of the brain implicated in aphasic symptoms

Table 9.1 Types of aphasia, their primary symptoms and the site of the associated brain lesion

Type of aphasia	Primary symptoms	Brain lesion to:
Sensory (Wernicke's) aphasia	General comprehension deficits, neologisms, word retrieval deficits, semantic paraphasias	posterior perisylvian region – postero-superior temporal, opercular supramarginal, angular and posterior insular gyri; planum temporale
Production (Broca's) aphasia	Speech production deficits, abnormal prosody, impaired syntactic comprehension	posterior part of the inferior frontal and precentral convolutions of the left hemisphere
Conduction aphasia	Naming deficits and impaired ability to repeat non-meaningful single words and word strings	arcuate fasciculus; posterior parietal and temporal regions – left auditory complex; insula; supramarginal gyrus
Deep dysphasia	Word-repetition deficits: verbal (semantic) paraphasia	temporal lobe, especially regions that mediate phonological processing
Transcortical sensory aphasia	Impaired comprehension, naming, reading and writing; semantic irrelevancies in speech	temporoparieto-occipital junction of the left hemisphere
Transcortical motor aphasia	Transient mutism and telegrammatic, dysprosodic speech	connection between Broca's area and the supplementary motor area; medial frontal lobe; regions anterolateral to the left hemisphere's frontal horn
Global aphasia	Generalised deficits in comprehension, repetition, naming and speech production	left perisylvian region, white matter, basal ganglia and thalamus

Sensory (Wernicke's) aphasia

Persons with sensory, or Wernicke's, aphasia are generally unable to comprehend speech produced by other people or themselves. Patients can produce speech fluently but the words are typically jargon-like. For example:

Doctor: 'What kind of work did you do before you came into the hospital?'
Patient: 'Never, now mista oyge I wanna tell you this happened when happened when he rent. His – his kell come down here and is – he got ren something. It happened. In these ropiers were with him for hi – is friend – like was. And it just happened so I don't know, he did not bring around anything. And he did not pay it. And he roden all o these arranjen from the pedis on from iss pescid. In these floors now and so. He hadn't had em round here.'

(Kertesz, 1981)

The locus of damage in Wernicke's aphasia is the first and posterior part of the second convolution of the superior temporal gyrus next to Heschl's gyrus (part of the auditory association cortex), and the planum temporale in the left hemisphere (Naeser *et al.*, 1981). The area is also called Wernicke's area, after Carl Wernicke who reported patients with the disorder that takes his name.

This region of the temporal lobe may be that which allows us to remember the constituent sounds of speech, and may mediate the link between the auditory representations of words and their meaning. The clinical findings are complemented by imaging studies that show increases in activation in Wernicke's area when people perform language tasks that have a semantic component (Petersen *et al.*, 1988). Object naming is associated with a spread of neural activity from Wernicke's area to the frontal motor systems responsible for activation of the muscles in the production of speech.

While the problems experienced by Wernicke's aphasics are essentially sensory, involving 'semantic-lexical' aspects of linguistic processing, problems with the articulatory aspect of linguistic processing are characteristic of patients with Broca's aphasia.

Production (Broca's) aphasia

Production or Broca's aphasia is also called non-fluent aphasia, expressive aphasia or motor aphasia, and describes difficulty in speech production. Symptoms can range from a complete inability to speak, to the ability to produce speech only with considerable effort. When speech is produced, it is slow and laboured. Language comprehension at a simple level, however, remains fairly normal.

The speech of a patient with Broca's aphasia is characterised by extreme verbal economy, an omission of prepositions and definite articles, little grammatical construction – it is 'telegrammatic' – and abnormal prosody. While patients have intact comprehension, their understanding may be impaired by syntactic ambiguities. The sentence 'The dog ate the bone' would cause a Broca's aphasic no problem, for example. It is clear that, in this sentence, the bone can be eaten by the dog, but the dog cannot be eaten by the bone. A more syntactically ambiguous sentence, such as 'The dog chased the cat', may not be so easily understood. The cat can chase the dog as easily as the dog can chase the cat.

Injury in Broca's aphasia is to the posterior part of the third frontal convolution and the adjacent part of the second frontal and precentral convolutions of the left hemisphere. As you saw in Chapter 1, Broca had originally observed a failure in speech production in patients who, at post-mortem, showed lesions to the left frontal cortex. This region, which is anterior to the motor cortex (specifically the region of the motor cortex responsible for facial movements), is labelled Broca's area.

However, it was Wernicke (1874) who explained the association between the cortical damage of Broca's aphasics and their symptoms. He suggested that sensory experiences are stored in the cortical regions adjacent to the areas responsible for those functions. As Broca's area is located near the region of the motor cortex responsible for the movements of the mouth, damage to this region will result in destruction of the memory traces of the movements required to produce speech. The impairment in articulation following damage to Broca's area is more variable than that of the language disturbances resulting from lesions to Wernicke's area.

Conduction aphasia

Patients with conduction aphasia display apparently normal speech comprehension and production. However, they are impaired at naming objects or repeating non-meaningful words and word sequences. The ability to repeat colloquialisms and stock phrases, however, may be preserved (Goodglass, 1993). The following example is an exchange between doctor and patient where the patient's task is to repeat what the doctor is saying (Margolin and Walker, 1981, cited in Carlson, 2001).

Doctor: 'Bicycle'
Patient: 'Bicycle'
Doctor: 'Hippopotamus'
Patient: 'Hippopotamus'
Doctor: 'Blaynge'
Patient: 'I didn't get it'
Doctor: 'Up and down'
Patient: 'Up and down'
Doctor: 'Yellow, big, south'
Patient: 'Yellen ... Can't get it'

Patients with conduction aphasia are aware of their language problems and will often make attempts to correct their errors. If presented with alternative pronunciations, patients are generally able to reject obviously inappropriate alternatives and will often accept the correct ones; this is taken as indicating that the phonological processing skills of these patients, their ability to process and integrate the sounds of speech, are intact and that the problem is confined to the process of retrieval (Goodglass, 1993).

Wernicke (1874) proposed that conduction aphasia was due to a disconnection of the arcuate fasciculus – the bundle of fibres that connects Broca's and Wernicke's areas. Later studies provided support for the hypothesis. Damasio and Damasio (1980), for example, found that patients showing symptoms of conduction aphasia were found to have damage to the association fibres of the inferior parietal lobe, which normally connects Wernicke's and Broca's areas.

Geschwind (1965) developed Wernicke's proposal into a fuller model of language processing. Geschwind suggested that when a conduction aphasic hears a word representing an object (e.g. bicycle), the patient produces a mental representation of the object. Information about this image is then sent from the visual association cortex to Broca's area (thus bypassing the damaged arcuate fasciculus) in order to initiate the movements necessary to produce the sounds that comprise the word. This strategy is only effective when repeating meaningful words and phrases, however. If the perception of a non-word fails to produce a visual image, the patient is unable to reproduce the word.

Dyslexia

The term dyslexia refers to a disorder involving impaired reading; it is one of the most common language disorders seen in children and adults. The incidence of the disorder lies between 5 and 17.5 per cent and boys are thought to be more affected than girls. Many different types of dyslexia have been described but there are two broad categories: acquired dyslexia and developmental dyslexia. Acquired dyslexia describes a reading impairment resulting from brain injury in individuals with previously normal language. Developmental dyslexia refers to a 'difficulty in learning to read despite adequate intelligence and appropriate educational opportunity' (Critchley, 1973). The types of dyslexia and their symptoms are described in Table 9.2.

Acquired dyslexia

The most important forms of dyslexia that result from brain injury are visual word form dyslexia, phonological dyslexia, surface dyslexia and deep

Table 9.2 The dyslexias and the brain regions associated with them

Types of dyslexia	Primary symptoms	Brain regions implicated
The acquired dyslexias		
Visual word form dyslexia	Impaired sight reading; some decoding is possible	Disconnection between the angular gyrus of the dominant hemisphere and the visual input system
Phonological dyslexia	Deficits in reading pseudo-words and non-words	Temporal lobe of the dominant hemisphere?
Surface dyslexia	Tendency to produce regularisation errors in the reading of irregular words	?
Deep dyslexia	Semantic substitutions, impaired reading of abstract words, inability to read non-words	Extensive damage to the dominant hemisphere
Developmental dyslexia	Impaired reading and spelling of words/non-words/pseudo-words, poor phonological processing skills, sequencing and short-term memory, some visuoperceptual defects	Temporoparietal regions of the dominant hemisphere

dyslexia. Visual word form dyslexia, one of three different types of reading impairment identified in Marshall and Newcombe's (1966) famous studies of missile wound injuries, describes an inability to recognise words immediately. Readers are able to make sense of the word gradually by naming each letter. Sometimes a patient might commit a letter-naming mistake, pronouncing 'c, a, t … cat' when the word to be read is 'mat'. The disorder is thought to result from a disconnection between the region of the left hemisphere, which mediates the recognition of word forms (the so-called visual word form area) and the visual input system (Warrington and Shallice, 1980). We'll return to the visual word form area in the section on neuroimaging and language below.

Phonological dyslexia refers to an inability to read pseudo-words and non-words, and is relatively rare (although phonological deficits are also seen in developmental dyslexia, described below). Phonological dyslexia provides evidence that whole-word reading and phonological reading involve different brain mechanisms. Phonetic reading, which is the only way we can read non-words or words we have not yet learned, entails some sort of letter-to-sound decoding. It also requires more than decoding of the sounds produced by single letters, because, for example, some sounds are transcribed as two-letter sequences (such as 'th' or 'sh') and the addition of the letter 'e' to the end of a word lengthens an internal vowel ('can' becomes 'cane').

Surface dyslexia is the inability to recognise and read words based on their physical characteristics. Individuals are able to apply the grapheme–phoneme correspondence rule (translating script into sound accurately), to regularly spelled words but have difficulties with applying the same rule to irregular words (so, 'yacht' is pronounced as it reads and sounds: [yaked], rather than yot; ache is read as [aikie], and so on). An over-reliance on reading by sound is the characteristic feature of surface dyslexia.

Deep dyslexia refers to a severe inability to read. Concrete words can sometimes be read but are commonly replaced by semantically related words. For example, a patient would read 'sleep' when the word is 'dream' or 'danger' instead of 'strife' (Coltheart *et al.*, 1980). Abstract words are rarely pronounced accurately and neither are pronounceable non-words. Words are often substituted for grammatically different ones. The word wise would be read as wisdom and warmth as warm. The deficit in deep dyslexia indicates an inability to apply grapheme–phoneme correspondence rules.

Developmental dyslexia: symptoms

The symptoms of developmental dyslexia resemble those of the acquired dyslexias but they are not caused by injury to the brain. Developmental dyslexia first manifests itself in childhood and tends to occur in families, which suggests (but only suggests) the presence of a genetic (and hence biological) component (Grigorenko *et al.*, 1997).

A fairly constant feature of developmental dyslexia is poor appreciation of the phonological features of sound – that is, poor phonological awareness. The segmentation of words into sounds, being aware of alliteration, and the ability to name objects quickly, are all impaired in developmental dyslexia. If children are asked to transpose the first sounds of the words 'mustard' and 'salad' (thereby producing 'sustard' and 'malad'), those with developmental dyslexia are very poor at this (Brunswick *et al.*). Similarly, individuals with developmental dyslexia may be unable to perform phonological tasks such as indicating what word is left when you take either the first or last sound away from a spoken word such as 'mice'.

There also seems to be a deficit in the verbal or phonological memory of developmental dyslexics. For example, several studies have shown that these individuals have a poorer memory span than good readers for letter strings, words in a sentence and strings of digits. The stimuli do not have to be printed, the deficit is purely language-based; memory for unfamiliar faces or abstract patterns is intact (Lieberman *et al.*, 1982).

Developmental dyslexia and the angular gyrus

A study of cerebral blood flow in 17 male dyslexics and a control group of 14 men, found that blood flow to the superior part of the temporal lobe – a region called the angular gyrus – increased in normal readers with good reading performance. Good reading skill was associated with greater blood flow to this area (Rumsey *et al.*, 1999). However, similar blood flow to this area was associated with poor reading skill in the dyslexic sample. This suggested that the good readers relied on this region to read and the region undertook the task adequately, but when the dyslexic readers also relied on the same region, it contributed to the task very poorly. Rumsey *et al.* suggest, therefore, that there is a functional 'lesion' in this region of the brains of people showing developmental dyslexia: the reliance on this area actually impairs performance in developmental dyslexia because the area itself is dysfunctional in some way.

Geschwind's (1965) model argued that the angular gyrus plays a role in mediating the relationship between the written aspects of language processing, which occur at the extrastriate sites (in particular, a region known as the lingual gyrus), and the lexical or linguistic representations found in or around the posterior superior temporal gyrus. This model predicts that these two areas should be connected in the intact brain. There is evidence of a breakdown in communication between these two areas in dyslexic readers (Horowitz *et al.*, 1998). The activation at the angular gyrus and the superior temporal lobe was found to be present in normal readers during word and non-word reading, but weak in dyslexic participants.

To examine whether this connectivity was specific to the phonological aspects of reading, Pugh *et al.* (2000) compared neuronal activation in impaired and normal readers who completed language tasks requiring minimal to considerable phonological processing. If tasks are print-related and involve no processing of the phonology of words, then there should be evidence of connectivity/activation between the angular gyrus and the superior temporal lobe in dyslexic participants. This is indeed what the study showed. There was disruption in the connections between the two regions in dyslexic participants when the tasks required phonological processing. However, when tasks did not involve phonological processing there was strong activation in both areas in normal and dyslexic readers. Is this poor phonological processing the cause of the reading disorder?

Developmental dyslexia and visual system pathways

Some psychologists have argued that phonological impairments do not explain the persistent and severe nature of dyslexia (Hulme and Roodenrys, 1995). Reading is a complex task that requires phonology, memory and visual perception, and there are various theories that attempt to explain developmental dyslexia in terms of dysfunctional neuronal systems in several areas of the brain (Habib, 2000). Stein and his colleagues (Stein and Walsh, 1997), for example, have suggested that developmental dyslexia is associated with poor visual processing, specifically poor visual direction sense, binocular convergence and visual fixation.

Stein's view argues that dyslexics are unable to process fast, incoming sensory information adequately in visual form. Most information from the retina to the cortex via the thalamus travels through one of three visual system pathways. One of these systems – the magnocellular (M) pathway – is thought to carry visual information about space, such as movement, depth and the relationships between the positions of stimuli as you saw in Chapter 5. Some researchers have implicated a malfunctioning M pathway in dyslexia but have had difficulty in explaining why the defective pathway makes reading difficult. Studies have shown that poor visual fixation, poor eye tracking from left to right and poor binocular convergence appear to hinder the development of normal reading (Eden *et al.* 1994).

In a functional Magnetic Resonance Imaging (fMRI) study of developmental dyslexics' ability to process visual motion, Eden *et al.* (1996) found that moving stimuli (such as dots) failed to activate the cortical area that receives projections from the magnocellular pathway (area V5 in the visual cortex). In competent readers, this area was activated in both hemispheres during the task. Furthermore, the presentation of stationary patterns did not produce different patterns of brain activation in dyslexics and controls, suggesting that the dyslexic sample had difficulties specifically with attending to moving stimuli. In a recent ERP study of good and poor congenitally deaf readers, an absence of contrast-sensitive responses at occipital areas in the early stages of visual perception was characteristic of the poor readers (Samar *et al.*, 2002). Given that the M pathway mediates this early perceptual response, it may also be impaired in deaf poor readers.

One recent hypothesis suggests that the M pathway plays an important role in selective attention. The reasoning is that the pathway acts as an attentional spotlight that focuses on important stimuli and ignores all the clutter surrounding these stimuli. To test this hypothesis, Vidyasagar and Pammer (1999) asked 21 reading-impaired children and age-matched normal readers to complete a standard visual search task that required participants to locate a stimulus characterised by a combination of colour and form (for example, looking for a grey triangle in a background of grey circles). The greater the number of distractors in this task, the greater the number of errors made by the reading-impaired group. When there were fewer than 36 distractors, the impaired readers did as well as their age-matched counterparts. When the number increased to 70, a significantly greater number of errors was committed by the impaired reading group, suggesting to the authors that in the dyslexic group, visual search mechanisms are compromised when a visual scene is cluttered. Because reading places great demands on the attentional spotlight – which detects the conjunction of features – an impairment in this process may be explained by deficits in the system that turns on and operates the spotlight.

Cellular anomalies

There may also be differences between normal and dyslexic readers at the structural, cellular level (Galaburda *et al.*, 1985). These researchers found that a part of the thalamus projected to by the magnocellular pathway was disordered in five dyslexics; this region was 20 per cent smaller than that of a control group. A reduction in the number of cells in a similar area has also been reported (Rae *et al.*, 1998). While it is too early to conclude for certain that this visual pathway is responsible for the impairments seen in dyslexia, the evidence suggests that some form of perceptual impairment related to vision may contribute to disordered reading.

Developmental dyslexia and the cerebellum

It has been estimated, however, that a quarter of dyslexics do not have an M pathway deficit. An impaired M pathway cannot, therefore, explain the reading deficits of all dyslexic individuals. Recent studies suggest that another brain region – the cerebellum – may be implicated in dyslexia. In a study of six dyslexic men and age-matched controls who were asked to execute familiar and novel motor movements, activation was significantly lower in the cerebellum of dyslexic participants than in the normal reading (Nicolson *et al.*, 1999). The authors suggest that this cerebellar dysfunction affects the learning of new skills and the 'performance of automatic, overlearned skills'. Reading, they argue, is a complex behaviour composed of a number of interacting motor behaviours that need to be learned and improved over time. The precise role of the cerebellum in dyslexia, however, is currently unclear and its significance to reading specifically has been challenged (Zeffirino and Eden, 2001).

Is developmental dyslexia a universal brain disorder?

The incidence of dyslexia is thought to be between 5 and 17 per cent, depending on the study you read. One reason for the variability in the disorder's appearance, especially in different countries, may be due to the depth of the orthographies studied. That is, languages with fairly transparent reading systems, such as Italian, are less likely to present readers with difficulties. When psychologists talk about the localisation of language, it is easy to forget that language is not a standard, unitary process but is heavily culture-bound. Russian and English, for example, have different orthographical and phonological rules. Some authors have suggested that this explains the differences in word reading speed in English and Italian individuals (Italians are faster).

Deep orthographies such as those found in English and French, however, are a minefield of rules and linguistic irregularities. In English, for example, there are 1120 ways of using graphemes (letters and strings of letters) to form 40 sounds (phonemes). Italian, on the other hand, has 33 graphemes representing 25 phonemes.

As you saw in Chapter 2, Eraldo Paulesu and his colleagues from the Institute of Neurology, London, and various Italian universities, examined whether such differences in reading would be reflected in different degrees or types of activation in the brain (Paulesu *et al.*, 2001b). In two PET studies, the researchers asked English and Italian university students to either read aloud words and non-words (Experiment 1) or to perform a feature detection task (Experiment 2), which involved paying attention to the physical aspects of words presented rather than to the words themselves. They were not asked to read the words in Experiment 2.

The researchers found that the Italian speakers showed greater activation in those areas responsible for processing phonemes (left temporal regions) whereas the English speakers showed greater activation in other areas of the temporal and frontal cortex (areas activated during word retrieval and naming), as Figure 9.2 illustrates.

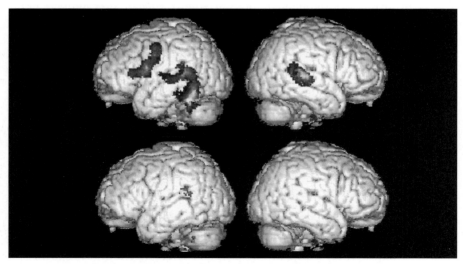

Fig 9.2 Regions of the brain that become active, during PET, when Italian and English participants read nonwords and words. The first row shows area of common activation in English and Italian participants during reading tasks; the second row shows how activation around the planum temporale was greater in the Italian readers. From Paulesu, E., McCrory, E., Fazio, F., Menoncello, L., Brunswick, N., Cappa, S.F., Cotelli, M., Cossu, G., Corte, F., Lorusso, M., Pesenti, S., Gallagher, A., Perani, D., Price, C., Frith, C.D. and Frith, U. (2000). A cultural effect on brain function. Nature Neuroscience, 3, 1, 91-96.

The study is the first to show cultural effects on brain function related to language, and the authors claim that the neurophysiological difference may explain the behavioural findings regarding word reading speed.

Paulesu *et al.* (2001a) subsequently reported that dyslexic English, French and Italian participants who read either bisyllabic words or non-words aloud (an explicit reading task), or made decisions about specific physical features of letters in words (an implicit reading task), showed a reduction in activation in the same region in the left hemisphere. The region included the left middle, inferior and superior temporal cortex.

Dyslexia and lateralisation

One model of developmental dyslexia suggests that dyslexics' language impairments occur because they have delayed or reduced left hemisphere function or show no hemisphere preference (Galaburda *et al.*, 1994). There is good evidence that function and structure are more symmetrical in dyslexic samples. When good and poor readers respond to visual or auditory stimuli, brain electrical activity tends to be symmetrical in dyslexics but typically left-based in controls (Brunswick and Rippon, 1994; Rippon and Brunswick, 1998).

The key region that shows greatest symmetry in dyslexics (but which is asymmetrical in normal readers) is the planum temporale (PT) – a region described in the section on aphasia and which corresponds to the auditory association cortex in the temporal lobe. This tends to be longer in the left hemispheres of most right-handers and more symmetrical in dyslexic readers (Galaburda *et al.*, 1994). A recent study compared the degree of planum temporale asymmetry in a group of young adult dyslexics having a known M pathway deficit, with that of a control group (Best and Demb, 1999). Using three methods of brain imaging, the authors found little difference between the controls and the dyslexics: both showed the typical leftward PT asymmetry. However, some methods did point towards greater symmetry in the dyslexics. What this (and other independent evidence) suggests, the authors conclude, is that a sub-type of dyslexia may have the characteristic leftward asymmetry but not the M pathway deficits.

Because of the PT's prominence in the left hemisphere (where it is longer) and because it contains an area that is functionally similar to Wernicke's area, some researchers have suggested that this structure is important for language. This idea, however, is speculative (Galaburda, 1995). For example, the leftward asymmetry of the planum temporale may simply be nothing more than a physical feature of the brain; it just happens to be larger on the left than the right. However, there do seem to be more anomalies in asymmetry in dyslexics than there are in normal readers.

9.5 LANGUAGE PROCESSING IN THE INTACT BRAIN

Neuroimaging studies using PET and fMRI have employed increasingly sophisticated designs to discover the neural basis of language disorders and normal language processing (Price, 1997) (see Figure 9.3).

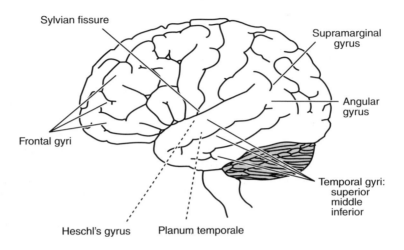

Fig 9.3 Areas of the brain involved in language processing

These studies generally conclude that the left hemisphere participates in language-related tasks more actively than does the right hemisphere, and that specific regions of the left hemisphere are involved in the different components of language such as speech production and comprehension, the processing of sound, the understanding of meaning, and so on.

The first PET study of language processing was carried out by Petersen *et al.* (1988) and was conceptually simple. The task involved asking participants to listen to and repeat words. The study found that the left posterior temporal cortex (including the primary auditory cortex and Wernicke's area) was significantly more active during the passive listening of words than during a control condition in which the participants performed no task. Repeating the words activated the primary motor cortex and Broca's area. Petersen *et al.* (1990) later reported that the auditory association cortex is activated by the sounds of words but not by other sounds.

When people were asked to think of verbs that were appropriate to use with the nouns, even more intense activity was seen in Broca's area. Price *et al.* (1994) have also reported that greater activation in the left inferior and middle frontal cortices was found during performance of a lexical decision task, whereas more temporal regions were activated during reading aloud and reading silently.

An important aspect of language analysis is, as the section on dyslexia showed, phonological processing – the putting together of sounds to make meaningful words. Neuroimaging studies have found that when individuals discriminate between spoken words on the basis of phonetic structure, when they discriminate between consonants and when they make judgements about rhyme or engage in phonological memory tasks, activation in the left frontal cortex near Broca's area is found (Zatorre *et al.*, 1996; Paulesu *et al.*, 1996). Other studies report involvement of the temporal cortex and angular gyrus especially during tasks that involve drawing analogies, repeating words, and reading words and pseudo-words (Nobre *et al.*, 1994; Karbe *et al.*, 1998).

This evidence suggests that Broca's area and the frontal cortex are necessary for the phonetic manipulation of language but that the posterior temporal cortex is responsible for the perceptual analysis of speech (Zatorre *et al.*, 1996). However, the picture may be a little more complex. Binder *et al.* (1997) compared the analysis involved in the phonetic and semantic perception of aurally presented words with the analysis of non-linguistic stimuli such as tones. A large network of left-hemisphere regions was activated during the semantic analysis, including areas in the frontal, temporal and parietal cortex. Activation was not limited to one specific region.

Damasio *et al.* (1996), in a comprehensive study, evaluated the effects of language processing in individuals with focal and stable brain lesions in both hemispheres, inside and outside the temporal regions. Damasio *et al.* hypothesised that there is no single mediating site for all words, but that there are separate regions within a larger network that are activated by different kinds of word. There were three categories of word: persons, non-unique animals and non-unique tools, each of which should be processed by different parts of the frontal and temporal lobe. Although 97 individuals showed normal language, 30 did not; 29 of these had brain injury to the left hemisphere. While impaired retrieval of words was associated with temporal cortex damage, abnormal retrieval of animal words was found in patients with left interior temporal lobe damage, and abnormal retrieval of tools was associated with posterolateral inferior temporal cortex damage.

Because we cannot infer normal function from brain damage, Damasio *et al.* conducted a second experiment in which healthy individuals performed the same language tasks while undergoing a PET scan. Although all words activated the left temporal cortex, specific categories were associated with activation of specific regions of the brain. Naming of tools activated the posterior, middle and inferior temporal gyri, for example, and animal naming activated other parts of the inferior temporal cortex.

Imageability of words

A number of different brain imaging studies demonstrate that the left temporal lobe is involved in the processing of words that differ in imageability, but various regions in the temporal lobe are activated during the hearing and reading of nouns that vary in imageability (Wise *et al.*, 2000).

Wise *et al.* presented nouns varying in imageability, at a rate of 40 per minute, to 18 right-handed men and women as they underwent a series of PET scans. The words were presented either auditorily or visually. As the imageability of the nouns increased, so did activity in various parts of the left temporal lobe (specifically, the left mid-fusiform gyrus and medial temporal lobes). The study identifies a key area that increased in activity regardless of whether the imagined word was read or listened to.

Is there a visual word form area?

As you saw in the section on acquired dyslexia, people with visual word form dyslexia are unable to recognise the form of words presented visually. Studies with healthy individuals have localised the ability to identify visual letter strings as words – the visual word form – in the left fusiform gyrus. Consequently, this area has been termed the visual word form area (Warrington and Shallice, 1980) because it responds to the visual, rather than auditory, forms of words (Giraud and Price, 2001).

Studies have suggested that damage to the ventral temporal lobe and fusiform gyrus is associated with an inability to recognise words, while the ability to recognise individual letters is intact (Binder and Mohr, 1992); patients with fusiform gyrus damage, for example, can engage in letter-by-letter reading (Beversdorf *et al.*, 1997). Neuroimaging studies show that this region is active during the perception of word and word-like forms but is less active during the perception of strings of letters that are unfamiliar, such as consonant-string non-words (Buchel *et al.*, 1998).

Whether this area responded to the abstract rather than the perceptual nature of words was investigated by Polk and Farah (2002). They reasoned that pseudo-words are pronounceable and that this is why the area was activated by these stimuli and real words. They presented words, non-words and word strings in normal form and with alternating case (e.g. AbLe) to nine healthy right-handed men. The left ventral visual cortex was active during pseudo-word and normal-case word recognition. Words and non-words that had alternating-case letters activated the area just as strongly as did the pseudo-words and words presented in regular form. Activation to these words was stronger in this region than it was to consonant strings presented in regular case. The findings suggest that this region may respond to abstract letter identities rather than the font, size or case of the letters. The results were supported by the findings of another fMRI study, which showed that activation in the left inferotemporal area was stronger when the person viewed an alphabetic letter string than a checkerboard, and was greater during word perception than the perception of consonants (Cohen *et al.*, 2002).

Research update ... do first and second languages recruit the same brain regions?

Bilingualism refers to a proficiency in two languages. The second language may be a native language – children may be reared bilingually – or it may be learned later in life. Bilingual language processing, like single-language processing, is thought to involve left hemisphere regions, but some researchers have suggested that the right hemisphere may be more important in the development of a second language. Bilinguals with right hemisphere lesions have been found to show a greater degree of aphasia than do bilinguals with left hemisphere lesions, for example (Hakuta, 1986).

Neuroimaging studies, however, suggest more left hemisphere involvement in bilinguals and that similar cortical areas may be recruited during the processing of both languages. A study of French and English speakers, for example, found that the processing in both languages was associated with activity in the left inferior frontal cortex (Klein *et al.*, 1995). Another study found that there was activation in different parts of Broca's area during language processing in adults who had learned the language in adulthood but not in those who had learned the language in childhood (Kim *et al.*, 1997). There was no differential activation in Wernicke's area.

These differences, of course, might reflect participants' proficiency in using language rather than the age at which the second language was acquired (Perani *et al.*, 1998). If there is an overlap in the language areas that mediate both tongues, this may be due to the similarity of the two languages spoken. Most studies, for example, have looked at bilinguals who speak Indo-European languages (English, French, Italian, and so on). Would the same overlap be seen if the two languages spoken differed in terms of syntax (meaning and grammar), morphology (physical construction of the language) and phonology (the sound of the language)? Evidence suggests that it would.

Klein *et al.* (1999), for example, found that a similar area in the left frontal cortex was activated during speech production in Mandarin and English. English and Mandarin are different types of language. Mandarin, for example, uses pitch and tone to a greater extent than does English. A similar area was found to be active during French and English language processing in Klein *et al.*'s previous study (1995). Further evidence to indicate that proficiency in a language may not explain differences in activation during the processing of these languages is reported by Perani *et al.* (1998). This study found that similar patterns of neural activation were observed in highly proficient bilinguals who spoke English/Italian and Catalan/Spanish. Current evidence, therefore, suggests that similar brain regions may be recruited in first and second language processing.

9.6 SEX DIFFERENCES

There is evidence to suggest that men's and women's brains respond differently during language processing, although this evidence is inconsistent. Neuroimaging studies of language show greater left hemisphere activation in men but a more symmetrical pattern of activation in women (Pugh *et al.*, 1996). Other data suggest greater activation in the left hemisphere in women during a phonological processing task (Pugh *et al.*, 1997), while still others report no difference between the sexes or have found left activation in both sexes (Frost *et al.*, 1999). The evidence for neurobiological sex differences in language processing, therefore, is mixed.

Focus on ... how the brain processes Braille and sign language

The origin of language probably lies in the motor system of our brain. Gesturing preceded the sophisticated vocal communication of evolutionary modern times but gesturing is still used to communicate. The congenitally deaf, for example, use American or British sign language. But to what extent does the brain have different systems for understanding the different types of communication – those that rely on our ability to hear and one that relies on our ability to decipher symbols or actions?

Individuals who are deaf but have learned sign language also appear to show activation in areas of the right hemisphere while signing. Neville *et al.* (1998) conducted an fMRI study of language in three groups of people: monolingual speakers of English who could hear; native deaf signers of American sign language (ASL); and bilingual users (of English and ASL) who could hear. Participants watched a videotape recording of a deaf signer producing sentences in ASL, and read English sentences presented on a computer monitor. The study found that although all groups activated the typical left hemisphere areas (Broca's and Wernicke's) when they processed English sentences, the native speakers of ASL also showed corresponding increases in the right hemisphere.

Could the results have been attributable to the possibility that deafness had led to a reorganisation of the cortex in the deaf participants? This is unlikely because both the hearing and deaf participants who were fluent ASL signers showed the same right hemisphere activation. Paulesu and Mehler (1998) have suggested that this pattern of activity may, instead, reflect the possibility that the right hemisphere holds the grammar for sign language because it requires representations of both sides of the body. Because neuroimaging studies of sign language are relatively rare, this hypothesis has yet to be tested. However, it seems reasonable given the role of the right hemisphere in processing spatial relationships (such as interpreting movement in space).

Mairead MacSweeney and a team of researchers from various English universities have carried out the first brain imaging study of the perception of British sign language (BSL) and compared the brain's response to this with its response to auditory stimuli in hearing individuals (MacSweeney *et al.*, 2002). Nine hearing and nine congenitally deaf individuals had their brain activity measured by fMRI during the perception of sentences presented in BSL. An analogous auditory task in English was completed by individuals who could hear.

Regardless of the modality of communication, there was activation in Broca's area and in Wernicke's area – both bilaterally – during the language perception tasks. However, differences did emerge between tasks in temporal and occipital areas. The auditory task in hearing individuals was associated with increased activity in the auditory cortices. This activation was not found during BSL. BSL, on the other hand, was associated with activity in area V5 at the junction of the temporal and occipital cortex. V5, as you saw in Chapter 5, is the region of the visual cortex that responds to movement and so activation here is consistent with what we know of the neurology of visual perception.

When hearing and deaf people's responses to BSL were compared, however, deaf signers showed greater activation in the left superior temporal cortex than did hearing signers. This result is intriguing because it suggests that the auditory cortex of the temporal lobe is active during an auditory language task in hearing individuals but that it may respond to visual input in congenitally deaf individuals.

This region of the temporal lobe has been described as a multi-modal language area (Büchel *et al.*, 1998) because it can be activated by language processed in different modalities. The MacSweeney study indicated that this was so for sign language. Büchel *et al.* observed a similar phenomenon when scanning blind participants who read Braille. When people engaged in tactile reading, the posterior left temporal area (Area 37) was active. Buchel *et al.* proposed that this area in blind, Braille-reading participants promotes activity in other parts of the brain that allows them access to words. However, this area was active only during written word recognition, not spoken word recognition.

9.7 HANDEDNESS AND LANGUAGE

Handedness refers to the degree to which individuals preferentially use one hand for certain activities (such as writing, unscrewing a jar, throwing a ball). It can also refer to the strength of hand skill. Handedness may be relevant to language because left- and right-handers may have speech localised in different hemispheres. According to a famous study by Rasmussen and Milner (1977), 96 per cent of right-handers and 70 per cent of left-handers in their study had left hemisphere speech. Other, recent estimates place the figures at 95.3 per cent and 61.4 per cent (Segalowitz and Bryden, 1983).

The implication of these figures is that left handers are less likely than right-handers to have left hemisphere speech and more likely to have right hemisphere or bilateral speech (this is why most neuroimaging studies of language indicate that their participants were all right-handed; this reduces the likelihood of variability in brain asymmetry). However, this evidence has largely come from brain injury or neuroimaging studies with small samples.

Recently, a large sample (N=188) of moderate and strong right-handers was studied in order to determine the strength of localisation in this group (Knecht et al., 2000). The participants' task was to think of as many words beginning with a given letter; 92.5 per cent of the sample showed left hemisphere language, with 7.5 per cent showing right hemisphere activation during the language task. There was no difference in lateralisation between men and women, and there were no differences in task performance between the sexes.

While the study shows a slightly greater number of individuals with right hemisphere language than previously reported, there was no scope for measuring the effect of degree of handedness on lateralisation – 75 per cent were strongly right-handed and the remainder were moderately right-handed. The percentage of right-handers with right hemisphere speech was similar to that reported in a previous study of language lateralisation in patients with epilepsy (Springer et al., 1999).

9.8 OTHER HIGHER FUNCTIONS

Reasoning

For most of our complex, intelligent behaviour a region in the front of the brain appears to be essential. Damage to the frontal lobes is associated with deficits in planning, putting stimuli in the correct order, behaving spontaneously and inhibiting incorrect responses (Adolphs *et al.*, 1996).

Antonio Damasio's studies of patients with frontal lobe damage, for example, suggest that these individuals have great difficulty in making correct decisions (Damasio, 1995). As you saw in Chapter 8, Damasio suggests that the ability to make decisions leading to positive or potentially harmful consequences depends on the activation of somatic (that is, bodily) states. Automatic, endocrine and musculoskeletal routes mark events as important, but appear to be impaired in certain frontal lobe patients. For example, patients with damage to a specific area of the prefrontal cortex are unable to make important, practical decisions in real life despite having intact cognitive ability. When the decision can have a positive or negative outcome, the degree of physiological activity commonly seen in healthy individuals when they make such decisions is absent in these patients (Bechara *et al.*, 1997).

Risky decision-making

In one study, frontal lobe patients and healthy controls were taught to play a card game which required them to make as much money as possible (Bechara *et al.*, 1997). There were four decks of cards and some had a high probability of delivering either a large immediate monetary reward, a large delayed monetary loss, a low immediate monetary reward or a low delayed monetary loss. No participant was told which deck contained the greatest probability of obtaining these outcomes and, therefore, had to learn from experience, turning over cards and remembering the outcomes. They had hunches. When a decision involved a high degree of risk, for example (such as losing a large amount of money), a healthy individual would show a characteristic increase in physiological arousal; the frontal lobe patient, however, would not. The patients would show a characteristic response after they had lost or gained, as would controls, and all patients were aware that they had lost money.

Bechera *et al.* (2000) were interested in determining whether their patients behaved in the way that they did because they were hypersensitive to reward, were insensitive to punishment or were insensitive to future consequences. In their modified task, advantageous decks of cards yielded high immediate punishment but even higher future reward. Disadvantageous decks yielded low immediate punishment but even lower future reward. Skin conductance response was measured after the participant had received reward or punishment.

The researchers found that the patients with ventromedial/orbitofrontal damage opted for the disadvantageous decks and failed to be sensitive to future consequences. Instead, they seemed to be guided by immediate reward. The researchers call this 'myopia for the future'. Even when the future consequences of behaving in a particular way are undesirable, these patients continue to behave in an inappropriate way.

A caveat?

New research, however, suggests that the role of the prefrontal cortex in this aspect of reward and risk-taking may be overstated. Manes *et al.* (2002) argue that although studies have ostensibly shown deficits in the gambling task (described above) in patients with frontal lobe damage, this damage is not restricted to the frontal cortex but extends beyond it. In Bechera *et al.*'s studies, for example, lesions were found in the medial orbitofrontal region but extended to the dorsolateral cortex and other neighbouring regions. Manes *et al.* (2002) studied the effects of restricted orbitofrontal cortex, dorsolateral, dorsomedial and large frontal lesions on a variety of neuropsychological measures, including the gambling task and a version of the task designed to increase the sense of risk further.

They found that dorsolateral lesions were associated with impairments in working memory, dorsomedial lesions with deficits in planning, and orbitofrontal lesions with performance at control level, although there was prolonged deliberation on another task, which required forward planning. The group with large frontal lesions, however, showed great impairment and was the only group to show risky decision-making. According to Manes *et al.*'s criteria, patients in the Bechara studies would be classified as having large frontal lesions.

The results suggest that the size of the lesion may be the critical predictor of risky decision-making: both the dorsal and ventral parts of the prefrontal cortex need to be damaged before impairments are observed. Four out of five patients with large frontal cortex damage had lesions to the right side, perhaps indicating that the impairment is lateralised.

Inductive and deductive reasoning in healthy individuals

If the frontal lobes are important for reasoning, then activation in these areas should be apparent when healthy individuals perform a reasoning task during neuroimaging. Goel *et al.* (1997; 1998) have recently reported two experiments in which they sought to test this hypothesis. In one experiment, they asked ten participants to undertake inductive and deductive reasoning tasks. Inductive reasoning involves the inference of general principles or rules from specific facts; deductive reasoning involves inferring specific instances from general principles or rules. The tasks in Goel *et al.*'s experiment involved reasoning tasks such as deciding whether the following logic was correct:

All carpenters are young
All woodworkers are carpenters
All woodworkers are young

and

George was a woolly mammoth
George ate pine cones
All woolly mammoths ate pine cones

The experimenters found that the frontal lobes were, indeed, involved. Significant increases in activation were reported in the left inferior and middle frontal gyri.

Intelligence

Studies published in the early twentieth century demonstrated that damage to the frontal cortex was associated with impaired cognitive and intellectual functioning. Rylander (1939), for example, reported that 21 out of 32 frontal lobe patients scored more poorly on tests of intellectual ability than did healthy controls. This impairment was not damage-general either. Patients with temporal, parietal and occipital lobe resection showed no difficulty on these tests.

These early studies did not, however, go unchallenged. Hebb (1945), for example, argued that there was no real significant difference between frontal and posterior damage patients on tests of intellectual ability (IQ tests). Although he did not argue that the frontal lobes had no part to play in intellectual behaviour, Hebb concluded that there was very little evidence to suggest that these areas were more involved than others.

And, 50 years on, Duncan (1995) suggested that the frontal lobes may not be necessarily involved in the operation of tasks requiring crystallised intelligence (knowing facts) but may be involved in the operation of tasks requiring fluid intelligence (the ability to engage in non-verbal tasks that do not assume previous semantic knowledge). Three of the frontal lobe patients he studied had normal intelligence test scores but reduced scores on a test of fluid intelligence. Scores on the fluid intelligence test were also lower than those of controls, suggesting that the frontal lobes are necessary for fluid intelligence.

If the frontal cortex is important to reasoning, would more or less activation in this region be apparent in very bright individuals? An early PET study indicated that individuals with high IQ had lower metabolic rates than those with low IQ during problem-solving (Haier *et al.*, 1988). When high- and low-IQ individuals were trained on a computer game, both groups' brain activity declined but the decline in the high-IQ group was more rapid, suggesting that the highly intellectually able may need to use less of their neural machinery to think (Haier *et al.*, 1992).

The less effort hypothesis also receives some support from EEG studies.

High-IQ individuals show consistently higher EEG alpha power (that is, less mental effort) during problem-solving and preparation for problem-solving than do low-IQ individuals (Jausovec, 1996). The most pronounced differences between high- and low-IQ individuals during working memory and arithmetic tasks were found across the frontal regions (Jausovec, 1998).

SOME USEFUL FURTHER READING

Brunswick, N. (1998) The neuropsychology of language and language disorders. In G.N. Martin, *Human Neuropsychology*. Harlow: Prentice Hall.

Fiez, J.A. and Petersen, S.E. (1998) Neuroimaging studies of word reading. *Proceedings of the National Academy of Sciences USA 95*, 914–21.

Funnell, E. (2001) *Case Studies in the Neuropsychology of Reading*. London: The Psychology Press.

Habib, M. (2000) The neurological basis of developmental dyslexia. *Brain* 123, 2373–99.

Posner, M.I. and Pavese, A. (1998) Anatomy of word and sentence meaning. *Proceedings of the National Academy of Sciences USA 95*, 899–905.

SOME USEFUL JOURNALS TO BROWSE

Aphasiology
Brain
Brain and Language
Cognition
Cognitive Neuropsychology
Dyslexia
International Journal of Psychophysiology
Journal of Experimental Psychology: Learning, Memory and Cognition
Journal of Memory and Language
Language and Cognitive Processes
Nature Neuroscience
Neuroimage
Neuroreport
Psycholinguistics
Psychological Review
Psychological Science
Quarterly Journal of Experimental Psychology
Reading and Writing: An Interdisciplinary Journal
Science
Trends in Cognitive Science

10 Consciousness

WHAT YOU WILL FIND IN THIS CHAPTER
- a discussion of what philosophers and psychologists mean by 'consciousness'
- a description and explanation of various states of altered consciousness, including sleep, pain and hypnosis
- a description of the main consciousness-altering drugs and their possible mechanism of action.

WHAT YOU SHOULD BE ABLE TO DO AFTER READING THE CHAPTER
- be aware of the difficulty in defining consciousness scientifically
- describe the major behavioural aspects of altered states of consciousness, such as sleep, pain and hypnosis, and their biological bases
- describe the main consciousness-altering drugs and how they might work

10.1 WHAT IS CONSCIOUSNESS?

Philosphers and psychologists have for centuries debated the meaning of consciousness and what it means to be conscious (Tassi and Muzet, 2001). According to William James (1890), 'all people unhesitatingly believe that they feel themselves thinking. This belief is the most fundamental of all postulates of Psychology.' We are aware of sights, sounds, smells and touches, and of discriminating within and between them; we are aware of people speaking to us, of picking up a glass of wine and savouring its flavour, of reading words on a page, and so on. That is, we have a good appreciation of the richness of our internal world. But what defines this as being consciousness? What is it to be conscious?

The centuries-long debate has not really arrived at a convincing answer (Block *et al.*, 1997). According to Sutherland (1985), 'Consciousness is a fascinating but elusive phenomenon: it is impossible to specify what it is, what it does, or why it evolved. Nothing worth reading has been written about it' (cited in Güzeldere, 1985). Psychologists generally neglected the problem of consciousness for many years. The rise of behaviourism at the beginning of the twentieth century, with its emphasis on studying only observable behaviour, swept aside the previous school of thought, introspectionism, which relied on self-report for data. The behaviourists had argued that the only subject matter for psychological investigation was behaviour, not consciousness.

Several psychologists continue to believe that consciousness is a side-effect of what we do – an epiphenomenon – and that it is not intrinsically interesting as a research question or a psychological topic. Over three decades ago, Jeffrey Gray (1971) published a paper outlining what he regarded as the hard problems of consciousness. Gray (1998) noted that in the years since the publication of the article, he had received just two requests for a copy of the paper!

The 1990s, however, saw a resurgence of interest in the topic, largely as a result of books published by mathematicians, physicists and philosophers (Penrose, 1989; 1994; Gray, 1998; Hameroff *et al.*, 1998) and landmark conferences – one of which, Towards a Science of Consciousness, held in Tucson, Arizona, saw a further snowballing of interest. Subsequent years, however, have seen the snowball melt a little and interest has waned (although the topic is still written about and discussed), possibly because scientists have realised that the questions they posed were either too difficult to answer or were unanswerable.

There are some aspects of consciousness, such as sleep and wakefulness, the effects of drugs on the CNS and the effect of pain on the body, that have always aroused scientific interest and, probably, always will. Other aspects, such as why and how consciousness exists, are less easy to answer and are difficult to put to the test experimentally.

Philosophical approaches to consciousness

Although the word 'consciousness' is a noun, 'consciousness' itself does not exist, in the same way that 'memory' does not exist or 'personality' does not exist. It is a label we attach to a collection of features or behaviours. Consciousness is a personal and private experience; we infer others' consciousness by referring to our own: we cannot directly experience another person's consciousness. We might think that this white page with black ink on it will also be perceived as such by another reader but we cannot be absolutely sure of this. You can appreciate why philosophers enjoy the problems of consciousness. Consciousness has a subjective quality that makes the subject difficult to study scientifically.

According to Chalmers (1995), consciousness investigators face easy problems and a hard problem. The easy problems include the ability to discriminate, categorise and react to stimuli, to integrate information by using a cognitive system, to report mental states and to access internal states, to control behaviour deliberately and to differentiate between wakefulness and sleep. These are the relatively easy topics of consciousness because they primarily involve the contents of consciousness; they refer to functions or abilities. Understanding (or discovering) the neural correlates of consciousness is also an easy problem, according to Chalmers. A mental state is said to be conscious when this state can be verbally reportable or internally accessible; the organism is able to be conscious of some information, react to it and explain it. This is another easy problem. But this is only one side of the story. The hard problem lies in studying the experience of these mental events – that is, explaining why we have the experience of consciousness in the first place. The distinction between easy and hard problems is a controversial one, and you would probably challenge the notion that the understanding of the neural correlates of consciousness, for example, represents an easy problem.

Neurobiological theories of consciousness

A number of neurobiological theories of consciousness has attempted to correlate conscious experience with physical or neural activity (Rolls, 1997; Gray, 1998). Chalmers (1998), for example, has listed over 20 possible neural correlates of consciousness (NCC).

The essence of the neurobiological approach is that consciousness arises from the neural activity of the brain. Neurobiological approaches diverge, however, when they begin to specify which parts or elements of the brain give rise to the activity that is meant to represent consciousness. Neurobiological theories of consciousness derive their data from neuroimaging and brain damage studies, as well as from studies in other branches of natural science such as mathematics and quantum physics. Each type of study has yielded a different perspective on the NCC, and some of the most important or influential of these theories are reviewed below.

10.2 CONSCIOUSNESS AND BRAIN DAMAGE

Brain damage can alter human consciousness. Patients with anterograde amnesia, for example, are unable to form new verbal memories but can learn some kinds of task. However, they remain unaware that they have learned something, even when their behaviour indicates that they have. The brain damage does not prevent all kinds of learning, but it does prevent conscious awareness of what has been learned.

As you saw in Chapter 5, there are individuals who, if they have damaged the posterior parts of their brain, show a lack of awareness of stimuli presented to their visual field. Brain damage that impairs the perception of visual stimuli also seems to impair the ability to be aware of perceiving these stimuli (Stoerig and Cowey, 1997). Individuals with blindsight have damage to the primary visual cortex and although they are able to perform some visual perception tasks, they report being unaware of the task stimuli that had been presented in their visual field. In Chapter 5, you saw how individuals with certain types of agnosia were unable to recognise objects or to ascribe meaning to such objects. People with prosopagnosia were unable to identify familiar faces by using facial cues alone. All of these disorders involve some lack of awareness and may help us to understand the regional contribution of the brain to conscious awareness.

Blindsight patients have damage to an area called V1, the primary visual cortex. This is the region in the brain to which information from the retina travels. Does the activity of V1 reflect conscious awareness of visual stimuli? Crick and Koch (1995) have proposed the controversial idea that it does not. They argue that it is not involved in conscious visual perception because V1 does not directly project to the frontal cortex (which integrates information from other parts of the cortex); the areas surrounding V1, however – the extrastriate cortex – do, and it is the activity of these areas that may reflect conscious processing. Crick and Koch (1995) admit that this is a subtle and speculative proposal, and have not undertaken an empirical test of this hypothesis; it remains an intriguing one.

Crick's astonishing hypothesis

Crick's theory (Crick, 1994), for example, suggests that consciousness is the result of the activity of collections of neurons called neural assemblies (this is the astonishing hypothesis). The behaviour of neurons is represented by 35–75 Hz oscillations in the cortex; these oscillations form the basis of consciousness and correlate with awareness in different sensory modalities. According to the theory, oscillation represents the way in which the information we process is bound. The concept of binding is important in consciousness; it refers to the process whereby separate pieces of information about a single entity are brought together and used for processing later (Chalmers, 1995).

Bringing together information about colour and shape to form an image of an object is an example of binding. When elements are bound together, Crick's theory argues, neural groups will oscillate in the same space and time. Such oscillations are the neural correlates of experience. While Crick's theory has received much attention and credit for specifically tying consciousness to specific brain activity, it has been criticised for not being able to explain the importance of these oscillations. If these oscillations give rise to conscious experience, why? Again, this exemplifies Chalmers' hard problem.

Penrose and Hameroff's quantum model

Another neurobiological approach to consciousness focuses on the importance of chaos or non-linear dynamics in explaining consciousness. Much of Penrose's work is rooted in some quite complex physics and mathematics, and we need not dwell on the detail here. In essence, Penrose (1989; 1994) argues that consciousness is a form of non-algorithmic processing, which is important to conscious mathematical insight (Penrose is a famous mathematician). That is, consciousness is not an all-or-nothing, straightforward, linear process; instead, it is an uneven, non-linear process.

Penrose's model relies on an understanding of quantum physics and Penrose's excellent books (1989; 1994) will fill in the quantum physics blanks here. Quantum physics suggests that although events are observable and seem to follow a logical order, these events themselves are altered by being observed (this is called the Heisenberg Uncertainty Principle). In a revision of the original model, Hameroff and Penrose (1996) and Hameroff (1998) have suggested that consciousness takes place in the skeletal structure of neurons (called the cytoskeleton), specifically in parts of the neuron called microtubules.

Hameroff is an anaesthetist and his ideas have been based on the processes involved in anaesthesia that induce loss of consciousness. For example, under general anaesthetic, individuals should not be able to move purposefully in response to a painful stimulus and should not be able to follow verbal commands (Franks and Lieb, 1998).

In Hameroff's model, microtubules are essential to consciousness. The function of microtubules is to transport material inside the neuron and define the shape of the processes they inhabit; they, therefore, serve an important neural function. The model suggests that quantum events occur in or around these microtubules and that these events give rise to our conscious experience. It suggests this for a number of reasons, not least the reason that microtubules are important for the functioning of the neuron. However, this model could be criticised on the same grounds as Crick's in the way that it does not explain why such neural events should be associated with consciousness. In fact, Churchland (1998) has suggested that these microtubules might just as well be called pixie dust in the synapses – essence that magically gives rise to consciousness – although Hameroff (1998) has argued that the mechanism by which microtubules give rise to consciousness is detailed and not as vague as pixie dust. The model, because it is derived from data from anaesthesia, is a highly specific neural model of consciousness and, because of this, holds great promise.

10.3 PAIN

One of the most dramatic and unpleasant changes in consciousness we can experience is pain. Pain is a feeling of acute discomfort that becomes unbearable. There are different types of pain experience; toothache, for example, is subjectively different to a headache, indigestion or the pain from a knife cut.

The body's pain receptors are called nocioceptors (from the Latin, 'to injure') and they are found all around the body. The most well studied are those in the skin and muscles. All nocioceptors are similar but they respond to different types of stimuli. Mechanical nocioceptors, for example, respond to serious mechanical challenge such as the pressure from a knife; heat receptors detect heat that is capable of burning the body; other receptors respond to other pain stimuli. Pain, as these examples show, is an adaptive mechanism. It helps us be aware of stimuli that can harm the body, and signals that if pain persists it will become worse and cause further damage.

The pain we experience is signalled by sensory fibres in the spinal cord, which receive information from the peripheral nervous system. Nocioceptors connect to the spinal cord via two types of nerve fibre: A-delta fibres and C fibres. A-delta fibres are small and thinly myelinated, and respond to rapid pain stimuli such as a pin-prick. C fibres are smaller and convey information about slow painful sensations such as dull ache, burning and nausea. They are not always involved in pain responses but no other fibres in the peripheral nervous system appear to be involved in pain.

From the dorsal roots of the spinal cord – where these fibres enter – fibres go further up the spinal cord to the dorsal horn. Here synapses with unmyelinated C fibres are made and Substance P, a neurotransmitter, is released. From the dorsal horn, signals are relayed to the brain, usually contralaterally. If this area (the dorsal horn) is surgically lesioned, for example, pain on the opposite side of the body is relieved, although not permanently. Stimulation of the A pathway causes experiences of pain but no other type of lesioning to parts of the spinal cord will relieve pain. It is informative that removal of the cortex does little to alleviate the experience of pain although the cortex does respond to painful changes in temperature.

An early influential theory of pain argued that the large, myelinated fibres that convey touch and A-delta and C fibres had different effects on a part of the spinal column called the substantia gelatinosa (Melzack and Wall, 1965). This was conceived as a 'gate' that controlled access to the ascending pain fibres of the spinal cord. Because of this conceptualisation, the proposal was called the 'gate control hypothesis'. The small pain fibres were thought to excite this area; but the touch fibres inhibited it. This is why, when a person rubbed the area of skin where there was pain, the pain was relieved. The touch fibres inhibited the area that was originally excited by the pain fibres. The brain was argued to exert some control over this gate. However, despite the plausibility of the theory, there is no direct evidence that such a mechanism exists.

The brain appears to play more of a role in pain than was originally imagined and a collection of regions, called the pain matrix (Melzack and Wall, 1965; Tracey *et al.*, 2000), is most involved. These regions are the somatosensory and motor cortices, the anterior cingulate cortex (ACC), the thalamus, the cerebellum, and the prefrontal and parietal cortex. Some of these areas are also involved in attention – the prefrontal cortex, thalamus, posterior parietal cortex and ACC, for example (Peyron *et al.*, 1999). These may be the regions that help us alleviate our pain because there is considerable behavioural evidence that if less attention is paid to the pain or the source of the pain, the less pain is actually experienced (Eccleston and Crombez, 1999; Petrovic *et al.*, 2000). A recent fMRI study has shown that if people are distracted from their pain and the distraction results in the experience of less intense pain, then this distraction is associated with increases in the prefrontal cortex and part of the ACC, but with decreases in the thalamus and another region of the ACC (Bantick *et al.*, 2002). The prefrontal cortex activity may reflect the active shifting of attention and the cognitive demands associated with it.

This distraction can be as simple as looking at pleasant pictures. De Wied and Verbaten (2001) presented pictures varying in emotional tone and arousal to a group of men each of whom kept an arm in a bucket of ice-cold water. (This procedure is called the cold-pressor test and is the most widely used pain-induction measure in the laboratory.) Exposure to pleasant pictures was associated with a greater tolerance of pain. In a second experiment in which unpleasant pictures, containing either pain-related or pain-unrelated stimuli, were presented, participants who viewed the pictures without pain cues tolerated the pain for longer than did those who viewed the pictures with pain cues. The results suggest that distraction by emotional cue may not be successful in reducing the experience of pain unless the distractor enhances positive mood (or does not produce a negative one, as the second experiment showed).

10.4 DRUGS AND ALTERED STATES OF CONSCIOUSNESS

Many drugs prescribed by physicians are administered to relieve a person of pain or distress; that is, their function is analgesic. While these drugs may have this effect they may also have other behavioural effects, such as heightening awareness or increasing euphoria. Drugs act on the brain's receptors and the study of the interaction between drug and receptor is called pharmacodynamics; the study of transport of drugs through the body is called pharmacokinetics. Finally, the mechanism by which the drug makes its way from the point of entry into the 'drug stream' is called absorption.

The most common way of administering drugs is via oral ingestion but drugs can be administered rectally, by injection, by inhalation through the lungs (as when a person receives general anaesthetic, nitrous oxide gas combined with five volatile liquids), through the skin (such as nicotine patches) or through the mucous membranes (such as via decongestant inhalers; another drug, cocaine, is often snorted and clings to the inside of the nose). Orally ingested drugs are dissolved in the stomach and are then carried to the small intestine where they are absorbed. When the drug is inside the body it exists in two forms: one form is soluble to water, the other is soluble to lipids and this solubility determines the rate of the drug's absorption. Lipid-soluble forms can cross lipid membranes but water-soluble forms cannot. All drugs described as psychoactive are lipid-soluble. The fastest method of administration is the injection – into veins (intravenous), muscles (intramuscular) or under the skin (subcutaneous) – but because of the speediness of administration, there is little time to respond to possible side-effects or to overdose.

Once absorption is complete, the drug is transported to its receptors but in doing so needs to cross various membranes or barriers depending on where the site of action is. Cell membranes are permeable to lipid-soluble drugs, and blood capillaries – very small, thin blood vessels surrounded by closely packed-together cells – have pores between these cells allowing drugs through. The blood–brain barrier protects the brain via a glial sheath (a fatty tissue layer) and a collection of tightly packed capillaries, so a drug would need to cross the wall of the capillary and then pass through the membrane of the glial cells in order to reach the brain's cells. Finally, in pregnant women, the placenta provides a barrier between the mother and child, and some drugs can penetrate this barrier.

The action of drugs ends with the elimination of the substance. Kidneys, lungs and skin eliminate drugs; the most common form of elimination is via urine. During anaesthesia, however, about 10 to 15 per cent of the drug is lost via sweat. Drugs have what is called a biological half-life: this refers to the time taken for the concentration of a drug in the blood to be reduced by half. Some drugs, such as the tranquilliser valium, have a half-life that can last several days.

Method of drug action

Drugs exert their effects largely by binding to relevant receptors and changing their function. These receptors tend to be specialised and respond to specific drugs. The strength of the receptor's response, therefore, depends on the drug that stimulates it, the amount of drug available and the number of receptors that can respond to the drug. By binding to a receptor specialised for a neurotransmitter, the drug can affect the amount of neurotransmitter made available to the synapse. If drugs help mimic the neurotransmitter system and enhance the ability of receptors to respond to a neurotransmitter, they are called agonists; if they prevent a neurotransmitter access to a receptor, they are called antagonists. Receptors for specific drugs are also selective for specific neurotransmitters. While a drug can affect the neurotransmission process, it does not create neurotransmission.

As you might expect, people will not respond universally to drug administration and so the dose–response relationship (the relationship between various doses of drug and the changes produced) depends on a number of factors, including previous experience with the drug, differences in the rates of drug absorption, differences in people's metabolism and whether drugs are combined (alcohol combined with tranquillisers such as benzodiazepines increases the sedation; other combinations have more fatal consequences). The notion of an average dose, therefore, means little to the pharmacologist or physician. The measure chemists use is an estimate of the amount of a drug that will have an effect in at least 50 per cent of people (this is called ED 50).

Drugs that produce sedation

Drugs that produce sedation, relief from anxiety or sleepiness are called central nervous system (CNS) depressants. Examples of these include barbiturates, alcohol and anaesthetics. The typical behavioural consequences of depressant administration is a blunting of sensory response, reduced cognitive function, feelings of sleepiness or drowsiness, and a reduction in physical activity. Unlike some other drugs, their effect is additive – taking two different kinds of CNS depressant produces greater sedation. CNS depressants are taken to relieve anxiety or produce sedation or sleep; they can also be used to relieve the effects of epilepsy. According to Julien (2000), depressants have an effect somewhere along the dimension between normal bodily state and death where the intervening stages comprise relief from anxiety, disinhibition, sedation, hypnosis/sleep, general anaesthesia and coma.

The first manufactured drugs to produce sedation were barbiturates in 1912. In the period since, tens of drugs have been tested until eventually the benzodiazepines, developed in 1961, replaced barbiturates as the sedative drug of choice. The most commonly available sedative, however, is alcohol.

Alcohol

Ethyl alcohol (ethanol) is very rapidly absorbed by the body. It takes between 30 to 90 minutes from the time of the last drink for the blood to reach its maximum concentration. If the stomach is empty, around 20 per cent of alcohol can be absorbed directly from the stomach; if the stomach is full, the rate of absorption is slower. Alcohol can easily cross the blood–brain and placental barriers, which means that it can be detected in a child's blood post-partum.

The majority of alcohol is metabolised by the liver where an enzyme converts the alcohol into acetaldehyde and where another different enzyme breaks down the acetaldehyde into acetic acid, and then to carbon dioxide and water. The liver performs its function at a steady, constant rate, regardless of the concentration of alcohol in the blood (about 10 mls of ethanol per hour). A tiny amount of alcohol (5 per cent) is exhaled through breath.

Intoxication, or being drunk, is achieved when blood alcohol concentration reaches 0.0 8g per cent – that is, when this percentage of ethanol is found in 100ml of blood. The actual figure, however, is arbitrary and different countries have different intoxication levels for driving competence purposes. Driving tends to be impaired at between 0.05–0.08g per cent and risk of accidents is four times higher than if no alcohol is present.

There is no one explanation for the psychopharmacological effects of alcohol and the mechanism of action is still discussed. Current models explain action in terms of alcohol's effect on the neurotransmitters NMDA and GABA. Ethanol can inhibit the action of a sub-type of NMDA glutamate receptor. It also has an effect on GABA receptors that is similar to that of barbiturates, and there is a frequent co-occurrence of symptoms of panic/anxiety and alcoholism. Alcohol also inhibits the release of acetylcholine, which might explain the memory impairment associated with alcohol use. Alcohol dilates the blood vessels in the skin, which results in warm flesh but a drop in internal temperature. Taking an alcoholic drink in the cold, therefore, is not really advisable. Alcoholics who stop drinking show withdrawal symptoms that include seizures, hyperexcitability, psychomotor disturbances and hallucinations. Excess alcohol use leads to liver damage – around two-thirds of alcoholic deaths are attributable to cirrhosis of the liver; as you saw in the chapter on memory, and will read about again in the next, excessive alcohol intake can also lead to neural destruction.

Psychostimulants

Cocaine and the amphetamines

Unlike sedatives, psychostimulants, as their name suggests, stimulate the activity of neurotransmitters. Specifically, they facilitate the action of catecholamines, dopamine and norepinephrine at synapses, usually at a region called the nucleus accumbens. Psychostimulants have some, but not much, therapeutic value but they have great psychological appeal – they create great euphoria in users, generate great arousal and provide an apparent increase in energy, all of which are attractive and reinforcing. These psychological effects are accompanied by physiological effects that include increased blood pressure, increased heart rate, pupil dilation, an increase in oxygen levels and a redirection of blood from the skin to muscles.

Two of the most well-documented psychostimulants are cocaine and amphetamine. Current estimates of use vary but cocaine users are thought to number 20–30 million in the United States; they tend to be between 12 and 39 years old, male and alcohol-dependent. Cocaine is derived from the leaves of the Peruvian and Bolivian *Erythroxylon coca* tree. An alkaloid in the leaf was isolated in 1859 and this was labelled cocaine; a leaf contains between 0.5 to 1 per cent. The drug became popular with the natives and with users overseas. Even at the turn of the twentieth century, Coca-Cola still marketed its soft drink with 60 mg of cocaine per eight-ounce serving.

When leaves are pulped, they produce around 80 to 90 per cent cocaine – the drug is, therefore, very potent. In diluted and powdered form, it is sold as cocaine hydrochloride, also known as 'crystal' or 'snow'. A line of cocaine provides around 25 mg of actual cocaine. When the hydrochloride form is boiled dry in a solution of baking soda or ammonia, the base form of the drug is obtained and this is commonly known as crack (so called because it makes a cracking noise when it is boiled). Cocaine can be absorbed by mucal membranes, the gastrointestinal tract and the lungs, and the drug can be snorted or injected. Around 20 to 30 per cent of the drug is absorbed when snorted, and the chemical peaks in blood plasma within 30 to 60 minutes (this parallels the change in behaviour). The fastest means of absorption is via intravenous injection – the drug reaches the brain in around a minute and penetrates the blood–brain barrier effortlessly. It has a half-life of 30 to 90 minutes and its metabolite can be measured in urine for up to 12 hours.

Cocaine effectively potentiates the action of monamines and blocks their reuptake. The key dopamine receptors are found in the midbrain. Dopamine-containing neurons in the ventral tegmental area of the midbrain project, as you saw in Chapter 3, to areas that include the prefrontal cortex, the nucleus accumbens, the amygdala and the hippocampus. One hypothesis is that cocaine acts at the presynaptic terminal of dopamine receptors and potentiates the release of the neurotransmitter.

Behavioural characteristics of cocaine use include alertness, hyperactivity, vasoconstriction, increased body temperature, pupil dilation, talkativeness, incoherent speech, enhanced self-esteem, extreme euphoria and boastfulness. These usually last around 30 minutes, followed by a milder period of 60 to 90 minutes, and then a period of anxiety lasting many hours. To alleviate the anxiety the user may take more of the drug to relive previous highs. If cocaine use is continued, it can result in tremors and seizures as well as psychological symptoms such as extreme suspiciousness and paranoia. Other physical side-effects can include sexual dysfunction, inflammation of the mucal membrane, destruction of the septum (the flesh separating the nostrils) and anosmia (loss of the sense of smell). A toxic dose is around 1–2 mg per kilogram of body weight.

Amphetamines have different psychological and behavioural effects but implicate the monoamine neurotransmitter system. They have effects on the CNS and PNS, and have similar physiological effects to adrenaline – constriction of blood vessels, hypertension and tachycardia (slowing of heart rate), restlessness, loss of appetite, increased motor activity and insomnia. People also experience euphoria, excitement and heightened arousal.

Amphetamines seem to exert most of their effects on presynaptic dopamine and norepinephrine neurons. Both neurotransmitters are released, and postsynaptic catecholamine receptors are also stimulated. This leaves more of the neurotransmitters in the synapse for take-up by the postsynaptic terminals. As you will see in the next chapter, amphetamines have been used to treat various illnesses and conditions including attention deficit hyperactivity disorder (ADHD), obesity, sea-sickness and morphine addiction. They are also used to treat sleep disorders such as cataplexy (discussed below). The drug can be detected in urine up to 48 hours after use.

Moderate use of amphetamines (20 to 50 mg) stimulates the respiratory system and provokes restlessness and insomnia, as well as the other symptoms described above. Chronic use is associated with increased repetitive motor behaviour, random aggression, paranoia and anorexia. Beyond this, users will experience weight loss, develop sores on the skin and become susceptible to infection. The toxicity of the drug is variable; some users react badly to moderate doses whereas other can tolerate doses of 400 mg or more.

Caffeine

The most popular and widely consumed drug is caffeine. An average cup of coffee contains about 50–150 mg of caffeine; a 12-ounce bottle of cola drink contains about 35–55 mg and a bar of chocolate around 25 mg. A lethal dose is around 10 grammes (or 100 cups of coffee). When 2 to 5 grammes are ingested, the spinal cord is stimulated and this is dangerous. Caffeine is absorbed very quickly and, within 90 minutes of ingestion, has been completely absorbed by the body. It has a half-life of about 3.5 to 5 hours, which means it remains in the system for that length of time after absorption. Caffeine in smokers tends to have a shorter half-life; in children, longer.

Caffeine has fairly dramatic effects on the CNS and behaviour. It increases cardiac contractions and dilates coronary arteries but constricts blood vessels, which results in reduced blood flow. It is a psychostimulant and stimulates the cortex, rather than the brainstem. It makes us mentally alert and wakeful, and makes our thinking clear; it also makes us restless and delicate movements difficult. Around two cups of coffee will produce these effects and around 12 will produce insomnia. The side-effects of excess caffeine include anxiety, insomnia, change in mood and hypertension.

Caffeine appears to exert these effects by blocking certain receptors, called adenosine receptors (i.e. it is an adenosine antagonist). Adenosine is a hormone that acts like a neurotransmitter that alters cell function: it acts by producing sedation (it also regulates delivery of oxygen to cells and produces asthma). Adenosine inhibits the release of neurotransmitters and by blocking its effects, caffeine makes more of these neurotransmitters available.

Research update … caffeine and memory

The decline in cognitive function across the day in elderly samples is well documented but researchers at the University of Arizona suggest that this could be halted or reversed by using a natural stimulant: caffeine. Lee Ryan and his colleagues tested a group of 65 year olds who considered themselves to be 'morning types' on memory recall and recognition measures, twice on two days, with 5–11 days' interval between testing sessions (Ryan et al., 2002). In each session, testing took place at 8 am and 4 pm. Individuals were randomly assigned to two groups: one received a 12-ounce cup of coffee; the other received the same amount of decaffeinated coffee. Testing took place 30 minutes after ingestion.

Participants who preferred the morning showed a significant decline in memory performance between morning and afternoon when caffeine was ingested 30 minutes before testing, however, the decline was halted. The researchers suggest that the improvement resulted from an increase in physiological arousal following caffeine administration, but caution that only coffee-drinkers were included in this study. This lays open the possibility that caffeine might have the same or different effects in non-coffee drinkers.

Nicotine

About 4000 compounds are released by cigarette tobacco when it burns, and nicotine is probably the best known of them because it is responsible for the pharmacological effects of smoking. The carcinogenic effects of smoking are due to other compounds. Nicotine is found in the smoke of burning tobacco (it is suspended in small bits of material, tars) and is quickly absorbed by the lungs. The average cigarette contains around 0.5 to 2 mg of nicotine and the lungs absorb around 20 per cent of this. Once absorbed, nicotine quickly reaches the brain and can cross the placenta. It has a half-life of around two hours in the chronic smoker.

People who have tried cigarette smoking at least once will probably have felt nauseous when inhaling their first cigarette. This is because nicotine stimulates the region of the brainstem that controls vomiting; it also stimulates receptors in the stomach. People can become very tolerant to nicotine, however, and its use can stimulate the hypothalamus to release a hormone that causes fluid retention. It also reduces muscle tone and weight gain. Behaviourally, it increases heart rate, blood pressure and contractions of the heart, and generates increased blood flow to the heart to meet the increase in contractions. In regular smokers, there is a low level of nicotine in the body when they wake up, which may explain the craving for the first cigarette of the morning.

At the neurophysiological level, nicotine acts on specific acetylcholine ('nicotinic') receptors that release acetylcholine in the CNS thereby increasing psychomotor activity, cognition and memory. Receptors for the drug may also exist on dopamine and serotonin-secreting neurons. Nicotine also acts on the PNS, hence the increase in blood pressure and heart rate; it also, via this system, stimulates the release of epinephrine from the adrenal glands.

Although nicotine is not carcinogenic it is reinforcing and this makes people continue to smoke despite the fact that other compounds in the cigarette are dangerous and are the principal cause of lung cancer (Denissenko *et al.*, 1996). Smoking is also associated with cardiovascular disease because the carbon monoxide in tobacco decreases the amount of oxygen that reaches the heart and the nicotine increases the amount of work the organ has to do. These compounds increase the narrowing of blood vessels (artherosclerosis) and blood clotting (thrombosis). The absence of nicotine makes withdrawal from smoking difficult, and people who try to give up smoking experience the typical abstinence syndrome: craving for tobacco, irritability, anxiety, anger, lack of consciousness, increased appetite and insomnia.

The opioids: morphine and other compounds

As you saw in an earlier section, pain is caused when nocioceptors on the skin or in organs are activated, and signals are sent to the spinal cord that releases the neuropeptide, Substance P. signals are relayed from the spinal cord to the brainstem and other brain areas. The brainstem, however, has two descending pathways, one of which can inhibit the pathway of the pain. When this pathway is activated, endorphins (see below) in the dorsal horn of the spinal cord are released, which inhibit Substance P.

There are substances that the body can externally absorb which relieve acute and chronic pain. These are called opioids and are pain-killers, most of which are derived from the opium poppy, *Papaver somniferum*. The opium poppy was used in fairly crude form before the nineteenth century in a medical and recreational context. Crude opium produced analgesia, euphoria and sedation in the user. At the turn of the nineteenth century, morphine was isolated from the opium and became one of the most effective, if not the most effective, means of alleviating pain.

The term, opiate, refers to any substance derived from the poppy; the two most important are morphine and codeine. Codeine acts on brainstem function and can suppress the coughing produced by the region (hence its use as a cough suppressant). The term endorphin is a generic word for any substance produced by the body that has a pain-killing effect and has the pharmacological effects of morphine. There are three basic types of endorphin: enkephalins, dynorphins and keta-endorphins.

The stronger opioids, such as morphine, act on specific types of receptor. There are three receptors that are specifically responsive to opioids – mu, kappa and delta – and it is the mu receptor that responds to morphine. Morphine's action at these receptors produces euphoria, analgesia, a slowness of breathing, constipation and miosis (where the pupils become like pin-points). Opioid receptors are widely distributed in the brain and each of the three types has a unique property. Mu opioid receptors are found in parts of the brain and spinal cord, specifically in the periaquaductal grey matter, caudate nucleus, geniculate nucleus, thalamus and the dorsal horn of the spinal cord. There are also receptors in the brainstem – especially the region controlling respiration – but few in the cortex itself.

The other two types of receptor are also associated with analgesia. Kappa receptors are found in the basal ganglia, nucleus accumbens, deep within the cortex and the dorsal horn of the spinal cord, and activate the release of dopamine at dopaminergic neurons. Some opioids are receptor agonists; some are antagonists. Morphine is an example of a pure agonist, as is methadone (a synthetic opioid that is used to help heroin users come off the drug) and fentanyl (which is used as an anaesthetic), and all bind to the mu receptor. Naltrexone is an opioid antagonist that blocks the access of drugs such as morphine. This is also used to treat heroin addiction – the patient takes the antagonist and then the heroin. Because the heroin has no euphoric effect – due to the antagonistic nature of the naltrexone – the patient receives no reinforcing hit from the drug.

The most effective analgesic is morphine and this can be administered orally, rectally, intravenously, subcutaneously and intramuscularly (the last three via injection). Injection allows the most rapid absorption of the drug but, like the problems discussed with other fast-acting, injected drugs, injection of morphine can lead to overdose. Around 20 per cent of morphine crosses the blood–brain barrier, whereas heroin crosses more easily and is, therefore, associated with more intense euphoria. Heroin (diacetyl morphine, diamorphine) is three times more powerful than morphine and reaches the brain more quickly because it is lipid-soluble. Morphine is metabolised by the liver and the metabolised form, which has the analgesic effect, is over 1000 per cent more potent than the unmetabolised form. It has a half-life of between three and four hours.

Morphine induces analgesia, relaxation, euphoria and shallow breathing. There is no loss of consciousness with the appropriate dose, despite the sedation, and people can still feel sensations of pain, although these sensations reduced and manageable. A vivid example of how morphine can be used to manage pain was that of the playwright, Dennis Potter, who, during his (last) television interview with Melvyn Bragg was seen to break off from the interview to take doses of morphine to alleviate his clearly distressing pain. Potter suffered from painful psoriasis and died shortly after the interview.

Morphine appears to act on mu receptors by facilitating the release of dopamine via the ventral tegmental–nucleus accumbens pathway. It also inhibits GABA neurons and thus disinhibits the production of dopamine from neurons that would be inhibited by GABA.

Marijuana

Marijuana is a mild sedative drug derived from the hemp plant, *Cannabis sativa*. There are various names for cannabis products (depending on its form): hashish, canga, hemp, and so on. The active ingredient in all of them, however, is delta-9-tetrahydrocannabinol (THC) and this is found in greatest concentration in the flowers of the female plant. A typical joint will contain between 150–300 mg of THC. About 50 per cent of THC in a joint of cannabis is inhaled through smoke (the amount is less when taken orally). Because of their composition, THCs can remain in fatty tissue for four to five days. THC has a half-life of seven days and can remain vital for up to 30 days. This means that traces of cannabis can be detected in the body up to a month after inhalation/ingestion has taken place.

THC acts by inhibiting the enzyme adenylate cyclase, which is found inside cells. In order to produce this inhibition, a complex called a G protein complex needs to be present. In the early 1990s, a specific complex receptor was identified that inhibited this enzyme and could bind to cannabinoids (Matsuda *et al.*, 1990). This receptor inhibits the flow of calcium ions and facilitates the flow of potassium. A large number of these receptors is found in the cerebellum, basal ganglia, frontal cortex and hippocampus. THC reaches the brain rapidly and affects the central nervous system (CNS), cardiovascular system and the immune system.

Doses of THC as low as 2.5 g in herbal cigarettes can produce a feeling of intoxication and a reduction in anxiety. Its use is associated with dissociation of ideas, infrequent hallucinations, intense emotional experiences (if the dose is high), heightened sensation and distorted sense of time. It can also produce panic attacks and paranoia. Its effects on psychomotor performance are similar to those of alcohol: behaviour becomes uncoordinated and reaction time slows. According to Thomas (1993), cannabis use includes 'experiences which in a non-intoxicated state would be considered as psychiatric symptoms'. In many European countries, the second most common substance found in the bodies of drivers involved in fatal accidents or drivers who drive poorly is cannabis. The majority of those who used cannabis showed no evidence of excessive or illegal alcohol consumption. Similar performance decrements are seen in pilots (even pilots who are seasoned cannabis users) 24 hours after cannabis intake (Ashton, 2001). A cross-sectional study, which compared the cognitive performance of old and young Costa Rican cannabis users and non-users, found that selective attention and memory recall was significantly more impaired in the older users than the other groups (Fletcher *et al.*, 1996).

10.5 SLEEP

You might think that sleep is a state of unconsciousness but it is, in fact, a state of altered consciousness. We can dream quite vivid dreams and yet forget about them as soon as we wake up (at other times, of course, we experience the opposite and may be surprised or horrified by the content of a dream). Why do we dream? We do not quite know. More importantly, why do we sleep? Again, we do not really know the answer. We do know, however, that sleep is not a constant experience and that there are distinct kinds, characterised by specific behaviours.

Getting to sleep and achieving slumber

Studies of sleep have utilised the psychophysiological techniques you read about in Chapter 2. By using EEG, researchers have been able to monitor changes in brain electrical activity as a person sleeps. Together with measures of eye muscle movement (by electrooculogram, or EOG), body muscle movement (by electromyogram, or EMG) and the activity of the heart (by electrocardiogram, or ECG), EEG has helped show that sleep progresses through several predictable stages.

The EEG is a very good measure of wakefulness. When the person is awake, the EEG tracing appears to be quite erratic. The person usually shows beta activity (high-frequency, low-amplitude activity; you see between 15–30 waves or cycles per second) when awake. When the person is relaxed, perhaps with eyes closed, beta activity reduces and alpha activity dominates. Alpha waves occur between 7 to 13 times a second, and are of medium frequency and amplitude.

Stage 1 of sleep, in which we are just drifting off into sleep, is characterised by theta activity (EEG activity of between 3.5 to 7.5 Hz or cycles per second). The EMG shows that there continues to be muscle activity and the EOG shows that the eyes are gently and slowly rolling. There may be a very slow opening and closing of the eyes. Stage 1 represents the precipice between sleep and wakefulness. After Stage 1, people fall into a deeper sleep and the EEG waves become large and slower. By Stage 4, the predominant EEG is delta activity, which occurs at between 1 to 4 cycles per second. During Stages 2 to 3, theta activity is displaced slightly by delta and, by Stage 4, it has been displaced almost completely by delta. By Stage 4, people are in deep sleep, are difficult to wake, appear oblivious to the environment around them and begin dreaming.

Stages 3 and 4 of sleep are called slow-wave sleep because the sleep is characterised by, not surprisingly, slow waves. It takes about an hour for a person to reach Stage 4 and this stage itself can continue for about half an hour. At this point, there is an interesting change in EEG. The person's brain activity appears to revert to how it was during the first stage of sleep. Heartbeat becomes irregular and there is a rapid, darting movement of the eyes. Eventually, the EEG recording shows signs of beta activity and the person shows signs of wakefulness and alertness. EMG shows that the muscles of the body are almost completely unresponsive but the feet and hands may twitch involuntarily. The body is asleep and yet the EEG record indicates wakefulness. Because of this apparent anomaly, this period of sleep is called paradoxical sleep.

When the rapid movement of the eyes occurs, the person is dreaming and has entered another stage of sleep: rapid eye movement (REM) sleep. According to James, the mental activity at this point represents a 'stream of consciousness' where the internal mental world is rich but where awareness of the outside world is absent. Voluntary control of events is lost but we seem to have a heightened awareness of the content of dreams (Posner and Rothbart, 1998). Stimuli that would normally be perceived during waking are not perceived during REM sleep (Llinas and Pare, 1991). If the person is awakened during REM sleep, they will report having had a dream and will be able to recollect many of its features with great clarity. Figure 10.1 shows some of these EEG changes during sleep.

Why is there this rich dreaming experience during REM? No scientist knows for sure, but some have suggested that there is a shift during REM in memory systems and these memory systems are different to those in non-REM sleep and wakefulness. These systems are associative because the imagery and action in the dream-state is often bizarre, creative and involves associations between events and symbols (Strickgold *et al.*, 1999). There are

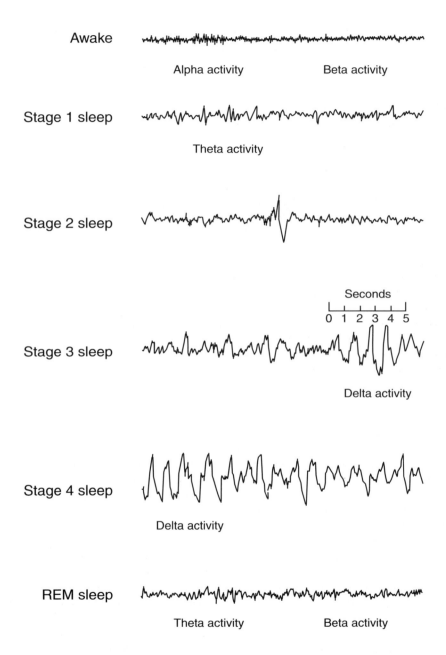

Fig 10.1 EEG changes that occur during the different stages of sleep

several anecdotal reports of problems being solved or of fictions being created during sleep. The story of Dr Jekyll and Mr Hyde, for example, came to the author Robert Louis Stevenson in a dream, and two Nobel Laureates have claimed to have solved complex biochemical problems during dreaming. The creativity may be circumscribed by sensory events or largely cognitive considerations, however. People with prosopagnosia, for example, appear to dream of faceless people.

During REM sleep, men may experience erections and women may release vaginal secretions, although these events are not associated with increased arousal. When REM sleep begins, it continues for about 20 to 30 minutes and then alternates with a period of slow-wave sleep. During the course of a night's sleep, REM sleep gets longer and slow-wave sleep gets shorter. The stages are, however, cyclical: the REM/slow-wave sleep period takes about 90 minutes. In a typical night's sleep of eight hours, therefore, a person will experience about four or five of these cycles.

Why do we sleep?

Sleep is a behaviour that is common to many species, and to all mammals and birds. The fact that it occurs with such regularity in many species suggests that it has some purpose, but what? One of the ways of answering this question is to observe the consequences of depriving a person of sleep. As Horne (2001) puts it,

> It may be a coincidence that renowned disasters or near-disasters due to human errors and concerning nuclear power plants, such as Chernobyl, Three Mile Island, Davis-Besse (Ohio) and Rancho Seco (Sacramento) all occurred in the early morning. ... But sleep deprivation certainly played a crucial role in the fateful dawn decision to launch the Space Shuttle Challenger. Key managers had less than two hours sleep the night before and had been on duty since 1 am.

Sleep deprivation appears to have no effect on physical exercise but it does affect brain and cognitive function. If cognitive tasks are short, sleep-deprived people can perform them as well as non-sleep deprived individuals, but longer tasks that involve allocating more cognitive resources are poorly performed (Horne and Minard, 1985). The 'Focus on ...' section that follows looks at how sleepiness can affect driving and how the effects of sleepiness on driving can be avoided.

During Stage 4 (slow-wave) sleep, the brain seems to show significantly reduced metabolism. When people are awoken during Stage 4, they appear confused, tired and want to go back to sleep. Perhaps the behaviour reflects a system that has shut down and is not functioning properly. Perhaps, therefore, sleep is a resting process allowing the brain to recuperate. If this hypothesis is correct, and the brain and body rests because of the activity it has previously undertaken, then we might further hypothesise that the more activity we engage in during the day, the more we will sleep. Conversely, the less we do, the less we sleep. There is little evidence for either of these hypotheses. Mental exercise, however, does seem to increase the amount of slow-wave sleep we produce. Horne and Minard (1985), for example, found that if a person's day was packed full of mentally stimulating activities, his or her sleep would be characterised by more slow-wave sleep than usual.

A curious phenomenon occurs when a person is deprived of REM sleep, however. If a person is deprived of it for several nights, its onset occurs more quickly when the person is allowed to sleep normally. It is as if a person has lost so much REM sleep that the body needs to engage in more of it, and sooner, when it has the chance to sleep. The body appears to be 'playing catch-up'. That said, if REM sleep is interrupted through brain injury, the interruption has no long-term consequences.

Other researchers have suggested that REM sleep plays a role in learning and consolidation. That is, REM sleep is the brain's way of consolidating or making sense of memories of the day and of removing what is unnecessary. Again, although deprivation of REM sleep is associated with slower learning, learning does take place, which suggests that it is not necessary for learning. Research with animals suggests that REM sleep may play an important part in brain development, however. When infant rats and kittens are deprived of sleep either via drugs or without drugs, respectively, abnormalities are found in the CNS of these animals. What the precise role of REM sleep is in development and why it should impair development in this way is unknown.

Slow-wave sleep has also been implicated in memory consolidation. The neurobiological idea behind this suggestion is that the hippocampus retreads the ground the person has gone over during the day and this replaying of memories leads to a strengthening of these memory traces (Wilson and McNaughton, 1994). Some have limited slow-wave sleep's involvement to declarative memory. Plihal and Born (1999) exploited the finding that slow-wave sleep is characterised by an inhibition of glucocorticoids to hypothesise that if this inhibition was reversed, declarative memory consolidation would be poorer than if inhibition was allowed as normal. They found that when a drug that inhibited glucocorticoid release was given before sleep but after participants had learned a series of word pairs, recall of the word pairs was significantly worse when the participants awoke than if inhibition had continued. Non-declarative memory was unaffected.

Focus on ... driving, sleep and fatigue

Most road traffic accidents occur between four and six o'clock in the morning, with a second, slightly smaller peak occurring in the middle of the afternoon (Horne and Reyner, 1999). Most researchers have attributed this pattern of accidents to sleeplessness and/or fatigue. A lack of sleep exacerbates driving performance, as does a feeling of fatigue (which appears to have the same detrimental effect on driving as alcohol, DeWaard and Brookhuis, 1991). Imagine a person who has completed a night shift for the first time after having slept little in the last 24 hours, and who then drives the long, monotonous road journey home. All of these conditions will present problems to the driver (Horne and Reyner, 1999) and studies have shown that driving performance is impaired in those people who cut short their sleep to make an early morning journey. Even in the wakeful driver, prolonged driving induces subjective feelings of tiredness (Summala *et al.*, 1999) and lane drifting (Brookhuis and DeWaard, 1993). Difficult driving conditions, however, seem to result in fewer driving mistakes than do monotonous ones, such as driving on a straight road (Matthews and Desmond, 2002).

Jim Horne and his colleagues at the sleep laboratories of Loughborough University have spent several years investigating how a lack of sleep affects our driving, as well as other aspects of our behaviour. EEG activity that is typical of the early stages of sleep is found in people who have been deprived of sleep and who are asked to simulate driving. The changes in physiology correlate with erratic driving; veering from one side of the road to the other is common, as is a lack of responsiveness to what is happening on the road (such as a change in traffic lights or the car in front braking). One obvious way of preventing this erratic, lack-of-sleep-induced driving is to avoid it completely; but if this is not practical, one solution may be to ingest substances that are psychoactive and that might stimulate wakefulness. The most obvious example of such a substance is caffeine.

To see if caffeine could reduce erratic driving brought on by a lack of sleep, Horne and Reyner (1996; Reyner and Horne, 1997) had participants who had been deprived of sleep complete a simulated driving exercise in the afternoon. In one study, the participants received either 150–200 mg of caffeine (in coffee), a placebo, or were asked to take a short nap before driving. In a second study, the nap and caffeine were combined. Both of the stimulating interventions – catching up on sleep and drinking caffeine – improved driving performance with significantly less lane drifting seen in these participants. The participants also reported feeling less sleepy after the interventions. In separate experiments, Reyner and Horne (1998) found that two common interventions when drivers feel sleepy – blowing cold air on the face or listening to the radio – had only short-term effects on sleepiness.

The data suggest that if a driver feels sleepy at the wheel, the first solution is to stop at a convenient place and take a nap. Coupling the nap with an intake of caffeine is an even better way of combating the potentially dangerous effects of sleepiness while driving.

How do we sleep?

There is a point in the day when most of us want to fall asleep for long periods; there are other points in the day when we want to be awake and when sleep is not desirable. What governs these behaviours? One factor may be the rhythmic changes that occur naturally in plants and animals. These changes are controlled by two internal clocks, and one of these appears to govern our daily, or circadian, rhythms – such as ensuring that we wake up and sleep at specific times of day, or that our temperature changes with these changes in wakefulness. Daylight appears to be the factor that sets our circadian clock.

The circadian clock is controlled by two small structures in the hypothalamus, called the suprachiasmatic nuclei (SCN), illustrated in Figure 10.2.

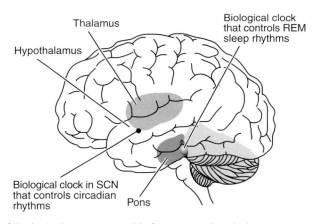

Fig 10.2 Areas of the brain that are responsible for our circadian clocks

The neurons here oscillate during the day and become inactive during the night; these oscillations control our periods of sleep and wakefulness. They are not resistant to change, however. If you placed a person in a windowless, permanently lighted room, their circadian rhythm would be present as normal but with continued exposure to the persistent light, the circadian rhythm would go a little out of synchrony with the 'real' world rather than the artificially lit one. When people leave such an environment, however, their circadian clock returns to normal. When we are exposed to daylight or turn on the lights when we wake up, our clock is reset and begins 'ticking'.

The other clock works for shorter periods – 90 minutes – and its discovery was made in the early 1960s when researchers noted that babies would demand feeding at regular intervals (Kleitman, 1961). Subsequent research has shown that other behaviours show a cyclical pattern: eating, drinking, urinating ... all follow a pattern of rest and activity. Kleitman (1982) called this the basic rest-activity cycle (BRAC). During the night, the BRAC controls the periods of slow-wave and REM sleep. The receptors that control this cycle, and thus REM sleep, appear to be located in the pons of the brainstem.

In mammals, the sensors that detect light and send signals to the circadian clock are located in the eyes and are called circadian photoreceptors. It was thought that the rods and cones of the eye were the parts that detected light in mammals, but studies with frogs with no rods and cones also show sensitivity to light. A pigment on the skin of the frogs appeared to be light-sensitive – this was called melanopsin – and later this pigment was also found in the retinas of these frogs and also in the retinal ganglion cells (RGCs) of mice (Provencio *et al.*, 2000).

When these neurons activate REM sleep, they release acetylcholine which has several effects on the CNS – activating neurons that cause REM sleep or activating the cortex. These RGCs receive signals from rods and cones and send information to the brain; about 1–2 per cent go to the SCN. However, when these RGCs are traced to the SCN in rats whose retinas have been removed and are exposed to light, they fire (Berson *et al.*, 2002). This suggests that these RGCs do not need rods and cones in order to demonstrate photosensitivity and that melanopsin may be the pigment which allows these RGCs to detect and respond to light.

Sleep disorders

Slumber sometimes does not go smoothly and people experience difficulties in sleeping. These difficulties include not being able to sleep, as well as being unable to stop sleep. Perhaps the most common sleep disorder is insomnia.

Insomnia

Insomnia is a symptom rather than a condition. It cannot be treated effectively by medication, for example, and in many cases is a symptom of a primary condition such as pain or discomfort. It is also a subjectively described phenomenon because some people can function happily on five regular hours of sleep a night whereas others cannot function on fewer than eight. A definition of insomnia, therefore, is difficult to make scientifically because different people need different amounts of sleep.

One of the conditions that can cause insomnia, especially in older people, is sleep apnoea where a patient is unable to breathe and sleep at the same time. When people fall asleep, they stop breathing and the build-up of carbon dioxide in the body leads to them waking up gasping for oxygen. With a session of deep breathing, however, these people are able to resume their sleep. The reasons for sleep apnoea are unclear although some restriction of oxygen via the air passages of the throat seems a likely factor.

Disorders associated with REM sleep

Two of the key features of REM sleep are dreaming and paralysis: the paralysis prevents a dream from being acted out but if the brain area responsible for its prevention – the pons – is damaged, an animal will 'act out' a dream although appearing asleep. Cats, for example, appear to walk around as if stalking prey and will respond to 'imaginary' foes (Jouvet, 1972).

Cataplexy is another disorder affected by the paralysing effects of the brain. People suffering from cataplexy become paralysed while engaging in normal day-to-day activity. These occurrences are described as attacks because they are sudden and last about a minute: as soon as the person becomes paralysed, they enter REM sleep. The attacks seem to be triggered off by emotional events such as laughter or crying. No one quite knows why they happen but they can be reduced by drugs that release inhibitory neurotransmitters.

Disorders associated with slow-wave sleep

The most common disorders of slow-wave/Stage 4/deep sleep are sleepwalking, talking in one's sleep, night terrors and bed-wetting (enuresis).

Sleepwalking can involve getting in and out of bed, or a more circuitous ramble around the house or to a car. Because sleepwalking occurs in Stage 4 of sleep, it appears not to be related to dreaming (because there is no REM). Sleepwalkers are difficult to awaken and, when woken, they appear confused and disorientated. The disorder causes no real harm – as long as the house is made as safe as possible.

Talking in one's sleep can occur during any stage of sleep but is more common during Stages 2 to 3. When people talk in their sleep, it is possible to converse with them but they will be unlikely to recall the conversation or its content when they have woken up. It is as if they are holding a conversation in the twilight zone between sleep and wakefulness.

Night terrors are more common in children than in adults and usually involve the child waking up screaming in terror. The child, however, is not capable of reporting having experienced any dream. Terrors are different to nightmares, which are frightening dreams. One theory suggests that the terrors result from a sudden awakening from Stage 4 sleep. Because the waking is sudden and occurs when the child is in deep sleep, the sudden change is terrifying to them.

Another slow-wave sleep disorder common to children is enuresis or bed-wetting. Bed-wetting has no single, identifiable cause but is thought to be triggered by emotional problems. It does not signify any psychological abnormality and it soon disappears as the child gets older (as do night terrors and sleepwalking). Feelings of anxiety may arise, however, because the behaviour has an outcome that needs clearing up and the child may feel guilty for necessitating the waking up of their parents and the time spent in changing the bed. A simple solution to the bed-wetting is to place moisture-sensitive sensors under the bedsheet that set off an alarm when they become wet. This wakes the child, who can then go to the toilet as normal.

10.6 ALTERED STATE OF CONSCIOUSNESS: HYPNOSIS

Hypnosis is a process whereby a person can be verbally instructed to behave in a particular way when he or she would not normally behave in that way. The ability to do this was first noted by the Austrian physician Franz Anton Mesmer, who coined the term mesmerism to describe it. He would pass magnets up and down the bodies of people to restore their magnetic balance and cure them of disease, and would notice that they would convulse or enter trance-like states. Mesmer noticed that his magnets had nothing to do with these behaviours but his suggestions during the magnet-dangling did.

There is no need to dangle objects such as a fobwatch in front of a person to induce a hypnotic state. A person may be alert or relaxed, lying down or sitting up. The process of induction normally involves suggesting that the person become relaxed or sleepy, followed by suggestions that the person lowers or lifts a limb. It may then be suggested that the person cannot lower their arm. They can also be convinced that they can or can't do other things.

Hypnotised people tend to be highly suggestible, but opinion is divided over whether hypnosis represents a trance-like state or whether it can be explained by more mundane psychological processes such as role-playing or compliance (Wagstaff, 1996).

Hypnosis has been used as an analgesic with mixed results: it appears to work for people who are hypnotically suggestible. Brain imaging studies have shown that during the hypnotic 'state', there are increases in blood flow to the occipital cortex and there is increased EEG delta activity (Rainville et al., 1999). There are also blood flow increases to the anterior cingulate cortex and in a part of the frontal cortex on both sides of the brain. During hypnotic suggestion, these increases are accompanied by significant increases in the frontal cortex on the left side, perhaps reflecting a process of disinhibition related to language, for which the frontal cortex takes responsibility.

Crawford et al. (1993) have reported that highly susceptible individuals show a bilateral increase in blood flow to the frontal cortex and somatosensory cortex during hypnotic analgesia and the experience of pain.

Studies of the brain's electrical activity have also implicated the frontal and temporal parts of the brain during hypnotically reduced pain perception (Crawford *et al.*, 1998). The evidence suggests that the frontal region deals with the active allocation of attention, whereas the posterior parts are concerned with the spatiotemporal aspects of pain perception (such as where and when the pain is experienced).

This neural activation, of course, does not demonstrate that hypnotic suggestion placed participants in an altered state of consciousness or placed them in a trance. In fact, the findings may have plausible, if mundane, cognitive explanations. Wagstaff (1987) has suggested that many of the effects seen in hypnotic analgesia are the result of the same factors that result in other forms of hypnotism. These factors include social support, relaxation, covert modelling, placebo and social compliance. Belief in the efficacy of the hypnosis is also an important factor. Wagstaff and Royce (1994) found that although hypnotic suggestions for the alleviation of nail-biting were better than non-hypnotic suggestions, the best predictor of abstinence from nail-biting was belief in the efficacy of the procedure. There may, therefore, be a strong placebo effect seen in these studies.

SOME USEFUL FURTHER READING

CONSCIOUSNESS: GENERAL
Baars, B.J. (1998) Metaphors of consciousness and attention in the brain. *Trends in Neurosciences* 21(2), 58–62.
Tassi, P. and Muzet, A. (2001) Defining the states of consciousness. *Neuroscience and Biobehavioural Reviews* 25, 175–91.

NEUROBIOLOGY OF CONSCIOUSNESS
Crick, F. and Koch, C. (2002) The problem of consciousness. *Scientific American* 12(1), 10–17.
Damasio, A.R. (1998) Investigating the biology of consciousness. *Philosophical Transactions of the Royal Society of London B, Biological Sciences* 353(1377), 1879–82.

DRUGS AND THE BRAIN
Julien, R.M. (2000) *A Primer of Drug Action* (ninth edition). New York: W.H. Freeman.

SLEEP
Horne, J. (2001) State of the art: sleep. *The Psychologist* 14(6), 302–6.
Winson, J. (2002) The meaning of dreams. *Scientific American* 12(1), 54–61.

HYPNOSIS
Maquet, P., Faymonville, M.E., Degueldre, C., Delfiore, G., Frank, G., Luxen, A. and Lamy, M. (1999) Functional neuroanatomy of hypnotic state. *Biological Psychiatry* 45(3), 327–33.

SOME USEFUL JOURNALS TO BROWSE

Addiction
British Journal of Psychiatry
Consciousness and Cognition
Imagination, Cognition and Personality
International Journal of Experimental and Clinical Hypnosis
Journal of Cognitive Neuroscience
Journal of Consciousness Studies
Pain
Psyche (see also http://psyche.cs.monash.edu.au/)
Psychopharmacology
Psychophysiology
Nature Neuroscience
Neuropsychobiology
Neuropsychologia
Trends in Cognitive Sciences
Trends in Pharmacological Sciences
Science
Sleep

11 Psychological and Degenerative Disorders

11.1 DISORDERS OF THE CENTRAL NERVOUS SYSTEM (CNS)

In some of the earlier chapters, you saw how damage to parts of the central nervous system (CNS) – especially the brain – affected functions such as vision, perception, language and emotion. There are other changes to the CNS that cause, or are associated with, more general psychological disorders. These disorders include psychiatric conditions such as dementia, depression and schizophrenia. This chapter describes some of the major types of disorder that involve the CNS.

11.2 DEMENTIA

Dementia describes a gradual, insidious and relentless loss of cognitive function and a diagnosis is made on the basis of clinical, histopathological and localisation factors. According to the American Diagnostic and Statistical Manual (DSM-IV, 1994), the diagnostic criteria for dementia are:

- a demonstrable impairment in short- and long-term memory

- at least one of the following – abstract thinking impairment, impaired judgement, higher cortical function disturbance (such as aphasia or agnosia) or personality change, the ability of memory/cognitive impairment to interfere with work, social activities and relationships, evidence of an organic factor that is 'aetiologically related' to the disturbance.

11.3 DEMENTIA OF THE ALZHEIMER TYPE (DAT)

Alzheimer's disease (AD) is the most common cause of dementia, occurring in approximately 45 per cent of demented patients in the USA (Cummings and Benson, 1992) and with an estimated prevalence of 3.75 million worldwide (Stuss and Levine, 1996). The disease was named after Alois Alzheimer who, in 1907, reported the case of a demented 56-year-old patient with abnormal formations called presenile plaques and tangles in her brain. This dementia is referred to as Dementia of the Alzheimer Type, or DAT. Other types of dementia occur with Parkinson's disease, Huntington's chorea, Pick's disease and other pathologies, discussed later.

It is estimated that between 5 and 10 per cent of individuals over 65 years of age will develop Alzheimer's disease (Rocca *et al.*, 1986) with the percentage quadrupling in the over-eighties. A recent study of the prevalence of DAT in Germany placed the estimate at 17 per cent (Riedel-Heller *et al.*, 2001). The disease can occur sporadically or in a genetic form called familial Alzheimer's disease. The familial form is thought to be autosomal dominant with the gene carried on chromosome 21 and, possibly, chromosome 19. It expresses itself by producing proteins that lead to malformations in neurons (see below). A positive family history of late-onset AD is a risk factor for developing the disease, and the most consistent genetic factor for late-onset AD is having one or more copies of the APOE4 allele (Holmes, 2002).

Psychological features of DAT

The major cognitive impairment in AD is loss of memory. Poor short-term memory and explicit memory are common features as is impaired episodic/autobiographical memory. Implicit memory is not as severely affected, neither is memory for remote events. Although public (famous face and name processing) and autobiographical memory is impaired in Alzheimer's patients, only public memory appears to deteriorate longitudinally (Greene and Hodges, 1996), which suggests that remote memory may be fractionated into components.

Language functions such as comprehension and naming, and coherent and semantically accurate speech are impaired. Both semantic knowledge and concept formation are poor in AD patients. Learning of new information is difficult and visual memory span is reduced (Albert and Moss, 1983). In the early stages, conversational speech is relatively normal with few solecisms. Speech content, however, is abnormal with a reliance on stock phrases. Reading ability is preserved. In the later stages, memory failure progresses, and judgement and the capacity for abstract thought disappear. In the final stage, all intellectual function breaks down and the patients reach the stage where they cannot recognise relatives, or even recognise themselves in a mirror.

Neuropathological features of DAT

Post-mortem brains of AD patients show a shrinkage of primarily frontal and temporal gyri (up to 20 per cent) and ventricle enlargement, although there is the possibility that the shrinkage is due to normal ageing because not all AD patients exhibit shrinkage. There is neuronal loss in the cortex, the hippocampal formation and the surrounding areas.

The classic pathological symptoms of AD are (1) neurofibrillary tangles, (2) senile plaques, (3) granulovacuolar degeneration, and (4) Hirano bodies. All are abnormal amyloid protein deposits in intracellular and extracellular sites (Muller-Hill and Beyreuther, 1989). Neurofibrillary tangles are straight or paired helical filaments that collect intracellularly, are made up of special proteins, and especially affect the temporal, parietal and frontal areas. The tangles do not appear with normal ageing, although they are found in other dementias.

Senile plaques are glia and abnormal nerve cell processes are more pronounced in AD patients than in age-matched controls. Some patients exhibit tangles but not plaques. Granuovacuolar degeneration occurs primarily in the hippocampus and, as the name suggests, results in neuronal tissue becoming full of holes. Brain imaging studies also indicate parietal lobe dysfunction, with extensive degeneration in this region and at temporal sites (Esiri et al., 1990).

Cholinergic dysfunction and dementia

One of the established neurochemical features of AD is the loss of acetylcholine, acetylcholinetransferase and nicotinic receptors. In the mid-1970s it was found that a loss of up to 70 per cent of choline acetyltransferase (CAT), the cholinergic marker enzyme that synthesises acetylcholine, was found in the temporal and parietal cortices of AD patients. This acetylcholine synthesis impairment is correlated with the severity of the dementia, and the loss is correlated with the number of senile plaques and the degree of dementia (Perry *et al.*, 1978). The cholinergic pathways linking the septum to the hippocampus are both lost in AD. This role of the cholinergic system in memory was encouraged by studies in which scopolamine, a cholinergic agonist, produced amnesia in healthy individuals. Despite this memory loss, the pattern of impairment seen with scopolamine is not identical to that seen in AD (Beatty *et al.*, 1986). The cholinergic system, however, is the key neurotransmitter targeted by putative drugs for alleviating DAT symptoms.

Treatment of AD

The current cost of caring for patients with DAT in the UK alone is estimated to be between £5 billion and £15 billion a year (McNamee *et al.*, 2001; Lowin *et al.*, 2001) but no current treatment is able to halt the progress of AD. Those treatments that have been attempted, have focused on alleviating the memory impairments in DAT. The cholinergic hypothesis of AD led to the development of drugs that specifically sought to redress the loss of cholinergic neurons and neurotransmitters. The mechanism of action for these drugs is the inhibition of the enzyme, acetylcholinesterase, which divides the neurotransmitter at its receptors (Bullock, 2002). Three compounds currently used are donepezil, rivastigimine and galantamine.

Patients who have been given a course of either donepezil or rivastigimine have shown some improvement in memory performance (Cameron *et al.*, 2000; Evans *et al.*, 2000). Other drugs under review are anti-inflammatory drugs (because the incidence of AD is low in sufferers of rheumatoid arthritis) and antioxidants such as vitamin E, but neither has been shown to demonstrate consistent efficacy (Bullock, 2002). Perhaps the most innovative treatment currently under investigation involves vaccinating the individual thereby giving him or her an antibody to remove the amyloid protein that causes cell degeneration. Trials in mice have been effective in relieving symptoms of AD and in preventing the development of plaques (Shenk *et al.*, 1999) but we have no such vaccine for humans, as yet.

Research update ... ageing and cognition

There is often a blurred line between the effects of normal ageing and the effects of Alzheimer's disease, and a clear diagnosis of DAT is difficult to make because the symptoms can be masked by the effects of normal ageing. Cognitive decline is common to both ageing and DAT (Horn,

1982). The difference between ageing and dementia, however, appears to be neurophysiological: ageing is not usually associated with the degree of plaques and tangles seen in patients with DAT.

Our processing capacity, however, seems to decline consistently with age, and this has been thought to underlie other examples of intellectual decline observed (Craik and Salthouse, 2000). The decline in ability to engage in working memory, to attend to stimuli and to process information speedily may explain the failure of older people on tests of fluid intelligence. All three types decline with age and appear to be linked with the loss of dopamine. Some researchers have suggested that the most important factor in information processing, and that underlies all cognitive decline with ageing is speed of processing (Salthouse, 1993). Salthouse (1991) has argued that speed of processing is a resource in the same way that working memory and attention is a resource.

A common neurophysiological feature of ageing is cell death and a reduction in the density of synapses. Dopamine levels also decline with ageing and the number of D2 receptors in the nigrostriatal region may be reduced by 10 per cent per decade from the age of 20 (Li et al., 2001). There may also be similar loss in other areas including the anterior cingulate cortex (found at the tip of the corpus callosum), the prefrontal cortex, the hippocampus and the amygdala.

The intellectual deficits seen with ageing have been attributed to a decline in prefrontal function (West, 1996). One area that is responsible for working memory – as you saw in the chapter on learning and memory – is the dorsolateral prefrontal cortex, and dopaminergic connections to this area may be reduced with increasing age (Arnsten, 1998). If ageing monkeys are given drugs that facilitate the working of the dopaminergic system (specifically, D1 agonists), the working memory deficits that are normally observed are reduced. With no intervention, D1 receptors continue to decline with age.

Interestingly, there is some evidence that older people may not be as efficient in using their neural resources as younger people. In neuroimaging studies where people are asked to engage in various cognitive tasks, activity is significantly more bilateral in older people than in younger people, especially when they are asked to retrieve material from memory (Reuter-Lorenz et al., 2000). One explanation for this finding is that more than one area of the brain is recruited in older people during task performance because the brain is compensating for the failure of the normal regions to function at optimum level.

11.4 PARKINSON'S DISEASE

Another degenerative disease, Parkinson's disease (PD) is a motor disorder in which individuals experience lack of spontaneous or voluntary movement (called akinesia), resistance to passive movement (called rigidity) and tremor when at rest. Parkinson's disease (PD) was first described by James Parkinson in 1817. The movement impairments can include general slowness of movement (called bradykinesia) as well as reduction of movement (called hypokinesia). Patients with PD can sometimes be seen pill-rolling: the forefinger and thumb move against each other as if a pill is being rolled between the two fingers. A clinical diagnosis of PD involves confirming the presence of two of the three classic symptoms outlined above. Onset normally occurs at around 60 years of age but there is a form called young-onset PD. The incidence of the disorder is around 0.5 per cent in those aged over 50.

The early symptoms appear as disturbed fine motor control in the hand; this makes activities such as writing or doing up buttons difficult. Speech becomes hoarse, the swing of the arm when walking might be reduced and making two simultaneous movements becomes problematic. The posture difficulties (such as falling over following a period of hesitation, or 'freezing') tend to be resistant to therapy.

Neuropathological features

The most prominent neuropathological feature of PD is a loss of the striatal dopamine pathway that runs from the substantia nigra to the neostriatum (caudate nucleus and putamen) and globus pallidus regions, as illustrated in Figure 11.1.

There is degeneration of the ventrolateral layer of the substantia nigra projecting to the striatum (Fearnley and Lees, 1991). Material, called Lewy bodies, is also found in the substantia nigra and locus coeruleus, which may be a diagnostic marker for the disease (although other diseases with Parkinsonian symptoms also show evidence of these Lewy bodies, and Lewy bodies are also found in other parts of the brain such as the cortex and raphe nuclei).

Dopamine has been found to be depleted in the caudate nucleus, putamen, substantia nigra and globus pallidus in patients with PD, with greater loss in the putamen (the loss is about 70–90 per cent) than in the caudate nucleus (Kish *et al.*, 1988). The residual striatal neurons may compensate for the loss of dopamine by increasing their activity, increasing dopamine or facilitating dopamine's release. These compensatory measures mean that clinical symptoms do not present themselves until dopamine levels have declined by

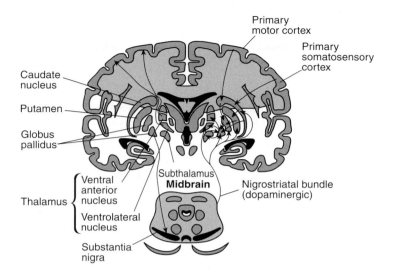

Fig 11.1 The basal ganglia

approximately 80 per cent, the 'threshold' for PD (Strange, 1992). There is also a reduction in GABA and 5-hydroxytryptamine in the striatum and substantia nigra (where these two transmitters predominantly exist).

The complex picture of neurotransmitter involvement in Parkinsonism has been accounted for, in part, by a model of basal ganglia circuitry, which suggests a complex arrangement of indirect and direct striatal outputs (Alexander *et al.*, 1990). The indirect pathway is thought to be over-stimulated in PD by an increase in glutamate release. This is normally inhibited by D2 receptors but the outer globus pallidus becomes overactivated. Meanwhile, the internal part becomes overstimulated, as is the pathway leading to the thalamus. This pallidothalamic projection is inhibitory but it is overactive; therefore, it has an overinhibitory effect on thalamic neurons. The direct pathway represents the inhibitory neurons of the striatopallidal pathway to the internal globus pallidus. This is excited by dopamine but the pathway is underactive. Both pathways increase activity of the internal globus pallidus.

Treatment for Parkinson's disease

Levodopa (L-DOPA), the precursor of dopamine and the first dopaminergic therapy for PD, significantly reduces the symptoms of PD. L-DOPA is taken up by nigrostriatal nerve endings where it is converted into dopamine. About 15 per cent of patients are unresponsive to treatment but these are not likely to have pure PD. After chronic treatment, improvement may also be seen to wane, with motor oscillations occurring either due to the drug 'wearing off' or to the fluctuating clinical state of the subject.

In recent years an alternative to drug therapy has been sought because patients experience 'off periods' when the symptoms recur. One promising new treatment involves surgical lesioning of the subcortical structures that give rise to the dopamine dysfunction and this is taken up in the 'Focus on ...' section below.

Focus on ... non-pharmacological treatment of Parkinson's disease

It has been estimated that around 70 per cent of patients who have been medicated for up to 15 years show fluctuations in treatment (Miyawaki *et al.*, 1997). Patients sometimes experience difficulties during the so-called 'off period' when the drug is not taken, and PD symptoms return when the drug apparently 'wears off'.

To try and combat these adverse effects, a different approach makes use of the fact that a specific regional neurotransmitter system is affected in PD. Two techniques explicitly utilising this knowledge are lesioning and deep-brain stimulation (DBS) in nerve cells in specific regions of the brain in PD patients. These regions include the thalamus, which acts as a relay station for sensory and motor input, a region near the thalamus (called the subthalamic nucleus) and a part of the globus pallidus (one of the three structures that make up the basal ganglia).

The lesioning approach involves destroying nerve cells in parts of the brain. Animal models of PD have shown improvements in symptoms when the neural regions responsible are destroyed. Human studies have shown that when the globus pallidus of a PD patient is lesioned, there is an improvement in drug-induced motor disorder and rigidity (Lang *et al.*, 1997). However, the technique is not free of problems. Some studies suggest that between 20 and 25 per cent of patients suffer some surgery-related complications (Obeso *et al.*, 1997). There is also the disadvantage that the procedure is irreversible.

Deep-brain stimulation, however, is reversible and has controllable side-effects (Schuurman *et al.*, 2000). In DBS, specific brain regions are electrically stimulated by inserting an electrode into the relevant brain area. This electrode is attached to a pulse-generating device that can deliver the stimulation. Studies have shown that DBS of the subthalamic nucleus and a part of the globus pallidus is associated with good improvement in tremor, bradykinesia and rigidity in PD patients (Limousin *et al.*, 1999; Galvez-

Jimenez *et al.*, 1998). Limousin *et al.* (1999), for example, electrically stimulated the subthalamic nucleus of 24 PD patients over a 12-month period. A 60 per cent improvement was seen in rigidity, tremor and gait.

Why (and how) should DBS work? There are various explanations, but most agree that some form of reduction in the excessive output of the globus pallidus to other brain regions is the key factor. Because electrical stimulation either reduces or inactivates nerve cells, it could directly inhibit these cells or cause other processes in the brain to inhibit nerve cells (Lozano, 2001).

11.4 OTHER CAUSES OF DEMENTIA

Pick's disease

Pick's disease is another degenerative condition associated with dementia but it differs symptomatically from AD in that there are marked changes in personality and social behaviour. Typically, the patient displays 'frontal lobe symptoms' such as lack of planning and perseveration, and lack of inhibition and attention. The histological characteristic of the disease is a collection of foreign bodies, called Pick bodies, in neurons (Wechsler *et al.*, 1982) and there is degeneration in the frontal and temporal cortex. Behaviourally, however, it is sometimes difficult to distinguish between AD and Pick's disease patients based on cognitive deterioration because this is similar in both. However, if the patient exhibits the classic frontal lobe characteristics, has asymmetrical frontal or temporal atrophy but normal EEG, Pick's disease is the more likely diagnosis (Whitehouse *et al.*, 1993).

Vascular complications

Another dementia, vascular dementia, arises from ischemia and haemorrhage, or from cerebral injury caused by cardiac arrest. It is also called multi-infarct dementia and results from many small cortical and subcortical infarcts, although the reason for their appearance is unclear. Features include slowing of cognition, memory impairment, executive dysfunction, and changes in personality and mood. Although it is thought to be the second most common type of dementia, there is still concern that the dementia is not very well defined (Stewart, 2002).

Korsakoff's psychosis

As you saw in the chapter on memory, Korsakoff's psychosis, or Korsakoff's syndrome, is a rare organic disorder in which alcohol has been a large source of caloric intake for many years. It is caused by thiamine (vitamin B1) deficiency, and damage to the medial diencephalon is common, especially in the dorsomedial nucleus of the thalamus and the mammillary bodies. Arendt and colleagues (1983) reported a reduction of 47 per cent in the nucleus basalis of Meynert (NbM) of patients with Korsakoff's psychosis (compared with 70 per cent loss in AD). Episodic and recognition memory deficits, concept formation, set shifting deficits and anterograde amnesia are common symptoms.

Recent as well as past memories may be affected. Korsakoff noted that the severity of the deficits varied, with mild cases showing an ability to remember recent memories, if only vaguely. Patients also invented fictions and repeated them. A consistent finding is that patients have difficulties in spatial memory. Although different forms of brain pathology may lead to amnesic syndromes, the term Korsakoff's syndrome is used to refer to cases of specific memory impairment which have a specific neuropathology and result from thiamine deficiency.

Huntington's chorea

Another well-known degenerative motor disorder is Huntington's chorea (HC), or Huntington's disease, first described by George Huntington who studied the incidence of chorea (jerky, dance-like movements) in families in Long Island, New York. The disease is inherited, autosomal dominant and appears to involve a mutation of a gene on the arm of chromosome 4. The result is degeneration of small and medium-sized neurons in the striatum, particularly GABAergic neurons, which project to the globus pallidus. The disorder can be traced back many years in a person's history and because of its inherited status, can be traced back many centuries. Historically, it has been thought that the 'witches of Salem' may have suffered from HC.

HC is rare and affects approximately 0.01 per cent of the population (the prevalence is two to seven individuals per 100 000). Age of onset is usually around 40 to 50 years, and the average duration of the disorder is 19 years. The most prominent feature of HC is involuntary, choreiform (dance-like) movement and dementia. Movements appear out of control and jerky, and the patient may also have difficulty speaking and standing. The first signs of the disease might manifest themselves in changes in personality or in gradual clumsiness or unsteadiness. There is also degeneration of the caudate nucleus.

A cognitive feature of HC is an impairment in executive function. The ability to plan, shift cognitive set and self-monitor, therefore, is poor in these patients. On the basis of this feature, some have suggested that the disease be described as a fronto-striatal dementia (Lawrence *et al.*, 1996). To determine whether executive dysfunction characterises HC and whether these deficits occur in the absence of other intellectual impairments, Crawford, *et al.* (2000) administered three 'frontal lobe' tests to 23 patients with HC and 22 healthy individuals. Crawford *et al.* found that the HC group's performance on the tests was significantly worse than that of the control group. However, its performance on standard intelligence tests was also significantly worse, which suggests that the executive deficit is not an exclusive characteristic of HC but one that may be related to general intellectual impairment.

In the late stages of the disorder, patients may be bed-ridden and in a vegetative state, and may often die of complications related to their immobility or difficulties in swallowing. Because the disease is inherited and is an autosomal dominant one, the child of an HC parent has a 50 per cent chance of developing the disease. If the gene is present, it will be expressed.

Motor neuron damage

Motor disorders that involve a dysfunction of the motor neurons include muscular paralysis and atrophy such as poliomyelitis, which is caused by a viral infection of the motor neurons of the spinal cord. Limb weakness, especially lower limbs or arms, result from loss of myelin in motor and sensory tracts (e.g. multiple sclerosis), and paralysis of both lower limbs can result from complete transection of the spinal cord (paraplegia). Paralysis can also occur in all four limbs (quadriplegia) and cerebral palsy describes motor dysfunction resulting from foetal brain damage.

11.5 DISORDERS OF THOUGHT AND EMOTION

Other CNS disorders present either more emotional features or different cognitive symptoms to those considered above. Clinical mood disorders, so-called affective disorders, are distinguished from normal emotional or mood changes in a number of ways. Most of us will experience mood changes occasionally: elation at having got a better-paid job, achieving an 'A' grade in an exam, becoming a parent, winning the lottery. We might experience sadness at the death of a friend or relative, at failing to win an important order, or at failing an exam. However, while momentarily upsetting, these experiences are not normally long-lasting and do not usually impair an individual's way of life permanently. Clinical emotional disturbances, if they go untreated, are long-lasting and do impair the individual's normal way of life.

The most common disorders of mood and affect are depression and mania. There are other emotional disorders, classed as anxiety disorders, and these include phobias, generalised anxiety disorder and obsessive-compulsive disorder (experiencing obsessional thoughts and impulses or obsessively performing behavioural rituals such as excessive washing of hands). These disorders involve an extreme emotional response – clinical anxiety or depression. Whereas normal mood shifts can disappear relatively easily; clinical mood changes are normally alterable only by medication or intensive behavioural or cognitive therapy. Another mental illness with emotional features, but which is not strictly a disorder of emotion, is schizophrenia. Schizophrenia is a disorder of thought and some biological factors may underlie its appearance.

11.6 DEPRESSION

The symptoms of depression depend on the degree of depression experienced. Some individuals will be miserable and show little interest in normally interesting activities (moderate depressive disorder). They might be pessimistic about the present, past and future, and feel helpless. Others might experience the same thoughts and feelings but with greater intensity (severe depressive disorder). Individuals may also experience bouts of mania that alternate with depressive episodes. Manic individuals are overactive, erratic, disinhibited, hypersexual, highly frustrated, demanding, flirtatious, insomniac and irritable. When manic episodes alternate with depressive episodes, the condition is described as a bi-polar disorder. When depressive episodes alone are observed, the condition is described as uni-polar. Manic episodes are never experienced alone.

Uni-polar, or major, depression is characterised by depressive symptoms that have spanned at least two weeks. It is twice as common in women than in men (bi-polar disorder shows no sex difference) and symptoms tend to be worse in the morning. According to DSM-IV, a major depressive syndrome is defined as one that has at least five of the manual's stated symptoms experienced within a two-week period. Mean age of onset for bi-polar disorder tends towards adolescence/young adulthood; uni-polar disorder has a later onset.

Neuropathology of depression

The region of the brain that seems to show greatest dysfunction in depression is the prefrontal cortex. Metabolic activity in frontal regions is found to be reduced in depressed patients (Austin *et al.*, 1992; Bench *et al.*, 1993), a feature called hypometabolism. Along similar lines, Davidson and colleagues (Schaffer, Davidson and Saron, 1983; Henriques and Davidson, 1991) have found less frontal EEG activation in clinically depressed patients.

Research update ... depression and the brain

In a series of pioneering studies, Drevets and his colleagues identified a specific region in the prefrontal cortex that was irregular in depressed individuals. In a neuroimaging study, they found that activity in the prefrontal cortex near the top of the corpus callosum was reduced in individuals with uni-polar and bi-polar depression (Drevets *et al.*, 1997). This part of the prefrontal cortex is called the anterior cingulate cortex, and a specific region within the cingulate – called subgenual region sg24 – is that which is reduced in people with mood disorder. Drevets *et al.* found that the volume of this region was lateralised to the left hemisphere, which is consistent with the data and model of normal emotion described in Chapter 8. These findings were subsequently replicated in a group of people with severe mood disorder (Hirayasu *et al.*, 1999).

When Drevets and his colleagues went on to explore the cellular nature of this region in people with mood disorder, they found the typical reduction in sg24 but also a reduction in the density of cells and in the number of glial cells (Ongur *et al.*, 1998). A further study, using a larger sample, found the same pattern of cell reduction in a group of individuals with major and bi-polar depression but only in a subset with a family history of the disorder (Torrey *et al.*, 2000). These cells carry neurotransmitter receptors and help transport neurotransmitters, which may explain why their reduction is associated with depression; the reduction might also explain why this area is seen as smaller in people with depression and bi-polar depression.

A second region thought to be implicated in depression is the hippocampal formation. As you saw in the chapters on memory and emotional stress, this region is important for many activities, including the formation of new memories and for regulating the glucocorticoids associated with stress. Some studies have reported smaller hippocampal volume in depressed individuals (Bremner *et al.*, 2000) and those with bi-polar disorder (Altshuler *et al.*, 2000). The significance of the loss, however, is unclear.

Neurochemistry of depression

The most influential neurochemical hypothesis of depression is based on the effects of two drugs administered to patients in the 1950s when a drug used to alleviate hypertension (reserpine) became associated with depressive symptoms in some patients. Animal studies indicated that the drug reduced levels of dopamine, noradrenaline and 5-HT in rats. Two others drugs that inhibited monoamine oxidase and were used to combat tuberculosis appeared to produce a lightening of the depression experienced by tubercular patients. So, a link was made between depression and a reduction in the monoamines, and it was proposed that returning monoamine levels to normal would lead to a removal of the depression. Anti-depressant drugs, called tricyclics, inhibit monoamine reuptake thus potentially increasing synaptic levels of the monoamines.

Neurochemical changes in depressed patients (usually seen as a change in neurotransmitter level and function, and neurotransmitter metabolite and receptor function) have been observed from four principal sources: the patient's blood plasma, urine, cerebrospinal fluid and post-mortem brain. The first three sources are not particularly informative since it is not known to what extent the level of neurotransmitter in these fluids is reflective of their level in the brain.

The principal chemicals studied have been the monoamines dopamine, noradrenaline, and their metabolites. Reduced levels of the dopamine metabolite homovanillic acid have been found in the cerebrospinal fluid of depressed patients. Early theories argued that presynaptic function in 5-HT neurons was decreased, although the absence of decreased levels of 5-HT argued for the hypothesis that postsynaptic neurons were not responsive to normal levels of 5-HT. There is no conclusive evidence either way.

Alleviating depression

The best-known pharmacological treatments for depression involve either preventing the blocking of the release of monoamine neurotransmitters or increasing the availability of these neurotransmitters in some way. The drugs are generally called monoamine oxidase inhibitors (MAOIs), tricyclic anti-depressants and serotonin-specific reuptake inhibitors (SSRIs).

Monoamine oxidase (MO) A and B are important for the metabolism of dopamine, noradrenaline and 5-HT. Drugs that inhibit this enzyme tend to have anti-depressant effects in mild but not severe depression (an inhibition of 80 per cent of MO must be observed before anti-depressant effects are observed). One major side-effect of MAOIs is the 'tyramine-cheese reaction', a hypertension resulting from the high concentration of tyramine in certain foods consumed, such as cheese, beer, chocolate and pickles. As the monoamine oxidase no longer metabolises tyramine, the tyramine displaces noradrenaline from adrenergic nerve endings. The behavioural result is that the patient might develop occipital headaches and begin vomiting, experience chest pain and become restless. Although a short-term reaction, this could lead to intracranial bleeding. If this occurs, it could be fatal.

Tricyclic antidepressants are the most popular antidepressant drugs. So-called because of their common three-ring structure, tricyclics, like MAOIs, take a few weeks to reach maximum effect and are thought to inhibit the reuptake of monoamines in the nerve terminal, resulting in an increased level of monoamine at the synapse. Side-effects of the drugs include blurred vision, dry mouth (an anticholinergic response), postural hypotension (an antiadrenergic response) and drowsiness (an antihistamine response). The different tricyclic drugs also inhibit reuptake of the three monoamines selectively, with one drug inhibiting one monoamine better than it would another.

Another group of drugs, so-called second-generation drugs, have been modelled on the presumed pharmacological action of previous anti-depressants. The original anti-depressants (MAOIs and tricyclics) were not specifically designed as anti-depressants but were found to have anti-depressant effects. The new drugs such as fluoxetine (Prozac) are called serotonin-specific reuptake inhibitors, and work by inhibiting the reuptake of serotonin, leaving more of that neurotransmitter in the synaptic cleft to stimulate postsynaptic receptors. This is the first drug of choice when tricyclic drug treatment has failed. SSRIs produce fewer negative side-effects than do tricyclics and the MAOIs, although some individuals do experience side-effects such as headache, gastrointestinal discomfort, insomnia, tremor and sexual dysfunction.

11.7 ANXIETY

Several important types of mental disorder are classified as anxiety disorders; these have fear and anxiety as their most prominent symptoms. Anxiety is a sense of apprehension or doom that is accompanied by certain physiological reactions, such as accelerated heart rate, sweaty palms and tightness in the stomach (Gray, 1982; 2000; DSM-IV, 1994). Anxiety disorders are the most common psychological disorders and the reported rate of anxiety disorder is twice as high in European women than in men (Weiller *et al.*, 1998). They include agoraphobia (fear of open spaces), panic disorder and generalised anxiety disorder.

The principal characteristic of generalised anxiety disorder (GAD) is excessive worry about all matters relating to the individual's life: health, money, work, relationships and so on. According to DSM-IV, these worries must be present on most days and will have occurred over a period of at least six months. The anxious individual finds it difficult to control the worry and shows at least three symptoms out of the following: restlessness, being easily fatigued, difficulty concentrating, irritability, muscle tension and sleep disturbance. Around 12 per cent of anxiety disorders are GAD (DSM-IV, 1994) and most individuals with GAD also experience depression, which sometimes makes a clear-cut diagnosis of GAD difficult.

Common to all anxiety disorders is an awareness of threat, tension, difficulty in concentration, fear, restlessness, sleep disturbance, increased muscle tension, gastrointestinal alteration (such as dry mouth, nausea and diarrhoea), difficulty in respiration, and increased sweating. The incidence of GAD is about 3–6 per cent; the lifetime risk for phobia is 10 per cent; for panic disorder, 1 per cent and for obsessive compulsive disorder, 2–3 per cent. A 40 per cent concordance rate for anxiety disorder is seen in monozygotic twins, whereas 15 per cent or less is found for dizygotic twins (Marks, 1986).

Cerebral blood flow studies suggest a role for the temporal lobe in anxiety. Reiman *et al.* (1986) found changes in rCBF at the polar temporal cortex in patients during a panic attack. Asymmetric rCBF activation in the parahippocampal gyrus was found in these patients before the attack (Reiman *et al.*, 1986). Temporal lobe abnormalities have also been found in MRI studies of patients with panic disorder (Fontaine *et al.*, 1990), with increased blood flow to the right parahippocampal gyrus (Reiman *et al.*, 1996). In a follow-on study, Reiman *et al.* (1989) observed rCBF changes in the polar temporal cortex in patients experiencing anticipatory anxiety. Various regions have been associated with increased activity during anxiety that has been provoked in healthy individuals, including the left anterior cingulate cortex and the left orbitofrontal and temporal cortex (Chua *et al.*, 1999). A problem with characterising anxiety neurochemically and neuropathologically is that the state is often a normal response to an event, object, person or situation. However, some indicator of the neurochemical substrates of the state may be gleaned from pharmacological treatment of the disorder (see below).

Alleviating anxiety

Barbiturates, derivatives of barbituric acid, are sedative drugs and include barbital and phenobarbital. Once a popular anxiolytic, their toxicity and their potential for fostering physiological and 'psychological' dependence led to a gradual reduction in their use. Since the effects of withdrawal were severe, the possibility of death with overdose was a possibility and since other new drugs such as the benzodiazepines became available, barbiturate prescription has become uncommon.

Benzodiazepines are sedative and anti-convulsant compounds, and are the most frequently prescribed drugs in medicine. They are, thus, the most widely used anxiolytics. The most common of them are chlordiazepoxide (Librium) and diazepam (Valium) and all are low in toxicity. They do produce side-effects if taken for a long period, however, and these include sedation and impaired memory/concentration. Depression and outbursts of violence may also be seen.

After about four weeks, however, the body becomes tolerant to benzodiazepines and the drug becomes ineffective. Withdrawal symptoms are marked after chronic administration and approximately 40 per cent of patients on long-term prescription experience them (the anxiety tends to be intensified post-administration). The tolerance to benzodiazepines and the withdrawal symptoms after its removal suggest the selective use of the drug (i.e. in the short-term alleviation of distress or in response to a stressful situation).

A model of anxiety

Based on a considerable review of animal data and the effects of anxiolytics in humans, Gray (1982; 2000) argued that anxiety is evoked by signals of punishment, signals of lack of reward, novel stimuli and innate fear stimuli. A behavioural inhibition system (BIS), the brain system responsible, allows the organism to evaluate the environment for threat or possible threat (the BIS is thought to be represented by the septum and hippocampal formation, or 'septohippocampal system'). Gray also suggested that noradrenergic pathways linking the locus coeruleus to the septohippocampal system and 5-HT pathways linking the raphe to it may control some of the BIS's activity. Threats activate these pathways which, in turn, send signals to the septohippocampal system.

However, there are other structures beyond those of the septohippocampal system that may mediate anxious responses. Electrical stimulation of the amygdala, for example, may provoke anxiety or fear in laboratory animals. This structure may be important in the detection of threat from the environment, as LeDoux's experiments have demonstrated. Also important is the periaqueductal grey region, which also results in fear/anxiety when stimulated electrically. Both the amygdala and periaqueductal grey region are innervated by 5-HT systems. These structures are important because, as Gray (1995) himself admits, the mechanisms that one postulates for the mediation of anxiety depend on which system one uses as a starting point. LeDoux's work on the amygdala, for example, concerns the formation of conditioned responses that are not significantly affected by anxiolytic drugs. The responses elicited by conditioned stimuli, however, can be alleviated by these drugs and this is the focus of Gray's model.

There is some evidence that drugs do affect the septohippocampal system. GABAa receptor modulators (such as the benzodiazepines) increase the inhibitory action of GABA. Noradrenergic neurons innervating the septohippocampal system are also inhibited in activating the septohippocampal system when these drugs are administered.

Does the BIS reflect the anxiety of the agoraphobic or the social phobic? According to Gray, it is plausible. The behavioural symptoms of anxiety may reflect the behavioural inhibition of the BIS. This inhibition results in a phobic avoidance when the individual responds to a threatening stimulus. Symbolic or linguistic threats such as fear of failure in an exam may be mediated by the pathway that links the cortical language areas to the prefrontal cortex and from there on to the motor programming circuits of the basal ganglia. From here, the pathway leads to the hippocampal formation via the entorhinal cortex. The inclusion of the basal ganglia here emphasises the importance of movement-related systems in anxiety. Both the basal ganglia and the limbic system are, according to Gray, responsible for the attainment of goals: sensory aspects are governed by the limbic system; motor aspects are governed by the basal ganglia. The maintenance and the monitoring of goals would be accomplished by the septohippocampal system.

11.8 SCHIZOPHRENIA

Schizophrenia is not a unitary disorder but a name given to a group of disorders characterised by distortions of thought, perception and emotion, bizarre behaviour, and social withdrawal. It appears to affect 1 per cent of the world population and has appeared in every country in which it has been studied. Schizophrenia is probably the most serious of the mental disorders.

The word 'schizophrenia' literally means 'split mind', although it is commonly misinterpreted as 'split personality'. The schizophrenic does not suffer from split personality or multiple personality (these are other mental disorders) but from disordered thought and affect. The man who invented the term, Eugen Bleuler (in 1911), intended it to refer to a break with reality caused by such disorganisation of the various functions of the mind that thoughts and feelings no longer worked together normally.

Bleuler divided the disorder into reactive and process forms. Patients with a general history of good mental health were categorised as having reactive schizophrenia because their symptoms were thought to be a reaction to stressful events. Recovery was good in these patients and people rarely experienced more than one episode. Patients who showed signs of mental illness early in life were categorised as having process schizophrenia, and this was considered to be a chronic disorder.

Schizophrenia is characterised by two types of symptom: positive and negative. Positive symptoms are those that include thought disorders, hallucinations and delusions. Thought disorders are a pattern of disorganised and irrational thinking, and are probably the most pronounced symptom of schizophrenia. Patients' logic is absurd and their conversation makes little coherent, logical sense, jumping as it does from one topic to another tenuously connected throughout. Delusions take the form of beliefs that have no basis in fact or reality. Delusions of persecution refer to patients' beliefs that others are plotting against them. Delusions of grandeur refer to a belief that the person is all-knowing, has god-like powers or knowledge that no other person has. Finally, delusions of control refer to beliefs that others are controlling the patient, usually though unusual means such as a receiver or radar planted inside the patient's brain.

Hallucinations are perceptions of stimuli that do not exist. The most common type in schizophrenia is auditory, but hallucinations can also involve distortions in other senses. Typically, the patient claims to hear voices talking to them. Sometimes, these voices order the person to commit an act; sometimes, they are reproving, make no sense at all, or provide a running commentary on their conduct.

The negative symptoms of schizophrenia, however, are characterised by the absence of normal behaviour. There is flattened affect or emotional response, poverty of speech, lack of initiative and persistence, an inability to experience pleasure, and social withdrawal (Crow, 1980; Frith, 1987). Negative symptoms are not specific to schizophrenia; they are seen in many neurological disorders that involve brain damage, especially to the frontal lobes, which may in fact be dysfunctional in schizophrenia (Selemon *et al.*, 1995).

Types of schizophrenia

DSM-IV identifies four types of schizophrenia: undifferentiated, catatonic, paranoid and disorganised (although these categories are not as clear as they seem; there are some patients who do not fall into any of the sub-types). The undifferentiated type experiences delusions, hallucinations and disorganised behaviour. The catatonic type (meaning 'to stretch or draw tight') is characterised by motor disturbances such as adopting unusual postures; waxy flexibility is a feature in which the patient's limb may be moved and the patient maintains the limb in that position. The paranoid type is characterised by delusions of persecution, grandeur or control. Finally, the disorganised type is characterised by disturbances of thought. Patients also exhibit inappropriate social behaviour such as laughing at inopportune times, and their conversation is sometimes a word salad, consisting of jumbles of seemingly random words.

Biological bases of schizophrenia

Interest in the biological basis of schizophrenia has focused on genetic, neuro-chemical and neuro-pathalogical factors. Twin studies of schizophrenia compare the concordance rates of monozygotic (MZ) twins with the concordance rates of siblings of different genetic relatedness who were reared either together or apart. According to Gottesman and Shields (1982) and Gottesman (1991), concordance rates for MZ twins are about 50 per cent, but they are less than about 20 per cent for dizygotic (DZ) twins. Identical twins are much more likely to be concordant for schizophrenia than are fraternal twins, and the children of parents with schizophrenia are more likely to become schizophrenic, even if adopted and raised by non-schizophrenic parents (Farmer *et al.*, 1987).

Neurochemical causes

Two classes of drug have been found to affect the symptoms of schizophrenia. Cocaine and amphetamine can cause symptoms of schizophrenia, both in schizophrenics and in non-schizophrenics; anti-psychotic drugs, however, can reduce symptoms, although both types of drug involve acting on the dopaminergic system. The dopamine hypothesis of schizophrenia states that the positive symptoms of schizophrenia are produced by overactivity of synapses that use dopamine as a transmitter substance.

Chlorpromazine and other anti-psychotic drugs are effective in alleviating the positive symptoms of schizophrenia because they inhibit or block the stimulation of dopamine receptors at synapses; drugs such as cocaine, on the other hand, stimulate these receptors. Anti-psychotic drugs are effective at reducing hallucinations and in reducing the amount of incoherent thought the patient engages in. Although dopamine-secreting neurons are located in several parts of the brain, most researchers believe that the ones involved in the symptoms of schizophrenia are located in the cerebral cortex and parts of the limbic system near the front of the brain. Because anti-psychotic drugs act on dopamine receptors (and the ones that may also be involved in Parkinson's disease), the use of drugs to treat schizophrenia may also result in temporary movement disorder. Long-term use, for example, is associated with a movement disorder called tardive dyskinesia, which is characterised by involuntary drooling and lip-smacking, and by a difficulty in talking.

Neurological causes

Anti-psychotic drugs alleviate the positive, but not the negative, symptoms of schizophrenia. Negative symptoms appear to be associated with brain dysfunction in patients exhibiting these symptoms. Weinberger and Wyatt (1982) found that the ventricles in the brains of schizophrenic patients were, on average, twice as large as those of normal individuals. The sulci (the wrinkles in the brain) have also been found to be wider in the brains of schizophrenic patients (Pfefferbaum *et al.*, 1988). Enlargement of the ventricles of the brain and widening of the sulci indicates the loss of brain tissue, which suggests the existence of some kind of neurological disease.

This enlargement in the ventricles has been confirmed in 50 studies (Lewis, 1990); MRI studies further indicate that the medial temporal lobes are affected (Chua and McKenna, 1995), although there appears to be a reduction in whole brain size, together with an increase in the occipital areas of the ventricles (Lawrie and Abukmeil, 1998).

There is also evidence that some form of frontal lobe dysfunction is characteristic of schizophrenia (Weinberger *et al.*, 1992). Semantic memory and 'frontal lobe' task performance is impaired in schizophrenic individuals (Shallice *et al.*, 1991). The dysfunction usually occurs in the form of hypofrontality – that is, a decrease in activity in the frontal cortex. Some researchers have suggested that the drugs taken by schizophrenics may have been responsible for the reduction (Gur and Gur, 1995) although a recent neuroimaging study of 17 neuroleptically naive (that is, 'drug-free') individuals found decreases in the lateral, orbital and medial areas of the frontal cortex (Andreasen *et al.*, 1997).

PET studies of schizophrenic patients suggest that there is a decrease in dopamine receptors in the prefrontal cortex (Okubo *et al.*, 1997). There is also evidence that the neuronal density in the prefrontal cortex is 17 per cent higher compared with patients with Huntington's chorea and patients with schizophrenia-related disorders (Selemon *et al.*, 1995). This 'squashing' of neurons results from abnormal brain development and may account for the frontal lobe deficits. The importance of the frontal lobe to schizophrenia is also suggested by studies of working memory in schizophrenics: schizophrenic patients perform poorly at keeping information in working memory over 30-second and 60-second delay periods (Keefe *et al.*, 1995).

Limbic and sublimbic activation has been found in schizophrenics during auditory verbal hallucination (Silbersweig *et al.*, 1995), and Gray and colleagues have proposed that schizophrenia may be the result of abnormal connections between the limbic forebrain (especially the hippocampal formation) and the basal ganglia, the region of the brain implicated in the regulation of movement (Gray *et al.*, 1995). These neuroanatomical abnormalities correspond to increases in dopamine in a part of the basal ganglia called the nucleus accumbens. A disruption in these connections means that steps in a motor programme are not confirmed by the brain, leading to the expected outcome of each step being perceived as novel or unexpected. Gray's model is consistent with that of Frith.

The evidence, therefore, indicates some role for the frontal and temporal cortices in schizophrenia, but the relevance of the structures is currently unclear. Crow (1998), for example, has controversially suggested that a deficit in the functional lateralisation of the brain, especially the lateralisation of language, may be the cause of schizophrenia, although the evidence for this is mixed.

Another possible neurological factor in schizophrenia may be interference with normal prenatal brain development. Weinberger (1996) has explicitly stated the neurodevelopmental hypothesis as follows: 'Schizophrenia is related to a defect in brain development. This defect predisposes to a characteristic pattern of brain malfunction in early adult life and to symptoms that respond to antidopaminergic drugs.' Complications at birth are associated with later development of schizophrenia (Hultman *et al.*, 1999) and Hultman *et al.*'s (1997) Swedish study of birth records of schizophrenic and control group infants reports the same pattern: increased risk of schizophrenia is associated with complications during pregnancy and birth, especially in boys. Why these complications should be a risk factor, however, is unclear.

SOME USEFUL FURTHER READING

DEMENTIA AND AGEING
Craik, F.I.M. and Salthouse, T.A. (2000) *The Handbook of Aging and Cognition*. London: Lawrence Erlbaum Associates.
Fleishman and Gabrieli (1999) Long-term memory in Alzheimer's disease. *Current Opinion in Neurobiology* 9, 240–4.
Grady, C.L. (2000) Functional brain imaging and age-related changes in cognition. *Biological Psychology* 54, 259–81.
Iqbal, K., Sisodia, S.S. and Winblad, B. (2001) *Alzheimer's Disease: Advances in Etiology, Pathogenesis and Therapeutics*. Chichester: John Wiley.
Li, S.-C., Lindenberger, U. and Sikstrom, S. (2001) Aging cognition: from neuromodulation to representation. *Trends in Cognitive Sciences* 5(11), 479–86.

DISORDERS OF THOUGHT AND EMOTION
Davidson, R.J. (2000) *Anxiety, Depression and Emotion*. Oxford: Oxford University Press.
Drevets, W.C. (2001) Neuroimaging and neuropathological studies of depression: implications for the cognitive-emotional features of mood

disorders. *Current Opinion of Neurobiology* 11, 240–9.

Gray, J.A. (2000) *The Neuropsychology of Anxiety*. Oxford: Oxford University Press.

Harrison, P.J. (2002) The neuropathology of mood disorder. *Brain* 125, 1428–49.

Harrison, P, and Roberts, G.W. (2000) *The Neuropathology of Schizophrenia*. Oxford: Oxford University Press.

SOME USEFUL JOURNALS TO BROWSE

American Journal of Psychiatry
Anxiety
Archives of General Psychiatry
Brain
British Journal of Clinical Psychology
British Journal of Psychiatry
Current Opinion in Neurobiology
Depression
Journal of Abnormal Psychology
Journal of Consulting and Clinical Psychology
Psychological Medicine
Schizophrenia Bulletin
Trends in Cognitive Sciences

Bibliography

Abel, T. and Lattal, K.M. (2001) Molecular mechanisms of memory acquisition, consolidation and retrieval. *Current Opinion in Neurobiology* 11, 180–7.

Adolphs, R., Russell, J.A. and Tranel, D. (1999) A role for the human amygdala in recognizing emotional arousal from unpleasant stimuli. *Psychological Science* 10, 167–71.

Adolphs, R., Tranel, D., Bechara, A., Damasio, H. and Damasio, A.R. (1996) Neuropsychological approaches to reasoning and decision-making. In A.R. Damasio *et al.* (eds), *Neurobiology of Decision-making*. Berlin: Springer-Verlag.

Adolphs, R., Tranel, D., Damasio, H. and Damasio, A. (1994) Impaired recognition of emotion in facial expressions following bilateral damage to the human amygdala. *Nature* 372, 669–72.

Adolphs, R., Tranel, D., Damasio, H. and Damasio, A. (1995) Fear and the human amygdala. *The Journal of Neuroscience* 15(9), 5879–91.

Aggleton, J.P. and Mishkin, M. (1986) The amygdala: sensory gateway to the emotions. In R. Plutchik and H. Kellerman (eds), *Biological Foundations of Emotion (Vol. 3)*. New York: Academic Press.

Aguirre, G.K. and D'Esposito, M. (1997) Environmental knowledge is subserved by separable dorsal/ventral neural areas. *Journal of Neuroscience* 17(7), 2512–18.

Aguirre, G.K., Zarahn, E. and D'Esposito, M. (1998) An area within human ventral cortex sensitive to 'building' stimuli: Evidence and implications. *Neuron* 21, 373–83.

Albert, M. and Moss, M. (1983) The assessment of memory disorders in patients with Alzheimer's disease. In N. Butters and L.R. Squire (eds), *Neuropsychology of Memory*. New York: Guilford Press.

Alexander, G.E., Crutcher, M.D. and DeLong, M.R. (1990) Basal ganglia–thalamocortical circuits: parallel substrates for motor, oculomotor, 'prefrontal' and 'limbic' functions. *Progress in Brain Research* 85, 119–46.

Allen, L.S. and Gorski, R.A. (1992) Sexual orientation and the size of the anterior commissure in the human brain. *Proceedings of the National Academy of Sciences* 89, 7199–202.

Altshuler, L.L., Bartzokis, G., Greider, T., Curran, J., Jimenez, T., Leigh, K.

(2000) An MRI study of temporal lobe structures in men with bipolar disorder or schizophrenia. *Biological Psychiatry* 48, 147–62.

Amunts, K., Schleicher, A., Burgel, U., Mohlberg, H., Uylings, H.B. and Zillies, K. (1999) Broca's region revisited: cytoarchitecture and intersubject variability. *Journal of Comparative Neurology* 412, 319–41.

Andreasen, N.C., O'Leary, D.S., Flaum, M., Nopoulos, P., Watkins, G.L. and Ponto, L.L.B. (1997) Hypofrontality in schizophrenia: distributed dysfunctional circuits in neuroleptically naive patients. *The Lancet* 349, 1730–4.

Arendt, T., Bigl, V., Arendt, A. and Tennstedt, A. (1983) Loss of neurons in the nucleus basalis of Meynert in Alzheimer's Disease, paralysis agitans and Korsakoff's Disease. *Acta Neuropathologica* 61, 101–08.

Arnow, B.A., Desmond, J.E., Banner, L.L., Glover, G.H., Solomon, A., Polan, M.L., Lue, T.F. and Atlas, S.W. (2002) Brain activation and sexual arousal in healthy, heterosexual males. *Brain* 125, 1014–23.

Arnsten, A.F.T. (1998) Catecholamine modulation of prefrontal cortical cognitive function. *Trends in Cognitive Sciences* 2, 436–47.

Ashton, C.H. (2001) Pharmacology and effects of cannabis: a brief review. *British Journal of Psychiatry* 178, 101–06.

Austin, M.P., Dougall, N., Ross, M., Murray, C., O'Carroll, R.E., Moffoot, A., Ebmeier, K.P. and Goodwin, G.M. (1992) Single photon emission tomography with 99m Tc-exametazime in major depression and the pattern of brain activity underlying the psychotic/neurotic continuum. *Journal of Affective Disorders* 26, 31–43.

Awh, E., Jonides, J., Smith, E.E., Schumacher, E.H., Koeppe, R.A. and Katz, S. (1996) Dissociation of storage and rehearsal in verbal working memory. *Psychological Science* 7, 25–31.

Baddeley, A.D. and Hitch, G.J. (1974) Working memory. In G.H. Bower (ed.), *The Psychology of Learning and Motivation: Advances in Research and Theory, Vol. 8.* New York: Academic Press.

Baddeley, A.D. and Logie, R.H. (1992) Auditory imagery and working memory. In R.S. Nickerson (ed.), *Attention and performance VIII.* Hillsdale, NJ: Lawrence Erlbaum Associates.

Baile, C.A., McLaughlin, C.L. and Della-Fera, M.A. (1986) Role of cholecystokinin and opioid peptides in control of food intake. *Physiological Review* 66, 172–234.

Bailey, J.M., Willerman, L. and Parks, C. (1991) A test of the maternal stress theory of human male homosexuality. *Archives of Sexual Behavior* 20, 277–93.

Bandura, A. (1977) *Social Learning Theory.* Upper Saddle River, NJ: Prentice-Hall.

Bantick, S.J., Wise, R.G., Ploghaus, A., Clare, S., Smith, S.M. and Tracey, I. (2002) Imaging how attention modulates pain in humans using functional MRI. *Brain* 125, 310–19.

Bartels, A. and Zeki, S. (2000a) The neural basis of romantic love. *Neuroreport* 11, 3829–34.

Bartels, A. and Zeki, S. (2000b) The architecture of the colour centre in the human visual brain: New results and a review. *European Journal of Neuroscience* 12, 172–93.

Basser, L. (1962) Hemiplegia of early onset and the faculty of speech with special reference to the effects of hemispherectomy. *Brain* 85, 427–60.

Battro, A.M. (2000) *Half a brain is enough.* Cambridge: Cambridge University Press.

Beatty, W.W., Butters, N. and Janowsky, D.S. (1986) Patterns of memory failure after scopolamine treatment: Implications for cholinergic hypothesis of dementia. *Behavioural and Neural Biology* 45, 196–211.

Bechara, A., Damasio, H., Tranel, D. and Damasio, A.R. (1997) Deciding advantageously before knowing the advantageous strategy. *Science* 275, 1293–5.

Bechara, A., Tranel, D. & Damasio, H. (2000) Characterization of the decision-making deficit of patients with ventromedial prefrontal cortex lesions. *Brain* 123, 2189–202.

Bench, C.J., Friston, K.J., Brown, R.G., Frackowiak, R.S.J. and Dolan, R.J. (1993) Regional cerebral blood flow in depression measured by positron emission tomography: the relationship with clinical dimensions. *Psychological Medicine* 23, 579–90.

Benedict, R.H., Lockwood, A.H., Shucard, J.L., Schucard, D.W., Wack, D., and Murphy, B.W. (1998) Functional neuroimaging of attention in the auditory modality. *NeuroReport* 9(1), 121–6.

Benoit, S.C. *et al.* (2000) A novel selective malanocortin-4 receptor agonist reduces food intake in rats and mice without producing aversive consequences. *Journal of Neuroscience* 20, 3442–8.

Benton, D. and Parker, P. (1998) Breakfast blood glucose and cognition. *American Journal of Clinical Nutrition* 67, 772S–8S.

Benton, D., Brett, V. and Brain, P.F. (1987) Glucose improves attention and reaction to frustration in children. *Biological Psychology* 24, 95–100.

Benton, D., Slater, O. and Donohoe, R.T. (2001) The influence of breakfast and a snack on psychological functioning. *Physiology & Behavior* 74, 550–71.

Bergman, H., Feingold A., Nini, A., Raz, A., Slovin, H., Abeles, M. and Vaadia, E. (1998) Physiological aspects of information processing in the basal ganglia of normal and parkinsonian primates. *Trends in Neurosciences* 21(1), 32–8.

Berlyne, D.F. (1966). Motivational problems raised by exploratory and epistemic behaviour. In S. Koch (ed.), *Psychology: A Study of Science, Vol. 5.* New York: McGraw-Hill.

Bermant, G. and Davidson, J.M. (1974) *Biological Bases of Sexual Behavior.* New York: Harper & Row.

Berson, D.M., Dunn, F.A. and Takao, M. (2002) Phototransduction by retinal ganglion cells that set the circadian clock. *Science* 295, 1070–3.

Beversdorf, D.Q., Ratcliffe, N.R., Rhodes, C.H. and Reeves, A.G. (1997) Pure alexias – clinical–pathologic evidence for a lateralized visual language association cortex. *Clinical Neuropathology* 16, 328–31.

Best, M. and Demb, J.B. (1999) Normal planum temporale asymmetry in dyslexics with a magnocellular pathway deficit. *NeuroReport* 10, 607–12.

Binder, J.R. and Mohr, J.P. (1992) The topography of callosal reading pathways: A case-control analysis. *Brain* 115, 1807–26.

Binder, J.R., Frost, J.A., Hammecke, T.A., Cox, R.W., Rao and Prieto (1997) Human brain language areas identified by functional magnetic resonance imaging. *Journal of Neuroscience* 17(1), 353–62.

Birch, L.L., McPhee, L. and Sullivan, S. (1989) Children's food intake following drinks sweetened with sucrose or aspartame: time course effects. *Physiology and Behaviour* 45, 387–95.

Black, S.L. and Biron, C. (1982) Androstenol as a human pheromone: No effect on perceived sexual attractiveness. *Behavioural and Neural Biology* 34, 326–30.

Blair, R.J.R. and Cipolotti, L. (2000) Impaired social response reversal: A case of 'acquired sociopathy'. *Brain* 123, 1122–41.

Blair, R.J.R., Morris, J.S., Frith, C.D., Perrett, D.I. and Dolan, R.J. (1999) Dissociable neural responses to facial expressions of sadness and anger. *Brain* 122, 883–93.

Bliss, T. and Gardner-Medwin, A. (1973) Long-lasting potentiation of synaptic transmission in the dendate area of unanaesthetised rabbit following stimulation of the perforant path. *Journal of Physiology* 232, 357–74.

Block, N., Flanagan, O. and Guzeldere, G. (1997) *The Nature of Consciousness*. Cambridge, MA: MIT Press.

Blundell, J.E., Green, S. and Burley, V. (1994) Carbohydrates and human appetite. *American Journal of Clinical Nutrition* 59, 728–34.

Boden, G., Chen, X., Mazzoli, M. and Ryan, I. (1996) Effect of fasting on serum leptin in normal subjects. *Journal of Clinical Endocrinology* 81, 3419–23.

Borod, J.C. (1992) Interhemispheric and intrahemispheric control of emotion: A focus on unilateral brain damage. *Journal of Consulting and Clinical Psychology* 60(3), 339–48.

Bottini, G., Corcoran, R., Sterzi, R., Paulesu, E., Schenone, P., Scarpa, P., Frackowiak, R.S.J. and Frith, C.D. (1994) The role of the right hemisphere in the integration of figurative aspects of language. *Brain* 117, 1241–53.

Bourtchouladze, R., Abel, T., Berman, N., Gordon, R., Lapidus, K. and Kandel, E.R. (1998) Different training procedures recruit either one or two critical periods for contextual memory consolidation, each of which requires protein synthesis and PKA. *Learning and Memory* 5, 365–74.

Boutelle, K.N., Kirschenbaum, D.S., Baker, R.C. and Mitchell, M.E. (1999) How can obese weight controllers minimize weight gain during the high risk holiday season? By self-monitoring very consistently. *Health Psychology* 18(4), 364–8.

Braun, A.R., Guillemin, A., Hosey, L. and Varga, M. (2001) The neural organization of discourse: A H2 15O-PET study of narrative production in English and American sign language. *Brain* 124, 2028–44.

Bremner, J.D., Narayan, M., Anderson, E.R., Staib, L.H., Miller, H.L. and Charney, D.S. (2000) Hippocampal volume reduction in major depression. *American Journal of Psychiatry* 157, 115–8.

Brewer, J.B., Zhao, Z., Desmond, J.E., Glover, G.H. and Gabrieli, J.D.E. (1998) Making memories: Brain activity that predicts how well visual experience will be remembered. *Science* 281, 1185–7.

Broadbent, D.E. (1958) *Perception and Communication*. London: Pergamon Press.

Brodmann, K. (1909) *Vergleichende lokalisationleht der grosshirnrinde in ihren prinzipien dargestellt auf grund des zelenbaues*. Leipzig: Barth.

Brookhuis, K.A. and DeWaard, D. (1993) The use of psychophysiology to assess driver status. *Ergonomics* 36(9), 1099–110.

Brooksbank, B.W.L., Brown, R. and Gustafsson, J.A. (1974) The detection of 5-alpha-androst-16-en-3alpha-ol in human male auxillary sweat. *Experientia* 30, 864–5.

Brown, G.L., Ebert, M.H., Goyer, D.C., Jimerson, D.C., Klein, W.J., Bunney, W.E. and Goodwin, F.K. (1982) Aggression, suicide and serotonin: Relationship to CSF amine metabolites. *American Journal of Psychiatry* 139, 741–6.

Brunswick, N. and Rippon, G. (1994) Auditory event-related potentials, dichotic listening performance and handedness as indices of lateralisation in dyslexic and normal readers. *International Journal of Psychophysiology* 18, 265–75.

Brunswick, N., McCrory, E., Price, C.J., Frith, C.D. and Frith, U. (1999). Explicit and implicit processing of words and pseudowords by adult developmental dyslexics: a search for Wernicke's wortschatz? *Brain* 122, 1901–17.

Bryden, M.P. and Ley, R.G. (1983) Right hemisphere involvement in imagery and affect. In Perceman (ed.), *Cognitive processing in the right hemisphere*. New York: Academic Press.

Buchel, C., Price, C. and Friston, K. (1998) A multimodal language region in the ventral–visual pathway. *Nature* 394 (6690), 274–7.

Buchner, A. and Wippich, W. (2000) On the reliability of implicit and explicit memory measures. *Cognitive Psychology* 40, 227–59.

Buck, L.B., Firestein, S. and Margolskee, R.F. (1994) Olfaction and taste in vertebrates: Molecular and organizational strategies underlying chemosensory perception. In G.J. Siegel, B.W. Agranoff, R.W. Albers and

P.B. Molinoff (eds), *Basic neurochemistry.* New York: Raven Press.

Bullock, R. (2002) New drugs for Alzheimer's disease and other dementias. *British Journal of Psychiatry* 180, 135–9.

Buss, D.M. (1995) Evolutionary psychology: A new paradigm for psychological science. *Psychological Inquiry* 6(1), 1–30.

Cabeza, R. and Nyberg, L. (2000) Imaging cognition II: An empirical review of 275 PET and fMRI studies. *Journal of Cognitive Neuroscience* 12(1), 1–47.

Calabrese, P., Markowitsch, H.J., Harders, A.G., Scholz, M. and Gehlen, W. (1995) Fornix damage and memory: A case report. *Cortex* 31, 555–64.

Cameron, I., Curran, S., Newton, P. *et al.* (2000) Use of donepezil for the treatment of mild-moderate Alzheimer's disease: an audit of the assessment and treatment of patients in routine clinical practice. *International Journal of Geriatric Psychiatry* 15, 887–91.

Campfield, L.A., Smith, F.J., Guisez, Y., Devos, R. and Burn, P. (1995) Recombinant mouse OB protein: evidence for a peripheral signal linking adiposity and central neural networks. *Science* 269, 546–9.

Cannon, W.B. and Washburn, A.L. (1912) An explanation of hunger. *American Journal of Physiology* 29, 444–54.

Cappa, S.E., Perani, D., Grassi, E., Bressi, S., Albertoni, M., Franceschi, M. (1997) A PET follow-up study of recovery after stroke in acute aphasics. *Brain and Language* 56, 55–67.

Caramazza, A. (1992) Is cognitive neuropsychology possible? *Journal of Cognitive Neuroscience* 4(1), 80–5.

Caramazza, A. and Hillis, A.E. (1990) Spatial representation of words in the brain implied by studies of a unilateral neglect patient. *Nature* 346, 267–9.

Caramazza, A. and Shelton, J.R. (1998) Domain-specific knowledge systems in the brain: The animate-inanimate distinction. *Journal of Cognitive Neuroscience* 10, 1–34.

Carlson, N.R. (2001) *Physiology of Behaviour* (seventh edition). Boston: Allyn and Bacon.

Carlson, N.R., Buskist, W. and Martin, G.N. (2000) *Psychology – The science of behaviour.* European edition. Harlow: Pearson Education.

Carlsson, K., Petrovic, P., Skare, S., Petersson, K.M. and Ingvar, M. (2000) Tickling expectations: neural processing in anticipation of a sensory stimulus. *Journal of Cognitive Neuroscience* 12, 691–703.

Casper, R.C. (1990) Personality features of women with good outcomes from restricting anorexia nervosa. *Psychosomatic Medicine* 52, 156–70.

Catalan, M.J., Honda, M., Weeks, R.A., Cohen, L.G. and Hallet, M. (1998) The functional neuroanatomy of simple and complex sequential finger movements: A PET study. *Brain* 121, 253–64.

Cecil, J.E., Castiglione, K., French, S., Francis, J. and Read, N.W. (1998) Effects of intragastric infusions of fat and carbohydrate on appetite ratings and food intake from a test meal. *Appetite* 30, 65–77.

Cecil, J.E., Francis, J., and Read, N.W. (1999) Comparison of the effects of a high fat and high carbohydrate soup delivered orally and intragastrically on gastric emptying, appetite and eating behaviour. *Physiology and Behavior* 67, 299–306.

Chalmers, D.J. (1995) Facing up to the problems of consciousness. *Journal of Consciousness Studies* 2(3), 200–19.

Chalmers, D.J. (1998) On the search for the neural correlate of consciousness. In S.R. Hameroff, A.W. Kaszniak and A.C. Scott (eds), *Towards a Science of Consciousness II*. Cambridge, MA: MIT Press.

Chiesi, M., Huppertz, C. and Hofbauer, K.G. (2001) Pharmacotherapy of obesity: Targets and perspectives. *Trends in Pharmacological Sciences* 22(5), 247–54.

Chua, P., Krams, M., Toni, I., Passingham, R. and Dolan, R. (1999) A functional anatomy of anticipatory anxiety. *Neuroimage* 9, 563–71.

Chua, S.E. and McKenna, P.J. (1995) Schizophrenia – a brain disease? A critical review of structural and functional cerebral abnormality in the disorder. *British Journal of Psychiatry* 166, 563–82.

Churchland, P.S. (1998) Brainshy: Nonneural theories of conscious experience. In S.R. Hameroff, A.W. Kaszniak and A.C. Scott (eds), *Towards a Science of Consciousness II*. Cambridge, MA: MIT Press.

Cicerone, K.D. and Tanenbaum, L.N. (1997) Disturbance of social cognition after traumatic arbitofrontal brain injury. *Archives of Clinical Neuropsychology* 12(2), 173–88.

Clark, R.E. and Squire, L.R. (1998) Classical conditioning and brain systems: The role of awareness. *Science* 280, 77–81.

Code, C., Wallesch, C.-W., Joanette, Y. and Lecours, A.R. (1996) *Classic cases in neuropsychology*. Hove: The Psychology Press.

Code, C., Wallesch, C.-W., Joanette, Y. and Lecours, A.R. (2001) *Classic cases in neuropsychology. Volume 2*. Hove, UK: The Psychology Press.

Cohen, N.J. and Squire, L.R. (1980) Preserved learning and retention of pattern analysing skill in amnesia: Dissociation of knowing how and knowing what. *Science* 210, 207–09.

Cohen, S., Frank, E., Doyle, W.J., Skoner, D.P., Rabin, B.S. and Gwaltney, J.M. (1998) Types of stressors that increase susceptibility to the common cold in healthy adults. *Health Psychology* 17(3), 214–23.

Cohen, L., Lehericy, S., Chochon, F., Lemer, C., Rivaud, S. and Dehaene, S. (2002) Language-specific tuning of visual cortex? Functional properties of the visual word form area. *Brain* 125, 1054–69.

Coltheart, M., Patterson, K. and Marshall, J.C. (1980) *Deep dyslexia*. London: Routledge and Kegan Paul.

Corbetta, M., Shulman, G.L., Miezin, F.M. and Petersen, S.E. (1995) Superior parietal cortex activation during spatial attention shifts and visual feature conjunction. *Science* 270, 802–05.

Cowell, S.F., Egan, G.F., Code, C., Harasty, J. and Watson, J.D. (2000) The functional neuroanatomy of simple calculation and number repetition: a parametric PET activation study. *Neuroimage* 12, 565–73.

Craik, F.I.M. and Salthouse, T.A. (2000) *The handbook of aging and cognition*. London: Lawrence Erlbaum Associates.

Crawford, H.J., Brown, A. and Moon, C. (1993) Sustained attentional and disattentional abilities: Differences between low and highly hypnotisable persons. *Journal of Abnormal Psychology* 102, 534–43.

Crawford, H.J., Knebel, T., Kaplan, L., Vendemia, J.M.C., Xie, M., Jamison, S. and Pribram, K.H. (1998) 1. Somatosensory event-related potential changes to noxious stimuli, and 2. Transfer learning to reduce chronic back pain. *International Journal of Clinical and Experimental Hypnosis* XLVI (1), 92–132.

Crawford, J.R., Blackmore, L.M., Lamb, A.E. and Simpson, S.A. (2000) Is there a differential deficit in fronto-executive functioning in Huntington's disease? *Clinical Neuropsychological Assessment* 1, 4–20.

Crick, F. (1994) *The Astonishing Hypothesis*. London: Simon & Schuster.

Crick, F. and Koch, C. (1995) Are we aware of neural activity in primary visual cortex? *Nature* 121–6.

Critchley, M. (1973) *The dyslexic child*. (First published 1970, Springfield, IL: Charles C. Thomas.) Redwood Press.

Crow, T.J. (1980) Molecular pathology of schizophrenia: More than one disease process? *British Medical Journal* 280, 66–8.

Crow, T.J. (1998) Nuclear schizophrenic symptoms as a window on the relationship between thought and speech. *British Journal of Psychiatry* 173, 303–09.

Cruz, A. and Green, B.G. (2000) Thermal stimulation of taste. *Nature* 403, 889–92.

Cummings, J.L. and Benson, D.F. (1992) *Dementia: A clinical approach*. Boston: Butterworth.

Curtiss, S. (1977) *Genie: a psycholinguistic study of a modern day 'wild child'*. New York: Academic Press.

Dabbs, J.M., Bernieri, F.J., Strong, R.K., Campo, R. and Milun, R. (2001) Going on stage: Testosterone in greetings and meetings. *Journal of Research in Personality* 35, 27–40.

Dabbs, J.M., Carr, T.S., Frady, R.L. and Riad, J.K. (1995) Testosterone, crime and misbehaviour among 692 male prison inmates. *Personality and Individual Differences* 18, 627–33.

Damasio, A.R. (1995) Toward a neurobiology of emotion and feeling: Operational concepts and hypotheses. *The Neuroscientist* 1, 19–25.

Damasio, H. and Damasio, A. (1980) The anatomical basis of conduction aphasia. *Brain* 103, 337–50.

Damasio, H., Grabowski, T., Frank, R., Galaburda, A.M. and Damasio, A.R. (1994) The return of Phineas Gage: Clues about the brain from the skull of a famous patient. *Science* 264, 1102–05.

Damasio, H., Grabowski, T.J., Tranel, D., Hichwa, R.D. and Damasio, A.R. (1996) A neural basis for lexical retrieval. *Nature* 380, 499–505.

Daneman, M. and Carpenter, P.A. (1980) Individual differences in working memory and reading. *Journal of Verbal Learning and Verbal Behaviour* 19, 450–66.

Davidoff, J. (1997) The neuropsychology of color. In C.L. Hardin and L. Maffi (eds), *Color Categories in Thought and Language*. New York: Cambridge University Press.

Davidson, J.M., Camargo, C.A. and Smith, E.R. (1979) Effects of androgen on sexual behavior in hypogonadal men. *Journal of Clinical Endocrinology and Metabolism* 48, 955–8.

Davidson, R.J. (1988) EEG measures of cerebral asymmetry: Conceptual and methodological issues. *International Journal of Neuroscience* 39, 71–89.

Davidson, R.J. (1992) Anterior cerebral asymmetry and the nature of emotion. *Brain and Cognition* 20, 125–51.

Davidson, R.J. (1998) Anterior electrophysiological asymmetries, emotion and depression: Conceptual and methodological conundrums. *Psychophysiology* 35, 607–14.

Davidson, R.J. and Fox, N.A. (1989) Frontal brain asymmetry predicts infants' response to maternal separation. *Journal of Abnormal Psychology* 98(2), 127–31.

Davitz, J.R. (1970) A dictionary and grammar of emotion. In M. Arnold (ed.), *Feelings and emotions: The Loyola symposium*. New York: Academic Press.

Dawson, G., Frey, K., Panagiotides, H., Osterling, J. and Hessl, D. (1997) Infants of depressed mothers exhibit atypical frontal brain activity: A replication and extension of previous findings. *Journal of Child Psychology and Psychiatry* 38(2), 179–86.

De Kloet, E.R., Oitzl, M.S. and Joels, M. (1999) Stress and cognition: Are cortocosteroids good or bad guys? *Trends in Neurosciences* 22(10), 422–6

Delahanty, D.L., Dougall, A.L., Hawkes, L., Trakowski, J.H., Schmitz, J.B., Jenkins, F.J. and Baum, A. (1996) Time course of natural killer cell activity and lymphocyte proliferation in response to two acute stressors in healthy men. *Health Psychology* 15, 48–55.

Denissenko, M.F., Pao, A., Tang, M. and Pfeifer, G.P. (1996) Preferential formation of benzo[alpha]pyrene adducts at lung cancer mutational hotspots in P53. *Science* 274, 430–2.

Dennis, M. and Whitaker, H.A. (1976) Language acquisition following hemidecortication: Linguistic superiority of the left over the right hemisphere. *Brain and Language* 3, 404–33.

DeRenzi, E. and Lucchelli, F. (1993) The fuzzy boundaries of apperceptive agnosia. *Cortex* 29, 187–215.

DeTurk, K.H. and Pohorecky, L.A. (1987) Ethanol sensitivity in rats: effect of prenatal stress. *Physiology & Behavior* 40, 407–10.

DeWaard, D. and Brookhuis, K.A. (1991) Assessing driver status: A demonstration experiment on the road. *Accident Prevention and Analysis* 23(4), 297–301.

de Wied, M. and Verbaten, M.N. (2001) Affective pictures processing, attention and pain tolerance. *Pain* 90, 163–72.

Dimberg, U. (1982) Facial reactions to facial expressions. *Psychophysiology* 19, 643–47.

Dimsdale, J.E. (1988) A perspective on type A behavior and coronary disease. *New England Journal of Medicine* 318, 110–12.

Donovan, A. and Oddy, M. (1982) Psychological aspect of unemployment: An investigation into the emotional and social adjustment of school leavers. *Journal of Adolescence* 5, 15–30.

Dorner, G., Greier, T., Ahrens, L., Krell, L., Munx, G., Sieler, H., Kittner, E. and Muller, H. (1980) Prenatal stress possible aetiogenic factor homosexuality in human males. *Endokrinologie* 75, 365–8.

Dorner, G., Schenk, B., Schmiedel, B. and Ahrens, L. (1983) Stressful events in prenatal life bi- and homosexual men. *Experimental and Clinical Endocrinology* 81, 83–7.

Doty, R.L., Appelbaum, S., Zusho, H. and Settle, R.G. (1985) Sex differences in odor identification ability: A cross cultural analysis. *Neuropsychologia* 23, 667–72.

Downing, P.E., Jiang, Y., Shuman, M. and Kanwisher, N. (2001) A cortical area selective for visual processing of the human body. *Science* 293, 2470–3.

Drevets, W.C., Price, J.L., Simpson, J.R., Todd, R.D., Reich, T., Vannier, M. and Raichle, M.E. (1997) Subgenual prefrontal cortex abnormalities in mood disorders. *Nature* 386, 824–7.

DSM-IV (American Psychiatric Association) (1994) *Diagnostic and statistical manual of mental disorders* (fourth edition). Washington, DC: ABA.

Duncan, J. (1995) Attention, intelligence and the frontal lobes. In M.S. Gazzaniga (ed.), *The Cognitive Neurosciences*, Cambridge, MA: MIT Press.

Eccleston, C. and Crombez, G. (1999) Pain demands attention: A cognitive-affective model of the interruptive function of pain. *Psychological Bulletin* 125, 356–66.

Eden, G.F., Stein, J.F., Wood, H.M. and Wood, F.B. (1994) Differences in eye-movements and reading problems in dyslexic and normal children. *Vision Research* 34(10), 1345–58.

Eden, G.F., VanMeter, J.W., Rumsey, J.M., Maisog, J.M., Woods, R.P. and Zeffiro, T.A. (1996) Abnormal processing of visual motion in dyslexia revealed by functional brain imaging. *Nature* 382, 66–9.

Ehrlichman, H. (1987) Hemispheric asymmetry and positive–negative affect. In D. Ottoson (ed.), *Duality and unity of the brain*. London: Macmillan.

Ekman, P. (1973) Cross-cultural studies of facial expression. In P. Ekman (ed.), *Darwin and facial expression: A century of research in review*. New York: Academic Press.

Ekman, P. and Friesen, W.V. (1969) Nonverbal leakage and clues to deception. *Psychiatry* 32, 88–105.

Ekman, P., Friesen, W.V. and Ellsworth, P. (1972) *Emotion in the Human Face: Guidelines for research and a review of findings*. New York: Pergamon Press.

Ellis, L., Ames, M.A., Peckham, W. and Burke, D. (1988) Sexual orientation of human offspring may be altered by severe maternal stress during pregnancy. *Journal of Sex Research* 25, 152–7.

Ellis, L. and Cole-Harding, S. (2001) The effects of prenatal stress, and of prenatal alcohol and nicotine exposure, on human sexual orientation. *Physiology & Behavior* 74, 213–26.

Epstein, R. and Kanwisher, N. (1998) A cortical representation of the local visual environment. *Nature* 392, 6676, 598–601.

Esiri, M.M., Pearson, R.C.A., Steele, J.E., Bowen, D.M. and Powell, T.P.S. (1990) A quantitative study of the neurofibrillary tangles and the choline acetyltransferase activity in the cerebral cortex and amygdala in Alzheimer's disease. *Journal of Neurology, Neurosurgery and Psychiatry* 53, 161–5.

Eslinger, P.J. and Damasio, A.R. (1985) Severe disturbance of higher cognition after bilateral frontal lobe ablation: Patient EVR. *Neurology* 35, 1731–41.

Evans, M., Ellis, A., Watson, D. *et al.* (2000) Sustained cognitive improvement following treatment of Alzheimer's disease with donepezil. *International Journal of Geriatric Psychiatry* 15, 50–3.

Evans, P., Bristow, M., Hucklebridge, F., Clow, A. and Walters, N. (1993) The relationship between secretory immunity, mood and life events. *British Journal of Clinical Psychology* 32, 227–36.

Evans, P., Bristow, M., Hucklebridge, F., Clow, A. and Pang, E-Y. (1994) Stress, arousal, cortisol and secretory immunoglobin A in students undergoing assessment. *British Journal of Clinical Psychology* 33, 575–6.

Evans, P., Clow, A. and Hucklebridge, F. (1997) Stress and the immune system. *The Psychologist* July, 303–07.

Everitt, B.J. (1990) Sexual motivation: a neural and behavioural analysis of the mechanisms underlying appetitive and copulatory responses of male rats. *Neuroscience and Behavioural Review* 14, 217–32.

Everitt, B.J., Cador, M. and Robbins, T.W. (1989) Interactions between the amygdala and ventral striatum in stimulus–reward associations: Studies using a second-order schedule of sexual reinforcement. *Neuroscience* 30, 63-75.

Farah, M.J. (1990) *Visual Agnosia: Disorders of Object Vision and What they Tell us About Normal Vision*. Cambridge, M.A: MIT Press.

Farah, M.J. and Aguirre, G.K. (1999) Imaging visual recognition: PET and fMRI studies of the functional anatomy of human visual recognition. *Trends in Cognitive Sciences* 3, 5, 179–86.

Farah, M.J., Rabinowitz, C., Quinn, G.E. and Liu, G.T. (2000) Early commitment of neural substrates for face recognition. *Cognitive Neuropsychology* 17, 1/2/3, 117–23.

Farah, M.J., Wilson, K.D., Drain, M. and Tanaka, J.N. (1998) What is 'special' about face perception? *Psychological Review* 105, 482–98.

Farmer, A., McGuffin, P. and Gottesman, I. (1987) Twin concordance in DSM-III schizophrenia. *Archives of General Psychiatry* 44, 634–41.

Farooqi, I.S. *et al.* (1999) Effects of recombinant leptin therapy in a child with congenital leptin deficiency. *New England Journal of Medicine* 341, 879–84.

Fearnley, J.M. and Lees, A. (1991) Ageing and Parkinson's disease: Substantia nigra regional selectivity. *Brain* 114, 2283–301.

Ferron, F., Considine, R.V., Peino, R., Lado, I.G., Dieguez, C. and Casanueva, F.F. (1997) Serum leptin concentrations in patients with anorexia nervosa, bulimia nervosa and non-specific eating disorders correlate with body mass index but are independent of the respective disease. *Clinical Endocrinology* 46, 289–93.

Fletcher, J.M., Page, J.B., Francis, D.J. *et al.* (1996) Cognitive correlates of long-term cannabis use in Costa Rican men. *Archives of General Psychiatry* 53, 1051–7.

Fletcher, P.C. and Henson, R.N.A. (2001) Frontal lobes and human memory: Insights from functional neuroimaging. *Brain* 124, 849–81.

Fletcher, P.C., Shallice, T. and Dolan, R.J. (1998) The functional roles of prefrontal cortex in episodic memory. I. Encoding. *Brain* 121, 1239–48.

Fontaine, R., Breton, G., Dery, R., Fontaine, S. and Elie, R. (1990) Temporal lobe abnormalities in panic disorder: an MRI study. *Biological Psychiatry* 27, 304–10.

Fowles, D.C. (1986) The eccrine system and electrodermal activity. In M.G.H. Coles, E. Donchin and S.W. Porges (eds), *Psychophysiology: Systems, Processes and Applications.* New York: Guilford.

Fox, N.A., Henderson, H.A., Rubin, K.H., Calkins, S.D. and Schmidt, L.A. (2001) Continuity and discontinuity of behavioural inhibition and exuberance: Psychophysiological and behavioural influences across the first four years of life. *Child Development* 72(1), 1–21.

Fox, N.A., Rubin, K.H., Calkins, S.D., Marshall, T.R., Coplan, R.J., Porges, S.W., Long, J.M. and Stewart, S. (1995) Frontal activation asymmetry and social competence at four years of age. *Child Development* 66, 1770–84.

Francis, S., Rolls, E.T., Bowtell, R., McGlone, F., O'Doherty, J., Browning, A., Clare, S. and Smith, E. (1999) The representation of pleasant touch in the brain and its relationship with taste and olfactory areas. *NeuroReport* 10, 453–9.

Franks, N.P. and Lieb, W.R. (1998) The molecular basis of general anesthesia:

Current Ideas. In S.R. Hameroff, A.W. Kaszniak and A.C. Scott (eds), *Towards a Science of Consciousness II*. Cambridge, MA: MIT Press.

French, S.J., Conlon, C.A., Mutuma, S.T., Arnold, M., Read, N.W., Meijer, G. and Francis, J. (2000) The effects of intestinal infusion of fatty acids on food intake in man. *Gastroenterology* 119, 943–8.

Friedman, M. and Rosenman, R.H. (1959) Association of specific overt behavior patterns with blood and cardiovascular findings – blood cholesterol level, blood clotting time, incidence of arcus senilis, and clinical coronary artery disease. *Journal of the American Medical Association* 162, 1286–96.

Frith, C.D. (1987) The positive and negative symptoms of schizophrenia reflect impairments in the perception and initiation of action. *Psychological Medicine* 17, 631–48.

Frith, C.D. (1992) *The Cognitive Neuropsychology of Schizophrenia*. Hove, UK: Erlbaum.

Frith, C.D., Friston, K.J., Liddle, P.E. and Frackowiak, R.S.J. (1991) Willed action and the prefrontal cortex in man: A study with PET. *Proceedings of the Royal Society of London* 244, 241–6.

Fromkin, V., Krashen, S., Curtiss, S., Rigler, S. and Rigler, M. (1972/3) The development of language in Genie: A case of language acquisition beyond the 'critical period'. *Brain and Language* 1, 81–107.

Frost, J.A., Binder, J.R., Springer, J.A., Hammeke, T.A., Belgowan, P.S.F., Rao, S.M. and Cox, R.W. (1999) Language processing is strongly left lateralised in both sexes. *Brain* 122, 199–208.

Furey, M.L., Pietrini, P. and Haxby, J.V. (2000) Cholinergic enhancement and increased selectivity of perceptual processing during working memory. *Science* 290, 2315–19.

Gainotti, G. (2000) What the locus of brain lesion tells us about the nature of the cognitive defect underlying category-specific disorders: A review. *Cortex* 36, 539–59.

Galaburda, A. (1995) Anatomic basis of cerebral dominance. In R.J. Davidson and K. Hugdahl (eds), *Brain Asymmetry*. Cambridge, MA: MIT Press.

Galaburda, A.M., Sherman, G.F., Rosen, G.D., Aboitiz, F. and Geschwind, N. (1985) Developmental dyslexia: Four consecutive patients with cortical anomalies. *Annals of Neurology* 18, 222–33.

Galaburda, A.M., Menard, M.T. and Rosen, G.D. (1994) Evidence for aberrant auditory anatomy in developmental dyslexia. *Proceedings of the National Academy of Sciences* 91, 8010–13.

Galvez-Jiminez, N., Lozano, A., Tasker, R., Duff, J., Hutchinson, W. and Lang, A.E. (1998) Pallidal stimulation in Parkinson's disease patients with a prior unilateral pallidotomy. *Canadian Journal of Neurological Sciences* 25(4), 300–5.

Gardner, D.L., Lucas, P.B. and Cowdry, R.W. (1990) CSF metabolites in borderline personality disorder compared with normal controls. *Biological Psychiatry* 28, 247–54.

Garner, D.M., Garfinkel, P.E. and O'Shaughnessy, M. (1985) The validity of the distinction between bulimia with and without anorexia nervosa. *American Journal of Psychiatry* 142, 581–758.

Gerlai, R. (2001) Behavioural tests of hippocampal function: simple paradigms complex problems. *Behavioural Brain Research* 125, 269–77.

Gerloff, C., Corwell, B., Chen, R., Hallett, M., and Cohen, L.G. (1997) Stimulation over the human supplementary motor area interferes with the organization of future elements in complex motor sequences. *Brain* 120(9), 1587–692.

Geschwind, N. (1965) Disconnexion syndromes in animals and man. *Brain* 237–94.

Gilman, A. (1937) The relation between blood osmotic pressure, fluid distribution and voluntary water intake. *American Journal of Physiology* 120, 323–8.

Giraud, A.L. and Price, C.J. (2001) The constraints functional neuroimaging places on classical models of auditory word processing. *Journal of Cognitive Neuroscience* 13, 754–65.

Glaser, R., Rice, J., Sheridan, J., Post, A., Fertel, R., Stout, J., Speicher, C. E., Kotur, M. and Kiecolt-Glaser, J.K. (1987) Stress-related immune suppression: Health implications. *Brain, Behavior, and Immunity* 1, 7–20.

Goebel, R., Khorram-Sefat, D., Muckli, L., Hacker, H. and Singer, W. (1998) The constructive nature of vision: Direct evidence from functional Magnetic Resonance Imaging studies of apparent motion and motion imagery. *European Journal of Neuroscience* 10, 1563–73.

Goel, V., Gold, B., Kapur, S. and Houle, S. (1997) The seats of reason? An imaging study of deductive and inductive reasoning. *NeuroReport* 8, 1305–10.

Goel, V., Gold, B., Kapur, S. and Houle, S. (1998) Neuroanatomical correlates of human reasoning. *Journal of Cognitive Neuroscience* 10(3), 293–302.

Goodale, M.A. and Milner, A.D. (1992) Separate visual pathways for perception and action. *Trends in Neurosciences* 15, 2–25.

Goodglass, H. (1993) *Understanding Aphasia*. New York: Academic Press.

Gorno Tempini, M.L. and Price, C.J. (2001) Identification of famous faces and buildings: A functional neuroimaging study of semantically unique items. *Brain* 124, 2087–97.

Gorno Tempini, M.L., Price, C.J., Josephs, O., Vandenberghe, R., Cappa, S.F., Kapur, N. and Frackowiak, R.S.J. (1998) The neural systems sustaining face and proper-name processing. *Brain* 121, 2103–18.

Gottesman, I.I. (1991) *Schizophrenia Genesis. The Origins of Madness*. New York: Freeman.

Gottesman, I.I. and Shields, J. (1982) *Schizophrenia: The Epigenetic Puzzle*.

Cambridge: Cambridge University Press.

Gould, A. and Martin, G.N. (2001) 'A good odour to breathe?' The effect of pleasant ambient odour on human visual vigilance. *Applied Cognitive Psychology* 15, 225–32.

Graf, P., Squire, L.R. and Mandler, G. (1984) The information that amnesic patients do not forget. *Journal of Experimental Psychology: Learning, Memory, and Cognition* 10, 164–78.

Graham, C.A., Janssen, E. and Sanders, S.A. (2000) Effects of fragrance on female sexual arousal and mood across the menstrual cycle. *Psychophysiology* 37, 76–84.

Grant, P.R. (1986) *Ecology and Evolution of Darwin's Finches*. Princeton, NJ: Princeton University Press.

Grant, V.J. (1994) Maternal dominance and the conception of sons. *British Journal of Medical Psychology* 67, 343–51.

Grant, V.J. and France, J.T. (2001) Dominance and testosterone in women. *Biological Psychology* 58, 41–7.

Gray, J.A. (1971) The mind–brain identity theory as a scientific hypothesis. *Philosophical Quarterly* 21, 247–54.

Gray, J.A. (1982) *The Neuropsychology of Anxiety*. Oxford: Oxford University Press.

Gray, J.A. (1995) A model of the limbic system and basal ganglia: Applications to anxiety and schizophrenia. In M.S. Gazzaniga (ed.), *The Cognitive Neurosciences*. Cambridge, MA: MIT Press.

Gray, J.A. (1998) Creeping up on the hard question of consciousness. In S.R. Hameroff, A.W. Kaszniak and A.C. Scott (eds), *Towards a Science of Consciousness II*. Cambridge, MA: MIT Press.

Gray, J.A. (2000) *The Neuropsychology of Anxiety*. Oxford: Oxford University Press.

Gray, J.A., Feldon, J., Rawlins, J.N.P., Hemsley, D.R. and Smith, A.D. (1991) The neuropsychology of schizophrenia. *Behavioural and Brain Science* 14, 1–84.

Green, S.M., Burley, V.J. and Blundell, J.E. (1994) Effect of fat- and sucrose-containing foods on the size of eating episodes and energy intake in lean males: Potential for causing overconsumption. *European Journal of Clinical Nutrition* 48, 547–55.

Greene, J.D.W. and Hodges, J.R. (1996) Identification of remote memory: Evidence from a longitudinal study of dementia of the Alzheimer type. *Brain* 119, 129–42.

Grigorenko, E.L., Wood, F.B., Meyer, M.S. *et al.* (1997) Susceptibility loci for distinct components of developmental dyslexia on chromosomes 6 and 15. *American Journal of Human Genetics* 60, 27–39.

Grill-Spector, K., Kushnir, T., Edelman, S., Itzchak, Y. and Malach, R. (1998) Cue-invariant activation in object-related areas of the human occipital lobe. *Neuron* 21(1), 191–202.

Gur, R.C. and Gur, R.E. (1995) Hypofrontality in schizophrenia: RIP. *The Lancet* 345, 1383–5.

Habib, M. (2000) The neurological basis of developmental dyslexia. *Brain* 123, 2373–99.

Hagemann, D., Naumann, E., Becker, G., Maier, S. and Bartussek, D. (1998) Frontal brain asymmetry and affective style: A conceptual replication. *Psychophysiology* 35, 372–88.

Hagemann, D., Naumann, E., Thayer, J.F. and Bartussek, D. (2002) Does resting electroencephalographic asymmetry reflect a trait? An application of latent state-trait theory. *Journal of Personality and Social Psychology* 82(4), 619–41.

Haier, R.J., Neuchterlein, K.H., Hazlett, E., Wu, J.C., Pack, J., Browning, H.L. and Buchsbaum, M.S. (1988) Cortical glucose metabolic rate correlates of abstract reasoning and attention studied with positron emission tomography. *Intelligence* 12, 199–217.

Haier, R.J., Siegel, B., Tang, C., Abel, L. and Buchsbaum, M.S. (1992) Intelligence and changes in regional cerebral glucose metabolic rate following learning. *Intelligence* 16, 415–26.

Hakuta, K. (1986) *Mirror of Language*. New York: Basic Books.

Halaas, J.L., Gajiwala, K.S., Maffei, M. and Cohen, S.L. (1995) Weight-reducing effects of the plasma protein encoded by the obese gene. *Science* 269, 543–6.

Halligan, P.W. and Marshall, J.C. (1994) *Spatial Neglect: Position papers on theory and practice*. London: Macmillan.

Halligan, P.W. and Marshall, J.C. (1997) The art of visual neglect. *Lancet* 350, 139–40.

Halpern, A.R. and Zatorre, R.J. (1999) When that tune runs through your head: A PET investigation of auditory imagery for familiar melodies. *Cerebral Cortex* 9, 697–04.

Halsband, U., Ito, N., Tanji, J. and Freund, H.J. (1993) The role of premotor cortex and supplementary motor area in the temporal control of movement in man. *Brain* 116(1), 243–66.

Hamann, S.B., Ely, T.D., Hoffman, J.M. and Kilts, C.D. (2002) Ecstasy and agony: Activation of the human amygdala in positive and negative emotion. *Psychological Science* 13, 135–41.

Hameroff, S.R. (1998) More neural than thou. In S.R. Hameroff, A.W. Kaszniak, and A.C. Scott (eds), *Towards a Science of Consciousness II*. Cambridge, MA: MIT Press.

Hameroff, S.R. and Penrose, R. (1996) Orchestrated reduction of quantum coherence in brain microtubules: A model for consciousness. In Hameroff, S.R., Kaszniak, A.W. and Scott, A.C. (1996), *Towards a Science of Consciousness*. Cambridge, MA: MIT Press.

Hameroff, S.R., Kaszniak, A.W. and Scott, A.C. (1998) *Towards a Science of Consciousness II*. Cambridge, MA: MIT Press.

Hammarstrom, A. and Janlert, U. (1997) Nervous and depressive symptoms in a longitudinal study of youth unemployment – selection or exposure? *Journal of Adolescence* 20, 293–305.

Harlow, J.M. (1848) Passage of an iron rod through the head. *Boston Medicine and Surgery Journal* 39, 389–93.

Harlow, J.M. (1868) Recovery from the passage of an iron bar through the head. *Massachusetts Medical Society Publications* 2, 327–46.

Harmon-Jones, E. and Allen, J.J.B. (1998) Anger and frontal brain activity: EEG asymmetry consistent with approach motivation despite negative affective valence. *Journal of Personality and Social Psychology* 74(5), 1310–6.

Harrison, L.K., Denning, S., Waston, H.L., Hall, J.C., Burns, V.E., Ring, C. and Carroll, D.G. (2001) The effects of competition and competitiveness on cardiovascular activity. *Psychophysiology* 38, 606ff.

Hebb, D.O. (1945) Man's frontal lobes: a critical review. *Archives of Neurology and Psychiatry* 54, 10–24.

Hebb, D.O. (1949) *The Organization of Behaviour.* New York: Wiley/Interscience.

Hecaen, H., Tzortzis, C. and Rondot, P. (1980) Loss of topographic memory with learning deficits. *Cortex* 16, 525–42.

Henriques, J.B. and Davidson, R.J. (1991) Left frontal hypoactivation in depression. *Journal of Abnormal Psychology* 100, 535–45.

Hertz-Pannier, L., Chiron, C., Jambaque, I., Renaux-Kieffer, V., Van de Moortele, P.-F., Delalande, O., Fohlen, M., Brunelle, F. and Le Bihan, D. (2002) Late plasticity for language in a child's non-dominant hemisphere. *Brain* 125, 361–72.

Hess, R.H., Baker, C.K., and Zihl, J. (1989) The 'motion-blind' patient: low level spatial and temporal filters. *Journal of Neuroscience* 9, 1628–40.

Higley, J.D. and Linnoila, M. (1997) Low central nervous system serotonergic activity is traitlike and correlates with impulsive behaviour. A nonhuman primate model investigating genetic and environmental influences on neurotransmission. *Annals of the New York Academy of Sciences* 836, 39–56.

Hirayasu, Y., Shenton, M.E., Salisbury, D.F., Kwon, J.S., Wible, C.G., Foster, I.A., Yurgelun-Dodd, Kikinis, Jolesz and McCorley (1999) Subgenual cingulate cortex volume in first-episode psychosis. *American Journal of Psychiatry* 156, 1091–3.

Holmes, C. (2002) Genotype and phenotype in Alzheimer's disease. *British Journal of Psychiatry* 180, 131–4.

Holmes, G. (1931) Discussion on the mental symptoms associated with cerebral tumors. *Proceedings of the Royal Society of Medicine* 24, 997–1000.

Horn, J.L. (1982) The theory of fluid and crystallised intelligence in relation to concepts of aging in adulthood. In F.I.M. Craik and S. Trehub (eds),

Aging and cognitive processes. New York: Plenum Press.

Hornak, J., Rolls, E.T. and Wade, D. (1996) Face and voice expression identification in patients with emotional and behavioural changes following ventral frontal lobe damage. *Neuropsychologia* 34(4), 247–61.

Horne, J. (2001) State of the art: Sleep. *The Psychologist* 14(6), 302–06.

Horne, J.A. and Minard, A. (1985) Sleep and sleepiness following a behaviourally 'active' day. *Ergonomics* 28, 567–75.

Horne, J.A. and Reyner, L.A. (1996) Driver sleepiness: Comparisons of practical countermeasures – caffeine and a nap. *Psychophysiology* 33, 306–09.

Horne, J.A. and Reyner, L.A. (1999) Vehicle accidents related to sleep: A review. *Occupational and Environmental Medicine* 56, 289–94.

Horowitz, B., Rumsey, J.M. and Donohue, B.C. (1998) Functional connectivity of the angular gyrus in normal reading and dyslexia. *Proceedings of the National Academy of Sciences* 95, 8939–44.

Hubel, D.H. and Wiesel, T.N. (1979) Brain mechanisms of vision. *Scientific American* 241, 159–62.

Hulme, C. and Roodenrys, S. (1995) Practitioner review: Verbal working memory development and its disorders. *Journal of Child Psychology and Psychiatry* 36(3), 373–98.

Hultman, C.M., Ohman, A., Cnattingius, S., Wieselgren, I.-M. and Lindstrom, L.H. (1997) Prenatal and neonatal risk factors for schizophrenia. *British Journal of Psychiatry* 170, 128–33.

Hultman, C.M., Sparen, P., Takei, N., Murray, R.M. and Cnattingius, S. (1999) Prenatal and perinatal risk factors for schizophrenia, affective psychosis and reactive psychosis of early onset: Case-control study. *BMJ* 318, 421–6.

Humphreys, G.W. and Riddoch, M.J. (1987a) *To See or Not To See: A case study of visual object processing*. Hove: The Psychology Press.

Hymphreys, G.W. and Riddoch, M.J. (1987b) The fractionation of visual agnosia. In G.W. Hymphreys and M.J. Riddoch (eds), *Visual Object Agnosia: A Cognitive Neuropsychological Approach*. London: Lawrence Erlbaum Associates.

Inglefinger, F.J. (1944) The late effects of total and subtotal gastrectomy. *New England Journal of Medicine* 231, 321–7.

Isaacs, E.B., Edmonds, C.J., Lucas, A. and Gadian, D.G. (2001) Calculation difficulties in children of very low birthweight: A neural correlate. *Brain* 124, 1701–07.

Ito, M. (1984) *The Cerebellum and Neural Control*. New York: Raven.

Ivnik, R.J., Sharbrough, F.W. and Laws, E.R. (1987) Effects of anterior temporal lobectomy on cognitive function. *Journal of Clinical Psychology* 43, 128–37.

Jackson, J.H. (1874) On the nature of the duality of the brain. *Medical Press and Circular* i(19), 41, 63.

Jacob, F. (1977) Evolution and tinkering. *Science* 196, 1161–6.

Jacob, S. and McClintock, M.K. (2000) Psychological state and mood effects of steroidal chemosignals in women and men. *Hormones and Behaviour* 37, 57–8.

James, W. (1884) What is emotion? *Mind* 19, 188–205.

James, W. (1890) *The Principles of Psychology*. New York: Henry Holt.

Jausovec, N. (1996) Differences in EEG alpha activity related to giftedness. *Intelligence* 23, 159–73.

Jausovec, N. (1998) Are gifted individuals less chaotic thinkers? *Personality and Individual Differences* 25, 253–67.

Jones-Gotman, M. and Zatorre, R.J. (1993) Odor recognition memory in humans: Role of the right temporal and orbitofrontal regions. *Brain and Cognition* 22, 182–98.

Jouvet, M. (1972) The role of monoamines and acetylcholine-containing neurons in the regulation of the sleep-waking cycle. *Ergebnisse der Physiologie* 64, 166–307.

Jueptner, M. and Weiller, C. (1998) A review of differences between basal ganglia and cerebellar control of movements as revealed by functional imaging studies. *Brain* 121(8), 1437–49.

Julien, R.M. (2000) *A Primer of Drug Action*. (ninth edition). New York: W.H. Freeman.

Kageyama, T., Nishikido, N., Kobayashi, T., Kurokawa, Y. and Kabuto, M. (1997) Commuting, overtime, and cardiac autonomic activity in Tokyo. *Lancet* 350, 639.

Kakihana, R., Butte, J.C., and Moore, J.A. (1980) Endocrine effects of maternal alcoholization: plasma and brain testosterone, dihydrotestosterone, estradiol and corticosterone. *Alcohol: Clinical and Experimental Research* 4, 57–61.

Kandel, D.B. and Udry, J.R. (1999) Prenatal effects of maternal smoking on daughters' smoking: nicotine or testosterone exposure? *American Journal of Public Health* 89, 1377–83.

Kandel, E.R. and Squire, L.R. (2000) Neuroscience: breaking down scientific barriers to the study of brain and mind. *Science* 290, 1113–20.

Kanwisher, N. (2000) Domain specificity in face perception. *Nature Neuroscience* 3(8), 759–63.

Kanwisher, N., Stanley, D. and Harris, A. (1999) The fusiform face area is selective for faces not animals. *Neuroreport* 10, 183–7.

Kanwisher, N., Tong, F. and Nakayama, K. (1998) The effect of face inversion on the human fusiform face area. *Cognition* 68, B1-B11.

Kaplan, M.S. (2001) Environment complexity stimulates visual cortex neurogenesis: Death of a dogma and a research career. *Trends in Neurosciences* 24(10), 617–20.

Karbe, H., Herholz, K., Weber-Luxenburger, G., Ghaemi, M. and Heiss, W.-D. (1998) Cerebral networks and functional brain asymmetry: Evidence from regional metabolic changes during word repetition. *Brain and Language* 63, 108–21.

Karmarck, T.W., Manuck, S.B. and Jennings, J.R. (1990) Social support reduces cardiovascular reactivity to psychological challenge: A laboratory model. *Psychosomatic Medicine* 52, 42–58.

Karnath, H.-O., Ferber, S. and Himmelbach, M. (2001) Spatial awareness is a function of the temporal not the posterior parietal lobe. *Nature* 411, 950–3.

Karnath, H.-O., Himmelbach, M. and Rorden, C. (2002) The subcortical anatomy of human spatial neglect: Putamen, caudate nucleus and pulvinar. *Brain* 125, 350–60.

Kaski, D. (2002) Revision: Is visual perception a requisite for visual imagery? *Perception* 31, 717–31.

Kaye, W.H. and Strober, M. (1999) The neurobiology of eating disorders. In D.S. Charney, E.J. Nestler and B.S. Bunney (eds), *Neurobiology of Mental Illness*. New York: Oxford University Press.

Kaye, W.H., Wetlzin, T.E., Hsu, L.K. and Bulik, C.M. (1991) An open trial of fluoxetine in patients with anorexia nervosa. *Journal of Clinical Psychiatry* 52, 464–71.

Keefe, R.S.E., Roitman, S.E.C. and Harvey, P.D. (1995) A pen-and-paper human analogue of a monkey prefrontal cortex activation task: spatial working memory in patients with schizophrenia. *Schizophrenia Research* 17, 25–33.

Keel, P.K. and Mitchell, J.E. (1997) Outcome in bulimia nervosa. *American Journal of Psychiatry* 154, 313–21.

Kempermann, G. and Gage, F.H. (2002) New nerve cells for the adult brain. *Scientific American* 12(1), 38–45.

Kertesz, A. (1981) Anatomy of jargon. In J. Brown (ed.), *Jargonaphasia*. New York: Academic Press.

Kessels, R.P.C., Postma, A., Wester, A.J. and deHaan, E.H.F. (2000) Memory for object locations in Korsakoff's amnesia. *Cortex* 36, 47–57.

Kessels, R.P.C., deHaan, E.H.F., Kappelle, L.J. and Postma, A. (2001) Varieties of human spatial memory: a meta-analysis on the effects of hippocampal lesions. *Brain Research Reviews* 35, 295–303.

Kettner, R.E., Marcario, J.K. and Port, N.L. (1996) Control of remembered reaching sequences in monkey II. Storage and preparation before movement in motor and premotor cortex. *Experimental Brain Research* 112(3), 347–58.

Kiecolt-Glaser, J.K., Marucha, P.T., Malarkey, W.B., Mercado, A.M. and Glaser, R. (1995) Slowing of wound healing by psychological stress. *Lancet* 346, 1194–6.

Kim, K., Relkin, N., Lee, K. and Hirsch, J. (1997) *Nature* 171–4.

Kim, M. and Davis, M. (1993) Lack of temporal gradient of retrograde amnesia in rats with amygdala lesions assessed with the fear-potentiated startle paradigm. *Behavioural Neuroscience* 107, 1088–92.

Kinsley, C. and Svare, B. (1986) Prenatal stress reduces intermale aggression in mice. *Physiology & Behaviour* 36, 783–6.

Kish, S.J., Shannak, K. and Hornykiewicz, O. (1988) Uneven pattern of dopamine loss in the striatum of patients with idiopathic Parkinson's disease: Pathophysiologic and clinical implications. *New England Journal of Medicine* 318, 876–81.

Klein, D., Milner, B., Zatorre, R.J. *et al.* (1995) *Proceedings of the National Academy of Science USA* 92, 2899–903.

Klein, D., Milner, B., Zatorre, R.J., Zhao, V. and Nikelski, J. (1999) Cerebral organization in bilinguals: A PET study of Chinese-English verb generation. *NeuroReport* 10, 2841–6.

Kleitman, N. (1961) The nature of dreaming. In G.E.W. Wolstenholme and M. O'Connor (eds), *The Nature of Sleep*. London: Churchill.

Kleitman, N. (1982) Basic rest–activity cycle – 22 years later. *Sleep* 4, 311–17.

Klimesch, W, Doppelmayr, M., Schimke, H. and Ripper, B. (1997) Theta synchonization and alpha desynchronization in a memory task. *Psychophysiology* 34, 169–76.

Kluver, H. and Bucy, P.C. (1939) Preliminary analysis of functions of the temporal lobes in monkeys. *Archives of Neurology and Psychiatry* 42, 979–1000.

Knecht, S., Deppe, E., Drager, B., Bobe, L., Lohmann, H., Ringelstein, E.-B. and Henningsen, H. (2000) Language lateralization in healthy right-handers. *Brain* 123, 74–81.

Kobasa, S.C. (1979) Stress life events, personality, and health: An inquiry into hardiness. *Journal of Personality and Social Psychology* 42, 168–77.

Kolodny, A. (1929) Symptomatology of tumor of the frontal lobe. *Archives of Neurology and Psychiatry* 21, 1107–27.

Kosslyn, S.M., DiGirolamo, G.J., Thompson, W.L. and Alpert, N.M. (1998) Mental rotation of objects vs hands: Neural mechanisms revealed by positron emission tomography. *Psychophysiology* 35(2), 151–61.

Kosslyn, S.M. and Intriligator, J.M. (1992) Is cognitive neuropsychology plausible? The perils of sitting on a one-legged stool. *Journal of Cognitive Neuroscience* 4(1), 96–106.

Kosslyn, S.M. and Van Kleek, M.H. (1990) Broken brains and normal minds: Why Humpty-Dumpty needs a skeleton. In E.L. Schwartz (ed.), *Computational Neuroscience*. Cambridge, MA: MIT Press.

Krashen, S.D. (1973) Lateralization, language learning and the critical period: Some new evidence. *Language Learning* 23, 63–74.

Kreiman, G., Koch, C. and Fried, I. (2000a) Imagery neurons in the human brain. *Nature* 408, 357–61.

Kreiman, G., Koch, C. and Fried, I. (2000b) Category-specific visual responses of single neurons in the human medial temporal lobe. *Nature Neuroscience* 3(9), 946–53.

Kruesi, M.J.P., Hibbs, E.D., Zahn, T.P., Keysor, C.S., Hamburger, S.D., Bartko, J.J. and Rapoport, J.L. (1992) A two-year prospective follow-up study of children and adolescents with disruptive behaviour disorder: Prediction by cerebrospinal fluid 5-hydroxyindoleactic acid, and autonomic measures. *Archives of General Psychiatry* 49, 429–35.

Krumpazsky, H.G. and Klauss, V. (1996) *Opthalmologica* 210, 1.

Kuskowski, M.A. and Pardo, J.V. (1999) The role of the fusiform gyrus in successful encoding of face stimuli. *Neuroimage* 9, 599–610.

Landrigan, C. (2001) Preventable deaths and injuries during Magnetic Resonance Imaging. *The New England Journal of Medicine* 345, 13, 1000–01.

Lang, A.E., Lozano, A.M., Montgomery, E., Duff, J., Tasker, R. and Hutchinson, W. (1997) Posteroventral medial pallidotomy in advanced Parkinson's Disease. *New England Journal of Medicine* 337(15), 1036–42.

Laplane, D., Talairach, J., Menninger, V., Bancaud, J. and Orgogozo, J.M. (1977) Clinical consequences of corticectomies involving the supplementary motor area in man. *Journal of Neurological Science* 34, 301–14.

Lawrence, A.D., Sahakian, B.J., Hodges, J.R., Rosser, A.E., Lange, K.W. and Robbins, T.W. (1996) Executive and mnemonic functions in early Huntington's disease. *Brain* 119, 1633–45.

Lawrie, S.M. and Abukmeil, S.S. (1998) Brain abnormality in schizophrenia. *British Journal of Psychiatry* 172, 110–20.

Lazarus, R.S. (1966) *Psychological stress and the coping process*. New York: McGraw-Hill.

Lazarus, R. S. and Folkman, S. (1984) *Stress, Appraisal, and Coping*. New York: Springer-Verlag.

Le, S., Cardebat, D., Boulanouar, K., Henaff, M.-A., Michel, F., Milner, D., Dijkerman, C., Puel, M. and Demonet, J.-F. (2002) Seeing, since childhood, without ventral stream: A behavioural study. *Brain* 125, 58–74.

Lechtenberg, R. and Ohl, D.A. (1994) *Sexual Dysfunction*. Philadelphia: Lea and Febiger.

LeDoux, J. (1995a) In search of an emotional system in the brain: Leaping from fear to emotion and consciousness. In M.S. Gazzaniga (ed.), *The Cognitive Neurosciences*. Cambridge: MIT Press.

LeDoux, J.E. (1995b) Emotion: Clues from the brain. *Annual Review of Psychology* 46, 209–35.

LeDoux, J.E., Cicchetti, P., Xagoraris, A. and Romanski, L.M. (1990) The lateral amygdaloid nucleus: sensory interface of the amygdala in fear conditioning. *Journal of Neuroscience* 10, 1062–9.

LeDoux, J.E., Sakaguchi, A. and Reis, D.J. (1984) Subcortical efferent projections of the medial geniculate nucleus mediate emotional responses conditioned by acoustic stimuli. *Journal of Neuroscience* 4(3), 683–98.

LeGrand, R., Mondloch, C.J., Maurer, D. and Brent, H.P. (2001) Early visual experience and face processing. *Nature* 410, 890.

Lenneberg, E. (1967) *Biological Foundations of Language*. New York: John Wiley.

Lepage, M., Habib, R. and Tulving, R. (1998) Hippocampal PET activations of memory encoding and retrieval: the HIPER model. *Hippocampus* 8, 313–22.

LeVay, S. (1991) A difference in hypothalamic structure between heterosexual and homosexual men. *Science* 253, 1034–7.

Levy, L.M., Reis, I.L. and Grafman, J. (1999) Metabolic abnormalities detected by 1H-MRS in dyscalculia and dysgraphia. *Neurology* 53, 639–41.

Lewis, S.W. (1990) Computerised tomography in schizophrenia: 15 years on. *British Journal of Psychiatry* 157 (suppl. 9), 16–24.

Li, S.-C., Lindenberger, U. and Sikstrom, S. (2001) Aging cognition: From neuromodulation to representation. *Trends in Cognitive Sciences* 5(11), 479–86.

Lichtensteiger, W. and Schlumpf, M. (1985) Prenatal nicotine affects fetal testosterone sexual dimorphism of saccharin preference. *Pharmacology, Biochemistry and Behaviour* 23, 439–44.

Lidberg, L., Tuck, J.R., Asberg, M., Scalia-Tomba, G.P. and Bertilson, L. (1985) Homicide, suicide and CSF 5-HIAA. *Acta Psychiatrica Scandinavia* 71, 230–6.

Lidow, M.S., Williams, G.V. and Goldman-Rakic, P.S. (1998) The cerebral cortex: A case for a common site of action of antipsychotics. *Trends in Pharmacological Sciences* 19, 136–40.

Lieberman, I.Y., Mann, V.A., Shankweiler, D. and Werfelman, M. (1982) Children's memory for recurring linguistic and non-linguistic material in relation to reading ability. *Cortex* 18, 367–75.

Lilenfeld, L.R., Kaye, W.H., Greeno, C.G., Merikangas, K.R., Plotnicov, K.H., Pollice, C., Rao, R., Strober, M., Bulik, C.M. and Nagy, L. (1997) Psychiatric disorders in women with bulimia nervosa and their first-degree relatives: Effects of comorbid substance dependence. *International Journal of Eating Disorders* 22, 253–64.

Limousin, P., Speelman, J.D., Gielen, F and Janssens, M. (1999) Multicentre European study of thalamic stimulation in Parkinsonian and essential tremor. *Journal of Neurology, Neurosurgery and Psychiatry* 66(3), 289–96.

Linnoila, M. and Charney, D.S. (1999) The neurobiology of aggression. In D.S. Charney, E.J. Nestler and B.S. Bunney (eds), *Neurobiology of Mental Illness*. New York: Oxford University Press.

Linnoila, M., Virkkunen, M., Scheinin, M., Nuutila, A., Rimon, R. and Goodwin, F.K. (1983) Low cerebrospinal fluid 5-hydroxyindoleactic acid concentration differentiates impulsive from nonimpulsive violent behaviour. *Life Science* 33, 2609–14.

Llinas, R.R. and Pare, D. (1991) Commentary on dreaming and wakefulness.

Neuroscience 44(3), 521–35.

Lomo, T. (1966) Frequency potentiation of excitatory synaptic activity in the dendate area of the hippocampal formation. *Acta Physiologica Scandinavica* 68, 128.

Lowin, A., Knapp, M.R.J. and McCrone, P. (2001) Alzheimer's disease in the UK: comparative evidence on cost of illness and volume of health services research funding. *International Journal of Geriatric Psycharity* (in press).

Lozano, A.M. (2001) Deep brain stimulation for Parkinson's disease. *Parkinsonism and Related Disorders* 7, 199–203.

Lydiard, R.B., Brewerton, T.D., Fossey, M.D., Laraia, M.T., Stuart, G., Beinfeld, M.C. and Ballenger, J.C. (1993) CSF cholecystokinin octapeptide in patients with bulimia nervosa and in normal comparison subjects. *American Journal of Psychiatry* 150, 1099–101.

Lynch, G., Muller, D., Seubert, P. and Larson, J. (1988) Long-term potentiation: Persisting problems and recent results. *Brain Research Bulletin* 21, 363–72.

McClintock, M.K. (1971) Menstrual synchrony and suppression. *Nature* 229, 244–5.

McHugo, G.J., Lanzetta, J.T., Sullivan, D.G., Masters, R.D. and Englis, B.G. (1985) Emotional reactions to a political leader's expressive displays. *Journal of Personality and Social Psychology* 49(6), 1513–29.

McKeffry, D. and Zeki, S. (1997) The position and topography of the human colour centre as revealed by functional magnetic resonance imaging. *Brain* 120, 2229–42.

McKenna, P. and Warrington, E.K. (1978) Category-specific naming preservation: A single case study. *Journal of Neurology, Neurosurgery and Psychiatry* 43, 571–4.

McNamee, P., Bond, J. and Buck, D. (2001) Costs of dementia in England and Wales in the 21st century. *British Journal of Psychiatry* 179, 261–6.

MacSweeney, M., Woll, B., Campbell, R., McGuire, P.K., David, A.S., Williams, S.C.R., Suckling, J., Calvert, G.A. and Brammer, M.J. (2002) Neural systems underlying British sign language and audio-visual English processing in native users. *Brain* 125, 1583–93.

Maffei, M., Halaas, J., Ravussin, E., Pratley, R.E., Lee, G. H., Zhang, Y., Fei, H., Kim, S., Lallone, R. and Ranganathan, S. (1995) Leptin levels in human and rodent: Measurement of plasma leptin and ob RNA in obese and weight-reduced subjects. *Nature Medicine* 11, 1155–61.

Maguire, E.A., Frackowiak, R.S.J. and Frith, C.D. (1997) Recalling routes around London: Activation of the right hippocampus in taxi drivers. *Journal of Neuroscience* 17, 7103.

Maguire, E.A., Burgess, N., Donnett, J.G., Frackowiak, R.S.J., Frith, C.D. and O'Keefe, J. (1998a) Knowing where and getting there: A human navigation network. *Science* 280, 921–4.

Maguire, E.A., Burgess, N., Donnett, J.G., Frackowiak, R.S.J., Frith, C.D.

and O'Keefe, J. (1998b) Knowing where things are: Parahippocampal involvement in encoding object locations in virtual large-scale space. *Journal of Cognitive Neuroscience* 10(1), 61–76.

Manes, F., Sahakian, B., Clark, L., Rogers, R., Antoun, N., Aitken, M. and Robbins, T. (2002) Decision-making processes following damage to the prefrontal cortex. *Brain* 125, 624–39.

Marks, I.M. (1986) Genetics of fear and anxiety disorders. *British Journal of Psychiatry* 149, 406–18.

Markus, R., Panhuysen, G., Tuiten, A. and Koppeschaar, H. (2000) Effects of food on cortisol and mood in vulnerable subjects under controllable and uncontrollable stress. *Physiology & Behavior* 70, 333–42.

Marmot, M.G., Bosma, H., Hemingway, H., Brunner, E. and Stansfeld, S. (1997) Contribution of job control and other risk factors to social variations in coronary heart disease incidence. *Lancet* 350, 235–9.

Marshall, J.C. and Newcombe, F. (1966) Syntactic and semantic errors in paralexia. *Neuropsychologia* 4, 169–76.

Martin, A., Wiggs, C.L., Ungerleider, L.G. and Haxby, J.V. (1996) Neural correlates of category-specific knowledge. *Nature* 379, 649–52.

Martin, G.N. (1996) Olfactory remediation: Current evidence and possible applications. *Social Science and Medicine* 43(1), 63–70.

Martin, G.N. (1998a) *Human Neuropsychology*. Hemel Hempstead: Prentice Hall Europe.

Martin, G.N. (1998b) Human electroencephalographic (EEG) response to olfactory stimulation: Two experiments using the aroma of food. *International Journal of Psychophysiology* 30, 287–302.

Martin, R.A. (2001) Humor, laughter and physical health: Methodological issues and research findings. *Psychological Bulletin* 127(4), 504–19.

Mason, W.T. (1980) Supraoptic neurones of rat hypothalamus are osmosensitive. *Nature* 287, 5778, 154–7.

Masters, W.H. and Johnson, V.E. (1970) *Human Sexual Inadequacy*. Boston: Little Brown.

Matsuda, L.A., Lolait, S.J., Brownstein, M.J. *et al.* (1990) Structure of a cannabinoid receptor and functional expression of the cloned cDNA. *Nature* 346, 561–4.

Matsumoto, N., Hanakawa, T., Maki, S., Graybield, A.M. and Kimura, M. (1999) Role of [corrected] nigrostriatal dopamine system in learning to perform sequential motor-tasks in a predictive manner. *Journal of Neurophysiology* 82(2), 978–98.

Matthews, G. and Desmond, P.A. (2002) Task-induced fatigue states and simulated driving performance. *The Quarterly Journal of Experimental Psychology* 55A, 2, 659–86.

Mayer, J. (1955) Regulation of energy intake and the body weight: The glucostatic theory and the lipostatic hypothesis. *Annals of the New York Academy of Science* 63, 15–43.

Mazur, A., Susman, E.J. and Edelbrock, S. (1997) Sex difference in testosterone response to a video game contest. *Evolution and Social Behaviour* 18, 317–26.

Meisel, R.L. and Sachs, B.J. (1994) The physiology of male sexual behaviour. In E. Knobil and J.D. Neill (eds), *The Physiology of Reproduction, Volume 2.* New York: Raven Press.

Melzack, R. and Wall, P.D. (1965) Pain mechanisms: A new theory. *Science* 150, 971–9.

Menon, V., Rivera, S.M., White, C.D., Glover, G.H. and Reiss, A.L. (2000) Dissociating prefrontal and parietal cortex activation during arithmetic processing. *Neuroimage* 12, 357–65.

Miller, B.L., Cummings, J.L., McIntyre, H., Ebers, G. and Grode, M. (1986) Hypersexuality or altered sexual preference following brain injury. *Journal of Neurology, Neurosurgery and Psychiatry* 49, 867–73.

Milner, A.D. (1998) Streams of consciousness: Visual awareness and the brain. *Trends in Cognitive Sciences* 2(1), 25–30.

Milner, A.D. and Goodale, M.A. (1995) *The Visual Brain in Action.* Oxford: Oxford University Press.

Milner, A.D., Perrett, D.I., Johnston, R.S., Benson, P.I., Jordan, T.R. and Healey, D.W. (1991) Perception and action in 'visual form agnosia'. *Brain* 114, 405–28.

Milner, B., Corkin, S. and Teuber, H.-L. (1968) Further analysis of the hippocampal amnesic syndrome: 14 year follow-up study of HM. *Neuropsychologia* 6, 217–24.

Miyawaki, E., Lyons, K, Pahwa, R. *et al.* (1997) Motor complications of chronic levodopa therapy in Parkinson's disease. *Clinical Neuropharmacology* 20, 523–30.

Money, J., Schwartz, M. and Lewis, V. G. (1984) Adult erotosexual status and fetal hormonal masculinization and demasculinization: 46,XX congenital virilizing adrenal hyperplasia and 46,XY androgen-insensitivity syndrome compared. *Psychoneuroendocrinology* 9, 405–14.

Monga, T.N., Monga, M., Raina, M.S. and Hardjasudarma, M. (1986) Hypersexuality in stroke. *Archives of Physiology, Medicine and Rehabilitation* 67, 415–7.

Montoussis, K. and Zeki, S. (1997) A direct demonstration of perceptual asynchrony in vision. *Proceedings of the Royal Society of London Series B* 264, 393–9.

Morley, J.E. and Blundell, J.E. (1988) The neurobiological basis of eating disorders: Some formulations. *Biological Psychiatry* 23, 53–78.

Morris, J.S., Frith, C.D., Perrett, D.I., Rowland, D., Young, A.W., Calder, A.J. and Dolan, R.J. (1996) A differential neural response in the human amygdala to fearful and happy facial expressions. *Nature* 383, 812–5.

Morris, R.G.M., Garrud, P., Rawlins, J.N.P. and O'Keefe, J. (1982) Place navigation impaired in rats with hippocampal lesions. *Nature* 182(297),

681–3.

Moss, H.E., Tyler, L.K., Durrant-Peatfield, M. and Bunn, E.M. (1998) Two eyes of a see-through: Impaired and intact semantic knowledge in a case of selective deficits in living things. *Neurocase* 4, 291–310.

Mountcastle, V.B., Talbot, W.H., Sakata, H. and Hyvarinen, J. (1969) Cortical neuronal mechanisms in flutter-vibration studied in unanaesthetised monkeys. Neuronal periodicity and frequency discrimination. *Journal of Neurophysiology* 32, 452–84.

Muellbacher, W., Ziemann, U., Wissel, J., Dang, N., Kofler, M., Facchini, S., Boroojerdi, B., Poewe, W. and Hallett, M. (2002) Early consolidation in human primary motor cortex. *Nature* 415, 640–44.

Muller-Hill, B. and Beyreuther, K. (1989) Molecular biology of Alzheimer's disease. *Annual Review of Biochemistry* 58, 287–307.

Murphy, K.J., Pacicot, C.I. and Goodale, M.A. (1996) The use of visuomotor cues as a strategy for making perceptual judgements in a patient with visual form agnosia. *Neuropsychology* 10, 396–401.

Naeser, M.A., Hayward, R.W., Laughlin, S.A. and Zatz, L.M. (1981) Quantitative CT scan studies in aphasia. I. Infarct size and CT numbers. *Brain and Language* 12, 140–64.

Nakamura, K., Sakai, K. and Hikosaka, O. (1999) Effects of local inactivation of monkey medial frontal cortex in learning of sequential procedures. *Journal of Neurophysiology* 82(2), 1063–8.

Nakamura, K., Kawashima, R., Sugiura, M., Kato, T., Nakamura, A., Hatano, K., Nagumo, S., Kubota, K., Fukuda, H., Ito, K. and Kojima, S. (2001) Neural substrates for recognition of familiar voices: a PET study. *Neuropsychologia* 39, 1047–54.

Neville, H.J., Bavelier, D., Corina, D., Rauschecker, J., Kami, A., Lalwani, A., Braun, A., Clark, V., Jezzard, P. and Turner, R. (1998) Cerebral organization for language in deaf and effects of experience. *Proceedings of the National Academy of Sciences of the USA* 95(3), 922–9.

Nicolson, R.I., Fawcett, A.J., Berry, E.L., Jenkins, I.H., Dean, P. and Brooks, D.J. (1999) Association of abnormal cerebellar activation with motor learning difficulties in dyslexic adults. *The Lancet* 353, 1662–7.

Nobili, R., Mammano, F. and Ashmore, J. (1998) How well do we understand the cochlea? *Trends in Neurosciences* 21(4), 159–67.

Nobre, A.C., Allison, T. and McCarthy, G. (1994) Word recognition in the human inferior temporal lobe. *Nature* 372, 260–3.

Nolde, S.F., Johnson, M.K. and D'Esposito, M. (1998) Left prefrontal activation during episodic remembering: An event-related fMRI study. *NeuroReport* 9, 3509–14.

Obeso, J.A., Guridi, J., Obeso, J.A. and DeLong, M. (1997) Surgery for Parkinson's disease. *Journal of Neurology, Neurosurgery and Psychiatry* 62, 2–8.

Ochsner, K.N. and Lieberman, M.D. (2001) The emergence of social cognitive neuroscience. *American Psychologist* 56(9), 717–34.

O'Craven, K. and Kanwisher, N. (2000) Mental imagery of faces and places activates corresponding stimulus-specific brain regions. *Journal of Cognitive Neuroscience* 12(6), 1013–23.

O'Doherty, J., Rolls, E.T., Francis, S., Bowtell, R., McGlone, F., Kobal, G., Renner, B. and Ahne, G. (2000) Sensory-specific satiety-related olfactory activation of the human orbitofrontal cortex. *NeuroReport* 11, 399–403.

O'Keefe, J. and Nadel, L. (1978) *The Hippocampus as a Cognitive Map.* Oxford: Clarendon.

Okubo, Y., Suhara, T., Suzuki, K., Kobayashi, K., Inoue, O., Terasaki, O., Someya, Y., Sassa, T., Sudo, Y., Matsushima, E., Iyo, M., Tateno, Y. and Toru, M. (1997) Decreased prefrontal dopamine D1 receptors in schizophrenia revealed by PET. *Nature* 385, 634–6.

Olson, J.M., Vernon, P.A., Harris, J.A. and Jang, K.L. (2001) The heritability of attitudes: a study of twins. *Journal of Personality and Social Psychology* 80(6), 845–60.

Olton, D.S., Becker, J.T and Handelsmann, G.E. (1979) Hippocampus, space and memory. *Behavioural and Brain Science* 2, 313–65.

Ongur, D., Drevets, W.C. and Price, J.L. (1998) Gial reduction in the subgenual prefrontal cortex in mood disorders. *Proceedings of the National Academy of Sciences USA* 95, 13290-5.

O'Toole, K., Abramowitz, A., Morris, R. and Dulcan, M. (1997) Effects of methylphenidate on attention and nonverbal learning in children with attention-deficit hyperactivity disorder. *Journal of the American Academy of Child and Adolescent Psychiatry* 36, 531–8.

Owens, D.S., Parker, P.Y., and Benton, D. (1997) Blood glucose influences mood following demanding cognitive tasks. *Physiology & Behavior* 62, 471–8.

Parkin, A.J. and Stewart, F. (1993) Category-specific impairments? No. A critique of Sartori *et al. Quarterly Journal of Experimental Psychology* 46A, 505–9.

Paulesu, E. and Mehler, J. (1998) Right on in sign language. *Nature* 392, 233–4.

Paulesu, E., Frith, U., Snowling, M., Gallagher, A., Morton, J., Frackowiak, R.S.J. and Frith, C.D. (1996) Is developmental dyslexia a disconnection syndrome? Evidence from PET scanning. *Brain* 119, 1, 143–57.

Paulesu, E., Demonet, J.-F., Fazio, F., McCory, E., Chanoine, V., Brunswick, N., Cappa, S.F., Cossu, G., Habib, M., Frith, C.D. and Frith, U. (2001a) Dyslexia: Cultural diversity and biological unity. *Science* 291, 2165–7.

Paulesu, E., McCrory, E., Fazio, F., Menoncello, L., Brunswick, N., Cappa, S.F., Cotelli, M., Cossu, G., Corte, F., Lorusso, M., Pesenti, S., Gallagher, A., Perani, D., Price, C., Frith, C.D. and Frith, U. (2001b) A cultural effect on brain function. *Nature Neuroscience* 3, 1, 91–6.

Peck, J.W. and Novin, (1971) Evidence that osmoreceptors mediating drinking in rabbits are in the lateral preoptic area. *Journal of Comparative and Physiological Psychology* 74, 134–47.

Pell, M.D. and Baum, S.R. (1997) The ability to perceive and comprehend intonation in linguistic and affective contexts by brain-damaged adults. *Brain and Language* 57, 80–99.

Pelleymounter, M. A., Cullen, M. J., Baker, M. B., Hecht, R. *et al.* (1995) Effects of the obese gene product on body weight regulation in ob/ob mice. *Science* 269, 540–3.

Penrose, R. (1989) *The Emperor's New Mind*. Oxford: Oxford University Press.

Penrose, R. (1994) *Shadows of the Mind*. Oxford: Oxford University Press.

Perani, D., Paulesu, E., Galles, N.S., Dupoux, E., Dehaene, S., Bettinardi, V., Cappa, S.F., Fazio, F. and Mehler, J. (1998) The bilingual brain: Proficiency and age of acquisition of the second language. *Brain* 121, 1841–52.

Perry, D.W., Zatorre, R.J., Petrides, M., Alivisatos, B., Meyer, E. and Evans, A.C. (1999) Localization of cerebral activity during simple singing. *NeuroReport* 10, 3448-3453.

Perry, E.K., Tomlinson, B.E., Blessed, G., Bergmann, K., Gibson, P.H. and Perry, R.H. (1978) Correlation of cholinergic abnormalities with senile plaques and mental test scores in senile dementia. *British Medical Journal* 2, 1457–9.

Persky, H., Lief, H.I., Strauss, D., Miller, W.R. and O'Brien, C.P. (1978) Plasma testosterone level and sexual behavior of couples. *Archives of Sexual Behavior* 7, 157–73.

Petersen, S.E., Fox, P.T., Posner, M.I., Mintun, M. and Raichle, M.E. (1988) Positron emission tomographic studies of the cortical anatomy of single-word processing. *Nature* 331, 585–9.

Petersen, S.E., Fox, P.T., Snyder, A.Z. and Raichle, M.E. (1990) Activation of extrastriate and frontal cortical areas by visual words and word-like stimuli. *Science* 249, 1041–4.

Petrovic, P., Petersson, K.M., Ghatan, P.H., Stone-Elander, S., and Ingvar, M. (2000) Pain-related cerebral activation is altered by a distracting cognitive task. *Pain* 85, 19–30.

Peyron, R., Garcia-Larrea, L., Gregoire, M.-C., Costes, N., Convers, P., Lavenne, F. *et al.* (1999) Haemodynamic brain responses to acute pain in humans. Sensory and attentional networks. *Brain* 122, 1765–80.

Pfaff, D.W., Schwartz-Giblin, S., McCarthy, M.M. and Kow, L.M. (1994) Cellular and molecular mechanisms of female reproductive behaviour. In E. Knobil and J.D. Neill (eds), *The Physiology of Reproduction, Volume 2*. New York: Raven Press.

Pfaus, J.G. and Everitt, B.J. (1995) The psychopharmacology of sexual behaviour. In F.E. Bloom and D.J. Kupfer (eds), *Psychopharmacology: The Fourth Generation of Progress*. New York: Raven Press.

Pfefferbaum, A., Zipursky, R.B., Lim, K.O., Zatz, L.M., Stahl, S.M. and

Jernigan, T.L. (1988) Computed tomographic evidence for generalized sulcal and ventricular enlargement in schizophrenia. *Archives of General Psychiatry* 45, 633–40.

Phillips, R.G. and LeDoux, J.E. (1994) Lesions of the dorsal hippocampal formation interfere with background but not foreground contextual fear conditioning. *Learning and Memory* 1, 34–44.

Pirke, K.M. (1996) Central and peripheral noradrenalin regulation in eating disorders. *Psychiatry Research* 62, 43–9.

Plihal, W. and Born, J. (1999) Memory consolidation in human sleep depends on inhibition of glucocorticoid release. *NeuroReport* 10, 2741–47.

Plomin, R. and Colledge, E. (2001) Genetics and psychology: Beyond heritability. *European Psychologist* 6(4), 229–40.

Plutchik, R. (1994) *The Psychology and Biology of Emotion*. London: HarperCollins.

Polich, J. and Kok, A. (1995) Cognitive and biological determinants of P300: An integrative overview. *Biological Psychology* 41, 103–46.

Poline, J.-B., Vandenberghe, R., Holmes, A.P., Friston, K.J. and Frackowiak, R.S.J. (1996) Reproducibility of PET activation studies: Lessons from a multi-center European experiment. *Neuroimage* 4, 34–54.

Polk, T.A. and Farah, M.J. (2002) Functional MRI evidence for an abstract, not perceptual, word-form area. *Journal of Experimental Psychology: General* 131(1), 65–72.

Popper, K.R. and Eccles, J. (1977) *The Self and its Brain: An Argument for Interactionism*. New York: Springer.

Posner, M.I. and DiGirolamo, G.J. (2000) Cognitive neuroscience: Origins and promise. *Psychological Bulletin* 126, 873–89.

Posner, M.I. and Rothbart, M.K. (1998) Attention, self-regulation and consciousness. *Philosophical Transactions of the Royal Society of London B: Biological Sciences* 353, 1915–27.

Price, C.J. (1997) Functional anatomy of reading. In R.S.J. Frachowiak, K.J. Friston, C.D. Frith, R.J. Dolan and J.C. Mazziotta (eds), *Human Brain Function*. New York: Academic Press.

Price, C.J., Wise, R.J.S., Watson, J.D.G., Patterson, K., Howard, D. and Frackowiak, R.S.J. (1994) Brain activity during reading: The effects of exposure duration and task. *Brain* 117, 1255–69.

Provencio, I. *et al.* (2000) A novel human opsin in the inner retina. *Journal of Neuroscience* 20, 600.

Pugh, K.R., Shaywitz, B.A., Shaywitz, S.E., Constable, R.T., Skudlarski, P., Fulbright, R.K., Bronen, R.A., Shankweiler, D.P., Katz, L., Fletcher, J. and Gore, J.C. (1996) Cerebral organisation of component processes in reading. *Brain* 119, 1221–38.

Pugh, K.R., Shaywitz, B.A., Shaywitz, S.E., Shankweiler, D.P., Katz, L., Fletcher, J.M., Skudlarski, P., Fulbright, R.K., Constable, R.T., Bronen, R.A., Lacadie, C. and Gore, J.C. (1997) Predicting reading performance from neuroimaging profiles: The cerebral basis of phonological effects in printed word identification. *Journal of Experimental Psychology: Human Perception and Performance* 23(2), 299–318.

Pugh, K.R., Mencl, W.E., Shaywitz, B.A., Shaywitz, S.E., Fulbright, R.K., Constable, R.T., Skudlarski, P., Marchione, K.E., Jenner, A.R., Fletcher, J.M., Lieberman, A.M., Shankweiler, D.P., Katz, L., Bronen, R.A., Lacadie, C. and Gore, J.C. (2000) The angular gyrus in developmental dyslexia: task-specific differences in functional connectivity within posterior cortex. *Psychological Science* 11(1), 51–6.

Purifoy, F.E. and Koopmans, L.H. (1979) Androstenedione, testosterone, and the free testosterone concentration in women of various occupations. *Social Biology* 26, 179–88.

Rae, C., Lee, M.A., Dixon, R.M., Blamire, A.M., Thompson, C.H., Styles, P., Talcott, J., Richardson, A.J. and Stein, J.F. (1998) Metabolic anomalies in developmental dyslexia detected by 1H magnetic resonance spectroscopy. *Lancet*, 351, 1849–52.

Ragland, D.R. and Brand, R.J. (1988) Type A behavior and mortality from coronary heart disease. *New England Journal of Medicine* 318, 65–9.

Raine, A. (1997) *The Psychopathology of Crime* (second edition). New York: Academic Press.

Raine, A., Buchsbaum, M. and LaCasse, L. (1997) Brain abnormalities in murderers indicated by positron emission tomography. *Biological Psychiatry* 42, 495–508.

Raine, A., Lencz, T., Bihrle, S., LaCasse, L. and Colletti, P. (2000) Reduced prefrontal gray matter volume and reduced autonomic activity in antisocial personality disorder. *Archives of General Psychiatry* 57, 119–27.

Rainville, P., Hofbauer, R.K., Paus, T., Duncan, G.H., Bushnell, M.C. and Price, D.D. (1999) Cerebral mechanisms of hypnotic induction and suggestion. *Journal of Cognitive Neuroscience* 11(1), 110–25.

Rasmussen, T. and Milner, B. (1977) The role of early left brain injury in determining lateralization of cerebral speech functions. *Annals of the New York Academy of Sciences* 299, 355–69.

Reiman, E.M., Raichle, M.E., Robins, E., Butler, F.K., Herscoritch, P., Fox, P.T. and Perlmutter, J. (1986) The application of positron emission tomography to the study of panic disorder. *American Journal of Psychiatry* 143, 469–77.

Reiman, E.M., Fusselman, M.J., Fox, P.T. and Raichle, M.E. (1989) Neuroanatomical correlates of anticipatory anxiety. *Nature* 305, 527-9.

Reuter-Lorenz, P.A. *et al.* (2000) Age differences in the frontal lateralization of verbal and spatial working memory revealed by PET. *Journal of Cognitive Neuroscience* 12, 174–87.

Reyner, L.A. and Horne, J.A. (1997) Suppression of sleepiness in drivers: Combination of caffeine with a short nap. *Psychophysiology* 34, 721–5.

Reyner, L.A. and Horne, J.A. (1998) Evaluation of 'in car' countermeasures to driver sleepiness: Cold air and radio. *Sleep* 21, 46–50.

Riddoch, G. (1917) Dissociation of visual perceptions due to occipital injuries, with special reference to appreciation of movement. *Brain* 40, 15–47.

Riedel-Heller, S.G., Busse, A., Aurich, C., Matschinger, H. and Angermeyer, M.C. (2001) Prevalence of dementia according to DSM-III-R and ICD-10. *British Journal of Psychiatry* 179, 250–4.

Rippon, G. and Brunswick, N. (1998) EEG correlates of phonological processing in dyslexic children. *Journal of Psychophysiology* 12, 261–74.

Ris-Stalpers, C., Kuiper, G.G.J.M., Faber, P.W., Schweikert, H.U., Van Rooij, H.C.J., Zegers, N.D., Hodgins, M.B., Degenhart, H.J., Trapman, J. and Brinkmann, A.O. (1990) Aberrant splicing of androgen receptor mRNA results in synthesis of a nonfunctional receptor protein in a patient with androgen insensitivity. *Proceedings of the National Academy of Sciences* 87, 7866–70.

Robbins, T.W., Mehta, M.A. and Sahakian, B.J. (2000) Boosting working memory. *Science* 290, 2275–6.

Robinson, R.G. and Benson, D.F. (1981) Depression in aphasic patients: Frequency, severity, and clinical pathological correlation. *Brain and Language* 14, 282–91.

Rocca, W.A., Amaducci, L.A. and Schoenberg, B.S. (1986) Epidemiology of clinically diagnosed Alzheimer's disease. *Annals of Neurology* 19, 415–24.

Rolls, B.J., Jones, B.P. and Fallowes, D.J. (1972) A comparison of the motivational properties of thirst induced by intracranial angiotensin and water deprivation. *Physiology and Behavior* 9, 777–82.

Rolls, B.J., Rowe, E.A., Rolls, E.T., Kingston, B. and Megson, A. (1981) Variety in the meal enhances food intake in man. *Physiology and Behavior* 26, 215–21.

Rolls, B.J., Rolls, E.T. and Rowe, E.A. (1982) How sensory properties of foods affect human feeding behaviour. *Physiology and Behavior* 29, 409–17.

Rolls, B.J., van Duijenvoorde, P.M. and Rolls, E.T. (1984) Pleasantness changes and food intake in a varied four course meal. *Appetite* 5, 337–48.

Rolls, E.T. (1989) Information processing in the taste system of primates. *Journal of Experimental Biology* 146, 141–64.

Rolls, E.T. (1990) A theory of emotion, and its application to understanding the neural basis of emotion. *Cognition and Emotion* 4(3), 161–90.

Rolls, E.T. (1997) Brain mechanisms of vision, memory and consciousness. In M. Ito, Y. Miyashita and E.T. Rolls (eds), *Cognition, Computation and Consciousness*. Oxford: Oxford University Press.

Rolls, E.T. and Baylis, L.L. (1994) Gustatory, olfactory, and visual convergence within the primate orbitofrontal cortex. *Journal of Neuroscience* 15, 5437–52.

Rolls, E.T., Murzi, E., Yaxley, S., Thorpe, S.J. and Simpson, S.J. (1986)

Sensory-specific satiety: Food-specific reduction in responsiveness of ventral forebrain neurons after feeding in the monkey. *Brain Research* 368, 79–86.

Rolls, E.T., Sienkiewicz, Z.J. and Yaxley, S. (1989) Hunger modulates the responses to gustatory stimuli of single neurons in the orbitofrontal cortex. *European Journal of Neuroscience* 1, 53–60.

Romo, R. and Salinas, E. (2001) Touch and go: Decision-making mechanisms in somatosensation. *Annual Review of Neuroscience* 24, 107–37.

Romo, R., Merchant, H., Zainos, A. and Hernandez, A. (1996) Categorization of somasthetic stimuli: sensorimotor performance and neuronal activity in primary somatic sensory cortex of awake monkeys. *NeuroReport* 7, 1273–9.

Rosenman, R.H., Brand, R.J., Jenkins, C.D., Friedman, M., Straus, R. and Wurm, M. (1975) Coronary heart disease in the Western Collaborative Group Study: Final follow-up experience of 8½ years. *Journal of the American Medical Association* 233, 872–7.

Rotton, J. (1983) Affective and cognitive consequences of malodorous air pollution. *Basic and Applied Social Psychology* 4, 171–91.

Rumsey, J.M., Horwitz, B., Donohue, B.C., Nace, K., Maisog, J.M. and Andreason, P. (1999) A functional lesion in developmental dyslexia: Left angular gyral blood flow predicts severity. *Brain and Language* 70, 187–204.

Russell, J.A. (1994) Is there universal recognition of emotion from facial expression? A review of cross-cultural studies. *Psychological Bulletin* 115, 102–41.

Ryan, L., Hatfield, C. and Hofstetter, M. (2002) Caffeine reduces time-of-day effects on memory performance in older adults. *Psychological Science* 13, 68–71.

Rylander, G. (1939) Personality changes after operations on the frontal lobes: clinical study of 32 cases. *Acta Psychiatrica et Neurologica Scandinavica Supplement* 20, 1–81.

Ryle, G. (1949) *The Concept of Mind*. New York: Barnes & Noble.

Sackheim, H.A., Greenberg, M.S., Weiman, A.L., Gur, R.C., Hungerbuhler, J.P. and Geschwind, N. (1982) Hemispheric asymmetry in the expression of positive and negative emotions: Neurologic evidence. *Archives of Neurology* 39, 210–18.

Sakata, H., Taira, M., Murata, A. and Mine, S. (1995) Neural mechanisms of visual guidance of hand action in the parietal cortex of the monkey. *Cerebral Cortex* 5, 429–38.

Samar, V.J., Parasnis, I. and Berent, G.P. (2002) Deaf poor readers' pattern reversal visual evoked potentials suggest magnocellular system deficits: Implications for diagnostic neuroimaging of dyslexia in deaf individuals. *Brain and Language* 80, 21–44.

Salthouse, T.A. (1991) *Theoretical Perspectives on Cognitive Aging*. London:

Erlbaum

Salthouse, T.A. (1993) Speed mediation of adult age differences in cognition. *Developmental Psychology* 29, 4, 722–38.

Schacter, D.L. (1987) Implicit memory: History and current status. *Journal of Experimental Psychology: Learning, Memory and Cognition* 13, 501–18.

Schacter, D.L. and Wagner, A.D. (1999) Medial temporal-lobe activations in fMRI and PET studies of episodic encoding and retrieval. *Hippocampus* 9, 7–24.

Schaffer, C.E., Davidson, R.J. and Saron, C. (1983) Frontal and parietal electroencephalographic asymmetry in depressed and non-depressed subjects. *Biological Psychiatry* 18, 753–62.

Schall, J.D. and Thompson, K.G. (1999) Neural selection and control of visually guided eye movements. *Annual Review of Neuroscience* 22, 241–59.

Schenk, D., Barber, R., Dunn, W. *et al.* (1999) Immunisation with B amyloid attenuates Alzheimer disease like pathology in the PDAPP mouse. *Nature* 400, 173–7.

Schierlitz, L., Dumanli, H., Robinson, J.N., Burrows, P.E., Schreyer, A.G., Kikinis, R., Jolesz, F.A. and Tempany, C.M.C. (2001) Three-dimensional magnetic resonance imaging in fetal brains. *The Lancet* 357, 1177–8.

Schleifer, S.J., Keller, S.E., Camerino, M., Thornton, J.C. and Stein, M. (1983) Suppression of lymphocyte stimulation following bereavement. *Journal of the American Medical Association* 15, 374–7.

Schmidt, G. and Clement, U. (1990) Does peace prevent homosexuality? *Archives of Sexual Behavior* 19, 183–7.

Schmidt, G. and Schorsch, E. (1981) Psychosurgery of sexually deviant patients: review and analysis of new empirical findings. *Archives of Sexual Behavior* 10(3), 301–23.

Schmidt, L.A. (1999) Frontal brain electrical activity in shyness and sociability. *Psychological Science* 10(4), 316–20.

Schmidt, L.A. and Trainor, L.J. (2001) Frontal brain electrical activity (EEG) distinguishes valence and intensity of musical emotions. *Cognition and Emotion* 15, 487–500.

Schneider, G.E. (1969) Two visual systems. *Science* 163, 895–902.

Schubert, K. and Siegel, A. (1994) What animal studies have taught us about the neurobiology of violence. *International Journal of Group Tensions* 24, 237–65.

Schuurman, P.R., Bosch, D.A., Bossuyt, P.M., Bonsel, G.J., van Sommeren, E.J. and de Bie, R.M. (2000) A comparison of continuous thalamic stimulation and thalamotomy for suppression of severe tremor. *New England Journal of Medicine* 342, 7, 461–8.

Schwartz, G.E., Brown, S.L. and Ahern, G.L. (1980) Facial muscle patterning and subjective experience during affective imagery: sex differences. *Psychophysiology* 17, 75–82.

Scott, T.R., Yaxley, S., Sienkiewicz, Z.J. and Rolls, E.T. (1986) Taste responses in the nucleus tractus solitarius of the behaving monkey. *Journal of Neurophysiology* 55, 182–200.

Scoville, W.B. and Milner, B. (1957) Loss of recent memory after bilateral hippocampal lesions. *Journal of Neurology, Neurosurgery and Psychiatry* 20, 11–21.

Searleman, A. (1977) A review of right hemisphere linguistic abilitites. *Psychological Bulletin* 84, 503–28.

Segalowitz, S.J. and Bryden, M.P. (1983) Individual differences in hemispheric representation of language. In S.J. Segalowitz (ed.), *Language functions and brain organisation*. New York: Academic Press.

Segarra, A.C. and Strand, F.L. (1989) Prenatal administration of nicotine alters subsequent sexual behaviour testosterone levels in male rats. *Brain Research* 480, 151–9.

Selemon, L.D., Rajkowska, G. and Goldman-Rakic, P.S. (1995) Abnormally high neuronal density in the schizophrenic cortex. A morphometric analysis of prefrontal area 9 and occipital area 17. *Archives of General Psychiatry* 52, 805–18.

Selye, H. (1956) *The Stress of Life*. New York: McGraw-Hill.

Selye, H. (1976) *Stress without Distress*. New York: Harper & Row.

Shallice, T., Burgess, P.W. and Frith, C.D. (1991) Can the neuropsychological case study approach be applied to schizophrenia? *Psychological Medicine* 21, 661–73.

Shapiro, A.H. (1975) Behaviour of Kibbutz and urban children receiving an injection. *Psychophysiology* 12, 79–82.

Sheridan, J. and Humphreys, G.W. (1993) A verbal–semantic category-specific recognition impairment. *Cognitive Neuropsychology* 10, 143–84.

Shima, K. and Tanji, J. (1998) Both supplementary and presupplementary motor areas are crucial for the temporal organization of multiple movements. *Journal of Neurophysiology* 80(6), 3247–60.

Silbersweig, D.A., Stern, E., Frith, C., Cahill, C., Holmes, A., Grootnoonk, S., Seaward, J., McKenna, P., Chua, S.E., Schnorr, L., Jones, T. and Frackowiak, R.S.J. (1995) A functional neuroanatomy of hallucinations in schizophrenia. *Nature* 378, 176–9.

Sirigu, A., Zalla, T., Pillon, B., Grafman, J., Agid, Y. and Dubois, B. (1995) Selective impairments in managerial knowledge following pre-frontal cortex damage. *Cortex* 31, 301–16.

Small, D.M., Jones-Gottman, M., Zatorre, R.J., Petrides, M. and Evans, A.C. (1997) A role of the right anterior temporal lobe in taste quality recognition. *Journal of Neuroscience* 17, 5136–42.

Small, D.M., Zatorre, R.J. and Jones-Gottman, M. (2001a) Increased intensity perception of aversive taste following right anteromedial temporal lobe removal in humans. *Brain* 124, 1566–75.

Small, D.M., Zatorre, R.J., Dagher, A., Evans, A.C. and Jones-Gotman, M.

(2001b) Changes in brain activity related to eating chocolate. *Brain* 124, 1720–33.

Smith, E.E., Jonides, J. and Koeppe, R.A. (1996) Dissociating verbal and spatial working memory using PET. *Cerebral Cortex* 6, 11–20.

Smith, T.W., Baldwin, M. and Christensen, A.J. (1990) Interpersonal influence as active coping: Effects of task difficulty on cardiovascular reactivity. *Psychophysiology* 27, 429–37.

Snowden, R.J. (2002) Visual attention to colour: Parvocellular guidance of attentional resources? *Psychological Science* 13(2), 180–4.

Sokejima, S. and Kagamimori, S. (1998) Working hours as a risk for acute myocardial infarction in Japan: Case-control study. *British Medical Journal* 317, 775–80.

Sparks, K., Cooper, C., Fried, Y. and Shirom, A. (1997) The effects of hours of work on health: A meta-analysis. *Journal of Occupational and Organizational Psychology* 70(4), 391–408.

Springer, J.A., Binder, J.R., Hammeke, T.A., Swanson, S.J., Frost, J.A., Bellgowan, P.S.F., Brewer, C.C., Perry, H.M., Morris, G.L. and Mueller, W.M. (1999) Language dominance in neurologically normal and epilepsy subjects. *Brain* 122, 2033–45.

Squire, L.R. (1987) *Memory and Brain*. Oxford: Oxford University Press.

Squire, L.R. (1994) Declarative and nondeclarative memory: Multiple brain systems supporting learning and memory. In D.L. Schacter and E. Tulving (eds), *Memory Systems*. Bradford: MIT Press.

Squire, L.R. and Moore, R.Y. (1979) Dorsal thalamic lesion in a noted case of human memory dysfunction. *Annals of Neurology* 6, 503–06.

Squire, L.R. and Zola-Morgan, S. (1988) Memory: Brain systems and behaviour. *Trends in Neurosciences* 11, 170–5.

Steele, R.J. and Morris, R.G. (1999) Delay-dependent impairment of a matching-to-place task with chronic and intrahippocampal infusion of the NMDA-antagonist D-AP5. *Hippocampus* 9, 118–36.

Stein, J.F. and Walsh, V. (1997) To see but not to read; the magnocellular theory of dyslexia. *Trends in Neurosciences* 20(4), 147–52.

Stern, K. and McClintock, M.K. (1998) Regulation of ovulation by human pheromones. *Nature* 392, 177–9.

Stewart, F., Parkin, A.J. and Hunkin, N.M. (1992) Naming impairments following from herpes simplex encephalitis: category-specific? *The Quarterly Journal of Experimental Psychology* 44A, 261–84.

Stewart, R. (2002) Vascular dementia: a diagnosis running out of time. *British Journal of Psychiatry* 180, 152–6.

Stoerig, P. and Cowey, A. (1997) Blindsight in man and monkey. *Brain* 120, 535–59.

Stone, A.A., Cox, D.S., Valdimarsdottir, H., Jandorf, L. and Neale, J.M. (1987) Evidence that secretory IgA antibody is associated with daily mood. *Journal of Personality and Social Psychology* 52, 988–93.

Strange, P.G. (1992) *Brain Biochemistry and Brain Disorders*. New York: Oxford University Press.

Strickgold, R., Scott, L., Rittenhouse, C. and Hobson, J.A. (1999) Sleep-induced changes in associative memory. *Journal of Cognitive Neuroscience* 11(2), 182–93.

Strosberg, A.D. and Issad, T. (1999) The involvement of leptin in humans revealed by mutations in leptin and leptin receptor genes. *Trends in Pharmacological Sciences* 20, 227–30.

Stuss, D.T. and Benson, D.F. (1986) *The Frontal Lobes*. New York: Raven Press.

Stuss, D.T. and Levine, B. (1996) The dementias: Nosological and clinical factors related to diagnosis. *Brain and Cognition* 31, 99–113.

Stuss, D.T., Gow, C.A. and Hetherington, C.R. (1992) 'No longer Gage': Frontal lobe dysfunction and emotional changes. *Journal of Consulting and Clinical Psychology* 60(3), 349–59.

Sugishita, M., Takayama, Y., Shiono, T., Yoshikawa, K. and Takahashi, V. (1996) Functional magnetic resonance imaging (fMRI) during mental writing with phonograms. *Neuroreport* 7(12), 1917–21.

Sullivan, M.J. and Brender, W. (1986) Facial electromyography: A measure of affective processes during sexual arousal. *Psychophysiology* 23, 182, 188.

Summala, H., Hakkanen, H., Mikkola, T. and Sinkkonen, J. (1999) Task effects on fatigue symptoms in overnight driving. *Ergonomics* 42, 798–806.

Sutton S.K. & Davidson R.J. (2000) Prefrontal brain electrical asymmetry predicts the evaluation of affective stimuli. *Neuropsychologia* 38, 1723–33.

Swaab, D.F. and Hofman, M.A. (1990) An enlarged suprachiasmatic nucleus in homosexual men. *Brain Research* 537, 141–8.

Tanji, J. and Evarts, E.V. (1976) Anticipatory activity of motor cortex neurons in relation to direction of an intended movement. *Journal of Neurophysiology* 39(5), 1062–8.

Tarr, M.J. and Gauthier, I. (2000) FFA: A flexible fusiform area for subordinate-level visual processing automatized by expertise. *Nature Neuroscience* 3(8), 764–9.

Tartaglia, L.A., Dembski, M., Weng, X., Deng, N.H., Culpepper, J., Devos, R., Richards, G.J., Campfield, L.A., Clark, F.T., Deeds, J., Muir, C., Sanker, S., Moriarty, A., Moore, K. J., Smutko, J.S., Mays, G.G., Woolf, E.A., Monroe, C.A. and Tepper, R.I. (1995) Identification and expression cloning of a leptin receptor, OB-R. *Cell* 83, 1263–71.

Tassi, P. and Muzet, A. (2001) Defining the states of consciousness. *Neuroscience and Biobehavioural Reviews* 25, 175–91.

Tatsumi, I.F., Fushimi, T., Sadato, N., Kawashima, R., Yokoyama, E., Kanno, I. and Senda, M. (1999) Verb generation in Japanese – a multicenter PET activation study. *Neuroimage* 9, 154–64.

Thayer, R.E. (1987) Energy tiredness and tension. Effects of a sugar snack versus moderate exercise. *Journal of Personality and Social Psychology* 52, 119–25.

Thomas, H. (1993) Psychiatric symptoms in cannabis users. *British Journal of Psychiatry* 163, 141–9.

Tiihonen, J., Kuikka, J., Kupila, J., Partanen, K., Vainio, P., Airaksinen, J., Eronen, M., Hallikainen, T., Paanila, J., Kinnunen, I. and Huttunen, J. (1994) Increase in cerebral blood flow of right prefrontal cortex in man during orgasm. *Neuroscience Letters* 170, 241–3.

Tippett, L.J., Miller, L.A. and Farah, M.J. (2000) Prosopamnesia: A selective impairment in face learning. *Cognitive Neuropsychology* 17, 1/2/3, 241–55.

Tohgi, H., Watanabe, K., Takahashi, H., Yonezawa, H., Hatano, K. and Sasaki, T. (1994) Prosopagnosia without topographagnosia and object agnosia associated with a lesion confined to the right occipitotemporal region. *Journal of Neurology* 241, 470–4.

Tomarken, A.J., Davidson, R.J. and Henriques, J.B. (1990) Resting frontal brain asymmetry predicts affective responses to films. *Journal of Personality and Social Psychology* 59(4), 791–801.

Torrey, E.F., Webster, M., Knable, M., Johnston, N. and Yolken, R.H. (2000) Foundation brain collection and Neuropathology Consortium. *Schizophrenia Research* 44, 151–5.

Tourney, G. (1980) Hormones and homosexuality. In J. Marmor (ed.), *Homosexual Behavior*. New York: Basic Books.

Tracey, I., Becerra, L., Chang, I., Breiter, H., Jenkins, L., Borsook, D. *et al.* (2000) Noxious hot and cold stimulation produce common patterns of brain activation in humans: A functional Magnetic Resonance Imaging study. *Neuroscience Letters* 288, 159–62.

Tramo, M.J. (2001) Music of the hemispheres. *Science* 291, 54–6.

Tranel, D. and Damasio, A.R. (1985) Knowledge without awareness: An autonomic index of facial recognition by prospopagnosics. *Science* 30, 235–49.

Tranel, D., Fowles, D.C. and Damasio, A.R. (1985) Electrodermal discrimination of familiar and unfamiliar faces: A methodology. *Psychophysiology* 22, 403–08.

Treasure, J. and Campbell, I. (1994) The case for biology in the aetiology of anorexia nervosa. *Psychological Medicine* 24, 3–8.

Tulving, E., Kapur, S., Craik, F.I.M., Moscovitch, M. and Houle, S. (1994) Hemispheric encoding/retrieval asymmetry in episodic memory: Positron emission tomography findings. *Proceedings of the National Academy of Sciences USA* 91, 2016–20.

Turner, J.R., Caroll, D. and Courtney, H. (1983) Cardiac and metabolic responses to 'Space Invaders': An instance of metabolically exaggerated cardiac adjustment? *Psychophysiology* 20, 544–9.

Ullian, E.M., Sapperstein, S.K., Christopherson, K.S. and Barres, B.A. (2001)

Control of synapse number by glia. *Science* 291, 657–60.

Ungerleider, L.G. and Mishkin, M. (1982) Two cortical visual systems. In D.J. Ingle, M.A. Goodale and R.J.W. Mansfield (eds), *Analysis of Visual Behavior*. Cambridge, MA: MIT Press.

Vaisman, N., Voet, H., Akivis, A. and Vakil, E. (1996) Effect of breakfast timing on the cognitive functions of elementary school students. *Archives of Paediatric Adolescent Medicine* 150, 1089–92.

Vallar, G. (1998) Spatial hemineglect in humans. *Trends in Cognitive Sciences* 2(3), 87–97.

Valzelli, L. (1971) Further aspects of the exploratory behaviour in aggressive mice. *Psychopharmacologia* 19, 91–4.

Vargha-Khadem, F., O'Gorman, A. and Watters, G. (1985) Aphasia and handedness in relation to hemispheric side, age at injury and severity of cerebral lesions during childhood. *Brain* 108, 677–96.

Vicari, S., Albertoni, A., Chilosi, A.M., Cipriani, P., Cioni, G. and Bates, E. (2000) Plasticity and reorganization during language development in children with early brain injury. *Cortex* 36, 31–46.

Vidyasagar, T.R. and Pammer, K. (1999) Impaired visual search in dyslexia relates to the role of the magnocellular pathway in attention. *NeuroReport* 10, 1283–7.

Virkkunen, M., DeJong, J., Goodwin, F.K. and Linnoila, M. (1989) Relationship of psychobiological variables to recidivism in violent offenders and impulsive fire setters: A follow-up study. *Archives of General Psychiatry* 46, 600–03.

von Cramon, D. and Kerkhoff, G. (1993) On the cerebral organization of elementary visuospatial perception. In B. Gulyas, D. Ottoson and P.E. Roland (eds), *Functional Organisation of the Human Visual Cortex*. Oxford: Pergamon.

Wagstaff, G.F. (1987) Hypnotic induction, hypnotherapy and the placebo effect. *British Journal of Experimental and Clinical Hypnosis* 4, 168–70.

Wagstaff, G.F. (1996) Methodological issues in hypnosis. In J. Haworth (ed.), *Psychological Research*. London: Routledge.

Wagstaff, G.F. and Royce, C. (1994) Hypnosis and the treatment of nail-biting: A preliminary trial. *Contemporary Hypnosis* 11, 9–13.

Ward, I.L. (1984) The prenatal stress syndrome: current status. *Psychoneuroendocrinology* 9, 3–11.

Ward, I.L. and Weisz, J. (1984) Differential effects of maternal stress on circulating levels of corticosterone, progesterone, testosterone in male and female rat fetuses and their mothers. *Endocrinology* 114, 1635–44.

Ward, I.L., Ward, O.B., Mehan, D., Winn, R.J., French, J.A. and Hendricks, S.E. (1996) Prenatal alcohol stress interact to attenuate ejaculatory behaviour, but not serum testosterone or LH in adult male rats. *Behavioural Neuroscience* 110, 1469–77.

Ward, I.L., Ward, O.B., Winn, R.J., and Bielawski, D. (1994) Male and female sexual behaviour potential of male rate prenatally exposed to the influence of alcohol, stress, or both factors. *Behavioural Science* 108, 1188–95.

Warr, P. (1987) *Work, Unemployment and Mental Health.* Oxford: Clarendon Press.

Warrington, E.K. (1975) The selective impairment of semantic memory. *Journal of Experimental Psychology* 27, 635–57.

Warrington, E.K. and McCarthy, R.A. (1987) Categories of knowledge: Further fractionations and an attempted integration. *Brain* 110, 1273–96.

Warrington, E.K. and Shallice, T. (1980) Word-form dyslexia. *Brain* 103, 99–112.

Warrington, E.K. and Shallice, T. (1984) Category specific semantic impairments. *Brain* 107, 829–54.

Wechsler, A.F., Verity, M.A., Rosenschien, S., Fried, I. and Sceibel, A.B. (1982) Pick's disease: A clinical, computed tomographic and histological study with Golgi impregnation. *Archives of Neurology* 39, 287–90.

Weiller, E., Bisserbe, J.-C., Maier, W. and Lecrubier, Y. (1998) Prevalence and recognition of anxiety syndromes in five European primary care settings. *British Journal of Psychiatry* 174 (suppl. 34), 18–23.

Weinberger, D.R. (1996) On the plausibility of 'the neurodevelopmental hypothesis' of schizophrenia. *Neuropsychopharmacology* 14, 1S–11S.

Weinberger, D.R. and Wyatt, J.R. (1982) Brain morphology in schizophrenia: In vivo studies. In F.A. Henn and G.A. Nasrallah (eds), *Schizophrenia as a Brain Disease* New York: Oxford University Press.

Weinberger, D.R., Berman, K.F., Suddath, R. and Torrey, E.F. (1992) Evidence for dysfunction of a prefrontal-limbic network in schizophrenia: An MRI and rCBF study of discordant monozygotic twins. *American Journal of Psychiatry* 149, 890–7.

Weiskrantz, L. (1986) *Blindsight: A Case Study and Implications.* Oxford: Oxford University Press.

Weiss, J.M. (1968) Effects of coping responses on stress. *Journal of Comparative and Physiological Psychology* 65, 251–60.

Wernicke, C. (1874) *Der aphasische symptomenkomplex.* Breslau, Poland: Cohn and Weigert.

Wessinger, C.M., Van Meter, J., Van Lare, J., Pekar, J. and Rauschecker, J.P. (2001) Hierarchical organization of the human auditory cortex revealed by functional Magnetic Resonance Imaging. *Journal of Cognitive Neuroscience* 13(1), 1–7.

West, R.L. (1996) An application of prefrontal cortex function theory to cognitive aging. *Psychological Bulletin* 120, 272–92.

Wheeler, R.W., Davidson, R.J., and Tomarken, A.J. (1993) Frontal brain asymmetry and emotional reactivity: A biological substrate of affective style. *Psychophysiology* 30, 82–9.

Whitehouse, P.J., Lerner, A. and Hedera, P. (1993) Dementia. In K.M.

Heilman and E. Valenstein (eds), *Clinical Neuropsychology* (third edition). New York: Oxford University Press.

Whiteley, A.M. and Warrington, E.K. (1978) Selective impairment of topographical memory: A single-case study. *Journal of Neurology, Neurosurgery and Psychiatry* 41, 575–8.

Whiteman, M.C., Deary, I.J., Lee, A.J. and Fowkes, F.G.R. (1997) Submissiveness and protection from coronary heart disease in the general population: Edinburgh Artery Study. *Lancet* 350, 541–5.

Wilensky, A.E., Schafe, G.E. and LeDoux, J.E. (1999) The amygdala modulates memory consolidation of fear-motivated inhibitory avoidance learning but not classical fear conditioning. *Journal of Neuroscience* 20, 7059–66.

Williams, R.B., Hanel, T.L., Lee, K.L. and Kong, Y.H. (1980) Type A behavior, hostility, and coronary atherosclerosis. *Psychosomatic Medicine* 42, 539–49.

Wilson, M.A. and McNaughton, B.L. (1994) *Science* 265, 676–9.

Wise, R.J.S., Howard, D., Mummery, C.J., Fletcher, P., Leff, A., Buchel, C. and Scott, S.K. (2000) Noun imageability and the temporal lobes. *Neuropsychologia* 38, 985–94.

Wood, R.J., Rolls, B.J. and Ramsey, D.J. (1977) Drinking following intracarotid infusions of hypertonic solutions in dogs. *American Journal of Physiology* 232, R88–92.

Woods, B.T. (1980) The restricted effects of right-hemisphere lesions after age one; Wechsler test data. *Neuropsychologia* 18, 65–70.

Wyon, D.P., Abrahamsson, J., Jarrtelius, M. and Fletcher, R.J. (1997) An experimental study of the effect of energy intake at breakfast on the test performance of 10-year-old children in school. *International Journal of Food Science Nutrition* 48, 5–12.

Yousem, D.M., Maldjian, J.A., Siddiqi, F., Hummel, T., Alsop, D.C., Geckle, R.J., Bilker, W.B. and Doty, R.L. (1999) Gender effects on odor-stimulated functional Magnetic Resonance Imaging. *Brain Research* 818, 480–7.

Zajonc, R.B. (1980) Feeling and thinking: Preferences need no inferences. *American Psychologist* 35, 151–75.

Zatorre, R.J. (1988) Pitch perception of complex tones and human temporal-lobe function. *Journal of the Accoustical Society of America* 84, 566–72.

Zattore, R.J., Berlin, P. and Penhune, V.B. (2002) Structure and function of auditory cortex: Music and speech. *Trends in Cognitive Sciences* 6(1), 37–46.

Zatorre, R.J., Meyer, E., Gjedde, A. and Evans, A.C. (1996) PET studies of phonetic processing of speech – review, replication and reanalysis. *Cerebral Cortex* 6(1), 21–30.

Zeffirino, T. and Eden, G. (2001) The cerebellum and dyslexia: perpetrator or innocent bystander? *Trends in Neurosciences* 24(9), 512–3.

Zeki, S. (1978) Functional specialization in the visual cortex of the monkey.

Nature 274, 423–8.

Zeki, S. (1990) A century of cerebral achromatopsia. *Brain* 113(6), 1721–77.

Zeki, S. (1993) *A Vision of the Brain*. Oxford: Blackwell.

Zeki, S. (2001) Localization and globalization in conscious vision. *Annual Review of Neuroscience* 24, 57–86.

Zeki, S. and Bartels, A. (1999) Towards a theory of visual consciousness. *Consciousness and Cognition* 8, 225–59.

Zeki, S. and ffytche, D. (1998) The Riddoch syndrome: insights into the neurobiology of conscious vision. *Brain* 121, 25–45.

Index

Reinforcement 121, 155
REM sleep 240–2, 247
Renin 128
Respiration 70
Resting potential 53
Reticular formation 115
Reticulospinal tract 115
Retina 85, 86–7
Retrieval/recall (see memory)
Retrograde amnesia 160
Reuptake 59–60
Ritalin (methylphenidate) 61
Rods 246
Rolandic fissure 65
Ryle, Gilbert 6

Salivary glands 72
Satiety 131–2
Scala tympani 105, 106
Schizophrenia 61, 268–72
Scientific method 12–4
Scotoma 88
Secondary taste cortex 112
Secretory immunoglobulin A 36,
    189, 190–1
Sedation 231–2
Semantic memory 159, 167–8
Semantic memory 82
Senile plaques 255
Sensory specific satiety 132–4
Septohippocampal system 267–8
Sequencing 82, 116–7
Serotonin (see 5-HT)
Serotonin specific reuptake
    inhibitors 264–5
Sex 139–46
Sex-linked genes 125
Sexual arousal 142–3
Short-term memory 158, 161
Shyness 184–5
Sign language 22–3
Single case study 4, 38–41
Single photon emission tomography

(SPECT) 20
Skeletal muscles 24
Skin conductance 29–30
Skin, receptors of 109–10
Sleep deprivation 242–5
Sleep disorders 246–8
Sleep 239–48
Sleepwalking 247
Slow wave sleep 240, 247–8
Smell (see odour, olfaction)
Smiling 25
Smooth muscles 24
Sociability 184–5
Sodium potassium pump 53
Sodium 52
Somatosensation 80, 108–111
Somatosensory cortex 109–10
Sommer's sector (see Ammon's horn)
Sound, processing of (see audition)
Spatial navigation 74, 79, 162–6
Spatial neglect 80, 97–8
Speech (see language)
Spinal cord 44
Split brain patients 12
Spurzheim, Caspar 7, 9
Staining 37
Stapes 105–6
Stereotaxic apparatus 38
Stomach 72, 129, 232
Stress 185–93
Stressor 186
Striate cortex 88
Stroke (see cardiovascular accident)
Substance P 228, 236
Substantia nigra 70, 256
Sulci 65
Superconducting Quantum
    Interference Device (SQUID) 23
Superior colliculi 70, 87–8, 89, 115
Supplementary motor area 115–7
Suprachiasmatic nulceus 245
Surface dyslexia (see dyslexia)
Sweat glands 30–1, 72
Sylvian fissure 65